Christ, the Spirit, and Human Transformation in Gregory of Nyssa's *In Canticum Canticorum*

OXFORD STUDIES IN HISTORICAL THEOLOGY

Series Editor
Richard A. Muller, Calvin Theological Seminary

Founding Editor
David C. Steinmetz †

Editorial Board
Robert C. Gregg, Stanford University
George M. Marsden, University of Notre Dame
Wayne A. Meeks, Yale University
Gerhard Sauter, Rheinische Friedrich-Wilhelms-Universität Bonn
Susan E. Schreiner, University of Chicago
John Van Engen, University of Notre Dame
Robert L. Wilken, University of Virginia

THE REGENSBURG ARTICLE 5 ON
JUSTIFICATION
*Inconsistent Patchwork or Substance of True
Doctrine?*
Anthony N. S. Lane

AUGUSTINE ON THE WILL
A Theological Account
Han-luen Kantzer Komline

THE SYNOD OF PISTORIA AND VATICAN II
Jansenism and the Struggle for Catholic Reform
Shaun Blanchard

CATHOLICITY AND THE COVENANT
OF WORKS
James Ussher and the Reformed Tradition
Harrison Perkins

THE COVENANT OF WORKS
*The Origins, Development, and Reception of the
Doctrine*
J. V. Fesko

RINGLEADERS OF REDEMPTION
How Medieval Dance Became Sacred
Kathryn Dickason

REFUSING TO KISS THE SLIPPER
*Opposition to Calvinism in the Francophone
Reformation*
Michael W. Bruening

FONT OF PARDON AND NEW LIFE
John Calvin and the Efficacy of Baptism
Lyle D. Bierma

THE FLESH OF THE WORD
The extra Calvinisticum *from Zwingli to Early
Orthodoxy*
K. J. Drake

JOHN DAVENANT'S HYPOTHETICAL
UNIVERSALISM
A Defense of Catholic and Reformed Orthodoxy
Michael J. Lynch

RHETORICAL ECONOMY IN AUGUSTINE'S
THEOLOGY
Brian Gronewoller

GRACE AND CONFORMITY
*The Reformed Conformist Tradition and the
Early Stuart Church of England*
Stephen Hampton

MAKING ITALY ANGLICAN
*Why the Book of Common Prayer Was
Translated into Italian*
Stefano Villani

AUGUSTINE ON MEMORY
Kevin G. Grove

UNITY AND CATHOLICITY IN CHRIST
The Ecclesiology of Francisco Suarez, S.J.
Eric J. DeMeuse

CALVINIST CONFORMITY IN POST-
REFORMATION ENGLAND
The Theology and Career of Daniel Featley
Gregory A. Salazar

RETAINING THE OLD EPISCOPAL
DIVINITY
*John Edwards of Cambridge and Reformed
Orthodoxy in the Later Stuart Church*
Jake Griesel

BEARDS, AZYMES, AND PURGATORY
The Other Issues that Divided East and West
A. Edward Siecienski

BISSCHOP'S BENCH
*Contours of Arminian Conformity in the Church
of England, c.1674–1742*
Samuel Fornecker

JOHN LOCKE'S THEOLOGY
An Ecumenical, Irenic, and Controversial Project
Jonathan S. Marko

THEOLOGY AND HISTORY IN THE
METHODOLOGY OF HERMAN BAVINCK
Revelation, Confession, and Christian Consciousness
Cameron D. Clausing

CHRIST, THE SPIRIT, AND HUMAN
TRANSFORMATION IN GREGORY OF
NYSSA'S *IN CANTICUM CANTICORUM*
Alexander L. Abecina

Christ, the Spirit, and Human Transformation in Gregory of Nyssa's *In Canticum Canticorum*

ALEXANDER L. ABECINA

OXFORD
UNIVERSITY PRESS

Oxford University Press is a department of the University of Oxford. It furthers the University's objective of excellence in research, scholarship, and education by publishing worldwide. Oxford is a registered trade mark of Oxford University Press in the UK and certain other countries.

Published in the United States of America by Oxford University Press
198 Madison Avenue, New York, NY 10016, United States of America.

© Oxford University Press 2024

All rights reserved. No part of this publication may be reproduced, stored in a retrieval system, or transmitted, in any form or by any means, without the prior permission in writing of Oxford University Press, or as expressly permitted by law, by license, or under terms agreed with the appropriate reproduction rights organization. Inquiries concerning reproduction outside the scope of the above should be sent to the Rights Department, Oxford University Press, at the address above.

You must not circulate this work in any other form and you must impose this same condition on any acquirer.

CIP data is on file at the Library of Congress

ISBN 978–0–19–774594–6

DOI: 10.1093/oso/9780197745946.001.0001

Printed by Integrated Books International, United States of America

Contents

Acknowledgements   ix

Abbreviations   xi

Introduction   1

PART I: TRINITY, CHRISTOLOGY, AND PNEUMATOLOGY: GREGORY OF NYSSA'S DOCTRINAL ACCOUNT OF HUMAN TRANSFORMATION AND UNION WITH GOD (*c.* 370–385)

1. Spiritual Marriage with Christ in *De Virginitate*   33

Introduction   33

Virginity in Trinitarian Perspective: Chapters I–II   34

Worldly Marriage, Heavenly Virginity: Chapters III–VI   39

The Holy Spirit, Demons, and Extreme Virginity: Chapter VII   41

Weak Virgins and the Power of the Spirit: Chapters VIII–XI   45

The Power of Death and the Power of the Spirit: Chapters XII–XIII   51

Spiritual Childbearing: Chapters XIIIb–XIV   55

Pneumatology in Chapters XIV–XXII   56

Conclusion   57

2. Baptism and Trinitarian Theology   59

Introduction   59

Ep. 5, *Ep. 24*, and *Adversus Macedonianos*   60

Adversus eos qui baptismum differunt and In baptismum Christi   67

Conclusion   75

3. Human Transformation and Christology in *Contra Eunomium* III   77

Introduction   77

The Economy and Restoration of Humanity: Interpreting Proverbs 8   78

Son(s) of God   86

The Firstborn and the First-fruit   89

Christology of Transformation   91

Conclusion   97

vi CONTENTS

4. **Spirit-based Christology in *Antirrheticus Adversus Apolinarium*** — 99
   Introduction — 99
   Apolinarius of Laodicea on the 'Spirit' and the Unity of Christ — 100
   Anointing in Eternity and the Exegesis of Psalm 44 (45):6–7 — 104
   Anointing after the Passion and the Exegesis of Acts 2:36/John 17:5 — 109
   Anointing at Conception and the Exegesis of Luke 1:35 — 114
   Beyond the *Antirrheticus adversus Apolinarium*: The Unity of Christ, the Spirit, and the Church — 118
   Conclusion — 120

5. **Tracing the Spirit: Christology in *Contra Eunomium* III Reconsidered** — 122
   Introduction — 122
   Spirit-based Christology in *ad Eustathium, de sancta trinitate*? — 123
   Tracing the Spirit in *Contra Eunomium* III — 130
   Conclusion — 143

PART II: ANALYSIS OF *IN CANTICUM CANTICORUM* (c. 391)

6. **The Baptismal Exegesis of the Song of Songs** — 153
   Introduction — 153
   Homily 1 (Song 1:1–4) — 153
      Baptismal Exegesis — 153
      Pneumatic Language, Pneumatology, and Purified Desire — 155
      The Baptismal 'Kiss' — 157
      Power, Activity, and the Spiritual Senses — 160
      Post-baptismal Virtue and the Unified Activity of Christ and the Spirit — 162
   Homily 2 (Song 1:5–8) — 165
      Baptismal Illumination — 165
      Illumination by Christ and the Spirit — 166
      Baptism, Pneumatology, and the Restoration of Humanity — 167
      The Spirit as 'Drink' Poured from Christ's Side — 170
   Homily 3 (Song 1:9–14) — 171
      Transformation through Baptismal Waters — 171
      The Spiritual Senses and the Unified Activity of Christ and the Spirit — 172
      Baptismal Exegesis of Christ's Anointing by 'Spikenard' — 176
      Unified Activity of Christ and the Spirit — 178
   Conclusion — 179

CONTENTS vii

7. **Advancement and Ascent: The Unified Activity of Christ and the Spirit** 181
   Introduction 181
   Homily 4 (Song 1:15–27) 181
     Purification and Advancement to Christ via the Spirit 181
     Seeing the Beauty of God in Christ with the Eyes of the Spirit 183
     Excursus: Sarah Coakley on Romans 8 and the 'Incorporative'
     Model of the Trinity 185
   Homily 5 (Song 2:8–17) 189
     The Spirit and the Coming of the Incarnate Christ 189
     Epektasis and Pneumatology 191
     Nourished by Christ and the Spirit 194
   Homilies 8 and 9 (Song 4:8–15) 196
     Burial and Resurrection with Christ through the Spirit 196
     Baptism and Transformation in Trinitarian Glory 197
   Homily 10 (Song 4:16–5:2a) 200
     The Mind Ruled by the Spirit 200
     Transformation by the Spirit of Pentecost 201
   Homily 12 (Song 5:5–7) 204
     The Choice to Be 'Buried with Christ' 204
     Choice, Faith, and Works 205
     Mortification and Vivification as Unified Activity of
     Christ and the Spirit 208
     Excursus: Baptismal Exegesis in the 'Middle Homilies' 212
   Conclusion 215

8. **Christ's Pneumatic Body in the Glory of the Trinity** 218
   Introduction 218
   Homily 7 (Song 3:9–4:7a) 219
     Christ's Pneumatic Body 219
     The Post-resurrection Glorification of Christ's Body 223
     Excursus: Christ's Pneumatic Body in *Hom. in 1 Cor. 15:28* 225
   Homilies 13, 14, and 15 (Song 5:8–6:9) 228
     Christ's Pneumatic Body in Trinitarian Glory 228
   Conclusion 237

Conclusion 238

Bibliography of Primary Sources 245
Bibliography of Secondary Sources 249
Scripture Index 259
Index 263

7. Advancement and Ascent: The Unified Activity of Christ and the Spirit

7. Advancement and Ascent: The Unified Activity of Christ and the Spirit	181
Introduction	181
Homily 4 (Song 1:15-2:7)	181
Purification and Advancement in Christ via the Spirit	181
Seeing the Beauty of God in Christ with the Eyes of the Soul	183
Excursus: Sarah Coakley on Romans 8 and the Incorporative Model of the Trinity	185
Homily 5 (Song 2:8-17)	185
The Spirit and the Coming of the Incarnate Christ	189
Prayer and Pneumatology	191
Nourished by Christ and the Spirit	194
Homilies 8 and 9 (Song 4:5-16)	196
Burial and Resurrection with Christ through the Spirit	196
Baptism and Transformation in Trinitarian Glory	197
Homily 10 (Song 4:6-5:2)	200
The Mind Ruled by the Spirit	200
Transformation by the Spirit of Pentecost	201
Homily 12 (Song 5:5-7)	204
The Choice to be Buried with Christ	204
Choice, Faith, and Works	205
Mortification and Vivification as Christ's Activity of Christ and the Spirit	208
Excursus: Baptismal Exegesis in the Macarian Homilies	212
Conclusion	216
8. Christ's Pneumatic Body in the Glory of the Trinity	218
Introduction	218
Homily 7 (Song 2:9-17)	219
Christ's Poem the Body	219
The Post-resurrection Characteristics of Christ's Body	223
Excursus: Christ's Pneumatic Body in 1 Cor. 15:35	226
Homilies 13, 14, and 15 (Song 6:4-6:9)	228
Christ's Pneumatic Body in Trinitarian Glory	228
Conclusion	237
Conclusion	238
Bibliography of Primary Sources	245
Bibliography of Secondary Sources	249
Scripture Index	259
Index	267

Acknowledgements

This book is the product of my doctoral research conducted at Peterhouse, University of Cambridge, between 2017 and 2020, generously funded by the Peterhouse Graduate Studentship and the Faculty of Divinity Crosse Studentship. My express gratitude goes to Steven Connor and Peter Harland for their assistance in securing extensions for both of these studentships in response to the interruption caused by the Coronavirus pandemic. I am also thankful to the Institute for Religion and Culture, Canada, for providing additional financial aid.

Many have made invaluable contributions at key stages along the way. Due credit must be given to my first-year doctoral examiners, Sarah Coakley and James Carleton Paget, who offered expert guidance in my project's early phase. I am indebted to my doctoral supervisor, Professor Thomas Graumann, who was instrumental in fine-tuning my research focus and without whose advice my thesis would not have reached completion. The Faculty of Divinity librarians, Clemens Gresser and Matthew Patmore, consistently went above and beyond the call of duty in locating and purchasing essential research materials. In 2018, I attended the 14th International Colloquium on Gregory of Nyssa, held at Les Collège des Bernardins, Paris, where I discussed my project with several experts, notably Giulio Maspero, Miguel Brugarolas, and Andrew Radde-Gallwitz. Opportunities to discuss aspects of my research with Michael Champion and Mark Edwards took place during the 18th International Conference on Patristic Studies, held at Oxford in 2019. The expenses for travel, accommodation, and registration for both conferences were generously covered by Peterhouse and Faculty of Divinity bursaries. My fellow doctoral student Austin Stevenson readily offered judicious observations on several draft chapters. Finally, I am grateful to my thesis examiners, Morwenna Ludlow and Mark Smith, who provided exacting feedback on all aspects of my research in their examiner's reports.

It has been a pleasure working with the editorial team of the Oxford Studies in Historical Theology series. I wish to express my thanks to Richard Muller for his endorsement of the work, and the two anonymous reviewers for their careful, detailed engagements. Likewise, I am greatly appreciative of

X ACKNOWLEDGEMENTS

the work of Tom Perridge, Rada Radojicic, and the editorial team at Oxford University Press for ensuring that the path to publication of this book was as smooth as possible.

Some sections of this book have been previously published elsewhere in articles. In chronological order, Chapter 4 was published in *Modern Theology*, 35/4 (2019), and Chapter 5 in the *Journal of Theological Studies*, 75/1 (2020); a significant portion of Chapter 1 was published in *Studia Patristica*, 115 (2021); and portions of Chapters 2 and 8 were published in the *International Journal of Systematic Theology*, 24/4 (2022). My thanks go to Oxford University Press, Peeters Publishers, and Wiley for granting permissions to reprint this material.

A number of friends are deserving of special mention for the joyful camaraderie during the period of my doctoral research. Firstly, my friends from Peterhouse MCR: Matthew Pawlak, Kan Gunawardena, Francisco Garita, Tom Langley, Jake Griesel, Eloise Davies, Daniel McKay, Jenny Ward, Tobias Cremer, Niahm Colbrook, Alex Tsompanidis, Adam Behan, Antoine Koen, Carolina Orozco, Peter Faul, Sam Woodman, Will Kaufhold, Theresa Jakuszeit, Fred Maeng, Alicia Mavor, Harry Spillane, Ephraim Levinson, William Simpson, James Thorne, Vincent Williams, Catherine Richards, Joanna Usher, and Matilda Gillis. Secondly, my friends and collaborators from the Cambridge Faculty of Divinity: Austin Stevenson, Roger Revell, Hannah Black, Ryan Gilfeather, Jessica Scott, Pui Ip, Isidoros Katsos, Jesse Grenz, Jonathan Platter, and Matthew Fell. Lastly, this book would not have been possible without the love and support of my family, especially Felix, Miguel, Theodor, Ana, and Jennifer.

Abbreviations

I. Gregory of Nyssa

anim. et res.	de anima et resurrectione [GNO III/3]
Apoll.	antirrheticus adversus Apolinarium [GNO III/1, 131–233]
	(English trans. = Orton)
ascens.	in ascensionem Christi oratio [GNO IX, 323–327]
bapt. Chr.	in baptismum Christi, in diem luminem [GNO IX, 221–242]
	(English trans. = NPNF II/5)
bapt. diff.	adversus eos qui baptismum differunt [GNO X/2, 355–370]
beat. 1-8	de beatitudinibus [GNO VII/2, 75–170]
	(English trans. = Graef)
ep. 1–25	epistulae [GNO VIII/2]
	(English trans. = Silvas)
Eun. I	contra Eunomium I [GNO I, 22–225]
	(English trans. = Hall I)
Eun. II	contra Eunomium II [GNO I, 226–409]
	(English trans. = Hall II)
Eun. III	contra Eunomium III [GNO II, 3–311]
	(English trans. = Hall III)
fid.	ad Simplicium, de fide [GNO III/1, 61–67]
	(English trans. = NPNF II/5)
hom. in 1 Cor. 15:28	homilia in illud: Quando sibi subjecerit; Tunc et ipse: in illud filius [GNO III/2, 1–28]
	(English trans. = Greer)
hom. in Cant.	in Canticum Canticorum [GNO VI, 3–469]
	(English trans. = Norris II)
Maced.	adversus Macedonianos [GNO III/1, 89–115]
	(English trans. = Radde-Gallwitz)
or. catech.	oratio catechetica magna [GNO III/4]
	(English trans. = Green)
or. dom.	de oratione dominica [GNO VII/2]

xii ABBREVIATIONS

	(English trans. = Graef)
perf.	*de perfectione* [*GNO* VIII/1, 173–214]
	(English trans. = Woods Callahan II; Greer)
Pss. titt.	*in inscriptiones Psalmorum* [*GNO* V, 24–175]
	(English trans. = Heine)
ref. Eun.	*Refutatio Confessionis Eunomii*
Steph. 1	*in sanctum Stephanum* I [*GNO* X/1, 75–94]
Trin.	*ad Eustathium, de sancta trinitate* [*GNO* III/1, 3–16]
	(English trans.= Silvas)
v. Mos.	*vita Moysis* [*GNO* VII/1]
	(English trans. = Malherbe and Ferguson)
virg.	*de virginitate* [*GNO* VIII/1, 247–343]
	(English trans. = Woods Callahan)

II. Other

Ar. 2	Athanasius, *orationes tres adversus Arianos*
	(English trans. = NPNF II/4)
BDGN	*Brill Dictionary of Gregory of Nyssa*
Cant.	Origen, *Commentarium in Cant.*
	(English trans. = Lawson)
corp. et div.	Apolinarius of Laodicea, *de unione corporis et divinitatis in Christo* [Lietzmann]
	(English trans.= Norris I)
d.e.	Eusebius of Caesarea, *demonstratio evangelica*
ep. 1–366	Basil of Caesarea, *epistulae* [PG 32]
Eun. 1–3	Basil of Caesarea, *adversus Eunomium libri tres*
	(English trans. = DelCogliano and Radde-Gallwitz)
fr. 1–115	Marcellus of Ancyra, *fragmenta* [Vinzent]
fr. 1–171	Apolinarius of Laodicea, *fragmenta* [Lietzmann]
	(English trans. = Norris I)
GNO	*Gregorii Nysseni Opera*
haer.	Epiphanius of Salamis, *panarion seu adversus lxxx haereses*
	(English trans.= Williams)
inc. et c. Ar.	pseudo-Athanasius, *de incarnatione et contra Arianos* [PG 26]
	(English trans. = Deferrari)
insomn.	Synesius of Cyrene, *de insomniis*

	(English trans. = Russell)
loc. aff.	Galen, *de locis affectis*
	(English trans. = Siegel)
NPNF	*Nicene and Post-Nicene Fathers*
	II/4 = Athanasius
	II/5 = Gregory Nyssa
PG	*Patrologia Graeca*
Spir.	Basil of Caesarea, *liber de Spiritu sancto*

Introduction

Between the early 370s and 390s, Gregory of Nyssa (*c.* 335–*c.* 394) served as a leading figure amidst the most pressing theological disputes of his time. In his capacity as bishop he produced a series of polemical treatises and personal correspondences defending what he held to be the orthodox account of trinitarian and christological doctrine. Within this same role, in a manner no less detached from theological controversy, Gregory acted as spiritual guide over his church. His body of works therefore includes a sizeable collection of homilies that expound upon scriptural teaching on both sound doctrine and the ethical life of virtue in which the church was to be formed. A common thread that unites the aims of both Gregory's technical, polemical works and his homiletical, spiritual writings during this entire period is his underlying interest in *soteriology*—that is, Gregory's basic concern rightly to articulate the conditions, theological and anthropological, under which finite and fallen humanity may be transformed, restored to its original state, and so united with God. One of the main tasks of the present work is to define, through a close analysis of several of Gregory's major writings, the main contours of this soteriological account of human transformation and union with God.

On the one hand, Gregory's account of human transformation and union with God has what we might call an *objective* aspect. This is the dimension of human salvation that, according to Gregory, is grounded in the divine initiative and activity, and can be considered independently of the 'first person' *subjective* experience of it. Gregory's polemical writings against the Macedonians, Eunomians, and Apollinarians, for instance, take for granted the possibility of articulating and defending *objective* grounds for human salvation in the economy with little to no reference to one's *subjective* experience of this reality. However, many of Gregory's more eirenic works, his homilies especially, reflect extensively upon a corresponding *subjective* experience of this same reality, encompassing the full ambit of the embodied, noetic, voluntary, and affective dimensions of human existence. How, then,

---

Christ, the Spirit, and Human Transformation in Gregory of Nyssa's In Canticum Canticorum. Alexander L. Abecina, Oxford University Press. © Oxford University Press 2024. DOI: 10.1093/oso/9780197745946.003.0001

2 INTRODUCTION

did Gregory understand the relationship between these two aspects—the *objective* and the *subjective*—of his account of human transformation and union with God; and, in particular, how does his understanding manifest itself across his doctrinal and homiletical writings? This is the question upon which I focus, culminating in an analysis of what is most probably Gregory's final written work, *hom. in Cant.* In turn, this question generates a number of other related queries that will be addressed along the way: To what degree is there coherence between the way Gregory relates the *objective* and *subjective* aspects? Are they logically or even 'systematically' related in a manner that crosses literary genres?

To this end, the present work is divided into two parts. In Part I (Chapters 1–5), I focus on a selection of Gregory's works written prior to *hom. in Cant.* By attending to the often-neglected role of pneumatology in these works, I argue that he held a largely coherent doctrinal account of the *objective* reality of human transformation and union with God grounded in:

- i. the unified activity of the Father, Son, and Holy Spirit; and
- ii. the incarnation of Christ, expressed in terms of what I call a Spirit-based christology.

In Part II (Chapters 6–8), I argue that Gregory wrote *hom. in Cant.* to guide his readers through a *subjective process* of interpreting the Song of Songs by which the *objective* reality of human transformation and union with God of which Gregory speaks throughout his corpus is experienced as a *subjective* reality within the depth of the whole person—heart, mind, body, and soul. I shall argue that, for Gregory, this *subjective process* of embodied, noetic, and affective transformation is itself grounded in both points (i) and (ii) and, in this way, completes and renders coherent his account of the *objective* reality of human transformation and union with God articulated in earlier works.

Chronology of Works

Gregory's works will be analysed in roughly chronological order, as best as this order can be determined. The approach is chosen *not* in order to chart the course of Gregory's 'development of thought' (more on this below), but rather because Gregory's literary-theological aims are conditioned by specific historical, polemical, and ecclesial contexts; and the natural sequence

INTRODUCTION 3

in which these contexts are arranged is chronologically. Furthermore, the chronological approach offers an orderly account of Gregory's thought *prior to* his exposition of the Song of Songs and can thus confidently be taken as a basis for Gregory's exegesis in *hom. in Cant.*

It is uncontroversial to begin this book, then, with an analysis of *virg.* as it is considered by a majority of scholars either to be early or Gregory's earliest.[1] In the introduction to this treatise, Gregory indicates that Basil, 'our most reverend bishop and father' is still alive,[2] so *virg.* must have been written after 370, the date of Basil's consecration as bishop, and prior to his death on 1 January, 379. This fact alone places *virg.* earlier than all other works considered in this book. Aubineau and Daniélou are of the view that the treatise was composed before Gregory became bishop, and hence they assign it a date of 371.[3] Cadenhead suggests that, owing to its prominent rhetorical features, *virg.* should be dated between 370 and 372, a period when Gregory was a practicing rhetorician.[4] However, Staats argues that, due to its apparent references to 'Messalians', *virg.* should be dated sometime between 375 and 378,[5] a period that falls within what Columba Stewart has called the first phase of the emergence of Messalianism.[6]

Staats' observation has merit, however it need not preclude an earlier dating. The link between *virg.* and Messalianism can be traced to Basil of Caesarea's longstanding friendship with Eustathius of Sebaste, who, at the Council of Gangra (*c.* 340), together with 'Eustathian' ascetics, was condemned for holding extreme views on marriage, fasting, and other church practices.[7] However, in 372 tensions began to rise between Basil and Eustathius' disciples; and by 375, after ongoing conflicts, Basil and Eustathius would come to sever their ties over a disagreement regarding the doctrine of the Holy Spirit. Between 373 and 375 Basil penned the 'eirenic' yet clearly

---

[1] Cf. Morwenna Ludlow, *Gregory of Nyssa: Ancient and [Post]modern* (Oxford: Oxford University Press, 2007), 184 n.6; Raphael A. Cadenhead, *The Body and Desire: Gregory of Nyssa's Ascetical Theology* (Oakland: University of California Press, 2018), 171.

[2] Virginia Woods Callahan, *Saint Gregory of Nyssa: Ascetical Works*, The Fathers of the Church 58 (Washington, DC: Catholic University of America Press, 1967), 7.

[3] Michel Aubineau, *Traité de la Virginité: Introduction, texte critique, traduction, commentaire et index*, Sources Chretiennes 119 (Paris: Les Éditions du Cerf, 1966), 31; Jean Daniélou, 'La chronologie des oeuvres de Grégoire de Nyssa', in *Studia Patristica 7*, ed. F. L. Cross (Leuven: Peeters, 1966), 160.

[4] Cadenhead, *Body and Desire*, 171.

[5] R, Staats, 'Basilius als lebende Mönchsregel in Gregor von Nyssa De Virginitate', *Vigiliae Christianae*, 39 (1985), 228–255.

[6] Columba Stewart, *'Working the Earth of the Heart': The Messalian Controversy in History, Texts, and Language to AD 431* (Oxford: Clarendon Press, 1991), 14–23.

[7] John Meyendorff, *The Byzantine Legacy in the Orthodox Church* (New York: St. Vladimir's Press, 1982), 200–201.

4 INTRODUCTION

anti-Eustathian work *On the Holy Spirit*, while, at the Council of Cyzicus of 376, Eustathius declared himself leader of the Pneumatomachian party.[8]

As Jason Scarborough notes, 'Basil's long association with *Eustathios of Sebaste* [*sic*] (and by association *Messalianism*) present themselves as the most pressing, and most obvious of Gregory's concerns [when writing *virg.*]'.[9] Moreover, 'the close connection between the earlier views of Basil and the Eustathians clearly informed the writing of the treatise [i.e. *virg.*]'.[10] From this vantage point, Gregory's emphasis in *virg.* on the Holy Spirit, demonic influence, and the necessity of baptism for the ascetical life of virginity (which I shall discuss in Chapter 1) probably reflects points of conflict that would have arisen among Basil, Eustathius, and their respective followers in the early to mid-370s. That Gregory composed a pro-Nicene treatise, critical of Eustathian proclivities for Messalianism, yet without the overt anti-Pneumatomachian polemics characteristic of the late 370s, fits the period between 373 and 375.

On a similar note, it is also uncontroversial that this book concludes with an analysis of *hom. in Cant.*, given that it is widely regarded as either late or the very last of Gregory's works. Some care needs to be taken with the dating as it is apparent that there are two stages of composition. In the first instance, there can be no doubt that the essential content of the homilies that comprise *hom. in Cant.* were actually preached by Gregory in person to his church in Nyssa, likely as part of a Lenten sermon series.[11] Only later did Gregory have a hand in editing the original content and determining the final form by consulting the 'notes' that were taken during his live preaching. The precise timeframe that elapsed between preaching and written composition is uncertain, though Norris offers a convincing case that it must have been relatively short.[12] In any event, it is a moot issue given that my interests in *hom. in Cant.* lie solely in its final form. As others have noted, *hom. in Cant.* was likely composed after *v. Mos.* since the former elaborates on ideas about Moses found

---

[8] Michael A. G. Haykin, *The Spirit of God: The Exegesis of 1 and 2 Corinthians in the Pneumatomachian Controversy of the Fourth Century* (Leiden: Brill, 1994), 9–49.

[9] Jason M. Scarborough, 'Asceticism as Ideology: Gregory of Nyssa's De virginitate', *Union Seminary Quarterly Review* 57 (2003), 131–150.

[10] Scarborough, 'Asceticism as Ideology', 144.

[11] J. Warren Smith, *Passion and Paradise: Human and Divine Emotion in the Thought of Gregory of Nyssa* (New York: Herder and Herder, 2004), 218.

[12] Richard A. Norris Jr., *Gregory of Nyssa: Homilies on the Song of Songs*, Writings from the Greco-Roman World 13 (Atlanta: SBL, 2012), xxii: 'Gregory himself suggests that he had little time to work on revisions "during the days of fasting" (which, I am inclined to suspect, means that is original delivery of the sermons and his revisions were undertaken during the same—busy—Lenten season)'.

INTRODUCTION 5

in the latter.[13] Regarding the dating of *v. Mos.*, Heine suggests that, because it deals with themes relevant to the Eunomian controversy, it should be dated between 380 and 384.[14]

There are reasons to believe, however, that *hom. in Cant.* was not written until well after this period, probably in the year 391. We know that Gregory's composition of *hom. in Cant.* was motivated by a request from Olympias, a woman of noble descent, with whom Gregory was already acquainted.[15] It is likely that Gregory did not receive this request from Olympias until after she was widowed at a young age in 386, and probably not until 391, when Emperor Theodosius I reneged on an earlier decision to temporarily confiscate Olympias' property and forbid her from associating with prominent church leaders.[16] With these considerations in mind, we can surmise that the homilies that form the basis for *hom. in Cant.* were probably preached sometime around 391, while *hom. in Cant.* itself was composed shortly thereafter. If Gregory died, as is believed, in the year 395, then *hom. in Cant.* could conceivably have been composed any time between 391 and the year of his death.[17] Whatever the precise date, the evidence suggests that it is significantly later than any of Gregory's other works considered in this book.

In Chapter 2, I cover several works in which baptismal theology is prominent. The first three works analysed—*ep. 5*, *ep. 24*, and *Maced.*—are clearly to be grouped together, and probably in this chronological order. We find in *ep. 5* a reference to Gregory's involvement in reconciling to the church 'those who came from the assembly of Marcellus [of Ancyra]' in response to instructions given to him by 'orthodox and fellow ministers in the East'.[18] Silvas is probably correct to trace these instructions to the Council of Antioch of 379, and so *ep. 5* was likely to have been written shortly thereafter. Regarding *ep. 24* and *Maced.*, several have noted there are clear parallels between the two works, but Radde-Gallwitz provides a compelling case that

[13] Cadenhead, *Body and Desire*, 178.
[14] R. E. Heine, *Perfection in the Virtuous Life: A Study in the Relationship between Edification and Polemical Theology in Gregory of Nyssa's De Vita Moysis* (Cambridge, MA: Philadelphia Patristic Foundation, 1975), 15.
[15] Norris, *Gregory of Nyssa: Homilies on the Song of Songs*, xx–xxi; Anne-Marie Malingrey, Jean Chrysostome, Lettres à Olympias, 2nd ed., *augmentée de la Vie Anonyme D'Olympias: Introduction, Texte Critique, Traduction et Notes*, Sources Chréttiennes 29 (Paris: Éditions du Cerf, 1968), 13–38.
[16] Norris, *Gregory of Nyssa: Homilies on the Song of Songs*, xx.
[17] Cf. J. B. Cahill, 'The Date and Setting of Gregory of Nyssa's Commentary on the Song of Songs', *Journal of Theological Studies*, 32/2 (January 1981), 447–460.
[18] Anna M. Silvas, *Gregory of Nyssa: The Letters: Introduction, Translation and Commentary*, Supplements to Vigiliae Christianae 83 (Brill: Leiden, 2007), 137; Cf. Andrew Radde-Gallwitz, *Gregory of Nyssa's Doctrinal Works: A Literary Study* (Oxford: Oxford University Press, 2018), 34.

6 INTRODUCTION

these are best explained if the latter work is understood to depend on the former. Beginning with the warranted assumption that *Maced.* 'has something to do with the Council of Constantinople in 381', he puts forth the plausible hypothesis that the work was 'provoked' by the Macedonian bishops that were in attendance.[19] This provides relevant background to Gregory's reference in *Maced.* to his opponents' objection to his 'confession' regarding the equal glory and honour of the Holy Spirit alongside the Father and the Son.[20] Rather than take this as a reference to Constantinople's 'reworked Nicene Creed', Radde-Gallwitz provides the more convincing case that the 'confession' to which his opponents object is the one contained in *ep. 24*. On this account, *Maced.* was composed in 381, while *ep. 24* was written in the same year or year before.[21]

The final two works analysed in Chapter 2—*bapt. diff.* and *bapt. Chr.*—can reliably be dated to the early 380s. According to Daniélou, the Epiphany sermon *bapt. diff.* is likely to have been delivered around 7 January 381, as may confidently be inferred from Gregory's reference to a Scythian invasion in the region of Comana Chryse.[22] Meanwhile, the sermon *bapt. Chr.* can reliably be dated to 383. Gregory refers to Christians who abandoned themselves to pagan amusements on the preceding Sunday, 1 January. The years during Gregory's ministry in which 1 January was a Sunday are therefore 372, 377, 383, and 394. Given that anti-Macedonian arguments feature prominently in this sermon, the most likely year in which it was written is 383.[23]

The remaining works upon which I focus are *Eun.* III, *Apoll.*, and *hom. in 1 Cor. 15:28*. We know that *Eun.* I was written after Basil's death (379), as Gregory mentions in *ep. 29*. There, he writes that after Basil died he 'inherited the controversy of Eunomius' and thus penned *Eun.* I in a mere seventeen days, probably in 380.[24] *Eun.* III must, therefore, have been written after this date, in reaction to a newly disseminated response to Basil from Eunomius. Cadenhead is correct that, given Gregory's eagerness to defend Basil and refute Eunomius, he would have no reason to delay his response to his opponent's final tome. Thus, the typical dating of *Eun.* III to sometime around 383 is highly plausible. Turning now to *Apoll.*, Daniélou claims this

---

[19] Radde-Gallwitz, *Doctrinal Works*, 63.

[20] Radde-Gallwtiz, *Doctrinal Works*, 63.

[21] Radde-Gallwitz, *Doctrinal Works*, 64–65.

[22] Cf. Jean Daniélou, 'La chronologie des sermons de Grégoire de Nysse', *Revue des Sciences Religieuses*, 29/4 (1955), 353–355.

[23] Cf. Daniélou, 'La chronologie des sermons de Grégoire de Nysse', 362.

[24] Silvas, *Gregory of Nyssa: The Letters*, 207.

INTRODUCTION 7

work was written between 382 and 383.[25] However, May proposes the date of 387 at the earliest, judging it to be later than *ad Theophilum*, which can be reliably dated to around 385.[26] Robin Orton's argument that *Apoll.* pre-dates *ad Theophilum* based on strong resemblances with *Eun.* III is sufficiently convincing, in my view, to side with Daniélou's earlier dating.[27] Regarding which work is earliest, however, it is likely that *Eun.* II predates *Apoll.* given the urgency with which Gregory sought to defend Basil against Eunomius.

Finally, in *hom. in 1 Cor. 15:28*, Gregory offers his exposition of the contested verse, 1 Cor. 15:28. While Daniélou claimed that Gregory turns his interest to this verse only in the mature stage of his thought,[28] and hence assigns it a date of 385, we know that Gregory already showed an interest in refuting the Eunomian interpretation of this verse in the *ref. Eun.*, which he wrote in response to Eunomius' presentation of a confession of faith at Council of Constantiople in 383. I suggest that Gregory would have been motivated to respond to Eunomius in haste, and so the *ref. Eun.* should be dated to around 383 also. The *hom. in 1 Cor. 15:28* should therefore be understood as a composition motivated by the Eunomian controversy and is plausibly dated to around 383/4.[29]

Summing up, then, the order in which Gregory's works are analysed in this book is chronological: *virg.* (373–375), *ep. 5* (379), *ep. 24* (380/1), *Maced.* (381), *bapt. diff.* (381), *bapt. Chr.* (383), *Eun.* III (383), *Apoll.* (383), *hom. in 1 Cor. 15:28* (383/4), *hom. in Cant.* (c. 391–395). To reiterate, I make no global claims about 'development' in Gregory's thought between the writing of *virg.* and *hom. in Cant*, but advance the more modest claim that Gregory's exegesis of the Song of Songs in his final work *hom. in Cant.* can be understood to be grounded in several key theological convictions discerned in his earlier works.

---

[25] Jean Daniélou, 'La chronologie des oeuvres de Grégoire de Nyssa', 163.

[26] Gerhard May, 'Die Chronologie des Lebens und der Werke des Gregor von Nyssa', in *Écriture et Culture Philosophique dans la Pensée de Grégoire de Nyssa*, Actes du Colloque de Chevetogne (22–26 Septembre 1969), ed. Marguerite Harl (Leiden: Brill, 1971), 51–67.

[27] Cf. Robin Orton, 'Struggling with Christology: Apolinarius of Laodicea and St Gregory of Nyssa', *Vox Patrum*, 37 (2017), 35–38; Radde-Gallwitz, *Doctrinal Works*, 194–200.

[28] Daniélou, 'La chronologie des oeuvres de Grégoire de Nyssa', 167.

[29] Cf. J. K. Downing, 'The Treatise of Gregory of Nyssa: 'In Illud: Tunc et ipse Filius'. A Critical Text with Prolegomena' (diss., Harvard University, 1947); Radde-Gallwitz, *Doctrinal Works*, 179.

8 INTRODUCTION

Unified Activity of the Trinity

A key concept that features throughout this book is Gregorys' notion of the unified activity of the Trinity. While the teaching is to be found throughout his works, a particularly clear statement of it is found in *De oratione dominica*:

> 'May Thy Holy Spirit come', he says, 'and purify us' (Luke 11:2, textual variant). The proper power and virtue of the Holy Spirit is precisely to cleanse sin; for what is pure and undefiled requires no cleansing. Now the very same thing the Apostle says about the Only-Begotten, who, *making purgation of our sins, sits on the right hand of the majesty* of the Father (Heb 1:3). Therefore one is the work of either (ἓν ἑκατέρου τὸ ἔργον), of the Spirit who cleanses from sin as well as of Christ who has made the purgation. But, if the two perform the same activity (ἡ ἐνέργεια μία), then their power must also be exactly the same (ἡ δύναμις πάντως ἡ αὐτή ἐστιν), for every operation is the effect of power (πᾶσα γὰρ ἐνέργεια δυνάμεώς ἐστιν ἀποτέλεσμα). If then there is one activity as well as one power (καὶ ἐνέργεια καὶ δύναμις μία), how can one assume a diversity of nature (ἑτερότητα φύσεως) in those in whom we can find no difference of power and operation (οὐδεμίαν κατὰ τὴν δύναμίν τε καὶ ἐνέργειαν διαφοράν)?[30]

A proper appreciation of the teaching, and the different uses to which Gregory puts it, requires some understanding of his metaphysical commitments, specifically with regard to the way 'power' (δύναμις) is understood within the nature-power-activity triad. The definitive study of Gregory's understanding of 'power' is that of Michel René Barnes. For Gregory, power (δύναμις) is 'the capacity to act that is distinctive to a specific existent and that manifests the nature of that existent'.[31] Thus, argues Gregory, if Father and Son have the same 'power' they must have the same 'nature'.[32] While the association of power and nature is commonplace in Gregory's Hellenistic philosophical milieu, the same cannot be said with regard to the connection Gregory draws between God's activity and God's nature. Thus, observes Barnes, 'the concept of the activity cannot, in itself, identify the kind of causal relationship between an existent and the effects the existent has, so that a specific

---

[30] *GNO* VII/2.40.13–41.10; Graef, 53, slight modifications.

[31] Michel René Barnes, *The Power of God: Δύναμις in Gregory of Nyssa's Trinitarian Theology* (Washington, DC: Catholic University of America Press, 2001), 13.

[32] Barnes, *The Power of God*, 13.

effect necessarily signals a specific nature'.[33] Barnes helpfully draws the example of a bicycle and a horse. Both perform the same activity of 'transportation', yet clearly do not share a common nature.[34] Thus, one cannot claim a common nature by simply naming *any* activity associated with Trinitarian persons. Rather, one must identify an activity that falls within a particular, well-defined class. To quote Barnes, '[o]nly when an activity is understood as *the activity produced by the power of an existent* is the class of activities specified in such a way that an activity is the expression of a nature'.[35] Lewis Ayres sums Gregory's view this way: 'if the activities of the three [i.e. Father, Son, and Holy Spirit] are the same, then the power which gave rise to them is the same and the ineffable divine nature in which that power is inherent must also be one'.[36]

Throughout this book I appeal several times to Gregory's notion of the unified activity of the Trinity, which further re-enforces the arguments of Barnes summarized here.[37] In Part I, where I examine a number of Gregory's earlier works, a key focus is the manner in which Gregory connects his teaching on the unified activity of the Trinity to his baptismal theology and, in turn, to human transformation. In Part II, I show how Gregory's baptismal theology, together with his teaching on trinitarian unity of activity, informs to a significant degree his understanding that the right reading of Song of Songs facilitates human transformation and union with God.

Chapter Overview

In Chapter 1, I lay the groundwork for my investigation with an analysis of *virg.* and argue that Gregory's pneumatology plays the primary role in achieving the work's *skopos*. He demonstrates that it is impossible for weak and fallen humanity to see God unless the power of death is overcome by the life-giving power of the Holy Spirit. With reference to baptismal illumination and regeneration, and the use of what I shall call 'baptismal exegesis' of scripture, Gregory shows that it is only by the Spirit that the virgin

---

[33] Barnes, *The Power of God*, 301.
[34] Barnes, *The Power of God*, 301–302.
[35] Barnes, *The Power of God*, 302.
[36] Lewis Ayres, *Nicaea and Its Legacy: An Approach to Fourth-Century Trinitarian Theology* (Oxford: Oxford University Press, 2004), 355.
[37] Cf. Ayres, *Nicaea and Its Legacy*, 347–359; Giulio Maspero, *Trinity and Man: Gregory of Nyssa's Ad Ablablium*, Supplements to Vigiliae Christianae 86 (Leiden: Brill, 2007), 56.

10 INTRODUCTION

ascetic may become spiritually married to Christ, and it is through the same Spirit that the spiritual offspring of the virtues that lead to the beatific vision are borne. We find that from the earliest moments of his writing career, Gregory conceives of marriage with Christ in emphatically anti-Macedonian terms, as a work initiated and perfected by the Spirit, who shares the essential attributes of the Father and the Son, a basic insight that he will carry into the writing of *hom. in Cant.*

In Chapter 2 I delve deeper into Gregory's understanding of baptism, and his use of baptismal exegesis, to conceptualize and articulate his trinitarian theology. First, I investigate *ep. 5*, *ep. 24*, and *Maced.*, where I analyse Gregory's arguments for the unity of the trinitarian persons, derived from his exegesis of the baptismal formula handed down by Jesus to his disciples (cf. Matt. 28:19–20). This uncovers what I will term Gregory's 'linear' and 'circular' models of trinitarian unity of activity. The former describes the 'linear' transmission of life-giving power to humanity *from* the Father, *through* the Son, *in* the Spirit, and is thereby concretely wedded to the economy of salvation. The latter describes the 'circular' intra-trinitarian exchange of 'glory'. While the latter model appears to stand independently of the economy, Gregory indicates that it is in fact by virtue of the process described by the 'linear' model that humanity can behold and, ultimately, be attached to the eternal exchange of 'glory' depicted by the 'circular' model. I advance as a working hypothesis that the precondition and ground for this attachment is not only baptism, but, according to Gregory's reference to John 17:5 at a crucial hinge-point in the baptismal argument of *Maced.*, the incarnate Christ himself, via his post-passion glorification by the Holy Spirit. The substantiation of this hypothesis is given in Chapter 4, where I show that, in parallel passages that appear in *Apoll.*, *hom. in 1 Cor. 15:28*, and *hom. in Cant.*, Gregory cites John 17:5 in a manner that directly supports my contention.

Second, I investigate two of Gregory's Epiphany sermons, *bapt. diff.* and *bapt. Chr.*, which focus upon Christ's baptism and regeneration by the Spirit in the Jordan river as the 'first-fruit' of the 'common lump' of restored humanity. These sermons, which view Christ as the prototypical recipient of the unified activity of the Father, Son, and Spirit through baptism, help to construct an emerging picture of the underlying structure of Gregory's doctrine on human transformation and union with God.

In Chapter 3, I turn to *Eun.* III with the aim of addressing some of the issues raised by my analysis of Gregory's baptismal theology in Chapter 2.

On the one hand, I show that, throughout this work, Gregory conceives of human transformation and union with God just as we would expect in light of his trinitarian-baptismal theology. Humanity is saved through the incarnation, which is made effective through the Holy Spirit's regeneration at baptism, whereby Christ's own baptism serves as the paradigm and precondition. However, when we attend to Gregory's christology proper, which constitutes the main theme of *Eun*. III, we find a conspicuous absence of the role of the Spirit in his account of the unity of the humanity and divinity in the incarnate Christ. This is particularly evident in Gregory's account of the post-resurrection transformation of Christ's flesh into unity with Only-begotten Son. Thus, the christology of *Eun*. III threatens to render Gregory's trinitarian and baptismal theology drastically incoherent, for while Gregory insists in his trinitarian theology and his theology of baptism that the Father, Son, and Spirit act in unity to transform and save humanity, the christology of *Eun*. III calls into question the basis for this unity of activity in the incarnation itself, upon which human salvation is supposedly grounded. In this work there appear to be two distinct accounts of human salvation that are not easily reconciled.

Does this offer yet further evidence of what some of Gregory's interpreters have claimed—that he is simply an incoherent thinker? We must consider, however, that the blatant incoherence might be explained by constraints placed on Gregory by the polemical context of *Eun*. III. After all, to assign an essential role to the Holy Spirit in his account of the unity of Christ's divine and human natures would have been a self-defeating strategy given that Eunomius held *both* the Son *and* the Spirit to be lower in status than the Father. This chapter thus brings into focus the fundamental question of how we ought to read Gregory. Do systematic readings of *Eun*. III introduce distortions to his christology by failing to account for subtle polemical strategies necessitated by the occasion? While Chapter 3 leaves this question momentarily unanswered, I address it at full length in Chapter 5.

In Chapter 4, I turn to Gregory's second major christological treatise, *Apoll*. Apolinarius argued that the divinity and humanity of Christ were united via the 'Spirit', by which he in fact meant the divine *Logos* that stood in the 'place' normally occupied by the human mind. I show that Gregory offered his own alternative account of Christ's unity via the Holy Spirit's anointing of Christ in eternity, at conception, and in the post-resurrection transformation of Christ's flesh. In this way, the Holy Spirit grounds both

12   INTRODUCTION

the 'static' and 'dynamic' unity of the divine and human natures in Christ. *Apoll.* therefore presents us with a significantly more coherent picture of the relationship between Gregory's trinitarian theology and his christology, vis-à-vis trinitarian unity of activity, than we find in *Eun.* III. When this Spirit-based christology is applied to his exegesis of 1 Cor. 15:28 in *hom. in 1 Cor. 15:28*, Gregory offers a view of human transformation much more coherent with this trinitarian theology and christology: just as the man assumed in the incarnation is united to the divinity of the Only-begotten Son by the Holy Spirit's anointing, and through this union to the Father, so too is the rest of humanity analogously united to the divinity of the Son, and hence to the Father, by one and the same Spirit. The analysis undertaken here offers substantial support to my hypothesis in Chapter 2 regarding Gregory's exegesis of John 17:5, namely that Gregory alludes to this verse in *Maced.* to mark the post-passion glorification of Christ's flesh by the Spirit as the basis for the rest of humanity's inclusion into the 'circular', intra-trinitarian exchange of glory.

The pronounced difference between the christology of *Eun.* III and *Apoll.* in turn raises the question of the supposed 'development' of Gregory's christology. In Chapter 5, I address the issue of development by returning to the problematic christology of *Eun.* III. With the Spirit-based christology of *Apoll.* in view, I ask if it is possible that Gregory already held a Spirit-based account of Christ's unity when he wrote *Eun.* III. I analyse Gregory's anti-Macedonian works *Trin.* and *Maced.* and show that there is a strong likelihood that this is indeed the case. I offer justification for this by formulating criteria for detecting probable traces of a Spirit-based christology in *Trin.*, *Maced.*, and *Eun.* III.

I conclude that Gregory probably concealed his Spirit-based christology in *Eun.* III for pragmatic reasons. Since Eunomius did not consider the Holy Spirit to be divine, any appeal that Gregory might have made to pneumatology to substantiate his christological argument for Christ's unity could only be self-defeating. Further, I suggest that Gregory's Spirit-based christology is in fact the foundation for his arguments for the Spirit's 'dignity' rather than the other way around, since the latter appears to rest on assumptions about the nature of 'anointing' that are integral to and explicitly articulated in the former. Thus, I will be able to show that this Spirit-based christology is the more original and authentic account of the unity of Christ's divine and human natures in Gregory's thought than the account found in *Eun.* III, and can be seen to underlie some of his arguments advanced in *Trin.* and *Maced.* In this way, it is with reference to Gregory's Spirit-based

INTRODUCTION 13

christology that we make best sense of the interconnecting structure of his doctrinal thought.

The analysis of Chapters 1–5 helps to define the main contours of what I refer to as Gregory's account of the *objective* reality of human salvation, grounded in (i) the unified activity of the Trinity and (ii) the incarnation of Christ, expressed in terms of a Spirit-based christology. It is an account of *objective* reality insofar as it articulates a vision of human transformation and union with God grounded in the divine initiative, independently of the perspective of the 'first person' *subjective* experience. Yet, Gregory's account of the *objective* remains incomplete, and thus incoherent, in an important sense in the absence of an account of the *subjective* dimension; for, as I show in my analysis of *virg.*, the *objective* reality of human transformation and union with God is, for Gregory, consequent upon humanity's *love* for God with the whole heart, mind, and soul. By viewing Gregory's theology once more from a systematic-theological vantage point, we see that his account of human transformation and union with God stated objectively therefore calls for a corresponding account of transformation and union from the perspective of *subjective* love for God. It is apparent that if theological coherence in this broader sense is to be preserved, this account of the *subjective* must also be grounded in trinitarian unity of activity and Spirit-based christology.

In Part II (Chapters 6–8), I argue that, in *hom. in Cant.*, Gregory offers an interpretation of the Song of Songs by which his account of the *objective* reality of human transformation and union with God becomes a *subjective* reality for his readers. Further, I show that Gregory's account of this subjective process of rightly reading the Song of Songs is itself thoroughly grounded in his understanding of trinitarian unity of activity and Spirit-based christology. In this way, *hom. in Cant.* completes and renders coherent his account of human transformation and union with God articulated in earlier doctrinal works from the perspective of human subjective experience.

Thus, Chapter 6 focuses on Gregory's use of baptismal exegesis in Homilies 1, 2, and 3 (with brief comment on Homily 6) to interpret the Bride of the Song as being initiated into this path to union via 'descending' trinitarian unity of activity. Chapter 7 focuses on Gregory's depiction of the unified activity of Christ and the Spirit in Homilies 4, 5, 8, 9, 10, 11, and 12, in bringing the Bride through progressive stages of 'ascending' spiritual advancement and ascent into union with Christ. Chapter 8 covers Gregory's teaching in Homilies 7, 13,14, and 15 on the church as Christ's pneumatic body united by the Spirit to the eternal 'circular' glory of the Trinity.

14   INTRODUCTION

Gregory as Systematic Thinker

Can Gregory's thought be considered 'systematic'? If we are merely enquiring into his ability to form more or less cogent expositions of doctrine within this or that stand-alone treatise, then it appears to be self-evidently true that it can. The more difficult problem with which this book engages is how we evaluate the 'systematic' quality of Gregory's thought over time, across multiple works, social and polemical contexts, and literary genres.

By way of definition, I regard Gregory to be systematic if his thought exhibits a significant degree of internal *coherence*. The theological claims by which we assess his thought are deemed coherent not only if they are *consistent* with one another (i.e. they do not lead to logical contradiction) but, more importantly, if they are logically *entailed* by one another—that is, if claims logically *follow* from other claims. To even begin to enquire into Gregory as a systematic thinker in this sense is, therefore, to admit that his thought can accurately be expressed as a set of theological propositions amenable to such analysis. But it is precisely on this note that we may already begin to question whether Gregory's thought is open to this kind of enquiry without falling foul of anachronism and unwarranted imposition of 'system'.

In response, I suggest that these dangers can be greatly minimized if we learn to think along *with Gregory* with a disciplined approach. Two factors are crucial—the *literary* and the *historical*. On this score, Andrew Radde-Gallwitz contends that the theological *content* of Gregory's claims is inseparable from the literary *form* in which the claims are communicated and, furthermore, that such claims cannot be properly understood in isolation from the works' occasion and *skopos*.[38] Ideally, when reading Gregory:

> each passage must be set within the part of the work in which it appears; each part must be nested within the whole work; the whole work must be set within Gregory's wider corpus, and in particular must be brought into dialogue with any works with relevant parallels; and then these parallel works must, to the extent possible, be read against the backdrop of their particular occasions and moments. If there *is* a system to be discovered, it lies in the structure of a given work: the arrangement (οἰκονομία) and ordering (τάξις, ἀκολουθία) that Gregory, with his rhetorical training, uses to unfold

[38] Radde-Gallwitz, *Doctrinal Works*, 8.

INTRODUCTION 15

his point . . . by attending to works' structures, convincing patterns across the works can emerge.[39]

While the approach outlined here will be reflected throughout this book, the systematic quality of Gregory's thought will not finally be settled at the level of works' *structures* but, rather, on the *propositional claims* that underpin such structures. If we learn to think *with Gregory*, in the sense delineated by Radde-Gallwitz, we greatly reduce the danger of isolating such claims from the larger thought-structures and the literary-historical contexts that determine what they mean and how they function.

My enquiry into systematic coherence of Gregory's thought is therefore grounded in literary-historical analysis and on this secure basis facilitates further probing into questions of systematic coherence. In doing so, however, the enquiry can begin to lose its literary-historical footing, and it is precisely here that the danger of artificial systematization and anachronism can rear its head. This suggests that, if we are to continue thinking *with Gregory*, the problem of systematic coherence must be solved *iteratively*, by moving *recursively* between the analysis of propositional claims and literary-historical analysis as new light is shed and new questions are raised during the enquiry process.

The methodological approach I advocate may be contrasted with that of Giulio Maspero in *Trinity and Man*, wherein he offers an analysis of Gregory's *Ad Ablabium*. About his work Maspero states:

> The commentary [i.e. on *Ad Ablabium*] will be essentially theological . . . the effort will be to situate the treatise [i.e. *Ad Ablabium*] at the centre of Nyssian theology, studying its central nodes in a largely synthetic perspective. Philological and historical analysis will thus be at the service of the theological one.[40]

Maspero methodologically subordinates history to theology. He is, of course, not alone in this manoeuvre, but is joined by several others who undertake theologically driven, synthetic readings.[41] This interpretive choice is not at

---

[39] Radde-Gallwitz, *Doctrinal Works*, 8–9.

[40] Maspero, *Trinity and Man*, xxviii.

[41] Cf. Sarah Coakley, 'Re-Thinking Gregory of Nyssa: Introduction—Gender, Trinitarian Analogies, and the Pedagogy of The Song', *Modern Theology*, 18/4 (2002), 431–443; Theo Kobusch, 'The Exegesis of the Song of Songs: a New Type of Metaphysics in the Homilies on the Song of Songs by Gregory of Nyssa', in *Gregory of Nyssa: In Canticum Canticorum: Analytical and Supporting Studies. Proceedings of the 13th International Colloquium on Gregory of Nyssa (Rome, 17–20 September 2014)*,

16   INTRODUCTION

all invalid per se, yet the emphasis placed upon a 'synthetic' reading runs the risk of smoothing over or perhaps overlooking literary and historical details that demand more fine-grained investigation. At the same time, synthetic readings of Gregory already *presuppose* from the outset that he *is* a systematically coherent thinker more or less.[42] Maspero does not offer any specific argument for holding this view but suggests that it is a fairly settled matter, here citing the views of Werner Jaeger: 'although Gregory has no closed system, there is a systematic coherence to his thought'.[43]

It should be clear from the comments above that my own approach to Gregory puts Maspero's interpretive choice in reverse. My aim is not to situate Gregory's *hom. in Cant.* 'at the centre of Nyssian theology' in order to elucidate its contents precisely because it is not known from the outset what this 'centre' is, or indeed even if there is anything that might warrant being called a 'centre'. Maspero suggests that this 'centre' is Gregory's interest in 'the connection between immanence and the Trinitarian economy'.[44] It would be difficult to argue that the subject is not of immense importance for Gregory, yet this choice already introduces significant interpretive bias from the outset, which I want to avoid. To repeat what I have already mentioned, I argue that literary-historical analysis comes first, and only secondarily (in order, not importance!) does the analysis give rise to more systematic-theological probing of Gregory's theological claims.

The issue of systematic coherence may be further illuminated by considering a specific set of doctrinal claims upon which I focus in this book. On the one hand, Gregory argues that humanity is transformed and united to God by the Holy Spirit, who acts in unity with the Father and the Son. Yet, Gregory also argues that Jesus of Nazareth is the basis for and 'first-fruit' of the rest of humanity's transformation and union with God. Here, then, we have Gregory offering two different accounts—one in a 'trinitarian' or 'pneumatological' register, and the other more 'christological'—of one and the same soteriological reality. The question of systematic *entailment* of theological claims invites us, as Gregory's interpreters, to now 'triangulate' these

---

Supplements to Vigiliae Christianae 150, ed. Giulio Maspero, Miguel Brugarolas, and Ilaria Vigorelli (Leiden: Brill, 2018), 155–169; Hans Boersma, *Embodiment and Virtue in Gregory of Nyssa: An Anagogical Approach* (Oxford: Oxford University Press, 2013); J. Warren Smith (2004).

[42] So, for instance, Maspero, *Trinity and Man*, 9, can claim: 'The procedure to understand the whole of Nyssian's theology is to move from above to below. Every analogy, every image that Gregory uses, is based in the profound and advanced elaboration of the doctrine of creation'.

[43] Maspero, *Trinity and Man*, xxx–xxxi.

[44] Maspero, *Trinity and Man*, xxviii.

INTRODUCTION   17

views: did Gregory believe that Jesus of Nazareth was transformed and united to God by the Spirit, in unity of activity with the Father and the Son? This is a genuinely *open question* that emerges from systematic-theological enquiry, but which thrusts us back onto literary-historical analysis. If the answer is no, then we might argue that Gregory's thought lacks systematic coherence since the 'christological' account will be found significantly to undermine the 'trinitarian' one by omitting pneumatology. If, however, the answer is yes (as I indeed argue), then we have evidence for systematic coherence, since Gregory's 'trinitarian' and 'christological' accounts of human transformation and union with God will be found to be strongly mutually *entailing*.

As briefly mentioned above, systematic coherence of Gregory's thought can plausibly be inferred if distinct 'patterns' of thought or 'resonant structures' of thought, whose underpinning propositional claims are systematically entailing, recur throughout Gregory's writings. Though I am aware of the complex hermeneutical issues at stake, it is my view that such patterns and resonances inhere *objectively* in Gregory's texts, and they do not emerge by mere accident or by the subjective projection of the reader, but by authorial intent. Moreover, if these 'resonant structures' of thought not only are found to occur diachronically across separate works, but are also integrated within the aims and organizing structure of a *single* literary composition, especially if the work is expansive enough that Gregory is compelled to showcase his full theological repertoire rather than display only a limited range of his thinking as is the case in his shorter works, then there is a strong case to be made that he intentionally aims for systematic coherence of thought. This is why my analysis of *hom. in Cant.* is especially important for adjudicating the claim to *intentional* systematic coherence—*hom. in Cant.* offers an expansive, integrative account of human transformation and union with God that exhibits deep resonances and coherence with patterns of baptismal, trinitarian, Christological, and pneumatological thought that recur throughout Gregory's earlier works, or so shall I argue. Ultimately, this thesis arrives at the measured view expressed by Morwenna Ludlow: 'Gregory's work demonstrates a fundamental coherence, despite its wide range of topics and genres and despite the presence of contradictions and changes of direction over some particular ideas'.[45]

---

[45] Morwenna Ludlow, *Universal Salvation: Eschatology in the Thought of Gregory of Nyssa and Karl Rahner* (Oxford: Oxford University Press, 2000), 10.

18   INTRODUCTION

As one further caveat, the argument for systematic coherence of Gregory's thinking that I seek to advance is *not* a claim about Gregory's theological output *in total*. Much of his writings are left unexplored here. Rather, I offer the more modest claim that intentional systematic coherence applies only to a specific but by no means insignificant *strand* of doctrinal, soteriological reflection that spans his works. It is likely that such coherence has further implications for other strands of Gregory's thinking, though substantiating this claim is not within the remit of this book.

Did Gregory's Thinking Develop?

As we can see, the subject of intentional systematic coherence naturally requires us now to reckon with a topic around which I have already been circling, namely supposed 'development' in Gregory's thinking. Because enquiry into systematic coherence is grounded in literary-historical analysis, it must also engage *as a matter of priority* with this issue. Development does not name just any kind of process of change, but rather denotes progression or evolution of thinking over time about some specific object or objects of thought, caused both by factors *intrinsic* to the process of thinking itself as well *extrinsic* influences derived from the culture and environment within which one's thinking is situated.

On face value it may seem that the relationship between intentional systematic coherence and development is one of *inverse proportion*: a low degree of developmental change in, say, Gregory's thinking about christology may suggest a high degree of intentional systematic coherence, while a high degree of developmental change might support a low degree of systematic coherence. Yet, the investigation undertaken in this book presents a complex set of data that does not admit of such straightforward formulation. For instance, I show in Chapters 3 and 4 that there is a significant difference between the accounts of christology found in *Eun.* III and *Apoll.* We may be compelled to suggest that the difference can straightforwardly be explained by a significant development in Gregory's thinking. Yet, since the alleged development would actually remove a substantial incoherence of propositional claims that underpin recurring patterns of his thought (i.e. among baptismal theology, trinitarian theology, christology, and pneumatology), the development in his christology supports the view that Gregory intentionally steers his thinking toward greater systematic coherence at a higher level. So, here, the relationship is *not* inversely proportional but rather *proportional*.

To posit another hypothetical example, it may be the case that Gregory begins his writing career with a very basic account of 'spiritual marriage' with Christ by the Spirit and ends with a philosophically robust, exegetically rich account of this same doctrine. If the former account, although basic, nevertheless *resonates* and *coheres* with the latter, the later account being *entailed* by certain claims not yet fully 'worked out' in the earlier one, we might wish to argue, once again, for a proportional relationship—*both* a high degree of intentional systematic coherence *and* a high degree of development. Here, the kind of development described is not so much a 'change of mind' as simple 'growth in understanding'. Radde-Gallwitz speaks of this kind of development when he notes that 'his [i.e. Gregory's] preaching seems to have prompted certain developments *in his understanding* of the incarnate economy'.[46] That Gregory experienced growth in understanding of doctrine is altogether uncontroversial. There is a possibility, however, that 'growth of understanding' can be mistaken for 'change of mind' in Gregory's works and thus we require criteria to sort out the differences.

It may be fruitful, therefore, to distinguish between at least two different kinds of theological development. There is, on the one hand, what we might call *convergent* development, whereby the overarching trajectory of an individual's thought smoothly or 'continuously' approaches, steers toward, and finally settles upon some theological destination at which the trajectory has consistently aimed. It seems to me that Raphael Cadenhead is representative of an argument for this kind of *convergent* development, which is more aligned with the notion of 'growth in understanding'. In his own words, 'Gregory adjusts and refines his thinking over time'.[47] On the other hand, a thinker might exhibit *divergent* development, characterized by more radical or 'discontinuous' shifts in this or that theological matter. Such *divergent* development, while disruptive or unpredictable, may yet climax at some higher synthesis or completion of earlier ways of thinking, though this end point is not straightforwardly commensurable with what came beforehand. This kind of development cannot be explained by Cadenhead's appeal to simple 'adjustment' and 'refinement'. Andrew Louth's suggestion that Gregory abandoned the Platonic idea of 'ecstatic' union with God held early in his career

[46] Radde-Gallwitz, *Doctrinal Works*, 27, my italics.
[47] Cadenhead, *Body and Desire*, 3.

20   INTRODUCTION

for an 'epektatic' view of perpetual progress later on may count as one such example.[48] Sarah Coakley's argument for the 'distinctively new dimensions of trinitarian thinking' found in *hom. in Cant.*, as outlined above, is also suggestive of this kind of *divergent* development, which is more aligned with the notion of development as 'change of mind'.

We may yet break this bipartite classification down further into two more categories: development that occurs only within the *short-term* and that which occurs over the *long-term*. Hypothetically, it might be possible to detect *short-term* development in Gregory's christology between the writing of *Eun.* III and *Apoll.* regarding the interpretation of a particular contested biblical passage like Acts 2:36 or Luke 2:52, thereafter reaching a settled view. By contrast, one may wish to argue for a more protracted, *long-term* development of, say, Gregory's pneumatology between the early *virg.* and the much later *hom. in Cant.* Additionally, *long-term* development in pneumatology may have an influence on *short-term* development in christology, or it may not. All this to say, the apparently simple issue of 'development' in Gregory's thought is in fact a highly complex, multi-faceted problem with many moving parts, whose precise mechanics have yet to be properly delineated in existing literature.

One more factor needs to be said about arguments for development of thought, namely that they are valid only if they have *explanatory power*. That is to say, such arguments must offer plausible reasons *why* organic changes in an individual's thoughts occur. Yet, there is one feature of large-scale arguments for development that significantly works against their explanatory power, as highlighted by Cadenhead. He offers his own robust account of alleged diachronic development in Gregory's ascetical theology spanning so-called early, middle, and late phases of his career. Yet, as Cadenhead has rightly acknowledged, arguments for development in Gregory's thinking are prone to circular reasoning. Thus:

It may be argued that commentators have interpretive biases or views that lend support to a particular idea of progression or development in Gregory's thought. They then arrange Gregory's writings to fit within their selected framework of development, grouping texts together based on perceived thematic convergences. The chronology is subsequently used to

---

[48] Andrew Louth, *Origins of the Christian Mystical Tradition: From Plato to Denys* (Oxford: Oxford University Press, 2007), 87.

INTRODUCTION   21

justify developments in Gregory's thought, thereby making the argument circular.[49]

Cadenhead aims to defeat the circularity argument by favouring the 'chronological phase' to which one of Gregory's texts belongs over and above the text's 'exact date' as the basis for building his theory of theological development.[50] This more measured approach, while offering some safeguards, does not completely succeed given that the very notion of 'chronological phase' is itself not immune to the critique of circularity. Cadenhead notes:

> By incorporating the theme of perpetual progress into the methodological nexus of this study, it is hoped that we will appreciate Gregory's ascetical theology as itself an evolving, mutable (*treptos*) intellectual project, subject to change (*metastasis*) and growth (*auxēsis*) over the course of his life.[51]

Here, by privileging one of Gregory's core doctrines, namely 'perpetual progress', within the heart of his 'methodological nexus', Cadenhead's study may be suspected of doing exactly what it consciously sets out to avoid. There is a real risk here of subjectively imposing a narrative of development onto Gregory to fit one's own interests.

For this reason, given that arguments in favour of *large-scale* development over the *long-term* are especially vulnerable to circularity and thus lack explanatory power, combined with the sheer complexity of mapping and rightly diagnosing 'development' of a particular sort, I remain hesitant about pronouncing *global* claims about development in Gregory's thinking. Furthermore, theories of development, while they often pose as sound alternatives to 'systematizing' readings, can in fact act in their own way to impose unwarranted 'systematization' upon the differences and diversity we find in Gregory's texts. *Both* highly synthetic readings *and* large-scale development narratives of Gregory's thought are but two sides of the one and the same 'systematizing' coin, the former being *statically* and *synchronically* systematizing and the latter being *dynamically* and *diachronically* so.

Therefore, we ought to be more open to the possibility that differences and diversity in Gregory's presentation of this or that theological matter do

[49] Cadenhead, *Body and Desire*, 2–3.
[50] Cadenhead, *Body and Desire*, 3.
[51] Cadenhead, *Body and Desire*, 3, my italics.

22   INTRODUCTION

not reveal development (or incoherence or inconsistency) so much as they offer evidence of the malleability, adaptability, or mobility of a stable core of Gregory's doctrinal convictions. For Gregory, key theological convictions can be stretched and nudged in different directions, muted or 're-mixed' in certain respects, depending on the occasion and context, without compromising overarching intentional systematic coherence, or so I shall argue. Development of thinking, whether understood as 'change of mind' or even as the more moderate 'growth in understanding', is ill-suited to explaining this phenomenon.

To conclude this section, I suggest that since *hom. in Cant.* is probably the last of Gregory's written works, it holds a special status in adjudicating the likelihood of both development and intentional systematic coherence regarding the *particular strand* of soteriological thought investigated in this book. The *hom. in Cant.* presents an 'upper limit' to alleged development in Gregory's thinking and is therefore a benchmark criterion for evaluating degrees of development over the long-term. Thus, if structures of thought found in earlier works, no matter their precise chronological dating, are found to be systematically coherent with those found in *hom. in Cant.*, this significantly diminishes the likelihood that there is *divergent* development of thinking relating to this structure of thought *in the long-term*. It does not, however, militate against the view that there may be either *convergent* or *divergent* developments in his thinking in the *short-term*; nor does it exclude the possibility that at the end of his writing career Gregory attained a significant *growth in understanding*. It does strongly suggest, however, if we are willing to grant that recurrent structures of thought do not emerge in Gregory's writings by accident but by authorial intent, that such smaller-scale developments, whether 'growth in understanding' or 'change of mind', are nevertheless constrained by a consistent aiming toward large-scale systematic coherence.

On the Relationship Between Doctrine and Exegesis

Parts I and II of this book draw a rough dividing line between what we might refer to as Gregory's 'doctrinal' and 'exegetical' works. Further, Part I is devoted to the *objective* aspect of Gregory's teaching on humanity's union with God, while Part II focuses on the *subjective* experience of this transformative process. This division, it must be said, is meant as a *heuristic* for the purposes

INTRODUCTION 23

of organizing the analysis of Gregory's works. It should not be taken to suggest that Gregory himself drew hard and fast boundaries between doctrine and exegesis, or a Cartesian dichotomy between subject and object. Neither should it be taken to imply that Gregory somehow believed that doctrine is objective while exegesis is subjective.

As we did with the term 'development', let us take a step back and disambiguate the terms 'doctrine' and 'exegesis' before proceeding further. Gregory's *doctrine*, in the straightforward sense, is simply *what he teaches*. Specifically, it is what Gregory teaches the church about God and humanity's relationship to God. Yet, there is a sense in which the term 'doctrine' applies most fittingly to Gregory's understanding of Christian faith as it relates to the *baptismal formula* of Matt. 28:19. In *ep. 5*, Gregory says, '[w]e confess that the doctrine of the Lord (τὴν τοῦ κυρίου διδασκαλίαν) which he gave to his disciples when he delivered to them the mystery of piety is the foundation and root of the right and sound faith'.[52] Thus, according to Radde-Gallwitz, for Gregory, '[t]he erudition, the dizzying array of imagery, the ornate rhetoric, and the length one encounters in Gregory's Trinitarian writings must not distract one from the foundational role played therein by the Matthean baptismal formula [i.e. Matt. 28:19]'.[53] Further, he argues that Matt. 28:19 is, for Gregory, 'meta-creedal: it is a confession about confessions, and in particular about their proper foundation in the baptismal tradition'.[54] If Gregory means what he says about the baptismal formula, then attending to his baptismal theology is likely to shed light on the relationship between his 'doctrinal works' and 'exegetical works'.

Since the affirmation of Gregory's doctrine was heavily contested in his day, he, along with other notable figures, took it upon themselves to produce writings in defence of their position. The nature of the debates, against philosophically astute combatants such as Eunomius of Cyzicus, meant that Gregory needed to formulate precise technical and philosophical concepts and frameworks to clarify his teaching. It is essentially those works, therefore, that take as their primary subject matter the triunity of God and the incarnation of the Son, and which tend to adopt a more polemical, apologetic, or philosophical style (e.g. *Maced., CE, Apoll., Ad Ablabium, or. catech.*) that are categorized in modern parlance as Gregory's 'doctrinal works'.

[52] *GNO* VIII/2.10–13; Silvas, *Gregory of Nyssa: The Letters*, 138.
[53] Radde-Gallwitz, *Doctrinal Works*, 44.
[54] Radde-Gallwitz, *Doctrinal Works*, 44.

24   INTRODUCTION

On the other hand, in continuity with the literary tradition that he inherited, Gregory produced a series of writings, often homilies, principally devoted to exegesis. Gregory read scripture *doctrinally*, which is to say, for what scripture *teaches* the church about God and humanity's relationship to God. Since, for Gregory, doctrine and Christian practice go hand in hand, his exegesis of scripture is marked by reflections on trinitarian theology and christology side-by-side with clear practical instructions on the Christian life. Among Gregory's modern interpreters, it is chiefly his homilies (e.g. *or. dom., beat., In Ecclesiasten homiliae, hom. in Cant.*) that tend to be categorized as 'exegetical works'.

With this terminological clarification, we are in a position now to enquire into the relationship between Gregory's 'doctrinal works' and his 'exegetical works'. In view of how I have framed the issue, the matter would appear to be relatively straightforward. On the one hand, Gregory's 'exegetical works' are thoroughly *doctrinal* works in the sense that they present to us Gregory's account of what scripture *teaches* the church about the triune God and humanity's relationship to God. On the other hand, Gregory's 'doctrinal works' are thoroughly *exegetical* works in that they present *Gregory's doctrine* to be none other than *scripture*'s doctrine. As a basic rule, therefore, the doctrinal works are exegetical and the exegetical works are doctrinal.

Why, then, we might ask is the issue of the relationship between Gregory's doctrine and his exegesis contested among Gregory of Nyssa scholars? As I have mentioned, those works normally identified as 'doctrinal', though they contain much by way of scriptural exegesis (as we shall see), nevertheless tend to engage in a mode of discourse and polemic that demands a high level of philosophical sophistication and precision, for instance Gregory's argument in *Ad Ablabium* against tri-theism and his arguments in *Eun.* I against temporal-spatial *diastēma* in the Trinity. Meanwhile, those works labelled 'exegetical', while not completely devoid of philosophical content and polemical undertones, are chiefly interested in allegorical or spiritual interpretation as a means to discern the life-giving nourishment of the Spirit veiled by the letter of scripture. The purpose of such readings is, in general terms, to assist in the listeners' or readers' anagogical contemplation of God and pursuit of divine virtue.[55] The problem of the relationship between 'doctrinal' and 'exegetical' works is, therefore, really a problem of the relationship between two different *modes* of 'theologizing', call them *Theologizing I* and *Theologizing II*. One of the difficulties that the modern interpreter of Gregory (and of patristic

[55] Cf. Verna E. F. Harrison, 'Allegory and Asceticism in Gregory of Nyssa', *Semeia*, 57 (1992b), 115: 'Virtue and communion with God are the central themes in Gregory of Nyssa's *Commentary on*

INTRODUCTION 25

theology in general) faces is the erroneous identification of *Theologizing I* as the remit of 'doctrine proper' formulated by the dogmatic-systematic theologian, and of *Theologizing II* as the province of Christian *spirituality* or *mysticism*. Although there have been various attempts to re-conceptualize the notion of 'doctrine', modern theology often equates it with positive propositional claims that are amenable to systematization. By contrast, in modern theology, 'mysticism' is often understood to denote those approaches to theology that cannot be systematized, since they are more apophatic, paradoxical, and experiential.

On the basis of this observation, the problems we face on this issue may be framed as a set of questions: How is Gregory's *doctrine* (teaching) that emerges from *Theologizing I* related to the *doctrine* (teaching) that emerges from *Theologizing II*? Do they merge into a coherent body of *doctrine*, or do they represent two disparate, irreconcilable strands of *doctrine* in Gregory's thought? Does the *doctrine* that emerges from *Theologizing II*, specifically in *hom. in Cant.*, have anything substantially new to add to the *doctrine* that emerges from *Theologizing I*? As we can see, the problem of the relationship between the doctrine that emerges from *Theologizing I* and *II* is a species of the problem of the systematic coherence of thought, and thus relatedly, of the problem of development.

The central question at stake has been extensively discussed by Sarah Coakley in an article of 2002. Coakley sets out to offer 'overarching principles that . . . should rightly guide our use of Gregory's *exegetical* writings in the explication of his full doctrinal position on the Trinity'. First, Coakley decries 'the false disjunction between exegesis and philosophical thinking' and between ' "spirituality" and "theology" '. Rather, Gregory's commentaries can be used as a 'source of insight' into Gregory's overarching 'doctrinal position'. Second, Coakley observes that, for Gregory, 'the exposition of doctrine does not unfold . . . on a *flat plane*'. Rather, there is a 'principle of diversification' in Gregory's account of doctrine in accord with 'different audiences, and different occasions'. Third, Gregory's understanding of 'spiritual ascent' suggests for Coakley that there is a 'doctrinal progression' that occurs in the life of each individual Christian over time. Hence, '[s]tages of spiritual growth are thus no less levels of doctrinal apprehension'. In particular, the Song of Songs

---

the Song of Songs and many of his other exegetical works. In other words, he uses Scripture to teach the ascetic life, and he acknowledges explicitly that this is his intention. Allegory, with its moral and mystical/theological interpretations, is what enables him to do this'.

26 INTRODUCTION

holds primacy of place as 'the apex of spiritual and doctrinal apprehension'. Fourth, Coakley argues that, for Gregory, 'ultimately philosophy is *subordinate* to Scripture'. As a result, we should therefore 'expect to find *deeper* insight, ultimately, into trinitarian doctrine in the exegetical writings than in the polemical or philosophical'. For Coakley, philosophical discourse is suited to Gregory's 'pagan interlocutor', while the 'mystical' insights of 'faith' depend on scriptural teaching regarding Christian 'inner transformation'. Fifth, the appeal to 'apophaticism' in Gregory's more polemical trinitarian expositions need to be linked to the more 'affective' enunciation of trinitarianism in the exegetical writings. Sixth, in view of Gregory's apophaticism, his exegesis of the Song of Songs exhibits 'a certain loosening up of imagery where trinitarian "analogies" are concerned' in comparison with those found in 'the more polemical and catechetical writings'. Seventh, matters of 'sex' and 'gender' are at the forefront of *hom. in Cant.*[56]

With these principles in place, Coakley proceeds to offer an analysis of trinitarian images in *hom. in Cant.* While Gregory does not wander away completely from the trinitarianism of *Ad Ablabium* (specifically the 'ordered causality of the divine operations *ad extra*), Coakley nevertheless suggests that there is a 'happy disregard' for precision, a 'freedom' and 'apparent carelessness' in his articulation of trinitarian analogies. Singled out, however, are four lengthier expositions of the Trinity's operations that are 'characterized by unusually visual and imaginative complexity'—the Spirit as 'wind' sent by the Father in the 'sails' of the church in contemplation of the Word in Homily 12; the Spirit as the bond of union between Father and Son overflowing to the church in Homily 15; the 'gender-modified' reflection on sonship-adoption in Romans 8, vis-à-vis the Bride's adoption by the Spirit as child of the Father and hence as 'sister' of the Son in Homily 4; and, finally, the 'shifting' and 'chaotically-related' images of the analogy of the wound of love in the human soul in Homily 4, depicted by 'the Father as the archer, the Son as the arrow, and the Spirit as that in which the arrow is dipped'. By attending to these trinitarian expositions, Coakley aims to broaden our understanding of 'the final *telos* of Gregory's more precise and philosophical trinitarian reflections'. In short, she argues, 'they find their completion in his exegetical account of *The Song* and supremely in the rich if chaotic images of incorporation into the life of the divine *energeia*', which are inseparably bound up with 'various gender shifts and transformations'.[57]

---

[56] Coakley, 'Re-Thinking Gregory of Nyssa', 436–438.
[57] Coakley, 'Re-Thinking Gregory of Nyssa', 438–440.

More recently, Coakley has written a sequel to her 2002 article 'to attempt a further clarification and assessment of the novel emphases of trinitarian thinking' found in *hom. in Cant*. Even more emphatically than her earlier article, she speaks of 'the distinctive new dimensions of trinitarian thinking which emerge only in the *Song* commentary'. On this note, Coakley not only seeks a 'clarification' but at the risk of 'anachronistic imposition' explicitly pursues a 'systematization' of Gregory's trinitarianism, even while acknowledging 'Gregory himself is no "systematic" thinker whatever ... but simply discourses freely in the *genre* appropriate to the particular context'. Retracing old ground, Coakley notes that 'it is certainly not the case that trinitarianism has disappeared from the text of the *Song*' but is rather manifest in 'new' and 'enigmatic' ways, illustrated by the same four passages already cited in her earlier article.[58] Among the shifts in Gregory's thought is the view that '[i]nstead of the Spirit inviting one into the *taxis* of the three-in-one on a linear or "chain" model of ascent' in *hom. in Cant.*, one is 'scooped up' by the Spirit through prayer into union with Christ, and is thus 'progressively "adopted" into the Son's filial posture' and hence into adoption by the Father.[59] Here, Coakley alludes to her notion of the 'incorporative' model of the Trinity about which I shall have more to say later. Therefore, contrary to modern sensibility, *hom. in Cant.* does not separate 'Trinity' and 'christology' as distinct categories but rather conjoins them. Finally, in commenting on Gregory's notion of the Spirit as the bond of union between the Father and the Son found in Homily 15, Coakley remarks that this is a 'breakthrough in trinitarian logic' and a 'last development in Gregory's trinitarian thinking'. In sum, Coakley remarks, 'we may be forgiven for scarcely recognizing what Gregory is now up to'. Further, 'Gregory now regards himself as agreed up to discourse trinitarianly in a new mode'.[60] In sum, to quote Coakley at length:

[T]he *Song* deserves not only to be taken seriously as a source for Gregory's trinitarian thought, but it actually changes the vision of the Trinity to be gleaned from Gregory's earlier trinitarian writings in some

[58] Sarah Coakley, 'Gregory of Nyssa on Spiritual Ascent and Trinitarian Orthodoxy: a Reconsideration of the Relation between Doctrine and Askesis', in *Gregory of Nyssa: In Canticum Canticorum: Analytical and Supporting Studies, Proceedings of the 13th International Colloquium on Gregory of Nyssa (Rome, 17–20 September 2014)*, Supplements to Vigiliae Christianae 150, ed. Giulio Maspero, Miguel Brugarolas, and Ilaria Vigorelli (Leiden: Brill, 2018), 361–364.

[59] Coakley, 'Gregory of Nyssa on Spiritual Ascent and Trinitarian Orthodoxy', 367.

[60] Coakley, 'Gregory of Nyssa on Spiritual Ascent and Trinitarian Orthodoxy', 371–373.

28   INTRODUCTION

significant ways: By its deliberate profusion of new metaphors for the Trinity; by the shift of emphasis away from a consistently ordered hierarchy or *taxis* (Father-Son-Spirit) to a dialectical 'adoptive child of God' incorporation via the Spirit into union with Christ; by the conjoined emphasis on Christological 'mingling', for the individual and for the church as a whole; and by his final vision of the Spirit as 'bond' of unity between Father and Son, subtly transforming thereby the idea of causality within the immanent Trinity.[61]

My analysis confirms the validity of Coakley's principles, with the exception that the claim to 'novelty' in *hom. in Cant.* is found to be overstated. Further, the observation that 'Trinitarianism' and 'christology' are conjoined in *hom. in Cant.* is shown not to be a consequence of the 'progressivist logic of the ascent of the *Song*' but rather the reverse: the 'progressivist logic' of *hom. in Cant.* is better understood as a result of the carefully articulated conjunction of Trinitarianism and christology *already found* in several of Gregory's earlier doctrinal works.[62] I shall contend, therefore, that it is only by emphasizing the underlying *continuity* of *hom. in Cant.* with earlier writings that we properly understand Coakley's insight that this final work 'completes' the theology of Gregory's earlier doctrinal works. This is not to deny that there are genuinely novel ways that Gregory expresses his trinitarian theology in *hom. in Cant.*, yet this must be understood as fundamentally continuous with his earlier doctrine.

We conclude, then, by returning to the set of questions posed above. First, how is Gregory's *doctrine* that emerges from *Theologizing I* related to the *doctrine* that emerges from *Theologizing II*? This book shows that if we focus our attention on Gregory's use of *Theologizing I* in several of his key 'doctrinal works', we are able to discern his *doctrine* of the *objective* reality of human transformation and union with God. By focusing on Gregory's adherence to *Theologizing II*, specifically as it is deployed in *hom. in Cant.*, we are able to discern his *doctrine* of the *subjective* reality of human transformation and union with God. We find that the *doctrine* that emerges from *Theologizing II* in *hom. in Cant.* is *systematically coherent* with, and thus completes, the *doctrine* that emerges from *Theologizing I* of the 'doctrinal works' considered in this book. This is because the doctrine that emerges from *Theologizing II*

---

[61] Coakley, 'Gregory of Nyssa on Spiritual Ascent and Trinitarian Orthodoxy', 373.
[62] Coakley, 'Gregory of Nyssa on Spiritual Ascent and Trinitarian Orthodoxy', 371.

INTRODUCTION 29

supplies the fully rounded account of the *subjective* reality of human transformation and union with God that is *entailed* by the correlated account of the *objective* reality that emerges from *Theologizing I*.

Now, regarding our second question: does the *doctrine* that emerges from *Theologizing II* in *hom. in Cant.* have anything substantially new to add to the soteriological *doctrine* that emerges from *Theologizing I*? Here, we find that the doctrine (teaching) that emerges from *Theologizing II* in *hom. in Cant.* certainly *does* add something new, though not primarily in the order of propositional content, nor by way of radical development in either trinitarian or christological thought. Rather, what is new about the *doctrine* that emerges from Gregory's guided exegesis of the Song of Songs is simply that it transposes *the same doctrine* rooted in the more philosophical, polemical mode of *Theologizing I* into a noetic-erotic register. It translates Gregory's teaching on the *objective* reality of union with God, based on the unified activity of the Trinity and Spirit-based christology, into a more *affective* mode of doctrinal catechesis of the heart, mind, and soul than can be expressed simply by argumentative means.

In addition, we find that the 'doctrinal works' considered in this book are *exegetical* works that emphasize *Theologizing I* while muting (not silencing) *Theologizing II*. They are exegetical in the sense that they are not merely Gregory's independent philosophical musings but rather explications of what, according to him, *scripture teaches*—and not in a flippant way, but in a disciplined manner that closely follows the scriptural text, as I shall show.

For the reasons already outlined in the preceding paragraph, the 'exegetical work' that is *hom. in Cant.* is found to be a *doctrinal* work that emphasizes *Theologizing II* while muting (not silencing) *Theologizing I*. Yet, it will be shown that *hom. in Cant.* is rightly denoted 'doctrinal' in the more fitting sense defined above inasmuch as the entire work, from beginning to end, appears to be motivated by Gregory's desire to expound the *baptismal* faith, or what he calls elsewhere 'the doctrine of the Lord (τὴν τοῦ κυρίου διδασκαλίαν) which he gave to his disciples when he delivered to them the mystery of piety (cf. Matt. 28:19; 1 Tim. 3:16)'.[63]

To sum up, my analysis finds that *both* 'modes' of theologizing are present in *both* kinds of works, albeit to different degrees, as is appropriate to the works' literary genres, aims, and audiences. As we would expect, we find that baptism is a key hub around which *Theologizing I* and *Theologizing II* revolve,

---

[63] GNO VIII/2.10–13; Silvas, *Gregory of Nyssa: The Letters*, 138.

30   INTRODUCTION

and thus functions as a concrete bridging point between 'doctrinal works' and *hom. in Cant*. We are not to suppose that the taxonomy outlined here can be applied to Gregory's works in their entirety since the texts analysed in this book are far from comprehensive. Nevertheless, the observations outlined here should contribute significantly to ongoing investigation on the relationship between doctrine and exegesis in Gregory's corpus.

PART I

TRINITY, CHRISTOLOGY, AND PNEUMATOLOGY

Gregory of Nyssa's Doctrinal Account of Human Transformation and Union with God (c. 370–385)

1

Spiritual Marriage with Christ in *De Virginitate*

Introduction

It is generally agreed that *virg.* is Gregory of Nyssa's first written work, composed sometime in the early 370s. Recent scholarly interest in the text has tended to focus upon Gregory's alleged 'ranking' of different forms of married and celibate life in relation to fourth-century Christian asceticism.[1] Rarely, however, has the overtly ascetical subject matter of the work been studied with regard to one of the most pressing doctrinal debates of the 370s and 380s, namely the dispute over the status of the Holy Spirit—a matter that the Cappadocian Fathers took up with great force against the Macedonians, who denied the Spirit's essential unity with the Father and the Son.[2]

This chapter therefore investigates the role Gregory assigns to the Holy Spirit in the virgin's 'spiritual marriage' or union with Christ. I will show that Gregory stresses throughout the work that such union with Christ is in fact impossible for the naturally weak and fallen virgin unless it is actualized by the life-giving power of the Holy Spirit, who shares in the very attributes of 'purity', 'incorruptibility', and 'virginity' that are proper to the Father and the Son. This he expounds with direct reference to baptismal theology. Thus, read in light of the debates with the Macedonians in the 370s and 380s, *virg.* can be understood to prescribe a form of ascetical life that rests upon the characteristically anti-Macedonian conviction that the Spirit, who is received at

---

[1] Mark D. Hart, 'Reconciliation of Body and Soul: Gregory of Nyssa's Deeper Theology of Marriage', *Theological Studies*, 51 (1990), 450–478; Mark D. Hart, 'Gregory of Nyssa's Ironic Praise of the Celibate Life', *Heythrop Journal*, 33 (1992), 1–19; Valerie A. Karras, 'A Re-evaluation of Marriage, Celibacy, and Irony in Gregory of Nyssa's On Virginity', *Journal of Early Christian Studies*, 13/1 (2005), 111–121; Susanna Elm, *Virgins of God: The Making of Asceticism in Late Antiquity* (Oxford: Oxford University Press, 1994), 113–124; Boersma (2013); Cadenhead (2018).

[2] Cf. R. P. C. Hanson, *The Search for the Christian Doctrine of God: The Arian Controversy, 318–381* (Grand Rapids, MI: Baker, 2006), 760–790.

34 TRINITY, CHRISTOLOGY, AND PNEUMATOLOGY

baptism, unites humanity to the Son and the Father because the Spirit is himself essentially united to the Son and the Father.

This analysis of pneumatology in *virg.* is of central importance to my study of *hom. in Cant*: both works portray humanity's union with Christ under the metaphor of marriage. That Gregory construes this nuptial union in thoroughly *pneumatological* and hence *baptismal* terms in his earliest work serves to attune my focus upon resonant pneumatological and baptismal themes that shed light on his exegesis of the Song of Songs in his final written work.

Virginity in Trinitarian Perspective: Chapters I–II

Gregory introduces *virg.* by stating that 'the aim (σκοπός) of this discourse is to create in the reader a desire for the life of virtue'.[3] He means by this the 'life of virginity', which he presents to his readers as a 'door or entrance into a nobler state'.[4] On the one hand, virginity is contrasted with 'the married life' (τῷ κοινοτέρῳ βίῳ) and hence refers quite literally to celibacy.[5] Yet, seeking to ignite his reader's desire for virtue, Gregory's notion of virginity goes well beyond the simply mundane definition. In Chapter I, he conceives of virginity as a participation in the divine attributes of 'incorruptibility' and 'purity'.[6] In Chapter II, Gregory elaborates upon this notion of virginity in terms of trinitarian doctrine, where the essential unity of the Spirit with the Father and the Son is grounded in the shared attributes of 'purity' and 'incorruptibility', both of which he takes to be synonymous with 'virginity' itself.[7] In addition to this trinitarian basis for virginity, Gregory's account is anchored in christology, since 'the Lord Jesus Christ, the source (πηγήν) of incorruptibility, did not come into the world through marriage'.[8] Mary's purity as a virgin was sufficient for receiving God's presence for 'the fullness of the divinity shone

---

[3] Wernerus Jaeger, Johannes P. Cavarnos, and Virginia Woods Callahan, eds., *Opera Ascetica*, GNO VIII/1 (Leiden: Brill, 1952), 247.1–2; Virginia Woods Callahan, trans., 'On Virginity', in *Saint Gregory of Nyssa: Ascetical* Works, The Fathers of the Church 58 (Washington, DC: Catholic University of America Press, 1967), 6.

[4] GNO VIII/1.247.5–6; Woods Callahan, 6; On this point see the illuminating article by Kristi Upson-Saia, 'Gregory of Nyssa on Virginity, Gardens, and the Enclosure of the Παράδεισος', *Journal of Early Christian Studies*, 27/1 (Spring 2019), 99–131.

[5] GNO VIII/1.247.3; Woods Callahan, 6.

[6] GNO VIII/1.252.10–11; Woods Callahan, 9.

[7] GNO VIII/1.254.1–6; Woods Callahan, 10.

[8] GNO VIII/1.254.17; Woods Callahan, 11. The christological focus is rightly noted in Amy Brown Hughes, 'The Legacy of the Feminine in the Christology of Origen of Alexandria, Methodius of Olympus, and Gregory of Nyssa', *Vigiliae Christianae*, 70 (2016), 67–71.

SPIRITUAL MARRIAGE WITH CHRIST IN *DE VIRGINITATE*   35

forth in Christ through virginity'.[9] By analogy, Gregory claims the incarnation event is imitated by every human soul being brought up in virginity.[10] Thus, alluding to John 14:23, Gregory claims, 'He [i.e. the Son] inhabits us spiritually (πνευματικῶς) and the Father along with Him'.[11]

It is worth pausing here to consider Gregory's use of the term πνευματικῶς. In light of the trinitarian context with which he opens *virg.*, together with his reference to the virgin Mary, it is plausible to infer that Gregory's use of the term, in connection with the Father and the Son, has the Holy Spirit within view. While further substantiation of this claim will be developed later in this book, we may note for now that support for this contention is given by his citations of John 14:23 in other works. In *beat.* 4, for instance, Gregory states that those who hunger and thirst for righteousness will receive God into themselves:

> if he has received God into himself, he is filled with Him for whom he has thirsted and hungered, as He has promised who said: I and my Father will come and will make our abode with him (cf. John 14:23). *The Holy Spirit of course had already been dwelling there before.*[12]

In *v. Mos.*, the reference to John 14:23 occurs in the context of an allegorical interpretation of Moses drawing water from the rock (an allusion to imbibing the 'spiritual drink' [πνευματικόν] from the 'rock' that was Christ in 1 Cor. 10:4), which he discusses with reference to those who are 'already capable of receiving God':[13]

> if one should employ the rod of faith he [i.e. Christ] becomes drink to those who are thirsty and flows into those who receive him, for he says, I and my Father shall come to him and make our home with him (cf. John 14:23).[14]

---

[9] *GNO* VIII/1.254.25–26; Woods Callahan, 11.

[10] *GNO* VIII/1.254.28; Woods Callahan, 11.

[11] *GNO* VIII/1.255.1–2; Woods Callahan, 11.

[12] Johannes F. Callahan, *De oratione dominica, De beatitudinibus*, GNO VII/2 (Leiden: Brill, 1992), 75–170; Hilda C. Graef, trans., *St Gregor of Nyssa: The Lord's Prayer, The Beatitudes*, Ancient Christian Writers 18 (New York: Paulist Press, 1954) 129, my italics.

[13] Herbertus, Musurillo, ed., *De vita Moysis*, GNO VII/1 (Leiden: Brill, 1964), 76.17–18; Abraham J. Malherbe and Everett Ferguson, trans., *Gregory of Nyssa: The Life of Moses*, The Classics of Western Spirituality (New York: Paulist Press, 1978), 87.

[14] *GNO* VII/1.76.21–22; Malherbe and Ferguson, 87.

36 TRINITY, CHRISTOLOGY, AND PNEUMATOLOGY

However, the reference to John 14:23 comes immediately after Gregory comments on the Red Sea crossing in terms of baptism and following the lead of the 'cloud', which stands for the Holy Spirit.[15]

In *hom. in Cant.*, the reference to John 14:23 is made in connection with Gregory's well-known metaphor of the archer's arrow:

> God is love, and he discharges his own chosen arrow—the Only-begotten God—at those who are being saved, having smeared over the triple point of the barb *with the Spirit of life* (the barb is the faith), so that, in the person in whom it is planted, it may introduce the archer together with the arrow, as the Lord says: 'I and my Father will come and make our dwelling with him' (cf. John 14:23).[16]

In these passages, the indwelling of the Son and Father is, for Gregory, always accompanied by the presence of the Holy Spirit, as in the original context of John 14:23 in John's gospel itself, and this strongly suggests that Gregory's use of πνευματικῶς in Chapter II of *virg.* is an oblique reference to the Holy Spirit's presence.

I shall argue that the term πνευματικῶς belongs, for Gregory, to a wider ensemble of terms that I refer to throughout this book as Gregory's 'pneumatic language', which he employs across his works to refer to realities directly dependent upon the activity of the Holy Spirit. Perhaps the key scriptural passage that governs Gregory's use of pneumatic language is John 3:6—'that which is born of the Spirit is spirit'.[17] This verse provides Gregory with a clear rationale for differentiating created human 'spirit' from the 'Spirit' as third person of the Trinity, while simultaneously stressing the direct causal dependence of the former upon the latter. In *fid.*, for instance, Gregory is aware that the term 'spirit' can be taken by Macedonian opponents to refer to the Holy Spirit when in fact only created *human spirit* is in view. Thus, in explaining the contested verse of Amos 4:13—'He who makes thunder strong and *creates spirit* (κτίζων πνεῦμα) and proclaims his Christ to men'—Gregory argues that 'thunder' refers to the message of the gospel, while created 'spirit' does not refer to the Holy Spirit, but rather to those *begotten of the Holy Spirit*

---

[15] *GNO* VII/1.70.17–74.9; Malherbe and Ferguson, 83–85.

[16] Hermannus Langerbeck, ed., *In Canticum canticorum*, *GNO* VI (Leiden: Brill, 1960), 127.11–128.3; Richard A. Norris Jr., *Gregory of Nyssa: Homilies on the Song of Song*, Writings from the Greco-Roman World 13 (Atlanta: SBL, 2012), 141, my italics.

[17] Gregory refers to John 3:6 in *virg.*, *GNO* VIII/1.304.21–305.6; Woods Callahan, 48.

SPIRITUAL MARRIAGE WITH CHRIST IN *DE VIRGINITATE*   37

who thereby become 'spirit' through the gospel. Here we see that Gregory's anti-Macedonian argument depends on the structure and logic of John 3:6 for his exegesis of Amos 4:13, and for formulating the distinction between created 'spirit' and that which begets 'spirit', namely the Holy Spirit.[18]

In a similar fashion, Rom. 8:16 also governs Gregory's use of pneumatic language. In *Eun.* III, Gregory debates Eunomius over the exegesis of 2 Cor. 3:17—'The Lord is the Spirit'—which leads him to comment once again on the relationship between human 'spirit' and 'the Spirit'. According to Gregory, Eunomius attempted to demote the status of the Only-begotten Son by claiming that the designation 'Lord' did not refer to his highly exalted 'dignity' (τῆς ἀξίας) but simply to his 'being' (τῆς οὐσίας), and that this 'being' according to 2 Cor. 3:17 is merely 'spirit'.[19] Gregory cites Rom. 8:16:

> He who says, 'The Spirit itself bears witness with our spirit' (cf. Rom. 8:16) is referring to none other than the Holy Spirit which is found in the understanding (τῇ διανοίᾳ) of believers; for to be sure he [i.e. Paul] often calls the mind (τὸν νοῦν) 'spirit' in his own writings, and when that [i.e. the mind] receives the fellowship of the Spirit (τὴν κοινωνίαν τοῦ πνεύματος), the dignity of adopted son (τὸ τῆς υἱοθεσίας ἀξίωμα) is bestowed on those who have received it.[20]

As with John 3:6, we see that Rom. 8:16 governs Gregory's understanding of pneumatic language, offering a clear rationale for distinguishing human 'spirit' from the Holy Spirit while maintaining the direct dependence of the former upon the latter.

---

[18] Fridericus Mueller, ed., *Gregorii Nysseni Opera Dogmatica Minora, Pars I, GNO* III/1 (Leiden: Brill, 1958), 67.7–23; William Moore and Henry Austin Wilson, trans., 'On the Baptism of Christ', in *Nicene and Post-Nicene Fathers: Select Writings and Letters of Gregory, Bishop of Nyssa*, Nicene and Post-Nicene Fathers, series 2, volume 5 (Grand Rapids: Eerdmans, 1994), 339; cf. Hanson, *Search for the Christian Doctrine of God*, 749–750. On the contested interpretation of this verse, cf. H. R. Smythe, 'The Interpretation of Amos 4 13 in St. Athanasius and Didymus', *Journal of Theological Studies*, 1/2 (October 1950), 158–168; cf. Mark DelCogliano, 'Basil of Caesarea, Didymus the Blind, and the Anti-Pneumatomachian Exegesis of Amos 4:13 and John 1:3', *Journal of Theological Studies*, 61/2 (October 2010), 644–658.

[19] Wernerus, Jaeger, ed., *Contra Eunomium Libra, Pars Altera: Liber III (Vulgo III--XII), Refutatio Confessionis Eunomii (Vulgo Liber II), GNO* II (Leiden: Brill, 1960), 160.1; Stuart G. Hall, trans., in Johan Leemans and Matthieu Cassin, eds., *Gregory of Nyssa: Contra Eunomium III. An English Translation with Commentary and Supporting Studies, Proceedings of the 12th International Colloquium on Gregory of Nyssa (Leuven, 14–17 September, 2010)*, Supplements to Vigiliae Christianae 124 (Leiden: Brill, 2014), 137.

[20] *GNO* II.161.3; Hall III, 137.

One may gather from the contested uses of the term 'spirit' that Gregory, who wrote *virg.* in the early 370s in the face of Macedonian opposition, like Athanasius, Didymus, and Basil before him, must have been extremely wary of the careless or unguarded use of pneumatic language. I shall assume as a rule, therefore, that when Gregory employs terms such as πνευματικῶς, and other instances of pneumatic language, these are always laden with pneumatological freight, necessitated by the agonistic environment within which he writes. At times Gregory employs pneumatic language with a deliberately polemical edge, as demonstrated in the passages from *fid.* and *Eun.* III. At other times, this polemical aspect recedes to the background, and yet reference to the Holy Spirit remains either *overt*, such as in Gregory's allusion to John 3:6 in Chapter XIII of *virg.*,[21] or *indirect*, as in Gregory's use of πνευματικῶς in Chapter II.[22] Even where such language refers primarily to created human 'spirit', the Holy Spirit as the agent who gives birth to the human 'spirit' and upon whom human 'spirit' depends for its constitution as 'spirit' is always presupposed. Those specific (rare) instances where the use of pneumatic language in Gregory's works do *not* have the Holy Spirit in view, either overtly or indirectly, will be clear from the context.

In any case, I shall assume that Gregory's use of pneumatic language, wherever it occurs, is never simply neutral. For instance, I take it that Gregory's notion of 'spiritual marriage' (πνευματικοῦ γάμου) in Chapter XX of *virg.* denotes the union of human 'spirit' with Christ in manner born of the Holy Spirit.[23] In *perf.*, I take it that Gregory refers to baptism as 'spiritual rebirth' (τῆς πνευματικῆς ἀναγεννήσεως) since it is the definitive event by which one is 'born of the Spirit' (cf. John 3:6).[24] And, in my analysis of *hom. in Cant.* in Chapter 6, I suggest that Gregory's reference to the allegorical 'spiritual (πνευματικόν) mountain' of the Lord in Homily 1[25] refers implicitly to the site at which the Holy Spirit begets human spirit. These are just a few of many more such instances we will encounter.

Setting aside the broad issue of pneumatic language for now, Gregory's main point in the present discussion in *virg.* is the claim that, from the point of view of the incarnation and the indwelling of the Son 'πνευματικῶς', virginity is to be desired since it plays a mediating role as a binding force between

---

[21] *GNO* VIII/1.304.24–25; Woods Callahan, 47.
[22] *GNO* VIII/1.255.1–2; Woods Callahan, 11.
[23] *GNO* VIII/1.325.7; Woods Callahan, 63.
[24] *GNO* VIII/1.202.9; Woods Callahan, 114–117.
[25] *GNO* VI.26.2; Norris II, 27.

SPIRITUAL MARRIAGE WITH CHRIST IN *DE VIRGINITATE*   39

God and humanity. Thus, for Gregory, 'the power (δύναμις) of virginity' that resides in heaven with the Father is said to 'bring God down to a sharing in human life' and then 'furnishes the man with wings' (πτερούσα),[26] bringing a 'desire for the heavens' and acting as a 'bond of union' (σύνδεσμός) (cf. Eph. 4:3) in humanity's 'inhabitation of God'.[27]

We see that Gregory's reflections on heavenly 'virginity' conceptualize two distinct 'movements' pertaining to humanity's union with God—the *descending* and the *ascending*. The downward movement is no doubt a reference to Christ's incarnation, while Gregory's reference to 'wings' suggests the upward movement is a reference to the Spirit's work, a point that he confirms in Chapter XI when he explicitly identifies the Spirit as the one who bestows 'wings' upon humanity for heavenly ascent to God. Hence, Chapters I–II reveal for us the basis upon which Gregory will seek to achieve the work's *skopos*. If a desire for a life of virtue is to be produced in the reader, Gregory suggests that it will be grounded upon a trinitarian basis and its two 'vertical' components—the christological and the pneumatological.

Worldly Marriage, Heavenly Virginity: Chapters III–VI

Having set his trinitarian framework in place, Gregory traces its implications for the social reality of married life. In Chapter III, he outlines how, on the one hand, marriage is a great delight and blessing that brings 'the joy of symbiosis (συμβιώσεως)'.[28] Importantly, the nuptial term 'symbiosis' will reappear in Chapter XV, where Gregory speaks of the soul becoming 'one spirit' with Christ. On the other hand, the goods of marriage are always accompanied by grief and fear, which arise from the ever-present expectation of impending death. Hence, for Gregory, the married state brings 'a constant mingling of opposites: laughter moistened by tears, grief mingled with joy, death, everywhere present, fastening itself upon each of our pleasures'.[29] The unmarried life of virginity, however, is said to be immune to all such troubles, since it is always accompanied by an incorruptible Bridegroom. Further, it always takes pride in the begetting (γεννήμασι), not of children, but of reverence. Further, in virginity, the master of the house is always present so that death

---

[26] Plato, *Phaedrus*, 246 A–D.
[27] *GNO* VIII/1.255.4–14; Woods Callahan, 11.
[28] *GNO* VIII/1.257.19–20; Woods Callahan, 13.
[29] *GNO* VIII/1.259.5–10; Woods Callahan, 14.

40 TRINITY, CHRISTOLOGY, AND PNEUMATOLOGY

actually effects a union (συνάφειαν) of what is longed for, since to die is to be with Christ (cf. Phil. 1:21–23).[30]

Thus, while the notion of virginity may be presented as an alternative *to* marriage, according to Gregory virginity is in fact to be understood as an alternative mode *of* marriage to Christ, the 'incorruptible Bridegroom'. Morwenna Ludlow notes that when Gregory praises virginity in the language of marriage, he is showing that 'the virgin life is *like* marriage', specifically in its 'social aspect'.[31] As such, the life of virginity that he endorses is understood as a kind of 'spiritual marriage', which naturally leads to a spiritual mode of 'begetting'.[32] Gregory will develop this idea extensively in the second half of his treatise where the role of the Holy Spirit will be central.[33] Here, he suggests that, for the virgin whose life is united to Christ, the power of death is annulled since dying only hastens the desired goal, namely union with the Bridegroom.

In Chapter IV, Gregory continues to magnify the desirability of virginity by means of a severe critique of earthly marriage. As a thoroughly worldly affair, beholden to earthly measures of status and success, marriage leaves one prone to being dragged down by a long chain of vices: 'greed, envy, anger, hatred, the desire for empty fame, and all such things'.[34] Moreover, marriage is bound up with 'the desire to excel other people', and thus the sin of pride is said to have its 'original cause' in marriage.[35] In this way, marriage exploits the various 'sicknesses of the soul'.[36] The effect is to tilt the soul's gaze downward toward bodily pleasures.[37] From here, the passions can take command of the soul, dragging it ultimately to 'condemnation which ends up in hell and darkness and fire'.[38]

If the life of marriage is a thoroughly worldly undertaking, plagued by vice and the fear of death, then the life of virginity is to be sought after, for

---

[30] *GNO* VIII/1.264.14–17; Woods Callahan, 18.

[31] Morwenna Ludlow, 'Useful and Beautiful: A Reading of Gregory of Nyssa's On Virginity and a Proposal for Understanding Early Christian Literature', *Irish Theological Quarterly*, 79/3 (2014), 229.

[32] This agrees with Ludlow's observation that, for Gregory, Christian ascetic communities embody traditional values better than traditional societies do, especially with regard to communal 'fecundity'. Cf. Ludlow, 'Useful and Beautiful', 229.

[33] The topic is comprehensively discussed in Verna E. F. Harrison, 'Gender, Generation, and Virginity in Cappadocian Theology', *Journal of Theological Studies*, 47/1 (1996), 38–68; and Cadenhead, *Body and Desire*, 44–52. However, neither emphasizes the role of pneumatology.

[34] *GNO* VIII/1.267.13–15; Woods Callahan, 20–21.

[35] *GNO* VIII/1.268.21–24; Woods Callahan, 22.

[36] *GNO* VIII/1.269.5; Woods Callahan, 22.

[37] *GNO* VIII/1.272.15–16; Woods Callahan, 24.

[38] *GNO* VIII/1.273.22; Woods Callahan, 25.

SPIRITUAL MARRIAGE WITH CHRIST IN *DE VIRGINITATE* 41

it moves the soul in the opposite direction, toward heavenly, incorruptible realities. In choosing to refrain from marriage, argues Gregory, such a person has thus 'elevated his soul above the whole world'.[39] It is not only the instability of human affairs that concerns Gregory but the impermanence of all of reality as such. Thus, the person who has 'purified his mind and rightly examined the truth of reality' is able to pass through life 'little affected by what he encounters'.[40] In this mode of existence, one contemplates the incorruptible Father and beautifies his own form in imitation of Him.[41]

Gregory's negative depiction of marriage and his positive portrayal of the life of virginity corresponds to the capacity within the human soul to move in *two directions*, which he discusses in Chapters V and VI—one *descending* toward judgment and destruction under the allure of worldly desire, and the other *ascending* toward God and immortality based on a heavenly desire for Him. Hence, Gregory's discussion of each of the main topics in Chapters I–VI (i.e. Trinity, virginity, marriage, desire, the soul) is oriented, so to speak, in the 'vertical plane'. Consequently, the *ascending* movement of the virgin's soul that desires to be united to the Bridegroom is strongly coupled with the *ascending* pneumatological movement on 'wings', to use Gregory's scriptural-platonic terminology in Chapter II. This is not an accidental feature of the work but, rather, a deliberate calibration of the pneumatological trajectory along which the remainder of the treatise will advance.

The Holy Spirit, Demons, and Extreme Virginity: Chapter VII

While Gregory spends Chapters I–VI of his treatise extolling the life of virginity, and warning against the pitfalls of marriage because of its material attachments and associations with the threat of death, he clearly does not reject marriage per se. For, as he says, marriage is 'not deprived of God's blessing'.[42] In Chapter VII, Gregory offers some brief comments on the good of marriage, yet, as he makes clear, this is only necessary because of a rival group of virgin ascetics who 'tamper with the teachings of the Church

[39] *GNO* VIII/1.267.20–21; Woods Callahan, 21.
[40] *GNO* VIII/1.272.4–5; Woods Callahan, 24.
[41] *GNO* VIII/1.276.18–20; Woods Callahan, 27.
[42] *GNO* VIII/1.282.1–5; Woods Callahan, 31.

42 TRINITY, CHRISTOLOGY, AND PNEUMATOLOGY

on marriage'.[43] While not made explicit in the text, it is likely that Gregory believed these 'extreme virgins' had become overly concerned with the status of the body. Instructive are his comments in Chapter XXII, where Gregory speaks of a group (possibly the same group of 'extreme virgins') who have adopted a strict diet, and who through 'excessive discipline, achieve the opposite effect of what they are aiming for'.[44] These, argues Gregory, descend into 'lowly thoughts' and the 'wearing out of the flesh' due to their extreme attention to 'bodily mortifications'.[45] Further, they 'concentrate on the suffering of the body'.[46] Gregory's highly polemical discourse on the good of marriage in Chapter VII should therefore be read not as a defence *of marriage* but, rather, as a critique of certain extreme views *about virginity*.

Crucially, Gregory frames the problem of 'extreme virginity' in terms of the choice to follow either the lead of the Holy Spirit or of demons. We therefore ought not to overlook, as have many commentators on *virg.*, the force of Gregory's allusion to 1 Tim. 4:1–2 whereby those who denigrate marriage in pursuit of an extreme form of the virgin life are 'forsaking the lead (ὁδηγίαν) of the Holy Spirit because of the teaching of demons' and thus 'make cuts (ἐγχαράσσουσι) and brands (ἐγκαύματα) upon their hearts'.[47] The original text of 1 Tim. 4:1–2, to which Gregory has alluded, refers only to what 'the Spirit expressly says (Τὸ δὲ πνεῦμα ῥητῶς λέγει)' about errors that will plague the church *in the future*. However, Gregory foregrounds the *active* role of the Spirit in the life of the virgin by defining the dispute over 'extreme virginity' as a problem of failure to follow the Holy Spirit's 'lead' *in the present*.

In addition, Gregory's denunciation of the 'extreme virgins' is expressed in terms of the classic Aristotelian view that virtue is 'the mean' between two evils. Those 'extreme virgins' who see marriage as 'disgusting' have failed to recognize that 'evil is the turning to extremes' of either 'deficiency' or 'excess'.[48] The relevant virtue in the present discussion of marriage is that of

---

[43] *GNO* VIII/1.282.12–13; Woods Callahan, 31. Some have suggested that Gregory is alluding to a Messalian faction, possibly associated with the followers of Eustathius of Sebaste, with whom his brother Basil and sister Macrina were closely associated. However, evidence is scant. Cf. Liesbeth Van der Sypt, 'Are There Messalian Syneisakts in Gregory of Nyssa's De virginitate 23,4?', in *Gregory of Nyssa: Contra Eunomium III: An English Translation with Commentary and Supporting Studies: Proceedings of the 12th International Colloquium on Gregory of Nyssa (Leuven, 14–17 September 2010)*, Supplements to Vigiliae Christianae 124, ed. Johan Leemans and Matthieu Cassin (Leiden: Brill, 2014), 704–717.

[44] *GNO* VIII/1.330.21–22; Woods Callahan, 66.

[45] *GNO* VIII/1.330.23–25; Woods Callahan, 66.

[46] *GNO* VIII/1.333.9; Woods Callahan, 68.

[47] *GNO* VIII/1.282.15–17; Woods Callahan, 31.

[48] *GNO* VIII/1.282.24–26; Woods Callahan, 32.

SPIRITUAL MARRIAGE WITH CHRIST IN *DE VIRGINITATE*   43

'moderation' (σωφροσύνη), which Gregory suggests is a certain 'strength of soul'.[49] This identification of 'moderation' with true 'strength' will become crucial, as we shall see.

Regarding a *deficiency* in the virtuous strength of moderation, Gregory says, 'the person who is deficient in the tension of his soul (ἐλλείπων κατὰ τὸν τῆς ψυχῆς τόνον) is an easy prey to the passion of pleasure, and, because of this, he does not go near the path of the pure and moderate (σώφρονος) life, being sunk down in the passions of dishonor'.[50] With regard to an *excess* in the strength of moderation, however, he says, 'the person who . . . goes beyond the mean of this virtue is thrown down by *the treachery of demons as if from a steep bank* (κρημνῷ)'.[51] Here, Gregory alludes to the account of demon possession in Mark 5:1–20, specifically the demon-possessed pigs who were driven off a 'steep bank (κρημνοῦ)' and drowned (cf. Mark 5:13).[52]

The term τόνος, which occurs in the quote above, simply means 'that by which something is stretched', such as that which puts tension in a string or in bodily tendons. However, it is also a technical term used in Stoic philosophy denoting the presence of *pneuma* in the soul.[53] According to this view, *pneuma* determines the soul's 'tension', either by tightening or loosening, and this corresponds to the propensity to virtue or vice. Regarding Stoic moral psychology and the tension of the soul, Teun Tieleman states, 'good tension (εὐτονία) is based on the right balance of the psychic pneuma enabling the soul to withstand the impact of incoming impressions, whereas lack of tension (ἀτονία) is linked to mental weakness (ἀκρασία) and a soul prone to emotion.'[54] We find that Galen, who did not subscribe to the Stoic theory of the pneumatic soul, nevertheless also speaks of the soul's tension and relates this directly to 'strength' and 'weakness'. Thus, in *de locis affectis VIII*, Galen remarks:

---

[49] *GNO* VIII/1.283.17; Woods Callahan, 32.

[50] *GNO* VIII/1.283.19; Woods Callahan, 32.

[51] *GNO* VIII/1.283.24; Woods Callahan, 32, my italics.

[52] Gregory's appeal to demonic teachings is likely to be genuine, not merely a rhetorical strategy. On demons in Gregory's works see Morwenna Ludlow, 'Demons, Evil, and Liminality in Cappadocian Theology', *Journal of Early Christian Studies*, 20/2 (2012), 179–211.

[53] Cf. Philip Van der Eijk, 'Galen on Soul, Mixture and Pneuma', in *Body and Soul in Hellenistic Philosophy*, ed. Brad Inwood and James Warren (Cambridge: Cambridge University Press, 2020), 62–88; Christelle Veillard, 'Soul, Pneuma, and Blood: The Stoic Conception of the Soul', in *Body and Soul in Hellenistic Philosophy*, ed. Brad Inwood and James Warren (Cambridge: Cambridge University Press, 2020), 145–170; Tamer Nawar, 'The Stoic Theory of the Soul', in *The Routledge Handbook of Hellenistic Philosophy*, ed. Kelly Arenson (New York: Routledge, 2020), 148–159.

[54] Teun Tieleman, 'Wisdom and Emotion: Galen's Philosophical Position in Avoiding Distress', in *Galen's Treatise Περὶ Ἀλυπίας (De indolentia) in Context*, Studies in Ancient Medicine 52, ed. Caroline Petit (Leiden: Brill 2019), 204–205.

44 TRINITY, CHRISTOLOGY, AND PNEUMATOLOGY

In those in whom the vital tension (ὁ ζωτικὸς τόνος) is weak (ἀσθενής) and who experience strong psychic affections from lack of education, the substance of the soul is easily dissoluble . . . But no magnanimous man ever met his death either as a result of forms of distress or other affections stronger than distress, for the tension of their soul (τόνος τῆς ψυχῆς) is strong (ἰσχυρός) and affections small.[55]

Given the likelihood that Gregory was aware of the Stoic usage, it seems he has transposed the notion of psychic *pneuma* to a new pneumatological register. Probably, as I suggest in Chapter 6, we see a similar transposition of the *pneuma* concept in Homily 4 of *hom. in Cant.*, where Gregory discusses seeing Christ with the imprint of the Spirit in eye of the soul.[56] In Homily 12 of *hom. in Cant.*, Gregory invokes the 'tension' and 'looseness' distinction in relation to the power that 'choice' (προαίρεσις) has to control humanity's dual nature—the 'fine and intelligible and light' (λεπτῆς καὶ νοερᾶς καὶ κούφης) and the 'coarse and material and heavy' (παχείας καὶ ἀτονίαν καὶ ὑλικῆς).[57] Thus, when these two aspects are battling each other, Gregory says 'choice' is able to 'work both *tension* (τόνος) in the nature that is being worsted in battle (τῷ κάμνοντι) and *looseness* (ἀτονίαν) in the nature that is overpowering (τῷ κατισχύοντι).'[58] As I shall show in Chapter 7, however, Gregory significantly relativizes the power of human choice in Homily 12 by emphasizing the necessary work of the Holy Spirit in achieving what human choice cannot, namely union of the soul in 'spiritual marriage' to Christ, the Bridegroom. In the present context of *virg.*, Gregory suggests that it is by following the Holy Spirit's lead that one's soul is in 'good tension' and thus virtuous. Like Galen, Gregory regards the soul's 'tension' as the determinant either of its 'weakness' or its 'strength' and, hence, of its survival or its ruin.

Returning now to *virg.*, in light of his earlier references to both 'incisions' (suggestive of extreme treatment of the body) and 'demons', it appears that Gregory associated the 'extreme virgins' of Chapter VII with the Gerasene demoniac, and his self-inflicted wounding and inhuman strength (cf. Mark 5:4).[59] In his view, they shun married life because, in wandering from the Holy Spirit's lead, they have fallen under the influence of an excessive

---

[55] Rudolph E. Siegel, trans., *Galen on the Affected Parts: Translation from the Greek Text with Explanatory Notes* (Buffalo: New York, 1976), 301–302.
[56] *GNO* VI.106.7–11; Norris II, 117.
[57] *GNO* VI.345.12–14; Norris II, 365.
[58] *GNO* VI.345.20–346.1; Norris II, 365, my italics, translation slightly adjusted.
[59] *GNO* VIII/1.282.15–17; Woods Callahan, 31.

SPIRITUAL MARRIAGE WITH CHRIST IN *DE VIRGINITATE*   45

'demonic' strength of soul. Rather than defeat the demons by their supposed 'strength', a feat achieved by the most admired Christian ascetics of Gregory's day, Gregory implies that they have instead been ruled, and ultimately destroyed, by them.[60] Alluding to 2 Tim. 2:26, he extends the comparison with demon possessed swine by naming the 'extreme virgins' captives 'in the stable (μάνδρᾳ) of the wicked one'.[61] Thus, to follow the Holy Spirit's lead toward a life lived at the 'mean' of virtue—that is, the life of *moderation*—even if that should lead to the married life and all its associations with mortality and death, is, in Gregory's estimation, yet the truer show of spiritual strength.

Weak Virgins and the Power of the Spirit: Chapters VIII–XI

At the conclusion of Chapter VII, Gregory has contrasted the way of the Holy Spirit with the way of demons. Further, he has defined virtue as the mean of moderation that one may fail to achieve through either a deficiency or an excess of spiritual strength. While Gregory clearly associates virtuous moderation with the way of the Holy Spirit, and while spiritual *deficiency* is clearly judged to fall short of virtue, it is only spiritual *excess* that he associates with the demonic. The asymmetry means that while both deficiency and excess deviate from the mean of virtue, spiritual *excess* is deemed to be destructive of humanity in a manner in which spiritual deficiency is not. To anticipate what I will argue below, for Gregory, *deficiency* of the mean of virtue is understood to be humanity's default state brought about by the fall into sin, while *excess* of the mean, of the kind found among the extreme virgins, results from the misguided attempt to overcome this deficiency independently of the Holy Spirit's power through a perverted notion of spiritual strength manifested as a kind of self-mastery.

This observation, I suggest, is the key to understanding Gregory's subsequent *reversal* and *redefinition* of his opponents' notions of spiritual strength and weakness in Chapters VIII–XI. Again, looking ahead to the argument that I will develop shortly, Gregory suggests that marriage is best suited to those who are *not* spiritually too weak, but rather spiritually *strong enough*

---

[60] Cf. David Brakke, *Demons and the Making of the Monk: Spiritual Combat in Early Christianity* (Cambridge: Cambridge University Press, 2006).
[61] *GNO* VIII/1.282.22–23; Woods Callahan, 30.

to undertake it, where true spiritual strength is now *redefined* as the mean of moderation (i.e. the way of the Holy Spirit). Conversely, the life of virginity will be suited not to the 'strong'—insofar as Gregory's opponents wrongly understand 'strength'—but to those who are in reality too weak to undertake marriage. Yet, although such persons are, in their default state of fallenness, too weak in heart, mind, soul, and strength to obey the Great Command to love God with an undivided self (cf. Mark 12:30), Gregory shows in Chapters VIII–XI how they might come to attain true strength; not of the excessive kind, which is demonic and hence ultimately ruinous, but the strength of virtuous moderation, which comes only from the Holy Spirit. That this suggestion of mine has not been pursued in scholarly literature on *virg.* arises from the fact that lack of attention has been given in general to Gregory's pneumatology. Hence, Gregory's use of the categories of the Holy Spirit and the demonic, and their relationship to ascetic strength and weakness in Chapters VII, have not adequately informed scholarly analyses of his argument in Chapters VIII–XI.

On this score, I specifically have in mind the work of Mark D. Hart and the myriad responses it has spawned.[62] He notes that, contrary to expectations, 'Gregory tells us that *celibacy* [i.e. not marriage] is a concession to human weakness' even though '[w]e might expect him to say the opposite, that celibates better than anyone else are able to oppose their sexual impulses and refuse temptations'. However, Hart proceeds to argue that the weakness of the celibates stems chiefly from their lack of 'courage'. Thus, he suggests, that for these weak celibates, according to Gregory's comments in Chapter IX, 'the only real solution to the problem of death is . . . the development of courage'. In Hart's view, therefore, Gregory thinks one is better off celibate than married only on the condition that one lacks courage or 'true virtue'. The 'enlightened marriage' represented by the 'allegorical Isaac' referenced by Gregory in Chapter VII of *virg.* proves that, for Gregory, '[enlightened] marriage may in fact be a higher realization of virtue than that generally found among the celibates'.[63]

Hart's analysis of weakness and strength in Gregory's theology of celibacy and marriage, though subtle and perceptive to the rhetorical twists of Gregory's treatise, is not without significant shortcomings. In particular, he overlooks completely the centrality of pneumatology to Gregory's discussion

---

[62] See footnote 1 in this chapter.
[63] Hart, 'Reconciliation of Body and Soul', 473–477.

SPIRITUAL MARRIAGE WITH CHRIST IN *DE VIRGINITATE*   47

of how weak virgins may become strong and truly virtuous. By overlooking pneumatology, Hart and his various respondents have been side-tracked by a preoccupation with the question of Gregory's 'ranking' of celibacy and marriage, resulting in distorted accounts of Gregory's literary aims.

As we shall see shortly, in view of the *universal* weakening of *all humanity* by sin and death, Gregory is much more concerned in *virg.* to show how the path to baptism and the post-baptismal life in the Spirit—what he calls spiritual marriage with Christ, which is potentially open to *all people*—is the path upon which weak and fallen young virgins bound for death are urgently called to pursue. Gregory does not so much 'rank' celibacy and marriage as hold them in temporal distension: marriage, *if it is to be pursued at all*, must come *later in life*, as the case of the aged 'allegorical Isaac' illustrates. But the path of ascent to the Father through marriage with Christ in the Spirit, which the post-baptismal life of virtue promises, must come *first* and without delay. If I am correct, then Hart's attempted ranking of celibacy and 'enlightened marriage' is misleading. The emphasis on pneumatology in *virg.* would suggest that it is precisely through post-baptismal formation in the Holy Spirit *while still young and unmarried* that one might even become suitably qualified for marriage in the order of 'Isaac' *at a later stage of life.*

Thus, in Chapter VIII, Gregory argues that 'the one who is weak (ἀσθενῶς) by disposition' should stay away from marriage 'rather than enter a contest which is beyond his strength'.[64] Further, 'because of the weakness (ἀσθενές) of nature, it is not possible for everyone to arrive at such a point of balance [i.e. marriage] . . . it would be profitable, as our treatise suggests, to go through life without the experience of marriage'.[65] Such a person is liable to 'turn his *mind* (voῦν)' toward fleshly pleasure, and to allow the passions to enter 'against the *soul* (ψυχῆς)'.[66]

In Chapter IX, Gregory builds upon his portrayal of the weak person by outlining how the human 'weakness' for worldly pleasure is also affected by the great power of 'habit' (συνήθεια), resulting in a person 'dividing his *heart*' between love for God and love for the world.[67] Thus, habit may lead even the 'lover of moderation' to delve into living a 'sordid life'.[68] Since one is prone to form worldly habits from within the married state, Gregory concludes that it

---

[64] *GNO* VIII/1.285.18–20; Woods Callahan, 34.
[65] *GNO* VIII/1.286.1–8; Woods Callahan, 34.
[66] *GNO* VIII/1.285.25; 286.8; Woods Callahan, 34, my italics.
[67] *GNO* VIII/1.288.5; Woods Callahan, 36.
[68] *GNO* VIII/1.287.4–9; Woods Callahan, 35.

48   TRINITY, CHRISTOLOGY, AND PNEUMATOLOGY

is 'advantageous for the very weak (τοῖς ἀσθενεστέροις) to flee for refuge to virginity'.[69]

This radical summons to a life of virginity is ultimately motivated by the call to obedience to the Great Command to love God with the 'whole heart and power (ἐξ ὅλης καρδίας καὶ δυνάμεως)' (cf. Mark 12:30), which Gregory claims is virtually impossible for the weak person to achieve from within the married state.[70] The present focus on Mark 12:30, however, initiates a chain of other references not only to 'the heart' but, quite fittingly, also to 'the mind' and 'the soul' throughout the following chapters of *virg.*, wherein Gregory will provide a solution to the weak person's inability to fulfil the Great Command that is grounded in the power of the Holy Spirit. Gregory appears to have alluded to either Mark 12:30 or Deut. 6:5 (LXX), which use δύναμις rather than ἰσχύς from the parallel passage Luke 10:27. While the term ἰσχύς means bodily strength or might, the term δύναμις denotes one's capacity to act. In moral discussion it denotes capacity to act either for good or for evil. Perhaps Gregory has alluded to δύναμις of Mark 12:30//Deut. 6:5 because it is better suited to the present discussion of the soul's virtuous obedience to the Great Command. Gregory does use the term in a more technical sense elsewhere in his trinitarian writings to denote a nature's capacity to act, as I shall discuss below.

It is necessary at this juncture first to look ahead briefly to a later part of *virg.* and note that Gregory's *second* allusion to the Great Command of Mark 12:30 occurs in Chapter XV. There, he warns that 'the *soul* clinging to the Lord for the purpose of becoming one spirit (ἓν πνεῦμα) with Him (cf. 1 Cor. 6:17) . . . having entered into a kind of symbiotic (συμβιωτικήν) agreement to love Him alone with its whole *heart* and *strength* (ὅλης καρδίας τε καὶ δυνάμεως) (cf. Mark 12:30), must not be involved in fornication'.[71] Gregory's reference to becoming 'one spirit' will certainly have the Holy Spirit in view by the time he comes to write *hom. in Cant*,[72] though presently this is at most only implicit in his present use of the pneumatic language of 1 Cor. 6:17. Importantly, the reference to entering into a 'symbiotic (συμβιωτικήν) agreement' with the Lord immediately recalls his earlier reference to the 'joy' of *earthly marriage* in Chapter III arising from what he also calls a 'symbiosis'.[73]

---

[69] *GNO* VIII/1.287.17–18; Woods Callahan, 35.
[70] *GNO* VIII/1.288.6–7; Woods Callahan, 36.
[71] *GNO* VIII/1.310.12; Woods Callahan, 51.
[72] Cf. *GNO* VI.467.1–2; Norris II, 495.
[73] Cf. *GNO* VIII/1.257.19–20.

SPIRITUAL MARRIAGE WITH CHRIST IN *DE VIRGINITATE*   49

Yet, this reference to 'symbiosis' in Chapter XV logically implies that the soul's entry into this 'symbiotic marriage' with the Lord has already been addressed by Gregory at some point *prior to* Chapter XV. The important question, therefore, is *where* in the treatise does Gregory first offer an account of the soul's 'marriage' with the Lord?

My analysis so far has shown that no such account occurs in Chapters I–VIII. The most natural answer is that Gregory's account of the soul's symbiotic marriage to Christ is first signposted at the conclusion of Chapter IX with his *first* allusion to the Great Command of Mark 12:30, which functions as an initial summons to the weak virgin to forego earthly marriage in order to enter into a 'symbiotic agreement' to love only Christ. This first allusion to Mark 12:30 in Chapter IX therefore facilitates the extended discussion in Chapters X–XI that immediately follows, detailing how the weak virgin may become strengthened in heart, soul, and mind in order to fulfil the Great Command to love God undividedly (cf. Mark 12:30; 1 Cor. 7:32–33). Chapters X–XI should therefore be read precisely as Gregory's account of the virgin's 'symbiotic marriage' to Christ, which I shall show is actualized by the Holy Spirit.

With the above observations in mind, in Chapter X we see that Gregory portrays the problem of human weakness as a universal one by framing it in terms of humanity's fall. Having identified the difficulty of obeying the Great Command to love God with the 'whole heart', he now draws attention to the weakness of 'the heart' once again, this time in order to emphasize humanity's inability to comprehend either by word or thought 'what is promised by the Lord in His beatitudes (cf. Matt. 5:8)', by which he means the beatific vision of God for those who are pure in *heart*.[74] Therefore, just as a 'verbal explanation' of light is useless to a person born blind, so a verbal explanation of God's beauty and light is useless for those whose 'purity of mental vision' is blinded by their fallen state.[75] Hence, he asks, 'what concept (ἐπίνοια) can possibly indicate the enormity of the loss for those who incur it?'.[76]

After establishing humanity's weakness of mind, Gregory introduces the 'solution' to humanity's inherent weakness via an extended discussion of the need for the Holy Spirit's power. David, though not a virgin himself, serves as the prime example of one whose *mind* was lifted to glimpse the divine

---

[74] *GNO* VIII/1.288.22–24; Woods Callahan, 36.
[75] *GNO* VIII/1.288.23; Woods Callahan, 36.
[76] *GNO* VIII/1.289.27; Woods Callahan, 37.

50 TRINITY, CHRISTOLOGY, AND PNEUMATOLOGY

beauty: 'when he was once lifted up in *mind* (τὴν διάνοιαν) by the power of the Spirit (τῇ δυνάμει τοῦ πνεύματος), he was, as it were, divorced from himself and saw that incredible and incomprehensible beauty in a blessed ecstasy'.[77] Yet, after David's brief heavenly vision is over, he is once again limited by 'the weakness (ἀσθενείᾳ) of his description' to account for what he had seen.[78] Gregory notes that while it is 'within our power (δύναμις)' to describe mere 'perceptible beauty' by the senses, divine beauty is well beyond our grasp.[79] In Chapter XI, Gregory notes the characteristic human 'weakness (ἀσθενείας) of knowing things' that needs to be overcome in order to 'direct our *mind* (τὴν διάνοιαν) to the unseen'.[80] Human weakness is further demonstrated by the fact that 'the sense faculties of the *soul* (τὰ τῆς ψυχῆς αἰσθητήρια) are not sufficiently trained to distinguish between the beautiful and the not beautiful'.[81] As a result, human beings 'squander [their] power of desire' on merely 'ephemeral' beauty.[82]

In light of fallen humanity's various weaknesses of heart, mind, and soul (cf. Mark 12:30), Gregory naturally asks how a redirection of desire and ascent toward God are even possible at all. Just as he has already suggested in the case of David, so Gregory reiterates once more that this only becomes possible for the weak human mind and soul through the 'power of the Spirit' (τὴν τοῦ πνεύματος δύναμιν) by which one flies up to heaven (ἀναπταίη) as if on 'heavenly wings' (πτερωθεὶς τῷ οὐρανίῳ πτερῷ).[83] Here Gregory employs the analogy of 'shooting stars'(ἀστέρας), which produce a 'firelike trail' (πυροειδῆ) when a 'wind is enflamed in the aether' (ἐν τῷ αἰθέρι τοῦ πνεύματος) and thus become 'light-like' (φωτοειδὴς).[84] The imagery of 'wings' and the lustrous 'aetherial' realm that Gregory evokes is borrowed from Plato's *Phaedrus* and finds direct points of connection with Neoplatonic teachings on the 'vehicle of the soul'.

Gregory clearly intends his pneumatology to play the central role in depicting the elevation of the weak and incompetent person to a position of true spiritual strength. Just as he had done previously in Chapter VII, Gregory employs pneumatology in Chapters VIII–XI to expound a rival

---

[77] *GNO* VIII/1.290.3; Woods Callahan, 37, my italics.
[78] *GNO* VIII/1.290.14; Woods Callahan, 37.
[79] *GNO* VIII/1.290.17–18; Woods Callahan, 37–38.
[80] *GNO* VIII/1.291.15–17; Woods Callahan, 38–39.
[81] *GNO* VIII/1.292.21–23; Woods Callahan, 39.
[82] *GNO* VIII/1.293.17; Woods Callahan, 39.
[83] *GNO* VIII/1.294.8–16; Woods Callahan, 40.
[84] *GNO* VIII/1.294.26–295.7; Woods Callahan, 40.

SPIRITUAL MARRIAGE WITH CHRIST IN *DE VIRGINITATE*   51

form of virginity that reverses and redefines the notions of spiritual strength and weakness espoused by his 'extreme' opponents. At the same time, I contend, he thereby offers an account of the virgin's 'spiritual marriage' with Christ, that is, a 'symbiotic agreement' to love the Lord with the whole heart, mind, and strength in fulfilment of the Great Command of Mark 12:30, so as to become 'one spirit' with him through the power of the Holy Spirit (cf. 1 Cor. 6:17).

The Power of Death and the Power of the Spirit: Chapters XII–XIII

So far, we have seen that Gregory, in Chapters VIII–XI, has outlined how the naturally weak and fallen person may be empowered by the Spirit to fulfil the Great Command to love God with the whole heart, mind, and soul (cf. Mark 12:30) and thus reach the final goal of virginity, the beatific vision of God (cf. Matt. 5:8). Up until now, however, he has not sufficiently offered a solution to the problem that occupied all of his attention in Chapters III–VI, namely death. Beginning at Chapter XII, and continuing to the conclusion of the treatise, therefore, Gregory addresses explicitly the problem of death by outlining the 'method' (μέθοδον) that overcomes death and leads to the vision of God.[85] In doing so, I suggest that Gregory continues to pursue the *skopos* of his treatise: to produce in his reader a desire for the life of virtue, now cast as a desire for the baptismal life actualized by the life-giving power of the Spirit.[86]

Gregory's account of baptismal life in the Spirit begins with the creation of man as outlined in the Genesis narrative. Of prime importance is man's creation as a 'living being' (ζῷον) (cf. Gen. 2:7), who 'from his first generation' (τὴν πρώτην γένεσιν) was without 'passion' or 'subjection to death'.[87] Gregory echoes his previous discussion of humanity's fall in Chapter X by noting that, as the image of God, man was endowed with 'choice' (τῆς προαιρέσεως) and, by choosing evil instead of good, fell into sin.[88] Man, as 'the inventor of evil', chose to 'shut off the perception of light' and thereby 'cut

---

[85] *GNO* VIII/1.297.13; Woods Callahan, 42.
[86] Cf. Boersma, *Embodiment and Virtue*, 117–145.
[87] *GNO* VIII/1.298.4–6; Woods Callahan, 42.
[88] *GNO* VIII/1.298.11–21; Woods Callahan, 43.

52 TRINITY, CHRISTOLOGY, AND PNEUMATOLOGY

himself off from the sun's rays' so as to 'make no provision for the rays of light to enter'.[89] Consequently, the godlike image of the soul became darkened.[90]

Importantly, however, this darkening is, according to Gregory, not essential to man, and is able to be removed so as to bring about the 'restoration to the original state (εἰς τὸ ἀρχαῖον ἀποκατάστασις) of the divine image'.[91] Hence, 'if, purified by water . . . the beauty of the soul may reappear again'.[92] Here, more clearly than anywhere else in the entire treatise, Gregory evokes baptism, anticipating that the work of the Holy Spirit will be central to the restoration to the original state of the divine image in the virgin.[93] Gregory appears to be referring to a literal act of baptism while simultaneously *theologizing* about baptism in order to prescribe the proper form of the spiritual-ascetical life. It is, therefore, appropriate to speak of Gregory's 'baptismal imagination' and an accompanying 'baptismal exegesis' of scripture, by means of which he explores the implications of baptism for the life of virginity and marriage with Christ.[94]

Gregory's application of his baptismal exegesis to the present context of Chapter XII also serves to show that human restoration is a divine, not human, work. Alluding to the Genesis creation narrative, he claims it is 'not possible to achieve unless one be created from the beginning (ἐξ ἀρχῆς ἐκτίσθη), so as to be born again (πάλιν γενόμενον)'.[95] Further, 'being like the divine is not our work (ἔργον), nor is it a product of human power (δυνάμεως ἀνθρωπίνης), but it is part of the generosity (μεγαλοδωρεᾶς) of God'.[96] Indeed, Gregory consciously limits and relativizes the scope of human strength by stating that 'human zeal extends only to this: the removal of the

---

[89] *GNO* VIII/1.299.4–5; Woods Callahan, 43.

[90] *GNO* VIII/1.299.5; Woods Callahan, 44.

[91] *GNO* VIII/1.302.6; Woods Callahan, 45; Cf. Ludlow, *Universal Salvation*, 38–44; Jean Daniélou, 'L'apocatastase chez Saint Grégoire de Nysse', in *Recherches de Science Religieuse*, 30/3 (1940), 328–347.

[92] *GNO* VIII/1.300.3; Woods Callahan, 44.

[93] Cf. Ilaria Ramelli, 'Baptism in Gregory of Nyssa's Theology and Its Orientation to Eschatology', in *Ablution, Initiation, and Baptism: Late Antiquity, Judaism, and Early Christianity*, Beihefte zur Zeitschrift für die neutestamentliche Wissenschaft und die Kunde der älteren Kirche, ed. David Hellholm, Tor Vegge, Øyvind Norderval, and Christer Hellholm (Berlin: De Gruyter, 2011), 1205–1231.

[94] This observation is reenforced by Ludlow's argument that *virg.* deliberately manipulates typical expectations of classical epithalamia. I suggest that, here, Gregory meets the expectations of classical wedding speeches by intentionally combining the topoi of rivers and associated 'watery myths' with an elaboration on the cosmic significance of marriage, and he does so by portraying 'spiritual marriage' between humanity and God in baptismal terms. In turn, my suggestion helps to reinforce Ludlow's contention that 'there is a theological purpose to Gregory's use of classical literary sources and motifs'. Cf. Ludlow, 'Useful and Beautiful', 231–233, 236.

[95] *GNO* VIII/1.300.7; Woods Callahan, 44.

[96] *GNO* VIII/1.300.8–10; Woods Callahan, 44.

SPIRITUAL MARRIAGE WITH CHRIST IN *DE VIRGINITATE* 53

filth which has accumulated through evil and the bringing to light again the beauty in the soul which we had covered over'.[97] In other words, the virgin's preparation for baptism is *only the first step*, and not even a particularly impressive one, on the way to regeneration through the Holy Spirit's power.

With the narrative sequence of Gen. 2–3 as his guide, Gregory suggests that the virgin must therefore begin to 'undo', *in reverse-order*, the initial sequence of events by which death entered into the world in the first place. For Gregory, this offers a justification for forgoing marriage. He argues that 'since the point of departure from the life in paradise was the married state (cf. Gen. 4:1), reason suggests to those returning to Christ (i.e. the virgins) that they, first, give this up as a kind of early stage of the journey'.[98] Gregory proceeds to outline further steps in the recovery of the divine image once the married life has been given up, closely adhering to the Genesis narrative, although in reverse order. Thus, the virgin is to:

1. forego marriage (cf. Gen. 4:1),
2. withdraw (ἀναχωρῆσαι) from the regular use (ταλαιπωρία) of the land (cf. Gen. 3:23),
3. put off the garments of skin (cf. Gen. 3:21),
4. reject the concealments of their shame . . . . the ephemeral leaves of life (cf. Gen. 3:7),
5. disdain the deceptions of taste and sight (cf. Gen. 3:6),
6. cease to follow the lead of the serpent (cf. Gen. 3:1–5), and
7. follow only the command of God (cf. Gen. 2:16–17).[99]

If we suppose that Gregory's retracing of the Genesis narrative ends at point (7), we miss the significance of the immediately following statements regarding the life-giving power of the Holy Spirit. He in fact appears to have retraced the narrative sequence back to Gen. 2:7.[100] Gregory asks, 'since paradise is a dwelling place of living beings (ζώντων) which does not admit those who are dead because of sin, and we are "carnal and mortal, sold to sin" (cf. Rom. 7:14), how is it possible for one who is ruled by the power (δυναστείᾳ) of death to dwell in the land of the living (τῶν ζώντων)?'[101]

---

[97] *GNO* VIII/1.300.13–15; Woods Callahan, 44.
[98] *GNO* VIII/1.303.9–12; Woods Callahan, 46.
[99] *GNO* VIII/1.303.9–14; Woods Callahan, 46–47.
[100] καὶ ἔπλασεν ὁ θεὸς τὸν ἄνθρωπον χοῦν ἀπὸ τῆς γῆς καὶ ἐνεφύσησεν εἰς τὸ πρόσωπον αὐτοῦ πνοὴν ζωῆς καὶ ἐγένετο ὁ ἄνθρωπος εἰς ψυχὴν ζῶσαν (Gen. 2:7 LXX).
[101] *GNO* VIII/1.304.15–21; Woods Callahan, 47.

54 TRINITY, CHRISTOLOGY, AND PNEUMATOLOGY

Restoration to the original paradisal state, Gregory argues, cannot depend on the human will, but upon the life-giving power of the Spirit, a term that Gregory has already utilized twice in this treatise. Therefore, with reference to Jesus' encounter with Nicodemus in John's gospel, Gregory recalls, 'That which is born of the flesh is flesh; and that which is born of the Spirit is spirit (cf. John 3:6)', noting that the flesh is subject to death, whereas the Spirit of God is incorruptible and life-giving (ζωοποιόν). Thus, says Gregory, just as the power (δύναμις) of death is born together with physical birth, so the Spirit gives a life-giving power (τὴν ζωοποιὸν . . . δύναμιν) upon those born (γεννωμένοις) through it.[102]

Gregory has most likely read the Genesis creation narrative (specifically Gen. 2:7) in light of John 3:6. Just as the first man in paradise was brought to life by God's 'breath of life' (πνοὴν ζωῆς) so as to become a 'living soul' (ψυχὴν ζῶσαν) (cf. Gen. 2:7 LXX), so sinful man overcomes death and is restored to the original paradisal state as 'spirit' by the life-giving power of 'the Spirit' of God. In the process, Gregory has quite clearly followed the Johannine lead by drawing the concept of human 'flesh' into the orbit of pneumatic language such that 'flesh' is opposed not only to the human 'spirit' but, at a more fundamental level, to the work of the 'Holy Spirit'. It is almost certainly the case, given Gregory's previous comments about 'purification by water' in the previous chapter, that his quotation of John 3:6 has baptism immediately in view. While Gregory has not addressed literal baptism, the retracing of Steps 1–7 of the Genesis narrative leading up to regeneration by the Spirit are strongly patterned after an actual baptismal ritual.[103]

Thus, baptismal life in the power of the life-giving Holy Spirit, and the overcoming of 'flesh', qualifies what Gregory meant earlier by the necessity for man to be 'created from the beginning' (ἐξ ἀρχῆς ἐκτίσθη) and to be 'born again' (πάλιν γενόμενον) so as to overcome death and attain the goal of the beatific vision of God. Chapters XII–XIII therefore round off the discussion Gregory introduced in Chapter VII, where true virginity is framed in terms of following the Spirit's lead. Further, Chapters VII–XIII offer the 'solution' to the problem of death that Gregory introduced in Chapters III–VI, underlining the fact that Gregory's pneumatology, informed by his baptismal imagination and baptismal exegesis of Gen. 2–3, does significantly more work in *virg.* than is often acknowledged.

---

[102] *GNO* VIII/1.304.21–305.6; Woods Callahan, 48.
[103] Compare with Gregory's list of liturgical ceremonies attached to baptismal regeneration in *Eun.* III, *GNO* II.285–6.57–8.

Spiritual Childbearing: Chapters XIIIb–XIV

If, as I have suggested, Chapters X–XI depict the virgin's marriage to Christ by the lifegiving power of the Holy Spirit culminating in the beatific vision, while Chapters XII–XIII outline how one enters into this marriage through the Holy Spirit initiated at baptism, we should expect this marriage to now bear the fruit of 'children' by means of the same Spirit's agency. And this is precisely the metaphor that Gregory introduces at the conclusion of Chapter XIII, continuing through to Chapter XIV and beyond. The point has been observed in Verna Harrison's extensive study on spiritual generation and spiritual marriage in Gregory's works. Commenting on *virg.*, she states, '[f]or Gregory, the virginal soul, like Mary, receives the entrance of God and brings forth Christ, though spiritually, not physically as she did. For Gregory, this is the essence of spiritual generation ... While bodily union produces mortal bodies, virginity generates life and incorruption through participation in the Holy Spirit'.[104] Furthermore, 'this spiritual mode [of generation] ... characterizes ascetic life in this world and the transformed human existence of the eschaton, and it is intrinsic to the process of human divinization and union with God'.[105] Harrison's analysis adds currency to my argument in this chapter. However, I wish to emphasize more strongly than she does the pneumatological aspect of 'spiritual' childbearing in *virg.*, which runs in continuity with the pneumatological and baptismal thread throughout the treatise.

Therefore, while bodily union between man and woman in physical marriage results in the birth of children that are mortal, Gregory explains that a different kind of union is possible that results in the birth of 'life and incorruptibility' themselves.[106] While Cadenhead offers a provocative analysis of Gregory's notion of spiritual begetting, one need not posit the highly speculative thesis that Gregory is giving an intentional critique and alternative to spiritual fecundity arising from the practice of Platonic pederasty. Pederasty is not explicitly mentioned in the text, and Cadenhead cites only one passing reference to *paiderastia* in Gregory's entire corpus (cf. *epistula canonica ad Letoium*). As I have shown, Gregory's discussion of 'spiritual begetting' is just

---

[104] Harrison, 'Gender, Generation, and Virginity in Cappadocian Theology', 57.
[105] Harrison, 'Gender, Generation, and Virginity in Cappadocian Theology', 67.
[106] *GNO* VIII/1.305.14; Woods Callahan, 48.

56 TRINITY, CHRISTOLOGY, AND PNEUMATOLOGY

the expected, natural outworking of the concept of the virgin's 'spiritual marriage' to Christ in the Spirit, introduced in the preceding chapters.[107]

The *ongoing work* of the Holy Spirit in the life of the baptized virgin is crucial, and thus he speaks of the 'offspring' of 'those who are united (τοῖς συναφθεῖσιν) in their fellowship in the Spirit (τῆς δὲ πρὸς τὸ πνεῦμα κοινωνίας)'.[108] To this Gregory adds a quote from 1 Tim. 2:15 about those virgins who are 'saved by childbearing', read in conjunction with a pneumatological interpretation of Ps. 112(113):9 whereby '[t]he virgin mother who begets immortal children through the Spirit (ἡ τὰ ἀθάνατα τέκνα . . . διὰ τοῦ πνεύματος) truly rejoices and she is called barren by the prophet because of her moderation'.[109] The 'immortal children' that Gregory speaks of are a likely reference to the virtues reflecting the divine attributes of 'life' and 'incorruptibility' cited above, and one cannot help but see here a parallel with Mary's begetting of Christ by the Spirit (cf. Luke 1:35). Hence, for Gregory, being 'born again' by the Spirit is generative of further spiritual begetting by the Spirit, a phenomenon he already signalled as early as Chapter III.

It is important to recall that Gregory had earlier described the life of virginity as suitable for those who are *weak* of soul. However, through their 'participation in the Spirit', we see how formerly weak virgins may now be elevated to the position of 'moderation' where the begetting of the 'immortal children' of the virtues is able to take place. As we saw in Chapter VII, 'moderation' is, for Gregory, the true strength of soul, being neither deficient nor excessive. Since it is strengthened by the Holy Spirit's 'life-giving power', it is, in his words, the form of life that is now 'stronger than the power of death (ὃς κρείττων τῆς τοῦ θανάτου δυναστείας ἐστίν)'.[110]

Pneumatology in Chapters XIV–XXII

In Chapters XIV–XXII, about which I can only be brief, Gregory continues to emphasize the role of the Holy Spirit in order to achieve the work's *skopos*. In Chapter XIV, he shows how the virgin's spiritual marriage to Christ results in childbearing through the agency of the Holy Spirit. Therefore, those who pursue the life of virginity like Mary also engender the fruit of virginity,

---

[107] Cadenhead, *Body and Desire*, 48–52.
[108] *GNO* VIII/1.305.13–14; Woods Callahan, 48.
[109] *GNO* VIII/1.304.20–22; Woods Callahan, 48.
[110] *GNO* VIII/1.305.26; Woods Callahan, 48.

SPIRITUAL MARRIAGE WITH CHRIST IN *DE VIRGINITATE*   57

which limits death. Alluding to John 1:13, Gregory states, 'birth comes, not of blood, nor of the will of the flesh, nor of the will of man, but of God alone. This occurs when someone, in the life of the heart, takes on the incorruptibility of the Spirit (τὴν ἀφθαρσίαν τοῦ πνεύματος) and begets wisdom and justice and holiness and redemption'.[111] In Chapters XV–XVIII, Gregory warns against spiritual adultery which would rend asunder the virgin's becoming of 'one spirit' with the Lord (cf. 1 Cor. 6:17), and thus he speaks of the risk of surrendering one's 'spiritual marriage' (τοῦ πνευματικοῦ γάμου).[112] The use of pneumatic language naturally recalls his remarks on the Holy Spirit throughout the treatise, and thus to commit adultery against Christ is simultaneously to turn away from the Spirit. In Chapter XX, Gregory refers to spiritual marriage with the Lord as the opportunity to 'perfect the power of the Spirit (τὴν τοῦ πνεύματος δύναμιν) in the weakness (ἀσθενείᾳ) of the body' while the dowry of such marriage is the 'fruits of the Spirit' listed by Paul.[113] In Chapter XXI, Gregory emphasizes the unified activity of Christ and the Spirit in guiding the virgin's course. Thus, he speaks of 'the good voyage using the breath of the Holy Spirit (τῇ ἐπιπνοίᾳ τοῦ ἁγίου πνεύματος) with Christ as the navigator at the rudder of moderation'.[114] Finally, in Chapter XXIII, Gregory portrays the virgin as a 'priest' who has 'been anointed (χρισθείς) for this very purpose of offering a gift to God', followed by some final exhortations on attaining the beatific vision (cf. Matt. 5:8).[115] Here, Gregory employs the key term 'anointing', which throughout his other works typically has the Holy Spirit in view.

Conclusion

My analysis of *virg.* shows that Gregory's pneumatology plays a much more significant role within the treatise than is often recognized. I have demonstrated that Gregory's conception of the virgin's 'spiritual marriage' with Christ, which culminates in the beatific vision of God, is grounded not only in Christ's incarnation but especially in the Holy Spirit's life-giving power. The christological and pneumatological components of the virgin's

---

[111] *GNO* VIII/1.308.15; Woods Callahan, 50. Gregory identifies the Holy Spirit as incorruptible at *GNO* VIII/1.304.21–305.6; Woods Callahan, 48.

[112] *GNO* VIII/1.312.13–21; Woods Callahan, 53.

[113] *GNO* VIII/1.327.19; Woods Callahan, 64.

[114] *GNO* VIII/1.341.3–5; Woods Callahan, 73.

[115] *GNO* VIII/1.342.4; Woods Callahan, 74.

58 TRINITY, CHRISTOLOGY, AND PNEUMATOLOGY

'spiritual marriage' are, for Gregory, two distinguishable and yet inseparable aspects of human salvation and transformation, which stem ultimately from his insistence upon the essential unity of Father, Son, and Spirit.

Second, Gregory's use of pneumatic language in this work is 'pneumatologically laden', by virtue of the yet unsettled disputes over the status of Holy Spirit that marked his era. Pneumatic language is thus used by Gregory in a careful, rather than ad hoc, naïve, or generic manner. He appeals to key scriptural passages (e.g. John 3:6, Rom. 8:16) clearly to demarcate the difference between human 'spirit' and the Holy 'Spirit', while simultaneously upholding the direct causal dependence of the former upon the latter. Thus, pneumatic terminology that Gregory employs throughout his works, such as 'πνευματικῶς' in Chapter II of *virg.* or 'πνευματικοῦ γάμου' in Chapter XX, should always be read with an eye to their pneumatological significance, unless the specific contexts in which they occur precludes such a reading.

Third, I showed that Gregory's pneumatology is the basis upon which he denounces the 'extreme' form of virginity espoused by his opponents via a redefinition of spiritual strength and weakness. Not only has this significant rhetorical hinge of *virg.* gone unacknowledged in secondary literature, but it demonstrates that, already in his first written work, Gregory's pneumatology of 'power in weakness' occupies a central place in his trinitarian doctrine and understanding of human transformation and union with God. It is his pneumatology that distinguishes his approach to the ascetical life of virginity from that of his rivals.

Fourth, and finally, I have uncovered how Gregory's pneumatology informs his baptismal imagination and baptismal exegesis, specifically in relation to Gen. 2–3. While at no point in the treatise does Gregory ever refer to a literal baptismal ritual, it is nevertheless the case that he views the ascetical life of the virgin who is spiritually married to Christ via the Spirit in thoroughly baptismal terms.

The features of *virg.* that I discerned in this chapter will assist my reading of *hom. in Cant.*, where, I shall argue, Gregory's appeal to pneumatology and his use of his baptismal imagination guide his exegesis of the Song of Songs.

2

Baptism and Trinitarian Theology

Introduction

In Chapter 1 I identified how Gregory's baptismal imagination facilitated a corresponding baptismal exegesis to expound the crucial role of the Holy Spirit in the virgin's spiritual marriage with Christ. As I shall show in the present chapter, he also exercised a similar imagination and exegesis in defending Nicene trinitarian doctrine. In this manner, Gregory followed the lead of Basil of Caesarea, who defended Nicene orthodoxy in explicitly baptismal terms. In *Letter 159*, for instance, Basil declares, 'as we were baptised, so we profess our belief. As we profess our belief, so also we make our confession'.[1] He proceeds to note that as baptism was handed down to us by Jesus 'in the name of the Father and of the Son and of the Holy Spirit', so the Holy Spirit is 'not separated from the divine nature' (τῆς θείας φύσεως) of the Father and the Son.[2] Basil's allusion here to Matt. 28:19 demonstrates that he understood the baptismal formula to teach the essential unity of trinitarian persons.

The very same verse could, of course, also be cited to arrive at the opposite conclusion. Hence, in *Contra Eun*, Basil names Eunomius of Cyzicus as one who taught that the Holy Spirit in fact *differs in nature* from the Father and the Son precisely because it is 'numbered third' in Lord's teaching on baptism.[3] Not surprisingly, Gregory also devoted significant attention in his writings to baptismal theology, both to prove his own orthodoxy against those were suspicious of his Nicene credentials and to reclaim the exegesis of the contested tradition of baptism based on Matt. 28:19–20.

This chapter focuses on the theology of baptism as a chief hub around which many of Gregory's most important reflections on the Trinity, christology, and pneumatology revolve. In particular I am interested in exploring

[1] Roy J. Deferrari, trans., *Letters: Volume II: Letters 59–185*, Loeb Classical Library 215 (Cambridge, MA: Harvard University Press, 1928), 392; PG 32.620C.

[2] *ep. 1–366*, PG 32.621A; Deferrari, 396.

[3] Mark DelCogliano and Andrew Radde-Gallwitz, trans., *St. Basil of Caesarea: Against Eunomius*, The Fathers of the Church Volume 122 (Washington, DC: Catholic University of America Press, 2011), 187.

60   TRINITY, CHRISTOLOGY, AND PNEUMATOLOGY

Gregory's constructive use of the traditional baptismal argument for trinitarian unity to shape his understanding of human transformation and union with God through Christ and the Spirit. The following investigation is important for my upcoming analysis of *hom. in Cant.*, for I contend that the structure of thought that emerges from Gregory's reflections on baptism and human transformation also underlie much of Gregory's baptismal exegesis of the Song of Songs.

Ep. 5, Ep. 24, and *Adversus Macedonianos*

Gregory wrote *ep. 5* around 379, possibly to a synod of bishops in Sebaste, and probably to disarm Macedonian followers of the recently deceased Eustathius of Sebaste, who took issue with Gregory's alleged Sabellianism and innovative teachings on the Holy Spirit.[4] The letter therefore serves as an opportunity to articulate the grounds for orthodox Christian belief. Importantly, Gregory's defence hinges on an interpretation of the baptismal instruction handed down by Jesus to the disciples (cf. Matt. 28:19–20), which he calls the 'foundation and root of the right and sound faith'.[5]

The dependence of Nicene trinitarian orthodoxy upon baptism leads Gregory in this letter to emphasize the key term 'life', which encompasses not only the new 'life' given to humanity via baptismal regeneration in the names of the Father, Son, and Spirit, but also 'life' proper to the Trinity itself. Thus, 'the lifegiving power' (ἡ ζωοποιὸς δύναμις) that comes through the Holy Trinity, says Gregory, brings 'eternal life' and 'perfection of life' to those who are 'reborn from death'.[6] Employing a baptismal exegesis of Ps. 35(36):9, Acts 3:15, and John 6:40, Gregory speaks of the Father as 'the fountain of life', the Son as 'the author of life', and the Holy Spirit as 'giver of life'.[7] Further, it is on the basis of the 'one life' that comes to the believer via all the three hypostases *in baptism* that Gregory stakes two Nicene trinitarian claims.[8] First, against the Macedonians, he asserts that neither the Son nor the Spirit is servile,

---

[4] Anna M. Silvas, *Gregory of Nyssa: The Letters: Introduction, Translation and Commentary*, Supplements to Vigiliae Christianae 83 (Leiden: Brill, 2007), 135–136. Cf. Andrew Radde-Gallwitz, *Doctrinal Works*, 32–37.

[5] Silvas, *Gregory of Nyssa: The Letters*, 138; according to Radde-Gallwitz, *Doctrinal Works*, 44: 'The sentence is meta-creedal: it is a confession about confessions, and in particular about their proper foundation in the baptismal tradition'.

[6] Georgio Pasquali, *Gregorii Nysseni Epistulae*, GNO VIII/2 (Leiden: Brill, 1959), 32.18; Silvas, 138.

[7] *GNO* VIII/2.33.5–8; Silvas, 138–139.

[8] *GNO* VIII/2.33.14–15; Silvas, 139.

BAPTISM AND TRINITARIAN THEOLOGY 61

created, or unworthy of the Father.[9] Second, guarding against any suspicion of Sabellianism directed toward himself, he claims that while there is only 'one life' that comes to the believer via the three persons, its transmission is to be understood to follow the particular *differentiated order* of names that were handed to the disciples by Jesus (cf. Matt. 28:19–20). Gregory speaks of trinitarian life 'gushing up *from* (ἐκ ... πηγάζουσα) the God of the whole of things (i.e. the Father), proceeding *through* (διὰ ... προϊοῦσα) the Son and becoming actual *in* (ἐν ... ἐνεργουμένη) the Holy Spirit'.[10] Only when 'the faith' is understood in this way does there exist an agreement (ὁμοφώνως) between 'the faith' handed to the disciples, the 'belief' of the Christian, and the corresponding 'glorification' of the holy Trinity.[11]

A similar account of the orthodox faith is also found in *ep. 24*, probably written after *ep. 5* in 380/1, to one 'heretic' named Heracleianus. Anna Silvas suggests that this letter is an invitation to Heracleianus to the orthodox faith from Macedonian circles. Here, too, the faith is defended on the grounds of the baptismal formula, though there appears some new arguments and terminology. Thus, as in *ep. 5*, the 'sound faith', says Gregory, is that which was transmitted from the Lord Jesus himself in the form of the baptism, the 'mystery of salvation in the bath of rebirth (παλιγγενεσίας)'.[12] Further, says Gregory, 'Jesus firmly established the doctrine of salvation in the tradition of baptism'.[13]

Once again, Gregory is intent to dispel any allegations of Sabellianism, claiming that the order of the divine names in the baptismal formula signifies three distinct and unconfused hypostases. The Father names 'the cause (αἰτίαν) of all', the Son names 'the power (δύναμιν)' coming from the first cause that upholds creation, and the Spirit names 'the power' (δύναμιν) that perfects all things created by the Father and the Son.[14] While the baptismal ordering of the divine names serves clearly to distinguish the hypostases, Gregory maintains that their substance (οὐσίας) remains incomprehensible to human thought and word.[15] And, since all three hypostases are 'equally incomprehensible' with respect to substance, Gregory argues that they share the one incomprehensible substance.[16]

---

[9] *GNO* VIII/2.33.9–14; Silvas, 139.
[10] *GNO* VIII/2.33.16–17; Silvas, 139.
[11] *GNO* VIII/2.33.17–20; Silvas, 139.
[12] *GNO* VIII/2.75.8–9; Silvas, 191.
[13] *GNO* VIII/2.75.15; Silvas, 192.
[14] *GNO* VIII/2.76.7–12; Silvas, 192.
[15] *GNO* VIII/2.77.1; Silvas, 193.
[16] *GNO* VIII/2.77.2–3; Silvas, 193.

62   TRINITY, CHRISTOLOGY, AND PNEUMATOLOGY

This rather weak 'negative' basis for trinitarian unity is complemented by a stronger 'positive' notion of unity in divine 'glory', a concept that did not feature in *ep. 5*, but is crucial to Gregory's trinitarian and christological reflections in later writings. Gregory argues that since Christian baptism and glorification of God (δόξα) are of one accord, then 'the glory (ἡ δόξα) of the Father, Son, and the Holy Spirit is not differentiated'.[17] Gregory makes the link between the important category of trinitarian glory and baptism explicit by introducing the technical notion of 'activity' that is said, once again, to flow *from* the Father, *through* the Son, and *in* the Holy Spirit. Hence, we can know the indivisibility of trinitarian glory from the activities (ἐκ τῶν ἐνεργειῶν) since the single 'power' of 'life' issues *from* the Father, *through* Son, and *in* Spirit in baptism (cf. John 5:21; 6:63).[18]

This brief analysis of *ep. 5* and *ep. 24* highlights the fact that Gregory's defence of the essential unity of trinitarian persons is concretely wedded to *the economy of salvation* by virtue of its grounding in the baptismal formula. As I turn now to an analysis of the much lengthier treatise, *Maced.*, we see the basis of Gregory's argument for trinitarian unity upon the economy of human salvation is ever more pronounced in light of statements he makes about both Christian spiritual formation and the post-passion glorification of the incarnate Christ.[19] Before I address these two aspects of *Maced.*, it is important not to lose sight of the polemical context within which they are situated, wherein the contested interpretation of the baptismal formula of Matt. 28:19–20 once again defines the contours of the dispute.

According to Gregory, the Macedonian opponents accuse him and his cohort of impiety (ἀσεβεῖν) for holding grandiose ideas about the status of the Holy Spirit.[20] He identifies three specific attributes that his opponents claim the Spirit does *not* share equally with the Father and the Son: 'power' (δυνάμει), 'glory' (δόξῃ), and 'dignity' (ἀξιώματι).[21] Significantly, his opponents find support for their claim regarding the Spirit's diminished status by appealing to the baptismal formula of Matt. 28:19–20. They

---

[17] *GNO* VIII/2.77.18–24; Silvas, 194.

[18] *GNO* VIII/2.78.26–79.6; Silvas, 195–196.

[19] Cf. Piet Hein Hupsch, *The Glory of the Spirit in Gregory of Nyssa's Adversus Macedonianos: Commentary and Systematic-Theological Synthesis*, Supplements to Vigiliae Christianae 163 (Leiden: Brill, 2020), now the most comprehensive study of this treatise.

[20] *GNO* III/1.89.16–18; Andrew Radde-Gallwitz, ed., *The Cambridge Edition of Early Christian Writings: Volume 1: God* (Cambridge: Cambridge University Press, 2017), 271.

[21] *GNO* III/1.90.5–10; Radde-Gallwitz, 270–271.

conclude from the fact that the Spirit is given 'third in order' (κατὰ τὴν τάξιν τρίτον) that he is estranged from the proper notion of God.[22]

Responding with an argument already employed in *ep. 24*, Gregory insists that 'numerical order' (ἀριθμὸν τάξιν) introduces no 'divergence in nature' because there is no variation in 'beneficent activity' (ἐνέργεια) among Father, Son, and Spirit.[23] Appealing to what I shall now call the 'linear' trinitarian transmission of divine power *from* the Father, *through* the Son, and *in* the Spirit, Gregory imagines three flaming torches, whereby both the second and the third light (φωτός) have been successively 'caused' (αἰτίαν) by the first.[24] He argues that even if the 'heat' produced by the first torch exceeded the heat of the others, it would be ridiculous to claim that the third could not be called fire just because it was lit third in sequence. The third torch does 'everything that fire does'.[25] By analogy, the Holy Spirit does not lack divine 'dignity' simply by being named third after the Father and the Son in the baptismal formula. Since this analogy constitutes Gregory's response to his opponent's exegesis of Matt. 28:19–20, the implication here is that it is *in baptism* that the Spirit completes the 'unified activity' transmitted *from* the Father, *through* the Son, thus establishing the Spirit's proper dignity (ἀξίας) and glory (δόξης).[26]

This conjunction of baptismal theology and trinitarian unity of activity in turn underpins Gregory's understanding of proper Christian spiritual formation, another point of dispute with the Macedonians.[27] He claims that just as an embryo is an imperfectly formed (ἀτελεσφόρητον) human being, so his opponents are not fully formed Christians, for they have 'not received a true formation in piety (τὴν ἀληθῆ μόρφωσιν τῆς εὐσεβείας)—one that extends through the entire [baptismal] mystery (δι᾽ ὅλου τοῦ μυστηρίου)'.[28] Just as one is properly a human being only if there is a 'completion in every attribute of the nature', so one is only properly a Christian, Gregory claims, if they are 'characterised (χαρακτηρίζεται) by faith in Father, Son, and Holy Spirit'.[29] Referring to baptism, Gregory speaks of this belief in the Trinity as the 'form (ἡ μορφή) of the one who has been formed (μεμορφωμένου) in

---

[22] *GNO* III/1.92.31–33; Radde-Gallwitz, 274.
[23] *GNO* III/1.92.34–93.3; Radde-Gallwitz, 274.
[24] *GNO* III/1.93.3–6; Radde-Gallwitz, 274.
[25] *GNO* III/1.93.8–10; Radde-Gallwitz, 274.
[26] *GNO* III/1.93.17–19; Radde-Gallwitz, 274.
[27] On unity of activity see Maspero, *Trinity and Man*, 53–60.
[28] *GNO* III/1.101.14–16; Radde-Gallwitz, 281.
[29] *GNO* III/1.102.2–5; Radde-Gallwitz, 281–282.

64 TRINITY, CHRISTOLOGY, AND PNEUMATOLOGY

the mystery of the truth'.[30] The one who denies the Holy Spirit is therefore deprived of the essential characteristic that the Holy Spirit brings, namely 'life', and is therefore 'not a living human being' but 'bones in the womb of a pregnant woman' (cf. Eccl. 11:5). Gregory paints for his reader the image of a still-born baptisand, who has not received the life-giving power of the Spirit that necessarily completes the unified transmission of life *from* the Father, *through* the Son.

This argument for trinitarian unity, which I again note is wholly dependent upon Christian formation *within the economy*, underscores the fact that, for Gregory, divine activity within the whole created order takes the 'linear' form '*from* the Father, *through* the Son, *in* the Holy Spirit', even when baptism is not directly in view. In other words, it can never be the case for Gregory that *any* divine activity within the created order ever takes a truncated form, say, '*from* the Father, *through* the Son, ___', or '*from* the Father, ___, ___', or '___, *through* the Son, ___', or '___, ___, *in* the Spirit'. This appears to be why, for instance, in *Maced.*, Gregory applies the logic of baptismal unity of activity to God's creation and bringing to perfection of the whole cosmos. Even here, where the bestowal of baptismal 'life' upon humanity or proper Christian formation is not directly in sight, and even where there appears to be no obvious scriptural support for holding such a view, Gregory states that all of created nature comes about as a result of 'a transmission of power (δυνάμεως διάδοσιν), which begins *from* the Father (ἀρχομένην), proceeds (προϊοῦσαν) *through* the Son, and is perfected (τελειουμένην) *in* the Holy Spirit'.[31] Gregory, it seems, imaginatively projected the insights of his baptismal theology and its accompanying metaphysical framework onto his cosmology. This feature of Gregory's notion of trinitarian unity of activity will resurface in both *hom. in 1 Cor. 15:28* and Homilies 13, 14, and 15 of *hom. in Cant.* in connection with his anti-Eunomian exegesis of 1 Cor. 15:28 regarding God's eschatological triumph over evil and his becoming 'all in all'.

I leave this issue aside for now and note that Gregory's instinct consistently to extend trinitarian unity of activity in baptism to cosmic order and teleology generally as a *cosmic principle* appears to have had direct implications on his christology and his views on the incarnation, which will in turn endow them with immediate cosmological significance.[32] Indeed, there is a subtle yet, I suggest, clear indication in *Maced.* that, via the crucial concept of divine

---

[30] *GNO* III/1.102.5–7; Radde-Gallwitz, 282.
[31] *GNO* III/1.100.8–11; NPNF II/5.320.
[32] Cf. Radde-Gallwitz, *Doctrinal Works*, 261.

BAPTISM AND TRINITARIAN THEOLOGY   65

'glory', Gregory extended the notion of trinitarian unity of activity in baptism to the post-passion glorification of Christ's human flesh, just as he extended this notion to God's activity in the creation of the world.

In *Maced.*, this christological feature of Gregory's thought emerges from his elaboration upon the 'linear' trinitarian model, where he argues that the *descending* unified transmission of power *from* the Father, *through* the Son, *in* the Holy Spirit at baptism is mirrored in a corresponding *ascending* movement such that humanity may come to behold the 'glory' of God. The person who has 'piously received the Spirit' (ὁ εὐσεβῶς τὸ πνεῦμα δεξάμενος) beholds the 'glory' of the Only-begotten in the Spirit, and through this image of the Son receives the impress of the archetype (i.e. the Father). Conversely, the person who grudges the Spirit's glory, 'by the same sequence' (διὰ τῆς αὐτῆς ἀκολουθίας) extends his blasphemy *to* (ἐπί) the Father *through* (διά) the Son.[33]

Crucially, Gregory's comments on beholding the Spirit's 'glory' together with the 'glory' of the Father and the Son is couched in terms of the ordered transmission of power *at baptism*, as indicated by his reference to those who have 'piously' (εὐσεβῶς) received the Spirit. Thus, it is the *baptismal framework* above all that provides the means of understanding Gregory's subsequent comments on the possibility of human persons beholding the 'intra-trinitarian' unity in 'glory'. According to this account of trinitarian unity, the Holy Spirit is 'glorified and has glory' and through such 'abundance of glory' glorifies the Father and the Son. Then, alluding to John 17:4–5 ('I have glorified you' . . . Glorify me with the glory that I had from the beginning (ἀπ' ἀρχῆς) from you, before the world began'), in conjunction with John 12:28 ('Indeed, I have glorified and will again glorify'), Gregory now envisages a 'circle of glorification' (τὴν ἐγκύκλιον τῆς δόξης) according to which the trinitarian persons are unified.[34]

We see that Gregory now offers an alternative account of trinitarian unity not yet found in either *ep. 5* or *ep. 24*. The familiar notion of trinitarian unity in terms of the 'linear' model is now supplemented with a 'circular' image aimed at depicting unity via intra-trinitarian glorification. Thus, I concur with Radde-Gallwitz's statement that the 'inner-Trinitarian exchange of

---

[33] *GNO* III/1.107.9–16; Radde-Gallwitz, 286.
[34] *GNO* III/1.108.30–109.15; Radde-Gallwitz, 287–288.

66   TRINITY, CHRISTOLOGY, AND PNEUMATOLOGY

glory . . . is not equivalent to the transmission of grace ad extra in the typical order—From Father, through Son, completed in the Spirit'.[35]

Nevertheless, it is important to note that the two trinitarian models— the 'linear' and the 'circular'—are, in Gregory's view, integrally connected. Indeed, the former is supposed to lead the baptized to the latter. Thus, it is according to the dynamic transmission of divine 'glory' within the economy of salvation depicted in the 'linear' model that Gregory suggests humanity may not only *behold* the trinitarian unity in glory depicted in the 'circular' model, but actually be *joined* to it. Hence, Gregory asks why his opponents cut themselves off from 'attachment' (προσκολλήσεως) to God, for humanity cannot be 'attached (προσκολληθήσεται) to the Lord unless the Spirit produces our connection (συνάφειαν) with him'.[36]

Crucially, his important allusion to John 17:5 suggests that the *incarnate Christ* himself somehow constitutes the original bridging point within the economy of salvation between the realities described by the 'linear' and 'circular' models of trinitarian unity. For the words of John 17:5 are spoken by the *human Jesus* in anticipation of his post-passion return to the eternal 'circular' intra-trinitarian unity in 'glory'. To be sure, Gregory passes over this intriguing reference to John 17:5 without much further elaboration, and it is easy to gain the impression, as a number of commentators have, that he uses it simply to make a point about the 'eternal' or 'immanent' Trinity, all the while brushing aside its obvious *economic* aspect.[37] However, this matter is worthy of further reflection since, in several later writings, Gregory cites this very same passage to demonstrate that the post-passion glorification of *the incarnate Christ's flesh* into unity of 'glory' of the Only-begotten Son and the Father is completed by the activity of the Holy Spirit.

Is it possible that, when he wrote *Maced.*, Gregory already viewed humanity's post-baptismal 'attachment' to the eternal 'circular' intra-trinitarian 'glory' of God via the unified activity of Father, Son, and Holy Spirit to have already taken place *prototypically* in the post-passion transformation

[35] Radde-Gallwitz, *Doctrinal Works*, 75; cf. Bernard Pottier, *Dieu et le Christ selon Grégoire de Nysse: Etude systématique de 'Contre Eunome' avec traduction inédite des extraites d'Eunome*, Ouvertures 12 (Paris: cultur et verité, 1994), 336–339.

[36] *GNO* III/1.109.21–22; Radde-Gallwitz, 288.

[37] Cf. Marie-Odile Boulnois, 'Le cercle des glorifications mutuelles dans la Trinité selon Grégoire de Nysse: De l'innovation exégétique à la fécondité théologique', in *Grégoire de Nysse: la Bible dans la construction de son discours*, Collection des Etudes Augustiniennes, ed. Matthieu Cassin and Hélène Grelier (Paris: Brepols, 2008), 33–34; Andrew Radde-Gallwitz, 'Gregory of Nyssa's Pneumatology in Context: The Spirit as Anointing and the History of Trinitarian Controversies', *Journal of Early Christian Studies*, 19/2 (2011), 281; and Hupsch, *The Glory of the Spirit*, 241, 319.

BAPTISM AND TRINITARIAN THEOLOGY   67

of the incarnate Christ's flesh by the Spirit?[38] This raises a further set of complex questions upon which I focus in upcoming chapters. For now, it is perhaps enough simply to observe that Gregory's passing reference to John 17:5 implies the view that Christ's post-passion glorification marks the definitive point of transition from the economy of salvation, where the 'linear' activity of Father, Son, and Spirit operates, to the 'circular' exchange of 'glory' characteristic of the inner trinitarian life.[39]

Adversus eos qui baptismum differunt and *In baptismum Christi*

As we turn now to two of Gregory's Epiphany sermons—*bapt. diff.* and *bapt. Chr.*—we discover further connections among his account of baptism, trinitarian unity of activity, and Christ's incarnation, though now from the perspective of Christ's own baptism in the Jordan.[40] As we find in comparable sermons of this period, Gregory urges his congregation to be baptized and, as is fitting with the liturgical season of Epiphany, Christ's own baptism is used as motivation to hasten them to action. Gregory invites his listeners to consider Christ baptized in the Jordan river as a 'type' of their own potential regeneration. Using Pauline imagery, they are to 'strip off the old man as a filthy garment' and to 'take the garment of incorruptibility which Christ stretched out unfolded' for them (cf. 1 Cor. 15:53; Eph. 4:22; Col. 3:9).[41] His congregation, then, is beckoned to come figuratively 'upon the Jordan', depicted by Gregory as a 'river of grace' flowing not only in Palestine, but everywhere.[42]

[38] So, Andrew Radde-Gallwitz, *Doctrinal Works*, 167: 'He views the life of Christ as the decisive hinge point in the history of the human race, the point where it was returned by divine grace to its original glory'.

[39] That Gregory only has the 'immanent' Trinity in view in his allusion to John 17:5 does not fit neatly with Gregory's uses of this passage elsewhere in his corpus. Contra Hupsch, that Gregory adds the gloss ἀπ' ἀρχῆς to his allusion to John 17:4–5 does *not* mean that he only has the *immanent* Trinity in view. Rather, I suggest that it reveals Gregory's instinct to safeguard the christological point that the *incarnate* Christ glorified by the Father with the Spirit in the economy is none other than the *eternal* Christ *eternally glorified* by Father with the same Spirit. The very same gloss on John 17:5 (ἀπ' ἀρχῆς) occurs in both *hom. in 1 Cor. 15:28* (cf. *GNO* III/1 222.1–7) and Homily 7 of *hom. in Cant.* (cf. *GNO* VI.242.17–19 (discussed in Chapter 8), where the incarnate Christ's death and post-passion glorification of his flesh are certainly in view. See Chapter 4, where I address the exegesis of John 17:4–5 in more detail.

[40] Everett Ferguson, 'Preaching at Epiphany: Gregory of Nyssa and John Chrysostom on Baptism and the Church', *Church History*, 66/1 (1997), 1–17; cf. Everett Ferguson, 'Exhortation to Baptism in the Cappadocians', in *Studia Patristica*, vol. 32, ed. E. A. Livingston (Leuven: Peeters, 1996), 112–120.

[41] Gunterus Heil, Johannes P. Cavarnos, and Otto Lendle, eds., *Sermones, Pars II. Post mortem Henrici Dörrie volume edendum curavit Friedhelm Mann, GNO* X/2 (Leiden: Brill, 1990), 360.16–22.

[42] *GNO* X/2.360.23–361.2.

68 TRINITY, CHRISTOLOGY, AND PNEUMATOLOGY

There they may approach Christ, the fount of 'sweet' and 'drinkable' water.[43] By coming to the river, where Christ is, they allow the Holy Spirit, represented by the 'dove', to fly over them.[44] Jesus himself, acting as a 'type' (τυπικῶς), is depicted here as the first (πρῶτος) to bring the Spirit down from heaven (ἐξ οὐρανοῦ κατήγαγε). Upon his descent, Gregory pictures the Spirit burning the soul of the baptized 'with fire' (cf. Matt. 3:11), transforming the baptized into an incense offering (ὡς πυρεῖον) to God. With the coming of the Spirit, who, as the dove, broods over her eggs, comes the birth of new life through the engendering of many children (πολλὰ τίκτει) into the world, or 'children of the Spirit' (τέκνα τοῦ πνεύματος), by which Gregory means the virtues and good works.[45] Here, the imagery is reminiscent of the virgin's post-baptismal engendering of the virtues by the Spirit in *virg*.

It is difficult to discern what influence, if any, Gregory's 'linear' model of trinitarian unity of activity plays in the formulation of this sermon on baptism. Certainly, given the force and consistency with which he argues for trinitarian unity of activity in baptism in the texts analysed above, it is difficult to imagine that Gregory is not cognizant of the principle when expounding upon Christ's own baptism in the Jordan. If he is to be consistent with the views expressed in *ep. 5*, *ep. 24*, and *Maced.*, then he must have viewed the baptism of Christ in the Jordan as being a unified activity of Father, Son, and Spirit. For otherwise, Christ's handing down of the baptismal formula to his disciples (cf. Matt. 28:19–20) would be said to ground orthodox faith in the essential unity of trinitarian person at the same time that Christ's very own baptism as 'prototype' denies it. In any case, Gregory's comments on Christ's baptism in this sermon are far too brief to lead to any concrete conclusions on this matter.

However, as we turn to a second of Gregory's Epiphany sermons, *bapt. Chr.*, we observe that Gregory probably did view Christ's own baptism in the Jordan in terms of the unified activity of Father, Son, and Spirit.[46] Preaching to his congregation as though Christ's baptism by John were contemporaneous with their present experience, Gregory announces that 'today' Christ is baptized by John to 'cleanse' humanity and to 'bring the Spirit from above' (πνεῦμα δὲ ἄνωθεν ἀγάγῃ) so as to 'exalt man to

---

[43] GNO X/2.361.2.
[44] GNO X/2.361.27.
[45] GNO X/2.361.27–362.8.
[46] Dated 6 January 383 by Daniélou, 'La chronologie des oeuvres de Grégoire de Nyssa', 362; Similarly, Ferguson, 'Preaching at Epiphany', 2; cf. discussion in Boersma, *Embodiment and Virtue*, 182–186.

heaven'.[47] Christ's baptism in the Jordan is here portrayed as the paradigm for all Christian baptism. Just as the Spirit comes down from heaven upon Christ at the Jordan, so the Spirit is brought down upon every person baptized, leading to their heavenly exaltation. Importantly, Gregory is adamant that the subject of baptism was 'he whose generation was before all things' (ὁ πρὸ πάσης οὐσίας ... γεννηθείς).[48] That is, it is the eternal *Only-begotten Son*, and not some 'second subject', who was baptized at the Jordan and thereby became 'adopted' into sonship. Nevertheless, this must be understood in a strictly qualified sense since, for Gregory, it is the Only-begotten Son *with respect to the man assumed* (τὸν ἄνθρωπον), rather than the Son according to his divinity, who receives the Spirit at baptism on humanity's behalf. Later in the sermon, Gregory speaks again of the 'dual aspect' of Christ's baptism. Thus, the Father's voice spoken from heaven upon the Son baptized (τῷ υἱῷ βαπτιζομένῳ) was to lead people *from his perceptible humanity* to the 'dignity' (ἀξίωμα) of nature of the Godhead.[49]

A fuller discussion of Gregory's christology, and his account of the unity of the divinity and humanity in Christ, will be undertaken in Chapters 3, 4, and 5. For now, it will suffice to observe that Gregory is intent on upholding the *single subject* of Christ according to the dual aspects of the perceptible humanity on the one hand and the imperceptible divinity on the other. Thus, Gregory understands Christ's baptism in the Jordan to be the baptism of the *Son*, who brings the Spirit down upon *the man assumed by the Son*, and in so doing forms the basis for the rest of humanity's exaltation by the Spirit at baptism. Here we catch a slight glimpse of Gregory's 'linear' notion of trinitarian unity of activity at baptism intersecting with his dual aspect christology.

Gregory does not immediately spell out how this process of humanity's heavenly exaltation via Christ and the Spirit works, nor over what timeframe it unfolds. However, a clue is given via his designation of the man assumed by Christ as the 'first-fruit' of humanity's regeneration. Thus, Christ 'assumes manhood' to 'cause' (αἰτία) a purification, renovation, and regeneration of humanity, and thus becomes a 'type' (τύπος) and 'figure' (χαρακτήρ) of us all, to 'sanctify the first-fruit' (ἀγιάσῃ τὴν ἀπαρχήν) of every action.[50] A little later on, he states that the Jordan, which receives 'the first-fruit of

---

[47] Ernestus Gebhardt, ed., *Sermones, Pars I*, GNO IX (Leiden: Brill, 1967), 223.13–16; NPNF II/5.518.

[48] *GNO* IX/1.223.12–13; NPNF II/5.518.

[49] *GNO* IX/1.237.14–18; NPNF II/5.523.

[50] *GNO* IX/1.224.2–5; NPNF II/5.519.

70 TRINITY, CHRISTOLOGY, AND PNEUMATOLOGY

sanctification and benediction' (τοῦ ἁγιασμοῦ καὶ τῆς εὐλογίας τὴν ἀπαρχήν) is like a 'fount' that conveys baptismal grace to the whole world.[51]

The notion of Christ as 'first-fruit' appears frequently in Gregory's writings, often in association with Rom. 11:16—'If the dough offered as first-fruits is holy, so is the whole lump'.[52] In several works, Gregory connects the notion of Christ as 'first-fruit' with the numerous Pauline statements concerning Christ as 'firstborn' (cf. Col. 1:15; 18; Rom. 8:29; Heb. 1:6). In *perf.*, he states that Christ baptized in the Jordan was 'the first-fruit (ὁ ἀπαρχή) of those who have fallen asleep' (cf. 1 Cor. 15:20) through his own 'birth from above' (διὰ τῆς ἄνωθεν γεννήσεως). He therefore 'leads the way' by 'drawing the grace of the Spirit upon the first-fruit of our nature ('ἐπὶ τὴν ἀπαρχὴν τῆς φύσεως ἡμῶν τὴν τοῦ πνεύματος χάριν ἐπισπασάμενος)'.[53] Gregory's point is not that the man assumed by Christ needed to be cleansed of sin, or adopted into sonship, but rather that if Christ's assumption of a human being is to sanctify the 'common lump' of humanity, then the man assumed as 'first-fruit' of human sanctification must himself also prototypically receive the Spirit. I shall delay until the final chapter my analysis of Gregory's prominent use of this theme in both *hom. in 1 Cor. 15:28*, and Homilies, 13, 14, and 15 of *hom. in Cant.*

To shed further light on Gregory's use of the 'first-fruit' concept, it is worth noting the close connection between pneumatology and the use of the concept in the Pseudo-Athanasian author of the *de incarnatione et contra Arianos*, who several scholars suggest directly influenced Gregory.[54] The author states that before the post-passion glorification of Jesus' flesh, the Holy Spirit had not yet come (Οὔπω ἦν Πνεῦμα ἅγιον) (cf. John 7:39).[55] Consequently, the Spirit of adoption was not yet among humanity, since the 'first-fruit' from human beings (ἀπαρχὴ ἐξ ἡμῶν) had not yet ascended to heaven.[56] Later, the author refers to 'the Spirit of our Father' in relation to humanity's adoption as sons of God.[57] The incarnation of Christ is essential to this adoption, and it is

---

[51] *GNO* IX/1.235.9–12; NPNF II/5.522.

[52] Cf. Lucas F. Mateo-Seco and Giulio Maspero, eds., *The Brill Dictionary of Gregory of Nyssa*, Supplements to Vigiliae Christianae 99 (Leiden: Brill, 2010), 612–614; Cf. Radde-Gallwitz, *Doctrinal Works*, 185–'188.

[53] *GNO* VIII/1.202.1–11; Woods Callahan, 114, modified. The more accurate translation in Greer, 38.

[54] Cf. Johannes Zachhuber, *Human Nature in Gregory of Nyssa: Philosophical Background and Theological Significance*, Supplements to Vigiliae Christianae 46 (Leiden: Brill, 2000), 139, 207–212; cf. Reinhard M. Hübner, *Die Einheit des Leibes Christi bei Gregor von Nyssa*, Philosophia Patrum 2 (Leiden: Brill, 1974), 53, 288f.

[55] *inc. et c. Ar*, PG 26.989B.

[56] *inc. et c. Ar*, PG 26.989B.

[57] *inc. et c. Ar*, PG 26.996B.

BAPTISM AND TRINITARIAN THEOLOGY   71

through Christ's becoming a 'perfect man' that human beings become united by the Spirit and thus become one Spirit (οἱ ἄνθρωποι ἐνωθέντες Πνεύματι, γένωνται ἓν Πνεῦμα) (cf. 1 Cor. 6:17).[58] Hence, just as God became flesh, so human beings become spirit (Αὐτὸς οὖν ἐστι θεὸς σαρκοφόρος, καὶ ἡμεῖς ἄνθροποι πνευματοφόροι).

Here, the concept of 'first-fruit' is once again important, for, as the author claims, when the Son receives the 'first-fruit' of humanity in the incarnation, he gives to humanity from the being of the Father the 'first-fruit' of the Holy Spirit (ἔδωκεν ἡμῖν ἐκ τῆς οὐσίας τοῦ Πατρὸς, ἀπαρχὴν ἁγίου Πνεύματος) in order that we might become like the Son of God (cf. Rom. 8:23).[59] Importantly, the Pseudo-Athanasian author also posits a link between the 'first-fruit' of the Spirit and Christ's baptism. Hence, with reference to Christ's baptism in the Jordan, the author recounts the descent of the Holy Spirit in the form of the dove upon Christ. Yet, whereas in humanity the divinity (i.e. the Spirit) dwells as 'first-fruit', Christ has the fulness of divinity (i.e. the Spirit).[60] In relation to the Eucharistic bread, the author interprets the 'daily bread' of the Lord's prayer (cf. Matt. 6:9–13//Luke 11:2–4) simultaneously as 'first-fruit', as 'flesh of the Lord', and as the Holy Spirit. Thus, concludes the author, 'the life-giving Spirit is the flesh of the Lord' (Πνεῦμα γὰρ ζωοποιοῦν ἡ σάρξ ἐστι τοῦ Κυρίου).[61] To be sure, there are clear differences between Gregory's use of the 'first-fruit' notion and that of the Pseudo-Athanasian author. Nevertheless, both seem to have held the view that the 'first-fruit' concept is to be understood in relation to the co-sanctifying work of both the incarnate Christ and the Holy Spirit.

According to Zachhuber, Gregory employs the concept of 'first-fruit' to express 'Christ's mediation of salvation to all humanity', with humanity identified as the 'common lump' of Rom. 11:16.[62] Following the influential thesis of Wilhelm Herrmann, which has been perpetuated by Albrecht Ritschl and Adolf von Harnack, Zachhuber argues that Gregory uses the 'first-fruit' concept in a dichotomous 'humanistic' and 'physical' manner. On the one hand, Christ is first-fruit 'in the sense of the perfect human model' that the rest of humanity is called to imitate through ethical-ascetical endeavour and the 'support' of the Holy Spirit.[63] On the other hand, it is

[58] inc. et c. Ar, PG 26.996C.
[59] inc. et c. Ar, PG 26.997A.
[60] inc. et c. Ar, PG 26.997 B.
[61] inc. et c. Ar, PG 26.1012B.
[62] Zachhuber, BDGN, 612.
[63] Zachhuber, BDGN, 613.

through the 'admixture' of the 'divine nature' to 'human nature' that 'Christ is "first-fruits" from which all humanity can grow into union with the divine', which Zachhuber views as 'a natural process accomplished in a necessary sequence'.[64] There are, thus, two distinct soteriological 'strands', so to speak, in Gregory's thought that are not easily reconciled.[65] Indeed, if Herrmann is to be believed, Gregory deliberately overcompensates for his 'physical' soteriology with his 'humanistic' one.

In upcoming chapters I shall provide reasons why the so-called physical and humanistic soteriological strands are more coherently integrated in Gregory's thought than we might at first be led to believe. There are reasons to suggest the distinction does not adequately characterize Gregory's authentic thought. One of the keys to discerning their closer unity is to realize that Gregory's use of the 'first-fruit' theme is often employed in the context of baptismal theology, as we have just seen, and is hence strongly connected to the regenerative activity of the Holy Spirit. I suggest that Zachhuber's analysis of the 'first-fruit' motif and its implications for Gregory's soteriology, while not at all inconsistent with what Gregory teaches in some texts, is somewhat limited in scope by overlooking the importance of pneumatology. For, in consistently framing the discussion of Christ as 'first-fruit' in connection with Jesus' baptism in the Jordan, Gregory highlights the *essential* rather than merely 'supporting' role of the Holy Spirit in constituting Christ as first-fruit and mediator of humanity's salvation.

The connection between the Spirit and the 'first-fruit' concept I am drawing attention to here is not a trivial point but, as I have argued above, goes to the very heart of Gregory's trinitarian theology and its coherence. As pointed out already, Gregory wed his argument for trinitarian unity to the economy of salvation via the notion of the unified activity of Father, Son, *and Spirit*. Consequently, in Gregory's view, there can be no salvation of humanity under the truncated form of divine activity '___, *through* the Son,

---

[64] Zachhuber, BDGN, 613. There is a longstanding discussion regarding Gregory's soteriological use of the concept 'human nature'. Zachhuber's study is, to date, the most comprehensive. It would require nothing less than a monograph to offer a proper response. The problem of pinning down Gregory's understanding of 'human nature' may prove to be ultimately intractable. Compare Andrew Radde-Gallwitz, 'Contra Eunomium III', in *Gregory of Nyssa: Contra Eunomium III: An English Translation with Commentary and Supporting Studies. Proceedings of the 12th International Colloquium on Gregory of Nyssa (Leuven, 14–17 September 2010)*, Supplements to Vigiliae Christianae 124, ed. Johan Leemans and Matthieu Cassin (Leiden: Brill, 2014), 305 with the significant change of mind in Radde-Gallwitz, *Doctrinal Works*, 173.

[65] This bifurcated soteriology is explored more fully in Zachhuber, *Human Nature*, 187ff.; cf. Ludlow, *Universal Salvation*, 92–95, who endorses Zachhuber's analysis.

_____', for according to Gregory's trinitarian theology, such truncated activity simply never occurs in the cosmos. Thus, to deny that the Spirit has an *essential* and *necessary* role in the process of human transformation and salvation, beginning with the incarnate Christ himself as 'first-fruit' of the 'common lump', and to conceive of this process as though it were something that in principle is actualized *exclusively* between Christ and humanity, either through ethical-ascetic imitation of Christ's human example, or through a necessary sequence at the level of universal *phusis* through the Son's assumption of human nature, is completely to undermine Gregory's notion of trinitarian unity and cosmic order. In other words, if Gregory really does posit that humanity can, in principle, undergo transformation and ultimate union with God through Christ's incarnation in any way that downplays the *unified activity* of the Spirit with the Father and the Son, then he undermines the very basis from which he argues that the Spirit is united to the Son and the Father in substance. And this in a manner that proves himself to be dangerously non-Nicene.[66]

The *bapt. Chr.* steers our attention acutely toward this matter as Gregory places the call to imitate Christ baptized as the 'first-fruit' of those sanctified by the Spirit in direct parallel with his typical anti-Macedonian account of baptism as the 'linear' transmission of power *from* the Father, *through* the Son, and *in* the Spirit. First, Gregory explains how Christian baptism is an 'imitation' (εἰς μίμησιν) of Jesus' own baptism, and that this in turn marks one's identification with his death and resurrection.[67] Just as Christ was raised on the third day, so the baptisand is immersed three times in water,

---

[66] The issue has recently been addressed by Miguel Brugarolas, 'Christological Eschatology', in *Gregory of Nyssa's Mystical Eschatology*, Studia Patristica CI, ed. Giulio Maspero, Miguel Brugarolas, and Ilaria Vigorelli (Leuven: Peeters, 2021), 31–46. In direct response to Zachhuber, he notes that, for Gregory, salvation cannot be reduced to either the merely ethical or the physical (41). However, Brugarolas' attempt to resolve the dilemma 'systematically' imports new concepts into Gregory's soteriology that do not have obvious textual support. Thus, according to Brugarolas, '[w]e can say that salvation is not a mere physical relationship . . . nor is it merely ethical; but rather it is mystical, that is personal. It is a union with God so strong that the divine gift dilates nature, and the virtue reaches a level at which it transcends its own possibilities: the union that makes the man son of God' (41–42). In the following chapters, I aim to show with stronger textual evidence that the alleged 'ethical-physical' divide in Gregory's soteriology rests on a misreading of how the soteriological implications of the christology of *Eun.* III stands in relation to Gregory's broader soteriological thought (see Chapter 5). To anticipate the argument developed in this book, the alleged soteriological dichotomy can be resolved *pneumatologically*. For Gregory, the same Spirit that unites the human nature of Christ to the divinity of the Son as baptized, crucified, and resurrected 'first-fruit' also unites the rest of humanity to the divinity of the Son, and through the Son to the Father, by means of baptismal imitation of Christ's death and resurrection and the post-baptismal, Spirit-empowered life of virtue. In short, *both* Christ *and* the Spirit save humanity 'physically' and 'ethically' in a single integrated activity.

[67] Cf. *GNO* IX/1.228.16; NPNF II/5.520.

74 TRINITY, CHRISTOLOGY, AND PNEUMATOLOGY

while the three names of the Trinity are spoken. Gregory then takes this as an opportunity to deliver his typical defence of the Holy Spirit's unity with the Father and the Son against those who 'contend boldly' and hold a 'grudge' against the 'glory of the Spirit' (τὴν δόξαν τοῦ πνεύματος). Alluding to the baptismal formula of Matt. 28:19–20, which is said to signify the Father as 'source (ἀρχή) of all things', the Son as 'the maker (δημιουργός) of the creation', and the Spirit as the one 'perfecting (τελειωτικόν) all things', Gregory argues 'there is not a distinction in the sanctification' (οὐκ ἔστι τοῦ ἁγιασμοῦ) among the trinitarian persons, who therefore cannot be divided into 'different natures' (φύσεις) or 'three Gods'.[68]

Thus, within one and the same train of thought, Gregory depicts Christian baptism *both* as an imitation of Christ baptized as 'first-fruit' of those sanctified by the Holy Spirit, *and* as the sanctification that comes by the unified activity of Father, Son, and Holy Spirit depicted by the 'linear' baptismal scheme. Depending on how systematic a thinker one takes Gregory to be, one may be tempted to draw from this the conclusion that the unified activity of Father, Son, and Spirit received in Christian baptism was already *prototypically* operative in like manner in the event of Christ's own baptism as 'first-fruit'. Gregory does not go so far as to make this connection explicit, yet when this passage is read in conjunction with *bapt. diff.*, where Jesus is said to be a 'prototype' of all those who receive the Spirit in baptism, the conclusion is difficult to avoid. In any case, he certainly appears to imply that Christ's baptism as first-fruit grounds the baptisand's own reception of the unified activity of the Trinity that leads eventually to resurrection. What can only be taken as an implication of Gregory's baptismal theology here will become a key structural motif in the final three homilies of *hom. in Cant.*, as I show in Chapter 8.

This perspective, in which *both* Christ *and* the Spirit jointly sanctify humanity, is now the proper basis on which we ought to understand Gregory's closing exhortation in this sermon on the post-baptismal life of transformation in virtue. Gregory summons those who have received 're-generation' (τῆς παλιγγενεσίας) to begin to demonstrate their 'change of ways' (μετακοσμήσεως).[69] Since baptism results in spiritual 'brightness'

[68] *GNO* IX/1.228.19–229.18; NPNF II/5.520; cf. Piet Hein Hupsch, 'Mystagogical Theology in Gregory of Nyssa's Epiphany Sermon *In diem luminum*', in *Seeing through the Eyes of Faith: New Approaches to the Mystagogy of the Church Fathers*, Late Antique History and Religion 11, ed. Paul van Geest (Leuven: Peeters, 2016), 131.

[69] *GNO* IX/1.237.23–27; NPNF II/5.523.

(λαμπρότητα)[70] and 'illuminates the man' (φωτίζει τὸν ἄνθρωπον),[71] then the proof of a transformed life of virtue is described in corresponding light terminology. Hence, 'as darkness is dispelled by light, and black disappears as whiteness is spread over it, so the old man also disappears when adorned with the works of righteousness'.[72] To be illuminated in baptism is simultaneously to be adopted as children of God. Therefore, says Gregory, 'we ought narrowly to scrutinize our Father's characteristics, that by fashioning and framing ourselves to the likeness of our Father, we may appear true children of Him who calls us to the adoption according to grace'.[73] Finally, quoting Isa. 6:10 at the conclusion of his sermon, Gregory speaks of baptism explicitly in nuptial terms reminiscent of *virg*. Gregory calls his congregation, now dressed in the 'robe' and 'garment' of salvation as both a 'bridegroom' and as a 'bride', to sing the hymn of Isaiah whose mouth was 'touched by the Spirit'.[74]

Gregory's concluding comments on the post-baptismal life of virtue is not, as we may be led to think, simply an exhortation to the Christian to choose to imitate Christ's ethical-ascetical example with the 'support' of the Spirit.[75] Rather, he depicts a life transformed in virtue as one brought about by the *co-essential* work of both Christ the 'maker' and the Spirit the 'perfector', whose joint activity flows from the one 'source' who is the Father.[76] Again, this understanding of salvation and human transformation will be much more apparent in *hom. in Cant.*, or so I shall argue.

Conclusion

In this chapter I have shown that Gregory conceived of trinitarian unity in terms of a 'linear' and a 'circular' model, both of which emerge organically from his reflections on baptism. According to Gregory, it is by means of the 'linear' transmission of divine activity *from* the Father, *through* the Son, and *in* the Holy Spirit, encountered in a specific salvific mode by the baptized, and perfected within the context of the post-baptismal life of virtue, that one

---

[70] *GNO* IX/1.224.25; NPNF II/5.519.
[71] *GNO* IX/1.227.15; NPNF II/5.521.
[72] *GNO* IX/1.238.17–20; NPNF II/5.523.
[73] *GNO* IX/1.239.8; NPNF II/5.524.
[74] *GNO* IX/1.241.23–242.3; NPNF II/5.524.
[75] Zachhuber, *Human Nature*, 190ff.
[76] Cf. Ludlow, *Universal Salvation*, 95–111 on salvation and human freedom in Gregory.

may come to behold and ultimately be joined in some sense to the eternal 'circular' exchange of glory among Father, Son, and Holy Spirit.

The analysis undertaken in this chapter confirms Khaled Anatolios' reading of *Maced.* regarding the relationship between the Trinity and the economy in Gregory's thought: 'Gregory's insertion of the Spirit into the trinitarian identity of operations tends to take its point of departure . . . in the trinitarian pattern of the Christian believer's relation to God'.[77] For Anatolios, the baptismal formula authorized a kind of 'sacramental logic' that in turn legitimized the formula's 'epistemological primacy'.[78] According to Gregory, then, 'the form of the baptismal formula is thus interpreted as directly indicating the "form" of the divine life, which is communicated through the rite'.[79]

While I concur with these observations, the scope of Anatolios' reflections needs to be broadened in view of Gregory's baptismal sermons analysed in this chapter. For, it appears that the epistemological primacy of the baptismal formula, and its accompanying sacramental logic, could not help but shape Gregory's understanding of Christ's own baptism and, by extension from this event, the activity of the Spirit in Christ's earthly ministry. If Christian baptism is a sharing in the benefits brought about by the Spirit's original descent upon Christ at the Jordan as first-fruit of humanity's sanctification, then every operation of the Spirit in Christ's ministry must also indicate, for the baptisand, the triune form of the divine life. It is on the basis of the sacramental logic of baptism, therefore, that Gregory understood the *economy* of Christ and the Spirit to mirror the *immanent* life of the Trinity. This explains why in *Maced.*, when arguing for the baptisand's incorporation into the intra-trinitarian exchange of glory, Gregory looked to the *incarnate* Christ's words in John 17:5 regarding his post-passion glorification by the Spirit.

To be sure, Gregory does not construct from the ideas explored in this chapter a rigorous theological 'system'. Nevertheless, these ideas all seem to spring from the common source of Gregory's baptismal theology, and consequently they are sufficiently interconnected and coherent to count as what we might call an underlying structure of thought. As I shall show in Part II, this structure of thought underpins much of Gregory's exegesis of the Song of Songs in *hom. in Cant.*

---

[77] Khaled Anatolios, *Retrieving Nicaea: The Development and Meaning of Trinitarian Doctrine* (Grand Rapids: Baker, 2011), 207.

[78] Anatolios, *Retrieving Nicaea*, 208.

[79] Anatolios, *Retrieving Nicaea*, 208.

3

Human Transformation and Christology in *Contra Eunomium* III

Introduction

At the Council of Constantinople (*c.* 360), Eunomius, who was at that time a deacon, became ordained bishop of Cyzicus. Almost immediately he faced criticism in his newfound role for propounding 'Heteroousian' theology and was compelled to write his *Apologia* in his own defence.[1] The work caught the attention of Basil, then still a presbyter, who responded with his rebuttal, *Contra Eun*, in 364 or 365. It was not until some thirteen years later, while enduring his extended exile from Constantinople during the reign of emperor Valens, that Eunomius wrote a second work, *Apologia Apologiae*, in direct response to Basil, who now held the role of bishop in the prominent see of Caesarea. Following Basil's death on 1 January 379, and within the same year of the publication of *Apologia Apologiae*, Gregory took up the mantle of his elder brother to rebut Eunomius' second treatise, resulting in the production of three works, *Eun.* I, II, and III, between the years 379 and 383. The third tome of this series of works, to which the present chapter is dedicated, was likely to have been written sometime around 383.

While *Eun.* III may be accurately described as a treatise on christology, it is nevertheless a wide-ranging work that touches upon several other topics, among which is the transformation of humanity and union with God. This chapter analyses the coherence between Gregory's account of ordinary human transformation and union with God, on the one hand, and, on the other hand, his account of the transformation and union with God of the man Jesus of Nazareth. The analysis undertaken in this chapter is intended to be read in conjunction with my forthcoming analysis of Gregory's christology and pneumatology in Chapters 4 and 5, while the overarching purpose

---

[1] Cf. Richard P. Vaggione, *Eunomius: The Extant Works* (Oxford: Oxford University Press, 1987).

Christ, the Spirit, and Human Transformation in Gregory of Nyssa's In Canticum Canticorum. Alexander L. Abecina, Oxford University Press. © Oxford University Press 2024. DOI: 10.1093/oso/9780197745946.003.0004

78 TRINITY, CHRISTOLOGY, AND PNEUMATOLOGY

of the cluster of Chapters 3–5 is to aide my eventual analysis of christological and pneumatological motifs that recur in *hom. in Cant.*

The Economy and Restoration of Humanity: Interpreting Proverbs 8

The exegesis of Proverbs 8 has a long history as a battleground for 'Arian' and 'Nicene' views on the status of the Son.[2] According to Arius the references to Wisdom being 'created' (ἔκτισέν), 'founded' (ἐθεμελίωσέν), and 'begotten' (γεννᾷ) in Prov. 8:22–25 proved that the Son was a creature, subordinate to the Father.[3] Marcellus of Ancyra (d. *c.* 374), in a work written against the 'Arian' Asterius, challenged this reading by arguing that 'created' (cf. Prov. 8:22) must be read as prophecy concerning the incarnation of the Word. This interpretive move therefore required a careful explanation of the proverb's temporal sequence. Regarding vs. 23, Marcellus argued that the phrase 'before the age he founded me' (πρὸ τοῦ αἰῶνος ἐθεμελίωσέν με) had two referents. First, 'the age' (singular) referred to the time immediately following the incarnation of the Word,[4] and not, as his subordinationist opponents suggested, to the Word's 'pre-cosmic' begetting by the Father. This being the case, he took 'before' (πρό) as a reference to God's eternal purposes for the incarnate Word, by virtue of which the Word (i.e. Wisdom) could be said to be 'founded' *in God's own mind* (πρότερον θεμελιώσας ἐν τῇ αὐτοῦ διανοίᾳ).[5] Finally, by taking the 'mountains' and 'hills' of vs. 25 as allegorical references to the Apostles, Marcellus argued that the proverb's reference to 'begetting' (vs. 24) points to Wisdom being incarnate *in the flesh* (περὶ τῆς κατὰ σάρκα γενέσεως), in anticipation of the Apostolic age. Regarding vss.

---

[2] Cf. Sara Parvis, 'Christology in the Early Arian Controversy: The Exegetical War', in *Christology and Scripture: Interdisciplinary Perspectives*, ed. Andrew T. Lincoln and Angus Paddison (London: T&T Clark, 2008), 120–137.

[3] Cf. M. J. Van Parys, 'Exégèse et théologie trinitaire: Prov. 8,22 chez les Pères Cappadociens', *Irénikon*, 43 (1970), 362–379; cf. M. J. Van Parys, 'Exégèse et théologie dans les livres contre Eunome de Grégoire de Nysse: Textes scripturaires controversés et élaboration théologique', in *Écriture et Culture Philosophique dans la Pensée de Grégoire de Nyssa. Actes du Colloque de Chevetogne (22–26 Septembre 1969)*, ed. Marguerite Harl (Leiden: Brill, 1971), 169–196; cf. Maurice Dowling, 'Proverbs 8:22–31 in the Christology of the Early Fathers', *Irish Biblical Studies*, 24 (2002), 99–117; cf. Hans Boersma, 'The Sacramental Reading of Nicene Theology: Athanasius and Gregory of Nyssa on Proverbs 8', *Journal of Theological Interpretation*, 10/1 (2016), 1–30.

[4] *Frag.* 35; Markus Vinzent, *Markell von Ankyra: Die Fragmente der Brief an Julius von Rom* (Leiden: Brill, 1997), 34: θεμέλιον μὲν τοῦτον ὀνομάζων, τὴν κατὰ σάρκα αὐτοῦ προορισθεισαν οἰκονομίαν.

[5] *Frag.* 37; Vinzent, 36.

HUMAN TRANSFORMATION AND CHRISTOLOGY 79

26–31, Marcellus abandons his 'incarnational' reading of Proverbs, taking the phrase 'I was present with him' (συμπαρήμην αὐτῷ) (cf. Prov. 8:27) as proof that the Word was eternally with the Father when he created the world.[6] Marcellus therefore offers a 'two-tiered' exegesis of Prov. 8:22–31 that alternates between references to both the incarnate and the eternal Word in order to refute his 'Arian' opponents.

An even more pronounced two-tiered approach to the interpretation of Prov. 8:22–31 belongs to Athanasius. In Discourse II of the *orationes tres adversus Arianos*, he read Proverbs 8 for its 'hidden' sense, arguing that 'created' in vs. 22 does not signify 'the essence of his godhead, nor his own everlasting and genuine generation from the Father', but rather, 'his manhood and economy towards us'.[7] Thus, 'the works' to which vs. 22 refers are the 'redemption from sins' and 'restoration' of humanity.[8] The term 'begets', however, is taken by Athanasius to signify what *precedes* his being 'created'. Therefore, ' "begat me" is prior to "created me" ' (τὸ δὲ γεννᾷ με πρὸ τοῦ ἔκτισέν ἐστιν).[9] Clearly, Athanasius has taken 'before' to mean Wisdom was begotten 'before all things'.[10] With regard to the line 'he founded me (ἐθεμελίωσέν με) before the world' (vs. 23), Athanasius reverts back to an 'incarnational' interpretation, arguing that 'Wisdom itself is founded for us, that it may become a beginning and foundation of our new creation and renewal'.[11]

Like Marcellus, Athanasius deals with the temporal sequence implied by the term 'before' by an appeal to God's *eternal purpose*. Thus, 'before the world', 'before he made the earth', and 'before the mountains were settled' signify that God's purposes for the 'economy according to the flesh' were all prepared before the world was made according to God's *foresight*, having been *predestined* 'according to election' (κατ᾽ ἐκλογήν).[12] Yet, intriguingly, Athanasius also provides an alternative interpretation of both the terms 'created' and 'established'. Since an image of divine Wisdom is said to be created *within humanity itself*, Athanasius argues that the words 'The Lord

---

[6] *Frag.* 110; Vinzent 104: πρὸ γὰρ τοῦ τὸν κόσμον εἶναι ἦν ὁ λόγος ἐν τῷ πατρί.

[7] *Ar.* 1–3; Karin Metzler and Kyriakos Savvidis, eds., *Athanasius Werke, Erster Band. Erster Teil Die Dogmatischen Schriften 2, Lieferung, Orationes I et II Contra Arianos*, Herausgegeben von der Patristischen Arbeitsstelle Bochum der Nordrhein Westfälischen Akademie der Wissenschaften unter der Leitung von Martin Tetz (Berlin: De Gruyter, 1998), 221.45.1; NPNF II/4.372.

[8] *Ar.* 1–3, 228.51.25; NPNF II/4.376.

[9] *Ar.* 1–3, 237.60.11; NPNF II/4.381.

[10] *Ar.* 1–3, 238.61.2; NPNF II/4.381.

[11] *Ar.* 1–3, 250.73.5–6; NPNF II/4.383.

[12] *Ar.* 1–3, 254.76.24; NPNF II/4.390.

80 TRINITY, CHRISTOLOGY, AND PNEUMATOLOGY

created me for his works' may be spoken *by eternal Wisdom* 'as if of himself' (ὡς περὶ ἑαυτοῦ λέγει). In a similar move, since the 'impress' of Wisdom upon the world God has made ensures that his created works remain 'settled and eternal', then the words 'before the world he founded me' are also said to apply to *eternal Wisdom*.[13] Athanasius therefore employs a more sophisticated 'two-tiered' exegesis than Marcellus, whereby eternal Wisdom is understood to take on flesh in the economy, while eternal Wisdom can also be spoken of in terms of created realities by virtue of the fact that such created realities bear eternal Wisdom's image (i.e. humanity) and impress (i.e. the rest of creation).

It is uncertain whether Gregory read either Marcellus or Athanasius directly, although, as we shall see, his interpretation of Proverbs 8 was likely influenced by the reception of the works of these two figures. Evidently, however, Gregory was familiar with Basil's interpretation of Proverbs 8, upon which the latter commented in his *Contra Eunomium*. Basil responds to his Eunomian opponents' claim, based on vs. 22, that the Lord is a mere 'creature'. Here, he advances three points: that the designation 'creature' is used only once in scripture; that this verse contains a 'hidden meaning' and hence any interpretation is neither 'indisputable' nor 'crystal-clear'; and finally, that the Hebrew is best rendered as 'he acquired me' rather than 'he created me'.[14] Basil's engagement with Proverbs 8:22 is so surprisingly brief that it can hardly form the basis for Gregory's extensive discussion of Proverbs 8 in *Eun.* III.[15] It may be the case that Gregory sought to make up for Basil's somewhat meagre attempt at interpreting this contested passage.

While Gregory shares many similarities with the reading of Athanasius and, perhaps to a greater extent, Marcellus, his exegesis is not 'two-tiered' like theirs, and in this way he stamps his own unique mark on the traditional interpretation. His exegesis remains, by and large, focused on the economy throughout. Importantly, Gregory appears concerned not only to combat 'Arian' exegesis, but also to interpret Prov. 8:22–31 as a guide in its own right to human transformation via both Christ and the Spirit.

---

[13] *Ar.* 1–3, 256.78.16; NPNF II/4.391.

[14] Cf. Mark DelCogliano, 'Basil of Caesarea on Proverbs 8:22 and the Sources of Pro-Nicene Theology', *Journal of Theological Studies*, 59/1 (April 2008), 187.

[15] Cf. extensive discussion in Matthieu Cassin, *L'Écriture de la Controverse chez Grégoire de Nysse: Polémique littéraire ett exégèse dans le Contre Eunome*, Collection des Études Augustiniennes, Série Antiquité 193 (Paris: Institut d'Études Augustiniennes, 2012), 229–274; cf. M. Canévet, *Grégoire de Nysse et l'herméneutique biblique: Étude des rapports entre le langage et la connaissance de Dieu* (Paris: Études Augustiniennes, 1983), 268–273.

HUMAN TRANSFORMATION AND CHRISTOLOGY   81

Gregory insists that Eunomius misunderstands Proverbs 8 because of a failure to uncover the text's 'hidden sense'[16] and 'higher meaning' (ἀναγωγὴν θεωρία).[17] That the text contains a 'hidden sense' is already suggested by the very term 'proverb' itself (παροιμίας), but also by the text's peculiar and potentially contradictory features.[18] What is required, says Gregory, is an interpretive 'turn' (στροφῆς) to uncover the text's 'hidden light'.[19] Hence, he begins by noting especially those parts of Proverbs 8 that are 'obscure (ἀσαφές) and hard to interpret (δυσθεώρητον)'.[20] For instance, he observes the 'odd order' of Wisdom in Prov. 8:22–25 being first 'created' (κτίζεται) (vs. 22), afterward 'founded' (θεμελιοῦται) (vs. 23), and then finally 'begotten' (γεννᾶται) (vss. 24–25).[21] In his words, 'to say that one is first created (κτίζεσθαι), finally born (γεννᾶσθαι), and in between these, founded (θεμελιοῦσθαι), what logic could one say there is in this, which fits the ordinary and literal meanings?'.[22]

His attempt to make sense of this strange logic leads Gregory to focus on an aspect of the text with which neither Marcellus nor Athanasius appeared to show much interest, namely the obscure references to the 'throne' set apart on 'winds' (ἀνέμων) (vs. 27) and the 'clouds' that become 'strong' (ἰσχυρά) (vs. 27). Gregory elaborates by noting that cloud is but a 'fine vapour' (μανότερος . . . ἀτμός) that is 'spread through the air (ἀέρα διαχεόμενος)', 'grows light (κοῦφος)', disappears 'in the airy wind (τῷ ἐναερίῳ πνεύματι)', and 'falls through the uplifting wind (τοῦ ἀνέχοντος πνεύματος)'.[23] He asks, therefore, from where the 'strength' (ἡ ἰσχύς) of the vaporous and airy winds is derived. Gregory will provide an answer to this question only later on, where the type of language used in vs. 27 will lend itself to a pneumatologically laden interpretation of the spiritual life of the Christian. Crucially, how Gregory makes sense of the mysterious order of verbs in Proverbs 8 appears already to be heavily influenced by the pneumatic imagery of vs. 27.

It is not simply that Gregory is interested in giving a pneumatological referent to this or that verse of Proverbs 8. Rather, Gregory's pneumatology provides the hermeneutical foundation for the exegetical approach itself. His first appeal to the role of the Holy Spirit relates not to any specific text as such

[16] GNO II.11.18–19; Hall III, 46.
[17] GNO II.13.15; Hall III, 47.
[18] GNO II.11.17; Hall III, 46.
[19] GNO II.12.11–20; Hall III, 47.
[20] GNO II.13.17–18; Hall III, 47.
[21] GNO II.15.22–23; Hall III, 49.
[22] GNO II.17.19–21; Hall III, 50.
[23] GNO II.17.101–5; Hall III, 50.

82 TRINITY, CHRISTOLOGY, AND PNEUMATOLOGY

but rather to the *reader* of the text, who in this case is Gregory himself. Thus, 'to grasp correctly the meaning of the passage is for those alone, who by the Holy Spirit search the depths (τὰ βάθη) and are skilled at uttering in the Spirit (ἐν πνεύματι) the divine mysteries'.[24] Gregory's reference to 'the depths' (τὰ βάθη) is clearly an allusion to 1 Cor. 2:10. He implies that he is able to grasp the meaning of Proverbs 8 because he has the Spirit that searches the depths of God, while Eunomius, who does not have the Spirit, remains a 'slave to the letter'.[25] Additionally, Gregory introduces a second notion of the Spirit's role, this time in relation to the *author* of the Proverbs, Solomon. He argues that 'it is not possible . . . for the wisdom which arises in a person from divine enlightenment (ἐλλάμψεως) to come quite alone without the other *gifts of the Spirit* (χαρισμάτων τοῦ πνεύματος); rather, the gift of prophecy must surely accompany it'.[26] Invoking the conventional association of the Spirit with illumination, Gregory argues that Solomon not only possessed wisdom as a gift of the Spirit, but also the gift of *prophecy* by the same Spirit.[27] On this basis Gregory will read Prov. 8:22ff. as *prophecy* concerning the future economy, an interpretative move based almost exclusively on the notion that the Holy Spirit operates jointly in *both the author and reader* of scripture to reveal the depths of the mysteries of God's economy of salvation. From the outset, therefore, we already have a significantly more pneumatologically charged reading of Proverbs 8 in Gregory than we find in either Athanasius or Marcellus.

Gregory proceeds to identify aspects of the Proverbs that he believes speak prophetically according to the Spirit. The first such example is Proverbs 9:1 (LXX)—'Wisdom has built a house for herself'—which he suggests speaks of 'the building of the Lord's flesh' with 'a dwelling from the body of the Virgin'.[28] Thus, Prov. 9:1 prophesies 'what was united (ἐνωθέν) . . . from the man and from the deity combined (ἀνακραθείσης) with the man'.[29] In this light, therefore, he claims that Prov. 8:22 likewise shows Solomon to be one 'prophetically moved' in his presentation of 'the whole mystery of the economy'.[30] Thus, while parts of the Book of Proverbs certainly do speak of the Only-begotten God as 'eternal' and 'uncreated' Wisdom, who 'laid the foundation

---

[24] *GNO* II.18.14; Hall III, 50.
[25] *GNO* II.15.9; Hall III, 48.
[26] *GNO* II.18.17–21; Hall III, 50.
[27] *GNO* II.18.11–25; Hall III, 50.
[28] *GNO* II.19.44; Hall III, 51.
[29] *GNO* II.19.11–12; Hall III, 51.
[30] *GNO* II.19/18–20; Hall III, 51.

HUMAN TRANSFORMATION AND CHRISTOLOGY   83

of the earth' (cf. Prov. 3:19), Gregory argues that the phrase ' "created me" is not spoken by the one who is pure and unmixed, but . . . by the one combined (ἀνακραθέντος) in the economy with our created nature (φύσεως).'[31]

The hidden sense of Prov. 8:22, as revealed to Gregory by the Spirit, therefore focuses almost exclusively on the transformation and salvation of humanity since the sole purpose of Wisdom's 'creation' in human flesh was to rectify the fall brought about by human disobedience to God's command.[32] It is for the 'restoration to your original state' (τὴν εἰς τὸ ἀρχαῖον ἀποκατάστασιν ὑμῶν), says Gregory, that Wisdom was 'created'.[33] It is with a *soteriological* focus, therefore, that Wisdom who has been 'created' as flesh becomes a 'beginning of ways' for God's works (cf. Prov. 8:22), that is to say, a 'new way' for fallen human beings to be made anew.[34]

With the soteriological emphasis in place, Gregory turns next to explain what the Proverb means by the remaining two terms, 'founded' (ἐθεμελίωσέν) (vs. 23) and 'begets' (γεννᾷ) (vs. 24). His unique contribution to the exegesis of this passage, when compared to Marcellus and Athanasius, lies in Gregory's choice to eschew any reference to eternal Wisdom, and thus to retain the 'economic' referent of each of these terms:

First therefore came the mystery of the virginity, and the Economy of the passion, and then the wise master builders of the faith laid down the *foundation* (τὸν θεμέλιον) of the faith and that means Christ, the father of *the age to come* (τοῦ μέλλοντος αἰῶνος) (cf. Isa. 9:5), on whom is built up the life of *unending ages* (ἡ τῶν ἀτελευτήτων αἰώνων ζωή). When this had happened, *in order that the divine desires of the gospel law and the manifold gifts of the Holy Spirit* (τὰ ποικίλα τοῦ ἁγίου πνεύματος χαρίσματα) *might be born* (γένηται) *in each of those believing*—all of which the divine scripture figuratively calls by a kind of naturally fitting signification 'mountains' and 'hills' (cf. Prov. 8:24–25), calling righteousness the 'mountains' of God, and naming his judgments 'deeps', and 'earth' (cf. Prov. 8:24–28) that which is sown by the Word and bears the fruit of plentiful *fruit* (καρπόν) (cf. 1 Cor.12:1–11), just as elsewhere we learn in David about *peace* by means of the 'mountains', *justice* by means of the 'hills' (cf. Ps. 71[72]:3)—it is necessary for Wisdom, the true Word, to be *begotten* (γεννᾶται) among believers

---

[31] *GNO* II.21.6–7; Hall III, 52.
[32] *GNO* II.21.51; Hall III, 52.
[33] *GNO* II.21.18–19; Hall III, 52.
[34] *GNO* II.20.21–24; Hall III, 52.

84 TRINITY, CHRISTOLOGY, AND PNEUMATOLOGY

(cf. Prov. 8:24–25); for the one who is in those who have received him has not yet been begotten (ἐγεννήθη) in unbelievers. So *in order that* these things may happen among us, the creator of these things must be begotten (γεννηθῆναι) (cf. Prov. 8:24–25) in us.[35]

It is important to note Gregory's advancement on the well-trodden exegesis of Prov. 8:23–25. Unlike his predecessors, Gregory radically elongates the temporal frame of this passage by interpreting Prov. 8:25 in light of Isa. 9:5 LXX. The passage thus takes on a distinctively *eschatological* orientation, whereby 'the age' (τοῦ αἰῶνος) is now understood not simply as the age of Christ's earthly ministry, but as the future 'age to come' (τοῦ μέλλοντος αἰῶνος) and also as 'the unending ages' (τῶν ἀτελευτήτων αἰώνων). This *eschatological* outlook we must take to be directly correlated to Gregory's earlier reference to humanity's ultimate restoration to the original state.[36]

By adopting this new eschatological time-scale, Gregory's exegesis is now entirely *future-oriented*, and thus, unlike either Marcellus or Athanasius, he is not at all compelled to look 'backward' in time to posit an eternal 'founding' of Wisdom's incarnation in God's mind nor in God's predestined election. Rather, it serves the eschatological reading of this passage to view Wisdom's 'founding' solely as the 'founding' of Christ by the Apostles. By the same token, unlike Athanasius, he does not require from the passage an eternal 'begetting' of Wisdom by virtue of Wisdom's impress upon created realities, for, again, it suits Gregory's *eschatological* and hence *ecclesial* reading to view Wisdom's 'begetting' as one that takes place *in those who believe*, namely the church.

The eschatological-ecclesial reading is now decisive for how Gregory interprets vss. 26–31 in terms of human transformation that is brought about by the 'gifts of the Spirit' (cf. 1 Cor. 12:1–11), such as 'peace' (cf. Gal. 5:22) and 'righteousness' (cf. Eph. 5:9), which he likens to 'fruit' (cf. Gal. 5:22–23). Importantly, far from playing a subsidiary role to the overtly 'christological' referent of Proverbs 8, the coming of the 'gifts of the Spirit' is crucial to his exegesis of the apparently strange ordering of the verbs 'created', 'founded', and 'begotten' that Gregory noted earlier. It is precisely *in order that* (ἵνα) the gifts of the Spirit come upon the church in anticipation of humanity's

---

[35] *GNO* II.23.9–27; Hall III, 53, my italics.
[36] Cf. *GNO* II.21.18–19; Hall III, 52.

HUMAN TRANSFORMATION AND CHRISTOLOGY 85

eschatological restoration that the Word must be 'created' in the flesh, 'founded' by the apostles, and finally 'begotten' in believers.[37]

In view of the coming of the Spirit's gifts in the church, the one in whom Wisdom is begotten now gains a heavenly orientation and is said to 'set his mind on things above' (cf. Col. 3:2), and 'prepare heaven for himself instead of earth'.[38] Here, Gregory returns finally to offer his interpretation of the pneumatic language that pervades Prov. 8:26ff., stating that this person 'may make strong for himself the teaching of the clouds above (τῶν ἄνωθεν νεφῶν)' (cf. Prov. 8:28), becoming 'airborne in his way of life' (διαέριος τῷ βίῳ).[39] Thus, they stand upon the 'spiritual way of life' (ἐπὶ τῆς πνευματικῆς βεβηκὼς πολιτείας), which the text calls 'winds' (ἀνέμους) (cf. Prov. 8:28) and in this way become the 'throne' (cf. Prov. 8:27) upon whom the Word sits.[40] Prompted by the pneumatic language of Proverbs 8, Gregory evokes similar imagery to that used in *virg.* to depict the ascent of the soul into the aethereal realms by the power of the Spirit.

Since Proverbs 8 tells of the establishing of 'mountains', 'hills', and the like, Gregory's reading frames the salvation and restoration of humanity as a narrative of 'new creation', where, once again, the focus is *eschatological*. Hence the one in whom Wisdom is born, and begets the gifts of the Spirit, becomes identified in light of Prov. 8:31 as 'the one who has in himself perfected God's world (τὴν οἰκουμένην τοῦ θεοῦ συντελέσαντα)'.[41] Alluding to the climactic point of the Genesis creation narrative, God is said finally to rejoice in becoming the parent of 'human beings (ἀνθρώπων)' (cf. Prov. 8:31) who stand, allegorically, for 'godly thoughts, which are being formed in the divine image by faith in the one who has been created, born, and founded in us (τὸν κτισθέντα ἐν ἡμῖν καὶ γεννηθέντα καὶ θεμελιωθέντα)'.[42]

It would be a mistake to conclude that the perfection of God's 'new creation' in humanity is accomplished solely by Christ's incarnation, for as Gregory's eschatologically oriented and pneumatologically laden exegesis of Proverbs 8 demonstrates, this is a transformation of humanity fundamentally inseparable from the activity of the Spirit. To be sure, for Gregory, the exegesis of the three contested 'verbs' of the Proverbs have a christological starting point, yet he is ultimately most interested in how the strange

---

[37] *GNO* II.23.14; Hall III, 53.
[38] *GNO* II.24.16–17; Hall III, 54.
[39] *GNO* II.25.1, Hall III, 54.
[40] *GNO* II 25.1–2, Hall III, 54.
[41] *GNO* II.25.8; Hall III, 54.
[42] *GNO* II.25.13; Hall III, 54.

ordering of these 'verbs' in fact points to the eschatological transformation of humanity in the age to come, where it is only through the gifts of the Spirit bestowed upon the church that humanity may gain a heavenly orientation and be restored to the original state.

Son(s) of God

That Gregory conceives of human transformation in terms of the essential, joint activity of Christ and the Spirit may be further observed in his response to Eunomius' alleged mishandling of the title 'Son'. According to Gregory, Eunomius claimed that 'Son' is the name of 'the begotten being' (τῆς γεννηθείσης οὐσίας),[43] and therefore the title signifies a 'difference of nature' (ἑτερότητα φύσεως) of the Only-begotten from the unbegotten Father.[44] In response, Gregory employs an argument based on an analogy of human generation. In the begetting of Abel by Adam (cf. Gen. 4:1–2), Gregory states, 'the first man had within himself the whole defining character of human nature (τῆς ἀνθρωπίνης οὐσίας), and the one begotten (γεννηθείς) by him is likewise classed under the same definition of his essential being (τῆς οὐσίας)'.[45] In a similar fashion, Gregory claims that once we 'remove every fleshly and material notion' from the analogy, we are led to believe that there is no variation in 'essential being' (οὐσίαν) of the divine Son who comes forth from the Father.[46]

A similar reasoning can then be extended, says Gregory, to our understanding of the titles 'Son of God' and 'Son of Man' as applied to the incarnate Christ. In both cases, the designation 'Son' signifies the 'sharing of nature' (τὴν τῆς φύσεως κοινωνίαν). Hence, the title 'Son of Man' suggests the sharing of human nature, while the title 'Son of God' suggest the 'bond' (συνάφειαν) of 'essential being' (τῆς οὐσίας) with the Father. Since these titles are attached to *one and the same subject*, Gregory suggests they point to the unity of divine and human nature in Christ. Hence, 'the same one' (ὁ . . . αὐτός) both is Son of God and became Son of Man by economy, so that by his own sharing (κοινωνίᾳ) in each he might join together (συνάψῃ) elements distinct in nature. Since 'the whole human compound' (πᾶν τὸ ἀνθρώπινον σύγκριμα)

[43] *GNO* II.28.8; Hall III, 56.
[44] *GNO* II.28.14; Hall III, 56.
[45] *GNO* II.30.7–11; Hall III, 57.
[46] *GNO* II.33.3–13; Hall III, 58.

HUMAN TRANSFORMATION AND CHRISTOLOGY   87

was in him, we ought to conclude, says Gregory, that the word 'Son' affirmed of him both 'the human in "man" and the divine in "God"'.[47]

While Gregory offers a robust alternative to Eunomius on the use of the title 'Son', he is forced to acknowledge the difficulty that arises from scripture's use of 'sonship' language in ways that in fact *do not* denote 'affinity of nature'.[48] Indeed, scripture can speak of those who are 'sons of light' and 'sons of day' (cf. John 12:36; 1 Thess. 5:5), indicating a kind of human, filial relationship with the divine that does *not* entail a unity of essential being.[49] Gregory employs two key ways of understanding this alternative type of 'sonship' language: one that appeals to the mediation of the Holy Spirit, and the other that refers to human free choice. Hence, those who are 'led' (ἀγόμενοι) by the Spirit of God are called 'sons of God', yet are not 'same in nature' as God.[50] Further, when scripture speaks of 'sons of power' or 'children of God' it speaks of 'kinship' arising from 'free choice' (προαιρέσεως)'. Thus, scripture can use the word 'son' in such a way that it may apply either 'by nature' (ἐκ φύσεως), or by 'construction' (ἐπισκευαστήν) or 'acquisition' (ἐπίκτητον)'.[51] Thus, for Gregory, a human being becomes a 'son of God' by being joined (συναπτόμενος) to Christ through the spiritual birth (τῆς πνευματικῆς γεννήσεως). However, the Son of God did not need to be adopted, but gets his name from what he is *by nature* (φύσιν). Whereas a human becomes a 'son of God' by being 'clothed' (ἐπενδύεται) in the divine nature (θείαν ... φύσιν), the Son of God did not require the addition of something external to himself. And whereas a human being becomes a 'son of God' as a 'chosen way of life' (ἡ τοῦ βίου προαίρεσις), the Son of God does not change according to 'free choice' (τῆς προαιρέσεως) but always wills (βούλεται) what he is and is what he wills.[52]

In this way, Gregory has clearly delineated two different ways that the 'sonship' concept functions in scripture. The first (*Sonship I*) is about how the title 'Son' signifies that Christ's *two natures*—divine and human—are *united* in 'the same subject'. The second (*Sonship II*) is about how the title 'son' applies to the rest of humanity, specifying *nothing about nature* as such, but rather the new, elevated rank or status that humanity may acquire in relation to

---

[47] *GNO* II.35.16–27; Hall III, 60–61.
[48] *GNO* II.42.11–14; Hall III, 65.
[49] *GNO* II.42.22–23; Hall III, 65.
[50] *GNO* II.42.26; Hall III, 65.
[51] *GNO* II.43.6–7; Hall III, 65.
[52] *GNO* II.45.19–46.10; Hall III, 66–67.

88 TRINITY, CHRISTOLOGY, AND PNEUMATOLOGY

God. Thus, *Sonship I* and *Sonship II* offer different accounts of the human relationship to God.

Importantly, while *Sonship I* guarantees that the divine and human natures are always inseparably *united* in the incarnate Christ, it tells us nothing about what 'rank' or 'status' that human nature has, so to speak, in relation to the divine nature vis-à-vis this union. In the case of *Sonship II*, however, Gregory could not be any clearer that, at least in the case of ordinary human beings, elevation to the rank of 'son' occurs only through a choice to be united with Christ via baptismal rebirth in the Holy Spirit. Did Gregory think that something similar happens—that is, an elevation of rank or status—in the case of the human nature that is united to the divine nature in the incarnate Christ himself?

As I showed in Chapter 2, Gregory certainly placed a great emphasis on Christ's reception of the Spirit at his own baptism as the very precondition for the reality described by *Sonship II* to be realized in the rest of humanity. He will reiterate this view in *Eun.* III, as we shall see shortly. Furthermore, it is certainly the case (also to be discussed momentarily in the present chapter) that Gregory understood the human nature of Christ to be elevated to a new 'rank', not at his baptism, but *after his passion* (cf. Acts 2:36).[53] These views suggest that Gregory was aware of the need not only to uphold the 'static' unity of the divine and human natures in Christ in a single subject, but also to account for the more 'dynamic' elevation in dignity that occurs in this union after the resurrection.

These are complex matters that, if handled poorly, lead to a variety of christological conundrums. It is therefore no surprise that Gregory, in the present response to Eunomius, chose, quite deliberately it seems, to focus only upon the *divine* 'single and uncompounded nature' and, hence, on *divine* 'free choice', which never deviates from the good. He steers well clear of dealing with the issue that the present dispute actually demands to be addressed, namely how Christ according to his *human nature* is affected by the reception of the Spirit. Gregory's apparent avoidance of this issue in the present context draws attention to it as a significant point of contention.

---

[53] *GNO* II.157.8–12; Hall III, 135.

The Firstborn and the First-fruit

Gregory's discussion of scriptural references to Christ as 'firstborn' and 'first-fruit', concepts that were briefly explored in Chapter 2, gives us what is arguably his clearest exposition in *Eun*. III of the relationship between the man assumed by Christ in the incarnation and the rest of humanity. The subject arises in response to his opponents' claim that 'whatever we perceive as the essential being (οὐσίαν) of "all creation", we say that its "firstborn" has the same (cf. Col. 1:15).'[54] Gregory, we recall, used this same style of argument to his advantage in claiming that the Son of God shares, via generation, the essential being of the Father. Yet, his opponents exploit the very same logic to argue that if the Son is firstborn of 'all creation' (cf. Col. 1:15) he must therefore share the *essential being* of 'all creation'.

Gregory's strategy is to show that scriptural use of the term 'firstborn' is subject to a different logic. This he demonstrates by undertaking a systematic analysis of the four Pauline references to the 'firstborn', wherein Paul speaks of Christ as 'the firstborn of all creation' (cf. Col. 1:15), the 'firstborn among many brothers' (cf. Rom. 8:29), the 'firstborn from the dead' (cf. Col. 1:18), and simply 'firstborn' (cf. Heb. 1:6).[55] Commenting first upon Heb. 1:6, he notes that it speaks of the *eschatological return* of the firstborn, whereupon he will be worshiped by the angels and reclaim humanity to its 'original grace'.[56] When read in light of Heb. 1:6, therefore, the other 'firstborn' references can be seen to 'all point to the same end' (σκοπόν), namely the *eschatological* restoration of humanity.[57] Thus, Christ is 'firstborn from the dead' (cf. Col. 1:18) since he is 'pioneer' (ὁδοποιήσῃ) of the resurrection. He is 'firstborn among brothers' (cf. Rom. 8:29) inasmuch as he is the first 'born of the water and the Spirit' (cf. John 3:5) and first 'born in the water of the new birth of regeneration (παλιγγενεσίας)' attended by the 'flight of the dove' (cf. Mark 1:10).[58]

In light of his various 'births' (i.e. bodily, baptismal, and resurrection), Gregory claims Col. 1:15 must be understood in terms of the 'two creations of our nature'.[59] In the incarnation, Christ himself was 'created' in the sense of 'becoming flesh' so as to reconstitute human flesh as 'spirit' (μετασκευάσῃ

[54] *GNO* II.66.18–25; Hall III, 80.
[55] *GNO* II.67.4–20; Hall III, 80.
[56] *GNO* II.68.12–13; Hall III, 81.
[57] *GNO* II.68.298–29; Hall III, 81.
[58] *GNO* II.69.1–20; Hall III, 81–82.
[59] *GNO* II.69.21; Hall III, 82.

90 TRINITY, CHRISTOLOGY, AND PNEUMATOLOGY

πρὸς πνεῦμα τὴν ἡμετέραν σάρκα).[60] Thus, Christ 'leads the way' (καθηγήσατο), as the 'firstborn' of the 'new creation' of humanity (cf. 2 Cor. 5:17). Subsequently, Gregory shows that the notion of Christ as 'firstborn' is essentially synonymous with the notion that he is 'first-fruit' (ἀπαρχή) who sanctifies the 'whole dough' (τὸ φύραμα) (cf. Rom. 11:16) of those born in life and made alive in resurrection.[61] In sum, the reference to 'firstborn of all creation' in Col. 1:15 does not apply to the Son in his 'pretemporal existence' (τὴν προαιώνιον ὕπαρξιν) or his 'transcendent nature' (ὑπερέχουσαν φύσιν) as the Eunomian opponents insist, but rather to the one who, 'by the philanthropic economy', comes to be 'in those who are being saved through the new creation'.[62]

Gregory's handling of the 'firstborn' and 'first-fruit' passages is governed by the scriptural narrative of human salvation, progressing from 'creation' to *eschatological* 'new creation', in a manner wholly consistent with his economic and *eschatologically oriented* exegesis of Proverbs 8. Importantly, just as we saw in his interpretation of that proverb, though even more emphatically here, the Holy Spirit plays an *essential* rather than peripheral role in Gregory's conception of eschatological 'new creation' and the restoration of fallen humanity through the incarnate Christ. For Gregory, the eschaton is the age in which flesh is reconstituted *as spirit* and in this sense depends not only the activity of Christ, but equally upon the activity of the Spirit who gives birth to spirit.

Yet, what makes this section in *Eun.* III doubly important for understanding Gregory's teaching on the eschatological transformation of humanity is his insistence that it is *Christ's own baptism*, by which he himself is said to be born of water and the Spirit, that serves as the precondition for the rest of humanity to share in a similar spiritual birth and thus attain its eschatological end. This appeal to Christ's baptism as a basis for human salvation cannot be dismissed as a merely theological trope that Gregory employs in his Epiphany sermons to suit the liturgical convention. Rather, it is a theological position that he must have been willing to defend in a technically precise sense given the polemical context of *Eun.* III and especially given the risky 'adoptionist' undertones this view entails. Gregory escapes the charge that the incarnate Christ is 'adopted' into divine sonship (via *Sonship II*) by viewing Christ's baptism as a purely 'philanthropic' event for the sake

---

[60] *GNO* II.70.12–13; Hall III, 82.
[61] *GNO* II.70.13–18; Hall III, 82.
[62] *GNO* II.70.18–71.2; Hall III, 82.

of humanity, only in his capacity as 'first-fruit' of the 'common lump' of humanity, and not one that is constitutive of his identity as 'Son of God'.

We have here, then, a *glimpse*, but no more than this, of the notion that human transformation by the Spirit, initiated at baptism, is grounded in Jesus of Nazareth's own prototypical regeneration by the Spirit in the Jordan. As for the role the Spirit plays in *this man's* other 'births'—specifically the bodily birth and the resurrection birth—this can only be guessed at this stage.[63]

Christology of Transformation

Gregory's exegesis of Proverbs 8, the christological titles 'Son of Man' and 'Son of God', and the 'firstborn' passages, clearly distinguish scriptural references to the Son of God in his pretemporal existence from those which refer to the Son in the 'philanthropic economy'. This method of interpretation also differentiates those scriptural references that speak of Christ according to his divine nature from those that pertain to his human nature. This approach to exegesis served to uphold Gregory's christological commitments, which insisted that while the divine and human natures were united in the single subject of the incarnation, this union introduced no diminution of the divine nature by introducing to it either change, passibility, or any of the other qualities that belong only to created natures. 'For just as we may not ascribe the peculiar properties (ἰδιώματα) of the flesh to the Word who is in the beginning', says Gregory, 'so conversely we may not observe the peculiarities of the deity in the fleshly nature.'[64]

There is, however, a price to be paid for adopting this kind of 'dual-aspect' exegesis and christology, namely that it runs the risk of being too divisive, implying that the incarnate Christ in fact consists of two separate 'subjects'— one human and one divine—or as Eunomius puts it, 'two Lords and Christs'. Gregory of course denies this, a point on which he debates Eunomius regarding the contested exegesis of Acts 2:36—'God has made him Lord and Christ, this Jesus whom you crucified'.[65] To deal with Eunomius' charge

---

[63] Cf. Cassin, *L'Écriture de la Controverse chez Grégoire de Nysse*, 279–292.

[64] *GNO* II.136.10–13; Hall III, 123; cf. Christopher A. Beeley, 'Gregory of Nyssa's Christological Exegesis', in *Exploring Gregory of Nyssa: Philosophical, Theological, and Historical Studies*, ed. Anna Marmodoro and Neil B. McLynn (Oxford: Oxford University Press, 2018), 96: 'Gregory defends an exegetical method of double predication'; cf. Christopher A. Beeley, *The Unity of Christ: Continuity and Conflict in Patristic Tradition* (New Haven, CT: Yale University Press, 2012), 206.

[65] Cf. Pottier, *Dieu et le Christ selon Grégoire de Nysse*, 44–46.

92 TRINITY, CHRISTOLOGY, AND PNEUMATOLOGY

Gregory must explain what it means for 'the man' Jesus of Nazareth to be 'made' Lord without backing down from the basic principles of his dual-aspect christology.

Gregory is partly motivated by the need to defend Basil of Caesarea's somewhat questionable explanation of this verse. In his *Contra Eunomium*, Basil argued that the use of the demonstrative pronoun in Acts 2:36 'makes a clear reference to his [i.e. Christ's] humanity'.[66] Yet, in what can only be explained as a careless lapse of judgment, Basil went on to state that the verse 'is not talking about the very substance of God the Word who was in the beginning with God' (cf. John 1:2) but, citing Phil 2:7, 'about *the one who emptied himself* in the form of a slave'.[67] Eunomius seized upon his adversary's slip-up by pointing out that if Phil 2:7 really does refer to the *humanity* of Jesus as Basil says, then this leads to the nonsensical conclusion that a slave emptied himself into a slave. Far from simply trying to score easy points against his opponent, Eunomius' chief aim was to show that Basil's interpretation of Phil 2:7 and Acts 2:36 implies the existence of two Christs and two Lords:

> If God the Word who was in the beginning is one (cf. John 1:14), and he who emptied himself and took a slave's form another (cf. Phil 2:7), and God the Word through whom are all things is Lord (cf. 1 Cor. 8:6), and 'this Jesus' (cf. Acts 2:36) who was crucified after all things were made is also Lord and Christ, then according to him there are *two Lords and Christs*.[68]

Eunomius thus asserts that there are three mutually exclusive ways that Acts 2:36 can be interpreted: *either* (i) the Word was 'made Lord' from the beginning, *or* (ii) there are in fact 'two Christs and two Lords' (one eternal, and another 'made' such via the economy), *or* (iii) the eternal Word was not after all Lord until he advanced to such status *after* the economy.[69] Eunomius nails his colours to the mast by choosing the first of these options and ruling out the other two. Hence, he claims, 'for us there is one Lord and Christ through whom all things were made (cf. 1 Cor. 8:6), who did not become Lord *by advancement* (κατὰ προκοπήν), but before all creation and before all ages existed as Lord Jesus'.[70]

---

[66] *Eun* 2.3; DelCogliano and Radde-Gallwitz, 134.
[67] *Eun* 2.3; DelCogliano and Radde-Gallwitz, 133.
[68] *GNO* II.115.19–116.24; Hall III.110–111.
[69] *GNO* II.115.19–116.10; Hall III, 111.
[70] *GNO* II.116.4–7; Hall III.111; cf. Radde-Gallwitz, *Doctrinal Works*, 171.

HUMAN TRANSFORMATION AND CHRISTOLOGY   93

When Gregory takes up the task of interpreting Acts 2:36, he claims, 'it is not good religion to apply 'made' (cf. Acts 2:36) to the divinity of the Only-begotten, but to the form of a slave (cf. Phil 2:7) which belonged by divine economy to the time of his presence in the flesh'.[71] Here, we see that Gregory has attempted to tidy up Basil's careless exegesis of Phil 2:7. Clearly, then, Gregory rules out the first of Eunomius' options. He does not thereby, however, accept either of Eunomius' other two options at face value. Gregory proceeds to show, in various ways, that Basil's interpretation of Acts 2:36 entails neither the existence of 'two Christs and two Lords', nor that the Word was not Lord until he had advanced to such rank via the economy. His basic strategy is to show that the term 'made' of Acts 2:36 refers strictly to 'the man' but only *after the passion*, whereupon he is exalted to the status of 'Christ and Lord', and his flesh is transformed into what the divinity is:

> The God appears in flesh, and the flesh having revealed God within it, *after the great mystery of death has been fulfilled in it*, is transformed (μεταποιεῖται) into the sublime and divine; by intermingling (ἀνακράσεως) it became 'Christ and Lord' (cf. Acts 2:36), transformed and changed (μετατεθεῖσα καὶ ἀλλαγεῖσα) into what he was, who had revealed himself in the very flesh.[72]

There is still a problem here, however, for Gregory's response leaves largely unanswered the question of the status of the humanity *before the passion*. For now, it is a question that Gregory can only answer in retrospect from the 'other side' of the passion, as it were. The issue could not be ignored for long, as Gregory's anti-Apollinarian debate would reveal. In any case, Gregory must have been satisfied that his argument was sufficient in the present context to rebut Eunomius' accusation that Basil taught the existence of 'two Christs and two Lords'.

Among several descriptions of the post-passion transformation and ascendency of Jesus to the status of 'Christ and Lord' that appear in *Eun.* III, one passage stands out as particularly intriguing because of its use of pneumatic language:

---

[71] *GNO* II.111.

[72] *GNO* II.150.21–27; Hall III, 131; cf. Radde-Gallwitz (2014); cf. Johannes Zachhuber, 'Gregory of Nyssa, Contra Eunomium III 4', in *Gregory of Nyssa: Contra Eunomium III: An English Translation with Commentary and Supporting Studies: Proceedings of the 12th International Colloquium on Gregory of Nyssa (Leuven, 14–17 September 2010)*, Supplements to Vigiliae Christianae 124, ed. Johan Leemans and Matthieu Cassin (Leiden: Brill, 2014), 313–334.

94   TRINITY, CHRISTOLOGY, AND PNEUMATOLOGY

Just as air (πνεῦμα) is not retained by water, when, forced downwards by same heavy object, it is taken down into the depth of the water, but flows upward to what is akin to it, and the water is often lifted up by the upward flow of the air (τοῦ πνεύματος), swelling up in the surrounding air with the appearance of a thin skin, so when after the passion the true Life (ἀληθινῆς ζωῆς) contained in the flesh flows back up to its own self, the flesh containing it is borne up with it, driven upwards from corruption to incorruption by the divine immortality. Just as fire, hidden from sight within the pile of wood, often escapes the view of those who look and even of those who handle it, but when being rekindled (ἀναζωπυρούμενον), it becomes apparent, so too when he was in death, he who separated soul and body operated with authority. He who said to his own Father, 'Into your hands I commit my spirit (τὸ πνεῦμά)' (cf. Luke 23:46), who also (as he says) has authority to lay it (i.e. his life) down, and has authority to take it again (cf. John 10:18), he is the one who despised shame among men because he was Lord of Glory, as it were concealing the tinder of life (τὸ τῆς ζωῆς ἐμπύρευμα) in the corporeal nature, in the economy of his death rekindled it (ἀνεζωπύρησε) and made it flare up (ἀνῆψέ) by the power of his own divinity, warming up what came from the dead. Thus, stirring up that small *first-fruit of our nature* (τῆς φύσεως ἡμῶν ἀπαρχήν) into the infinity of the divine power, he made that also just what he himself was.[73]

There are two analogies that Gregory employs here. The first, involving the air bubble, is reminiscent of the pneumatic language he employed in his exegesis of Prov. 8:26–31, and harks back to a similar usage of such language in *virg.*[74] It is a tantalizing possibility, though we cannot be certain, that Gregory's reference to 'spirit' and the parallel term 'life' have the Holy Spirit in view. The second analogy involves the rekindling of fire, in connection with two scriptural allusions, which again implies a parallel between 'spirit' (cf. Luke 23:46) and 'life' (cf. John 10:18). Presumably, it is the same 'spirit' that Jesus lays down that is taken up again as the rush of 'air' that rekindles 'fire' in the resurrection.

It is vital to note that, here, Gregory again uses the notion of Christ's humanity as the 'first-fruit' of our nature, once more in the context of the post-resurrection transformation of his flesh. This is an important text, for it links

---

[73] *GNO* II.131.22–132.21; Hall III, 120–121.
[74] Cf. commentary in Pottier, *Dieu et le Christ selon Grégoire de Nysse*, 266–267, though the pneumatological significance is not mentioned.

HUMAN TRANSFORMATION AND CHRISTOLOGY 95

the post-resurrection transformation of Jesus directly to Gregory's earlier discussion of the 'firstborn' and 'first-fruit' passages that typically appear in a *baptismal* context. Evidently, therefore, Gregory saw the post-passion transformation of Christ's flesh by the uplifting, rekindling, and life-giving power of 'pneuma' as part of one *unified sequence* of events in continuity with Christ's baptism and resurrection, and in which the rest of humanity may have a share.

One final dispute over the exegesis of Acts 2:36 is worth mentioning for what it reveals about Gregory's conception of Christ's 'advancement'. According to Gregory, Eunomius took the term 'made' in Acts 2:36 to refer to 'the one who is in the beginning'. For the sake of argument, Gregory momentarily concedes the point to Eunomius and then proceeds to show that, even if this were the case, one still cannot conclude from this anything about the Word's 'essential being'.[75] If, as Eunomius argues, it really is the Only-begotten Son who is 'made' Lord and Christ, then this 'making' is merely analogous, says Gregory, to David's transition from private citizen to king (cf. 1 Sam. 16:13). Therefore, this transition is:

> rather like the story about David, which says that, being son of Jesse and in charge of the sheep, he was anointed (ἐχρίσθη) king, when the anointing (χρίσεως) did not at that time make him a man, but retaining the nature (φύσιν) he already had, he was changed (μετατιθείσης) from a private citizen (ἰδιώτου) into a king (cf. 1 Sam. 16:13).[76]

Hence, even if one concedes that Acts 2:36 refers to 'the one who was in the beginning', rather than the 'the man' Jesus, one still cannot infer from it anything about the Word's 'being'. This is because 'lordship' is not a title of 'being' but of 'authority', while the title 'Christ' indicates 'kingship' and not 'nature'.[77] This being said, Gregory acknowledges that 'these things are what scripture says came to be in the case of the Son of God'.[78] At this point, Gregory's argument shifts from the merely hypothetical to one that reflects his actual position on this matter. Thus:

[75] *GNO* II.157.1; Hall III, 135.
[76] *GNO* II.157.26; Hall III, 135.
[77] *GNO* II.157.3–6; Hall III, 135.
[78] *GNO* II.157.6–7; Hall III, 135.

96 TRINITY, CHRISTOLOGY, AND PNEUMATOLOGY

We should therefore consider what is more devout and logical: of which is it religiously correct to say that by advancement (προκοπήν) he shares some exalted status, the God, or the man (τὸν ἄνθρωπον). Whose mind is so infantile that he thinks the divinity advances toward perfection? It is not unreasonable to think such a thing of the human nature (τῆς ἀνθρωπίνης φύσεως), when the gospel text attests his growth as a human being (τὴν κατὰ τὸ ἀνθρώπινον αὔξησιν): 'Jesus advanced (Ἰησοῦς γὰρ προέκοπτεν)', it says, 'in stature, wisdom and grace' (cf. Luke 2:52).[79]

Hence, the Only-begotten Son does *not* become 'Christ' and 'Lord' by advancement (ἐκ προκοπῆς).[80] Drawing upon his dual-aspect christology, Gregory notes, 'What God the Word was in the beginning, that he is now and remains for ever, for ever King, for ever Lord, for ever Most High and God'.[81] However, 'the one who is elevated from manhood (ἐξ ἀνθρώπου) by assumption to the divine (πρὸς τὸν θεῖον), being one thing and made another, is correctly and truly said to have been made Christ and Lord' (cf. Acts 2:36).[82]

In light of Gregory's reference to the 'anointing' of Christ in the context of his post-passion 'advancement', it is tempting to speculate about a possible allusion to the Holy Spirit here. It is difficult to imagine that one of the main points of David's anointing by Samuel, documented in 1 Sam. 16:13—'and from that day the Spirit of the Lord came upon David'—would have been lost on Gregory. In many other contexts, to make such a link between Christ's 'anointing' and the Holy Spirit would be automatic and instinctive for him. In the anti-Macedonian works, for instance, Gregory's so-called anointing argument is used to establish the proper dignity of the Holy Spirit against those who demote the Spirit's status relative to the Father and the Son.

Thus, in *Trin.*, Gregory points out that the Spirit is the eternal 'anointing' (χρῖσμα) of the Only-begotten, indicating their shared dignity. In *Maced.*, Gregory makes a similar argument, showing that since the Holy Spirit is the 'anointing' and hence the 'kingship' of Christ, they share equal glory.[83] I will

---

[79] GNO II.157.8–12; Hall III, 135.
[80] GNO II.158.18; Hall III, 136.
[81] GNO II.158.16–18; Hall III, 136.
[82] GNO II.158.20–22; Hall III, 136.
[83] Cf. Pottier, *Dieu et le Christ selon Grégoire de Nysse*, 333–335; cf. Miguel Brugarolas, 'Anointing and Kingdom: Some Aspects of Gregory of Nyssa's Pneumatology', *Studia Patristica*, 67 (2013), 113–119; cf. Lewis Ayres, 'Innovation and Ressourcement in Pro-Nicene Pneumatology', *Augustinian Studies*, 39/2 (2008), 201–202; Giulio Maspero, 'The Spirit Manifested by the Son in Cappadocian Thought', *Studia Patristica*, 67 (2013), 3–12; Christopher A. Beeley, 'The Holy Spirit in the Cappadocians: Past and Present', *Modern Theology*, 26/1 (2010), 105–108; Anthony Meredith, 'The

return to these two passages from *Eun.* III in Chapter 5, where I will argue that Gregory's references to 'pneuma' and to 'anointing' are in fact veiled references to a Spirit-based account of Christ's unity. I will have to suspend my discussion of this claim until I have discussed in more detail what I mean by Gregory's Spirit-based christology via an analysis of *Apoll.* in the following chapter.

Conclusion

As I have shown in this chapter, we have in *Eun.* III an account of human transformation and union with God that is at variance with the account of the transformation and union with God of 'the man' Jesus of Nazareth. The former is largely consistent with my analysis in Chapters 1 and 2, where human transformation was found to be grounded in the economy of Christ's incarnation and brought to completion in the Spirit via the post-baptismal life of virtue. The proper initiation into this life of transformation and ulti-mate union with God is, of course, baptism.

Gregory certainly posits an analogy in *Eun.* III between the man united to the divine nature in the economy and the lives of his followers. Christ is, after all, the 'firstborn' and 'first-fruit' of a transformed and restored hu-manity. Gregory even draws explicit connection between Christ's baptism, understood as regeneration by the Holy Spirit, and the regeneration of his followers. Yet, there are inconsistencies. While the Spirit's descent upon Christ at his baptism serves to benefit the rest of humanity vicariously through Christ as 'first-fruit', the Spirit appears to play little role within the incarnate life of Christ himself, either before or after this brief episode in the Jordan. In the texts where Gregory speaks most explicitly about the transfor-mation of the human being who is 'made' Lord and Christ (cf. Acts 2:36), he makes no further reference to the Spirit. There is no mention of John 17:5, for instance, which in *Maced.* signified the incarnate Christ's re-entry into the eternal glory of the Trinity through the glorification of the Spirit (or so I argued in Chapter 2).

There are, however, instances where Gregory appears to be on the verge of assigning the Spirit an active role in the transformation of the 'the man' Jesus

Pneumatology of the Cappadocian Fathers and the Council of Constantinople', *Irish Theological Quarterly*, 48/3–4 (1981), 205–209.

98 TRINITY, CHRISTOLOGY, AND PNEUMATOLOGY

through the intriguing use of his signature pneumatic language. Christ's flesh is made airborne by 'pneuma'. Arguably, it is the 'pneuma' of Christ, which he has authority to take back up, that rekindles the flame of life in his body and soul in the resurrection. However, Gregory's uses of pneumatic language in these contexts, while enticing to speculate about, are highly elusive. On another occasion, Gregory speaks of Jesus' 'advancement' to the authoritative rank of 'Lord' and 'Christ' in terms of kingly 'anointing', yet makes no connection to the activity of the Spirit, even though such a link is immediately warranted by 1 Sam. 16:13, which he cites, and comes as second nature to Gregory in other contexts via an appeal to the 'anointing argument'.

It is worth highlighting here just how problematic this is for the systematic coherence of Gregory's trinitarian theology and christology. While Gregory argues quite forcefully for trinitarian unity on the basis of a single transmission of saving activity *from* the Father, *through* the Son and *in* the Spirit that transforms humanity and ultimately unites humanity to God, it appears that such unified activity is absent in the case of the incarnate Christ himself who is supposed to be a prototype or 'first-fruit' of ordinary human transformation. Gregory's christology in *Eun.* III is thus dangerously 'non-Nicene' in this regard: it truncates the activity of the Spirit from the economy of salvation in Christ, and it thereby undermines 'Nicene' trinitarian unity. In terms of Johannes Zachhuber's analysis of Gregory's soteriology, in *Eun.* III there certainly does appear to be a sharp bifurcation between 'humanistic' and 'physical' accounts of human salvation. This charge of incoherence in Gregory's thought remains unless it can be shown that Gregory assigns the Spirit a more prominent role in his christology elsewhere in his writings. I investigate this issue in the following chapter.

4

Spirit-based Christology in
Antirrheticus Adversus Apolinarium

Introduction

Apolinarius of Laodicea is perhaps best known for his allegedly heterodox account of christological unity. According to fragmentary remains of his teachings, mostly gleaned from quotes and paraphrases recorded in the writings of his opponents, he taught that in the incarnate Christ the divine Logos stood in the 'place' normally taken by the ordinary human mind. This attempt to explain the union of the divinity and humanity in Christ was found wanting by the Cappadocian Fathers. Around 377 or 378, Apolinarius was anathematized by pope Damasus after a complaint about his teaching was raised by Basil of Caesarea. However, Apolinarius and the Apollinarians escaped any such official condemnation at the Council of Constantinople in 381. The toleration of Apollinarian views between 382 and 387 allowed Apollinarians to flourish in the city of Nazianzus, resulting in an attempt to appoint an Apollinarian bishop there in 383. An aging Gregory of Nazianzus, who had actively opposed the Apollinarians throughout this period, became instrumental in their eventual condemnation by Theodosius in 388. Gregory of Nyssa was himself directly involved in anti-Apollinarian polemics in the years leading up to the decree of Theodosius.

The following chapter investigates Gregory of Nyssa's key anti-Apollinarian christological treatise, *Apoll.*, a work written in direct response to Apolinarius' *Apodeixis* and his christology more broadly. My analysis in the present chapter further pursues the question raised in Chapter 3 regarding the role that Gregory assigns to the Holy Spirit in his christology. In doing so I will focus upon Gregory's use of the 'anointing argument' to subvert Apolinarius' appeal to the 'Spirit' as the ground for the unity of the divinity and humanity in Christ. It is worth restating that the analysis undertaken here will eventually prove useful in interpreting christological and pneumatological themes that appear in *hom. in Cant.*

Christ, the Spirit, and Human Transformation in Gregory of Nyssa's In Canticum Canticorum. Alexander L. Abecina,
Oxford University Press. © Oxford University Press 2024. DOI: 10.1093/oso/9780197745946.003.0005

100 TRINITY, CHRISTOLOGY, AND PNEUMATOLOGY

Apolinarius of Laodicea on the 'Spirit' and the Unity of Christ

I begin my analysis of Gregory's christology and the anointing motif in *Apoll.* with a brief sketch of Apolinarius of Laodicea's account of the unity of the divine and human in Christ in his *corp. et div.* This account is what I shall call a 'Spirit-based' one for reasons soon to become clear. What follows does not aim for comprehensiveness, but to highlight some aspects of Apolinarius' christology that will bring Gregory's own account of the unity of Christ in *Apoll.* into sharper relief.[1]

In the *corp. et div.*, Apolinarius opens with the claim that Christ was unlike any other human being.[2] The uniqueness of Christ, he argues, is testified by Luke 1:35: 'he [i.e. Christ] differs from every other body, for he was conceived in his mother not in separation from the divinity (θεότητος) but in union (ἡνωμένος) with it, just as the angel says, "The holy Spirit shall come upon you, and the power of the Most High shall overshadow you, so that your holy offspring will be called Son of God"' (cf. Luke 1:35).[3] For Apolinarius, Christ's birth was unique since, according to John 3:13, it was characterized by the heavenly descent of the Son of Man from heaven.[4] In conjunction with this view, Apolinarius claims that Christ's body cannot be called 'creature' for 'it is conjoined into unity with God (πρὸς ἑνότητα θεῷ συνῆπται)'.[5] This is what it means for the Word (λόγος) to have become flesh (cf. John 1:14) and for the Last Adam to have become a life-giving Spirit (πνεῦμα ζωοποιοῦν) (cf. 1 Cor. 15:45).[6] Thus, the strong claim to Christ's uniqueness is, for Apolinarius, conditional upon the comprehensive and inseparable union of the divine and human.

---

[1] For a more in-depth analysis of Apolinarius than is offered here, see Hélène Grelier, *L'Argumentation de Grégoire de Nysse contre Apolinaire de Laodicée: Étude littéraire et doctrinale de l'Antirrheticus adversus Apolinarium et de l'Ad Theophilum adversus apolinaristas* (2008), January 16, 2023, http://theses.univ-lyon2.fr/documents/lyon2/2008/grelier_h/pdfAmont/grelier_h_these.pdf; cf. Kelly McCarthy Spoerl, 'Apolinarius and the Holy Spirit', *Studia Patristica*, 37 (2000), 571–592; Kelly McCarthy Spoerl, 'Apolinarian Christology and the Anti-Marcellan Tradition', *Journal of Theological Studies*, 45 (1994), 545–568; Kelly McCarthy Spoerl, 'Apolinarius and the Response to Early Arian Christology', *Studia Patristica*, 26 (1993), 421–427.

[2] *corp. et div.*, Hans Lietzmann, *Apollinaris von Laodicea und seine Schule* (Tübingen: J. C. B. Mohr, 1904), 185.1.12; Richard A. Norris Jr., ed. and trans., 'On the Union in Christ of the Body with the Godhead', in *The Christological Controversy*, Sources of Early Christian Thought (Philadelphia, PA: Fortress, 1980), 103.

[3] *corp. et div.*, Norris I, 103.

[4] *corp. et div.*, Norris I, 103.

[5] *corp. et div.*, Lietzmann, 186.2.5–6; Norris I, 103.

[6] *corp. et div.*, Norris I, 103.

SPIRIT-BASED CHRISTOLOGY   101

Already we see here the crucial role that biblical references to 'Spirit' play in Apolinarius' understanding of the unity of Christ. In the biblical passages cited above, Apolinarius takes 'Spirit' not to refer to the third person of the Trinity. Rather, 'Spirit' is synonymous with the divine 'Word', which, in the incarnation, stands in the 'place' normally occupied by the ordinary human mind.[7] This view on the Spirit is reflected, for instance, in Fragment 19 of the *Apodeixis*: 'But he is God in virtue of the Spirit which is enfleshed but human in virtue of the flesh assumed by God'; and also in Fragment 25 of the *Apodeixis*: 'So Christ, having God as his Spirit (πνεῦμα)—that is his intellect (τὸν νοῦν)—together with soul and body, is rightly called "the human being from heaven"'.[8]

The particular interpretation of biblical references to 'Spirit' in relation to the unity of Christ plays an important role in Apolinarius' interpretation of John 17:5, where Christ calls upon his Father, 'Glorify me':

When he says, 'Glorify me', this utterance stems from the body (ἀπὸ σώματος), and the glorification touches the body (περὶ σῶμα ὁ δοξασμός), but the reference is to the whole (ἐπὶ τοῦ ὅλου), because the whole is one (τὸ ὅλον ἐστιν ἕν). He adds, '. . . with the glory which I possessed with you before the existence of the world' (cf. John 17:5) and manifests the eternally glorious divinity (θεότητα), but though this expression peculiarly befits the divinity (θεότητι), it was spoken inclusively with reference to the whole (ἐπὶ τοῦ ὅλου). Thus he is both coessential with God (θεῷ ὁμοούσιος) in the invisible Spirit (τὸ πνεῦμα τὸ ἀόρατον), the flesh (σαρκός) being comprehended in the title because it has been united to that which is co-essential with God (πρὸς τὸν θεῷ ὁμοούσιον), and again coessential with men (ἀνθρώποις ὁμοούσιος), the divinity being comprehended with the

---

[7] See Grelier's comprehensive analysis of Apolinarius' interpretation of Luke 1:35 in *L'Argumentation de Grégoire de Nysse contre Apolinaire de Laodicée*, 338–381. According to Grelier, 'Le πνεῦμα qui est présent dans le texte Lc 1, 35 n'est donc pas compris par Apolinaire comme étant l'Esprit Saint . . . Mais le πνεῦμα désigne l'élément divin qui vient animer et assumer la chair de l'homme qui est formé. Cela revient à dire qu'il désigne le Logos (le divin qui s'incarne)' (342). Further, 'Contrairement à l'interprétatioin plus récente de ce passage dans l'histoire de l'exégèse . . . celle d'Apolinaire fait du πνεῦμα un synonyme de la δύναμις ὑψίστου, qui désigne le Logos préexistant qui vient prendre chair' (343). The notion that, for Apolinarius, the Spirit is synonymous with the Word is affirmed by Christopher A. Beeley, 'The Early Christological Controversy: Apollinarius, Diodore, and Gregory Nazianzen', *Vigiliae Christianae*, 65 (2011), 376–407: 'Christ is himself the divine spirit (the Word as divine "spirit", versus Christ's flesh) in his own nature as God-made-man'. Cf. Aloys Grillmeier S.J., *Christ in Christian Tradition: Volume One: From the Apostolic Ages to Chalcedon (451)*, trans. John Bowden (Westminster: John Knox, 1975), 331.

[8] *fr. 25*, Lietzmann, 210.25.23–25; Norris I.108.

body (τῷ σώματι) because it has been united to what is coessential with us (πρὸς τὸ ὑμῖν ὁμοούσιον ἥνωται). And the nature of the body (τῆς τοῦ σώματος φύσεως) is not altered by its union (ἐνώσει) with what is coessential (ὁμοούσιον) with God and by its participation in the title of *homoousios*, even as the nature of the divinity (τῆς θεότητος) is not changed by its participation of a human body and by bearing the name of a flesh coessential with us.[9]

It is clear from Apolinarius' interpretation of John 17:5 that the 'glory' that Christ receives from the Father must apply to Christ 'as a whole, because the whole is one'. So complete and inseparable is the unity of Christ for Apolinarius that one could naturally take him to teach that Christ's flesh pre-existed, and hence always shared in the eternal 'glory' of divinity, though this needs to be held in tension with his understanding that Christ's flesh still needed to be 'brought from humiliation to glory' in some manner he leaves undefined.[10] Apolinarius' reference to John 17:5 is significant since we learn that he takes 'glory' and 'glorification' as categories not only in a 'trinitarian' sense expressing the unity of the Son with the Father, as in the plain meaning of John's gospel, but also in a 'christological' sense expressing the unity between the divine and the human. As Apolinarius says in an earlier section of *corp. et div.*, 'we attribute glory to the body (τὰ ἔνδοξα τῷ σώματι) by reason of the divine conjunction (ἐκ τῆς θείας συλλήψεως) and its unity with God (τῆς πρὸς θεὸν ἑνότητος).'[11] Once more, it is important to note how, in connection with John 17:5, 'Spirit', in connection with the category of 'glory', operates as a key term securing Christ's inseparable unity.

To be sure, Apolinarius did not doggedly take every scriptural reference to 'Spirit' as synonymous with the divine Word. Indeed, in *corp. et div.*, he refers to the Holy Spirit, the third person of the Trinity, numerous times, but always with one specific purpose in mind: to deny that the divine Word receives the Holy Spirit in order to be sanctified. Hence, 'the divinity (ἡ θεότης) was not named "Jesus" before his birth from a virgin; neither did it receive the anointing of the Holy Spirit (τὴν ἐν ἁγίῳ πμεύματι χρίσιν), because the Word

---

[9] *corp. et div.*, Norris I, 105; Lietzmann, 188.7.4–18.

[10] *corp. et div.*, Norris I, 107; Commentary in Orton (2015), 103; Apolinarius, in *Fragment* 32 of the *Apodeixis*, states, 'the man Christ pre-exists (προϋπάρχει). The Spirit that is God does not exist as distinct from him, but the Lord is the divine Spirit in the nature of the God-man'. Cf. *fr.* 32; Lietzmann, 211. That Apolinarius did not teach the pre-existence of Christ's flesh, cf. Beeley, 'The Early Christological Controversy', 380–381.

[11] *corp. et div.*, Lietzmann, 186.3.8–9; Norris I, 103.

of God is the giver of the Spirit, not the one who is sanctified by the Spirit'.[12] While we cannot be certain, it seems likely, given the preceding reference to the virgin, that the anointing of the Word by the Spirit that Apolinarius refers to here corresponds to the moment of Jesus' conception. By inference, however, it must surely be the case that Apolinarius believed that at no point either in the economy or in eternity is the Word ever in need of the Spirit's anointing. He says, 'the Word sanctifies and illuminates through the Spirit, being in no wise sanctified, for the Logos is Creator and not creature'.[13]

Apolinarius does, however, find one acceptable way in *corp. et div.* to speak of sanctification in relation to the incarnation. Hence, 'the incarnation itself is in every way a sanctification', but by this he means 'the sanctification of the flesh by the divinity'.[14] Once again, Apolinarius refers to the key verse of Luke 1:35 to explain what is meant by sanctification in this strictly delimited sense. Thus, '[e]lsewhere he [i.e. Christ] explains this sanctification [by saying] that it was the birth from a virgin'.[15] While the ordinary man is conceived by a 'spermatic substance (σπερματικῆς ὕλης)' that carries the 'life-giving power (τὴν ζωοποιὸν δύναμιν)', 'the holy child born of the virgin was constituted by the coming of Spirit (ἐκ δὲ πνεύματος ἐφόδου)'.[16] Here, Apolinarius refers to 'Spirit' as the ground for the sanctification of the flesh at conception and of the union of the human and divine, though he has of course reverted back to his earlier interpretation of 'Spirit' as synonymous with the divine Word.

As will be argued momentarily, in *Apoll.* Gregory of Nyssa rebuts virtually every key point of Apolinarius' Spirit-based account of Christ's unity, as outlined in *corp. et div.*, further underscoring the highly contested use of pneumatic language in Gregory's milieu. Gregory will challenge the Laodicean's interpretation of 'Spirit' in relation to both John 17:5 and Luke 1:35; he will argue, against Apolinarius, that the eternal Word and the man Jesus of Nazareth do in fact receive the anointing of the Holy Spirit; using Apolinarius' own terms, he will offer a rival account of the conception of Christ and the role of the Holy Spirit with regard to Christ's constitutive elements (i.e. body and soul) in the incarnation; and, while Gregory will adopt 'glory' in connection with 'Spirit' as a category fit for expressing Christ's unity, he will argue that Christ's flesh receives a transforming glorification

---

[12] *corp. et div.*, Lietzmann, 189.9.7–8; Norris I, 105.
[13] *corp. et div.*, Norris I, 106.
[14] *corp. et div.*, Norris I, 106.
[15] *corp. et div.*, Norris I, 106.
[16] *corp. et div.*, Lietzmann, 191.6–8; Norris I, 106.

104 TRINITY, CHRISTOLOGY, AND PNEUMATOLOGY

from the Holy Spirit's anointing after the passion, an event that constitutes the final phase in the dynamic union between the Word and the flesh. As a result, we will see that Gregory seeks to supplant Apolinarius' Spirit-based account of the unity of Christ and will articulate his own account of Christ's unity grounded in the Holy Spirit's anointing.[17]

Anointing in Eternity and the Exegesis of Psalm 44 (45):6–7

Gregory's first use of the Spirit's anointing motif arises in direct response to Apolinarius' accusation that the orthodox', with whom Gregory aligns himself, hold that 'Christ did not exist from the beginning' and that 'they therefore deny that he [i.e. Christ] was God the Word'.[18] Robin Orton helps to make sense of this peculiar claim suggesting that, '[i]f Apolinarius really did say anything along these lines, his point was presumably that "the orthodox", by separating Christ's divinity and his humanity in a such a crude way, deny in effect that Christ who lived and died on earth can actually be identified . . . with the Word who existed from before all ages'.[19] Gregory's first use of the Spirit's anointing motif is therefore best read as the first stage in a mounting counter-response to Apolinarius' accusation of a 'divisive' christology.[20]

In order to grasp how this counter-response functions, it is helpful to refer to an earlier section in *Apoll.* where Gregory deals with what he perceives to be one of the fatal implications of Apolinarius' radically unitive christology. Namely, 'that the Godhead of the Only-begotten Son is mortal . . . that his impassible, immutable nature was changed so as to participate in passion'.[21]

---

[17] *Apoll.* was written in direct response to Apolinarius' *Apodeixis*, yet, as this chapter will show, the high degree of correlation between the arguments of *Apoll.* and the content of *corp. et div.* is unlikely to be accidental. Either Gregory was familiar with the *corp. et div.* or the complete text of the *Apodeixis*, which we do not possess, contained material that overlapped significantly with the *corp. et div.*

[18] GNO III/1.219.14–15; Robin Orton, trans., 'Refutation of the Views of Apolinarius', in *St. Gregory of Nyssa: Anti-Apollinarian Writings*, The Fathers of the Church 131 (Washington, DC: Catholic University of America Press, 2015), 237. For the sake of brevity, but at the cost of historical accuracy, I designate Apolinarius' direct targets throughout this article as 'the orthodox' (in scare quotes) following Orton's convention in his commentary, and distinguish them from Gregory who was not the direct target.

[19] Commentary in Orton, 237.

[20] On the alleged 'divisive' character of Gregory's christology, see Beeley, *Unity of Christ*, 197–221.

[21] GNO III/1.136.19–22; Orton, 99–100.

He responds to this issue via an appeal to divine simplicity. According to Gregory, 'Since God is simple (ἀπλοῦς), undivided and uncompounded, whatever he is said to be he is as a whole. He does not have different attributes in different parts. If one attribute exists, all the others can be understood in light of it; if it does not exist, all the others are erased at the same time.'[22] Hence, if it was the Only-begotten God who died on the cross, which Gregory takes to be the absurd logical consequence of Apolinarius' christology, then 'all the characteristics that can be understood as associated with his divinity perished as well.'[23] The scriptural warrant for this argument is based on 1 Cor. 1:24, which states that Christ is 'the power of God and the wisdom of God'. Thus, says Gregory, 'if both of these [i.e. God's power and wisdom] had been extinguished in death at the same time as the divinity of the Son, neither wisdom nor power nor life nor any other of those characteristics of God that we call good would have remained with the Father'.[24]

As Michel Barnes has noted, Gregory understood the term 'power' (δύναμις) of 1 Cor. 1:24 in a technical philosophical sense. Thus, Gregory describes the Son's relationship to the Father 'by the analogy of a power to an existent: as long as the existent is what it is, it has the effective power by which it is identified and without which it ceases to be itself'.[25] Andrew Radde-Gallwitz's work on divine simplicity in Gregory of Nyssa's thought is helpful for understanding what the Nyssen means by the related notion of the divine 'goods'. He notes that Gregory's list of 'the goods', which includes power (δύναμις) among others such as wisdom (σοφία), light (φῶς), life (ζωή), justice (δικαιοσύνη), and truth (ἀλήθεια), holds the status of 'propria', by which he means 'unique and identifying properties that are inseparably linked to the divine nature', and which are notions that 'one naturally has of divinity'.[26] Each of the goods are 'inter-entailing but not, to all appearances, identical'.[27] Further, 'they necessarily inhere in the natures of which they are propria'.[28]

[22] *GNO* III/1.136.30; Orton, 100.

[23] *GNO* III/1.137.8–10; Orton, 100. Cf. Grelier, *L'Argumentation de Grégoire de Nysse contre Apolinaire de Laodicée* for a comprehensive survey of alleged caricaturizing of Apolinarius; cf. Robin Orton, '"A Very Bad Book"? Another Look at St Gregory of Nyssa's Answer to Apolinarius', *Studia Patristica*, 72 (2014), 171–189.

[24] *GNO* III/1.137.7; Orton, 100–101.

[25] Barnes Michel René, 'Contra Eunomium III 6', in *Gregory of Nyssa: Contra Eunomium III. An English Translation with Commentary and Supporting Studies. Proceedings of the 12th International Colloquium on Gregory of Nyssa (Leuven, 14–17 September, 2010)*, ed. Johan Leemans and Matthieu Cassin (Leiden: Brill, 2014), 374; cf. Barnes (2001).

[26] Andrew Radde-Gallwitz, *Basil of Caesarea, Gregory of Nyssa, and the Transformation of Divine Simplicity* (Oxford: Oxford University Press, 2009), 184–185.

[27] Radde-Gallwitz, *Divine Simplicity*, 198.

[28] Radde-Gallwitz, *Divine Simplicity*, 202.

106 TRINITY, CHRISTOLOGY, AND PNEUMATOLOGY

According to Radde-Gallwitz, the divine goods 'entail one another reciprocally', which is to say, 'if one of them exists, they all must exist'.[29] Additionally, the divine goods are 'perfect' insofar as they are not mixed with their opposite. On this basis, therefore, Radde-Gallwitz notes that Gregory's understanding of the divine goods is closely related to his understanding of divine simplicity, understood as 'the unmixed divine perfection'.[30]

Equipped with this way of understanding Gregory's notion of simplicity and the divine goods, we are now in a position to analyse his first use of the Spirit's anointing motif. As noted above, it occurs in direct response to Apolinarius' accusation that the alleged divisive christology of 'the orthodox' prevents the incarnate Christ from being identified with the eternal Word. Therefore, Gregory begins by stating:

> we do not deny that in these last days the power of God and his wisdom, his light, and his life—and all these things are Christ—become manifest through the flesh (διὰ σαρκὸς πεφανερῶσθαι) . . . Anyone who said that Christ did not exist from the beginning—Christ, who is 'the power of God and the wisdom of God' and whose name is supremely exalted and totally appropriate to God—would be denying that any of these other things that we knew through this great name existed from the beginning . . . Thus the power and the wisdom and every name that is appropriate to God are co-eternal with the Godhead; nothing that was not there from the beginning can be joined by way of addition to the glory of the divine nature.[31]

How should we understand the logic of Gregory's argument? Robin Orton suggests that it takes the following form:

a. God's eternal divine properties (power, wisdom, light, life, etc.) were manifested in the enfleshed Christ.
b. Therefore, Christ can be identified with these eternal divine properties.
c. Therefore, Christ can be identified with God.
d. Therefore, Christ existed from all eternity.[32]

---

[29] Radde-Gallwitz, *Divine Simplicity*, 208.
[30] Radde-Gallwitz, *Divine Simplicity*, 212.
[31] *GNO* III/1.219.15–220.9; Orton, 238.
[32] Commentary in Orton, 238.

SPIRIT-BASED CHRISTOLOGY   107

I contend that this is in fact not quite the argument that Gregory has advanced. Rather, his reference to the list of 'divine goods' suggests that the present argument points back to his earlier one based on divine simplicity. Just like the former argument, I take the present argument also to be a *reductio ad absurdum* which proceeds as follows:

a. God has eternal properties or divine 'goods' (power, wisdom, light, life, etc.).
b. According to 1 Cor. 1:24, Christ is the 'power' and 'wisdom' of God.
c. God is simple.
d. Therefore, since the divine goods entail one another reciprocally, if Christ did not exist eternally, *none* of the divine properties existed eternally.
e. Therefore, Christ existed from all eternity.

For Gregory, it is because of divine simplicity that God's power and the other 'goods' all exist inseparably together from eternity, or none exist at all. If Christ does not exist eternally, then God, who is very wisdom, power, light, and life, does not exist eternally either.

Gregory's first use of the anointing motif now stands in direct continuity with the argument from simplicity above. Thus, reflecting on the very title of 'Christ' itself, Gregory proceeds to observe 'the name of Christ expresses, from all eternity, the concept of the Only-begotten in a special way'.[33] According to Gregory, 'Confession of this name implies the Church's teaching on the Holy Trinity, as each of the Persons in whom we believe is . . . indicated by this title'.[34] Gregory's argument, based on the exegesis of Ps. 44(45):6–7, is intricate, and so for the sake of clarity I quote it in full:

> The term 'throne' means rule over all things. The 'sceptre of righteousness' means incorruptibility of judgment. The 'oil of gladness' represents the power of the Holy Spirit (τὴν τοῦ ἁγίου πνεύματος . . . δύναμιν), by whom God is anointed (χρίεται) by God, that is, the Only-begotten by the Father, because he 'loved justice (δικαιοσύνην) and hated' injustice. If there had even been a time when he was not a friend of justice (δικαιοσύνης) or an enemy of injustice, it would follow that he who is said to have been anointed

---

[33] *GNO* III/1.220.9–11; Orton, 239.
[34] *GNO* III/1.221.12–15; Orton, 239.

108   TRINITY, CHRISTOLOGY, AND PNEUMATOLOGY

because he loved justice (δικαιοσύνην) could be said at one time not to have been anointed—as he himself was justice (αὐτὸς δικαιοσύνη ὤν), he can hardly have hated himself—he must always be considered as having been anointed (ἐν τῷ χρίσματι). As he who is just cannot be unjust (ὁ δίκαιος οὐκ ἄδικος), so Christ could never be unanointed, and he who had never been unanointed must necessarily always have been Christ. Everyone must believe (or, at any rate, everyone whose heart has not been covered with the veil of the Jews) that it is the Father who anoints and the Holy Spirit who is the anointing.[35]

Orton provides only a brief commentary on this section of Gregory's work, but nevertheless finds it wanting. He suggests that Gregory employs a 'doubtful logic' and 'beg[s] the question' by supplying the premise 'he [i.e. Christ] himself was justice' to assure the outcome of his argument.[36] However, Gregory is rescued from this charge if, as I suggest, we understand this first use of the anointing argument to stand in direct continuity with his preceding argument. In that case, Gregory is seen here to be interpreting Ps. 44(45):6–7 in light of his understanding of divine simplicity and its implications for how the divine goods are interrelated within the Trinity. Indeed, he appears to have interpreted the Psalm as referring to the Only-begotten as the exemplification of divine 'justice' (δικαιοσύνη), one of the attributes that he lists throughout his works to be among the divine goods.[37] This explains his statement 'he who is just cannot be unjust', for according to Gregory the divine goods are perfect, and hence eternally unmixed by their opposites. Just as God is never without his 'power' and 'wisdom', so is he never without 'justice'. According to divine simplicity, either all 'the goods' exist together, or none of them exist at all. Psalm 44 (45):6–7 must therefore be speaking of an *eternal* anointing of the Only-begotten by the Spirit, which for Gregory can only mean one thing: the Only-begotten is eternally anointed by the Father with the Holy Spirit and is hence eternally *Christ*. If he is not eternally Christ in this sense, then, according to the doctrine of divine simplicity, the Trinity

---

[35] *GNO* III/1.220.21–221.5; Orton, 240.

[36] Commentary in Orton, 239.

[37] Cf. *GNO* VIII/1.134.17; cf. Wernerus Jaeger, ed., *Contra Eunomium Libri, Pars Prior: Liber I et II (Vulgo I et XIIB), GNO* I (Leiden: Brill, 1960), 295.11; 373.5; the Psalm was interpreted christologically by Justin, Theophilus of Antioch, Tertullian, Cyprian, Novatian, Hippolytus, Origen, Eusebius, Athanasius, and Basil, among others. Origen understood Psalm 44 (45):7 as a reference to the anointing of the Holy Spirit. Ronald E. Heine, 'Origen on the Christological Significance of Psalm 45 (44)', *Consensus*, 23/1 (1997), 33 n.20, suggests Gregory 'is dependent on Origen's exegesis'.

SPIRIT-BASED CHRISTOLOGY 109

does not eternally exist either. This I suggest is the force of Gregory's biblical exegetical argument.

I showed above how Gregory's application of divine simplicity to his reading of 1 Cor. 1:24 demonstrated his belief in Christ's eternal existence, while simultaneously exposing how Apolinarius' strongly unitive christology, in view of Christ's crucifixion, called God's eternal existence into question. Here, divine simplicity, applied to the exegesis of Ps. 44(45):6–7, now in connection with the Spirit's anointing motif, performs an identical function. Once again, Gregory exposes how Apolinarius' strongly unitive christology, precisely because it denies that the Word receives the anointing of the Holy Spirit, ends up denying not only eternal existence of Christ but also of the Trinity. Gregory's counter-response directly turns the tables on his opponent. It is important to remember that this is not just a *generic* defence of Christ's eternal existence, nor is it an out-of-place defence of Trinitarian orthodoxy. Rather, Gregory's subtle transposition of his earlier 'simplicity argument' into a pneumatological register must be understood as the first step in a mounting response to Apolinarius' accusation that the allegedly divisive christology of 'the orthodox' means that the incarnate Christ could not strictly be identified with the eternal Word.

Anointing after the Passion and the Exegesis of Acts 2:36/John 17:5

In the very next stage of Gregory's response, it is clear that he seeks to build upon the previous argument by continuing to tackle Apolinarius' allegation of a divisive christology held by 'the orthodox'. Hence, Gregory introduces the next phase of his argument by referring once again to the alleged denial of Christ's eternal existence by 'the orthodox': 'How can Apolinarius claim that we say that Christ did not exist from the beginning?'[38] Whereas the first stage of his response focused on Christ *eternally* anointed by the Spirit, Gregory's focus now shifts to the *economy*, and in particular upon Christ's flesh, which will in turn lead to his second use of the Spirit's anointing motif.

In Gregory's words, 'that we confess that Christ is eternal does not mean that we believe that he always had the flesh (σάρκα) that Apolinarius has invented.'[39] Gregory's reference to Christ's 'eternal flesh' may be a caricature

[38] Orton, 237.
[39] *GNO* III/1.221.8; Orton, 240.

110 TRINITY, CHRISTOLOGY, AND PNEUMATOLOGY

of Apolinarius' position, but perhaps not without some justification, as I suggested above.

The ensuing discussion of Christ's flesh is closely bound up with one of Apolinarius' accusations, which Gregory partially dealt with earlier in *Apoll.*, and which resurfaces here once more—namely, that 'the orthodox' extend the concept of the Trinity into a so-called 'Quaternity' (τετράδα) consisting of Father, Spirit, and 'two Sons', one from eternity and the other human.[40] If Gregory's quotation of Apolinarius is reliable, the latter objected that, 'if God, who is complete, had been joined to a complete man, there would have been two of them, the one Son of God by nature and the other by adoption'.[41] It is apparent elsewhere that by 'two of them' Apolinarius means 'two persons' (δύο πρόσωπα).[42]

As we saw in the previous chapter, Gregory had countered a very similar accusation previously in writing *Eun.* III, where the discussion revolved around the proper interpretation of Acts 2:36. This is the context in which we encounter Gregory's well-known analogy of the drop of vinegar in the ocean where 'by mingling with the divine, the mortal nature is renewed to match the dominant element, and share the power of deity, as if one might say that the drop of vinegar mingled with the ocean is made into sea by the mixing, because the natural quality of this liquid no longer remains in the infinity of dominant element'.[43] I assume that Gregory believed this account was, at least at the time of writing *Eun.* III, sufficient to counter Eunomius' accusation of belief in 'two Christs and two Lords'. By showing how 'the man', Jesus of Nazareth, is transformed into the divine, Gregory was highlighting the unity of the subject of the incarnation. In the apt words of John Behr, 'This is neither adoptionism nor the deification of a man. Rather, the crucified Jesus, as man, becomes that which he, as God, always is'.[44] And, in the words of Brian Daley, 'Gregory's point is that the process of transformation which the gospels show to have taken place in Christ . . . although it is a change only in his humanity, reveals precisely whose humanity this has been from the beginning'.[45]

---

[40] *GNO* III/1.201.25; Orton, 108.

[41] *GNO* III/1.199.18–20; Orton, 205.

[42] *GNO* III/1.185.1; Orton, 177.

[43] *GNO* I.101.151–134.69; Hall II, 102–121.

[44] John Behr, *The Case against Diodore and Theodore: Texts and their Contexts* (Oxford: Oxford University Press, 2011), 14.

[45] Brian E. Daley, '"Heavenly Man" and "Eternal Christ": Apolinarius and Gregory of Nyssa on the Personal Identity of the Savior', *Journal of Early Christian Studies*, 10 (2002b), 481; On Gregory's christology of transformation see also Brian E. Daley, 'Divine Transcendence and

SPIRIT-BASED CHRISTOLOGY   111

Yet, it is apparent that Gregory had not fully escaped the accusation of 'two Christs and two Lords' as the anti-Apollinarian context now makes abundantly clear. When Apolinarius raises the same type of objection against 'the orthodox', it is not the interpretation of Acts 2:36 that is at the centre of the dispute, but rather the nature of the assumption by the Son of the human flesh *as such*, and therefore the relationship between the divinity and Christ's human constitutive elements (i.e. his body and soul). Hence, the battle ground over the so-called Quaternity concerns not only the time after the passion but the time *before* and *during* it as well—the time of Jesus' conception and the time period of his death. I shall return to this matter in more detail below.

In responding to the Apollinarian context, however, it is clear that several of Gregory's anti-Eunomian rejoinders still remain useful for articulating his basic position. For instance, he restates the drop of vinegar analogy in order to dispel the notion that he teaches a 'Quaternity'.[46] Speaking of the transformation of Christ's flesh he states, 'the flesh's own nature (τῆς δὲ σαρκὸς τῇ ἰδίᾳ φύσει) was changed into the sea of incorruptibility . . . the mixture (ἀνακράσεως) with the divine takes up the lowliness of the fleshly nature (τῆς σαρκώδους φύσεως) into the divine attributes. So there is no danger, as Apolinarius claims, of our extending the concept of the Trinity into that of a Quaternity (τετράδα)'.[47] At the same time there is a notable difference in the way Gregory communicates this perspective on the transformation of Christ's flesh as he augments his earlier account, reframing the transformation of humanity now in terms of the Holy Spirit's anointing. This is his second use of the anointing motif in *Apoll*. Thus, prefacing his comments with a passing reference to the contested teaching of Acts 2:36, he states:

> The Word was both Christ and Lord, and that is what he who was combined
> with him (ὁ ἐμμιχθείς) and taken up into the divinity became. The Word
> is Lord already; he is not re-ordained into lordship, but rather the form of
> the slave becomes the Lord. So the text 'one Lord, Jesus Christ, through
> whom are all things' applies similarly to him who before all ages (πρὸ τῶν

Human Transformation: Gregory of Nyssa's Anti-Apolinarian Christology', *Modern Theology*, 18 (2002a), 497–506; cf. Brian E. Daley, *God Visible: Patristic Christology Reconsidered* (Oxford: Oxford University Press, 2018), 138–149.

[46] *GNO* III/1.221.11; Orton, 240.
[47] *GNO* III/1.201.16–25; Orton, 208.

112 TRINITY, CHRISTOLOGY, AND PNEUMATOLOGY

αἰώνων) was clothed with the glory of the Spirit (τὴν δόξαν τοῦ πνεύματος περικείμενος) (for that is what his anointing (ἡ χρῖσις) symbolically means). After the Passion he makes the man (ἄνθρωπον) whom he has united with him (ἐνωθέντα) into Christ, making him beautiful with the same anointing (χρίσματι). 'Glorify me', he says (it is as if he said 'anoint me'), 'with the glory that I had in your presence before the world existed' (cf. John 17:5). But that glory that is posited here, existing before the world, before all creation, before all ages (πρὸ πάντων αἰώνων), that glory in which the Only-begotten God is glorified, is, in our opinion, no other than the glory of the Spirit. For orthodox doctrine teaches that the Holy Trinity alone exists before the ages (προαιώνιον) . . . the glory attributable to the Only-begotten God, which is posited to exist before all the ages (πρὸ τῶν αἰώνων) is the Holy Spirit. Therefore, what belongs to Christ, who was with the Father before the world came to being, also belongs to the end of the ages (ἐπὶ τέλει τῶν αἰώνων), to him who is united to Christ (τῷ ἐνωθέντι πρὸς τὸν Χριστὸν). Scripture speaks of 'Jesus of Nazareth', whom 'God anointed with the Holy Spirit' (cf. Acts 10:38). So let Apolinarius not maliciously misrepresent our views by claiming that we say that the Only-begotten God was not always Christ.[48]

Gregory speaks of the transformation of the man, Jesus of Nazareth, not merely as absorption into divinity but, with reference to John 17:5, as glorification and anointing by the Spirit. This interpretation of John 17:5 immediately recalls Gregory's exegesis of the same passage in *Maced.* in relation to the 'circular' exchange of trinitarian 'glory', and it is not out of the question, as I suggested earlier, that Gregory's Spirit-based christology underpins his allusion to this verse in the anti-Macedonian treatise. In the present context we see that he has responded to the accusation of teaching a 'Quaternity' by showing that the post-passion glorification of Jesus of Nazareth by the Holy Spirit mirrors the (eternal) 'past' glory of the Only-begotten Son by the same anointing of the Spirit. Hence, Gregory leads us to the conclusion that, after the passion, there can be only a single subject of the incarnation.[49]

[48] *GNO* III/1.222.5–25; Orton, 241–242.

[49] That Gregory's allusion to John 17:5 develops an argument for the unity of divinity and humanity in Christ via his post-passion anointing by the Spirit seems to have been misunderstood by a number of scholars. Marie-Odile Boulnois (2008), 35–36, suggests the allusion to John 17:5 relates only to Christ *before the economy* and thus mirrors the anointing of Jesus *during the economy* vis-à-vis his interpretation of Acts 10:38. Piet Hupsch (2020), 243–244, suggests that Gregory's christological argument only has in view other 'human beings' who are connected to the eternal Son through salvation history rather than the man Jesus of Nazareth. Gregory's use if John 17:5 is rightly understood

SPIRIT-BASED CHRISTOLOGY   113

This Spirit-based account of human transformation, which now incorporates the category of 'glory' from John 17:5 (understood as symbolic of 'anointing'), would of course have been pointless against Eunomius who denied the Spirit's divinity. However, it must be asked what difference, if any at all, does the reference to John 17:5 and the Spirit's anointing make to his current debate against Apolinarius and the issue of 'two Christs and two Lords'? It seems to me that the answer must lie in the direct challenge that Gregory's Spirit-based account of Christ's unity presents to Apolinarius' own Spirit-based account by using the Laodicean's own terms against him. On the one hand, Gregory can be seen to agree with Apolinarius' position in *corp. et div.* that the category of 'glory', as derived from John 17:5, is indeed an appropriate category for speaking of the unity of the divine and human in Christ. In the past, Gregory had only applied this category to trinitarian debates, usually centred upon the divine status of the Spirit.[50] Here, rising to the challenge presented by the anti-Apollinarian context, we see that 'glory' functions as a properly christological category. Yet, whereas the 'glory' of John 17:5 functions as a static concept for Apolinarius that, according to Gregory, would absurdly entail the eternal existence of Christ's flesh, Gregory's concept of 'glory' is dynamic and transformational, applying to Christ *from eternity*, and then only in the course of the economy to the flesh of the incarnate Christ *after the passion*.

Having established 'glory' as both a trinitarian and a christological category, Gregory is now in a position to launch a further attack on Apolinarius' reference to the 'Spirit'. We recall that in his exposition of John 17:5 in *corp. et div.*, Apolinarius grounded the unity of Christ's flesh and divinity not only in 'glory' but also in the 'Spirit' by which he meant the divine 'Word'. Gregory, on the other hand, can be seen here to offer a rival account of Christ's unity using Apolinarius' own terminology, though with reference to the Holy Spirit, the third person of the Trinity, as the unifying agent of the divinity and the human flesh. Gregory's own Spirit-based account of christological unity, in which the incarnate Christ of Acts 2:36 is found to be identical with

---

by Miguel Brugarolas, 'The Holy Spirit as the "Glory" of Christ: Gregory of Nyssa on John 17:22', in *The Ecumenical Legacy of the Cappadocians*, ed. Nicu Dumitrascu (New York: Palgrave MacMillan, 2015), 252.

[50] Here I assume that *Apoll.* pre-dates *hom. in 1 Cor. 15:28* and the use of the Spirit's anointing motif found there, which I discuss briefly below.

114   TRINITY, CHRISTOLOGY, AND PNEUMATOLOGY

the eternal Christ of Ps. 44(45):6–7, is superior, or so he would claim, since it does not entail the pre-existence of Christ's flesh.

Anointing at Conception and the Exegesis of Luke 1:35

We turn our attention now to Gregory's final use of the anointing motif in *Apoll.*, which immediately follows his account of the transformation of Christ's flesh by the Spirit's anointing and centres on the exegesis of Luke 1:35. As Hélène Grelier notes, Luke 1:35 goes to the heart of the Apollinarian controversy.[51] Not surprisingly, Gregory's response to Apolinarius made extensive reference to this verse. Grelier remarks that of the twenty references to this verse in Gregory's entire corpus, thirteen of them occur in *Apoll.*[52] It appears that Apolinarius' dependence on Luke 1:35 forced Gregory to undertake a sustained reflection on the multiple ways this verse applied to his understanding of the incarnation. It results in a newfound emphasis within his writings upon the Holy Spirit's role in the union of the divine nature and human constitutive elements (i.e. body and soul) at the moment of Christ's conception.

As already hinted above, Gregory's second use of the Spirit's anointing motif provides only a partial solution to the accusation of teaching 'two Christs and two Lords'. His earlier argument, based on Acts 2:36/John 17:5 and the glorification of Christ's flesh by the Spirit's anointing *after the passion*, is still vulnerable to the objection that there is an unaccounted 'gap' in the incarnate life of Jesus. *Before the passion*, 'the man' Jesus of Nazareth holds an undetermined status—is he the same Spirit-anointed 'Christ' of Ps. 44(45):6–7 and Acts 2:36/John 17:5, and, if so, how is this to be understood? If it is only *after the passion* that the humanity is elevated into unity with the divinity through the Spirit's glory, then who does Gregory say Jesus is *before* the passion, and even *during* the passion?[53] Until Gregory can resolve this glaring issue he is still open to the charge of positing 'two Christs and two Lords'.

---

[51] Grelier, *L'Argumentation de Grégoire de Nysse contre Apolinaire de Laodicée*, 340.
[52] Grelier, *L'Argumentation de Grégoire de Nysse contre Apolinaire de Laodicée*, 338–381 provides an exhaustive analysis.
[53] Radde-Gallwitz, 'Gregory of Nyssa's Pneumatology in Context', 283, comments on the significance of the Spirit's anointing argument *after the passion*, but not prior to it.

SPIRIT-BASED CHRISTOLOGY 115

It seems to me that Gregory is himself completely aware that his exegesis of Acts 2:36 leaves unresolved issues. Thus, in *Apoll.*, Gregory offers a more expansive reading of Acts 2:36 in light of his earlier exegesis of Ps. 44(45): 6–7, John 17:5, and his anti-Apollinarian interpretation of Luke 1:35, focussing now on the time *before* and *during* the passion, 'filling the gap', so to speak, of his exegesis of this passage in *Eun.* III. The immediate context in which this occurs is Gregory's reply to Apolinarius' accusation that 'the orthodox' understanding of the passion implies the existence of 'two Christs'—on the one hand, there is 'the man' (τὸν ἄνθρωπον) who alone suffers in the passion, and, on the other hand, there is the divine Christ, who does not suffer.[54] Gregory aims to show how the divine presence, by remaining 'in' the man who suffers (ἐν τῷ πάσχοντι) without itself being subject to passion, secures the indissoluble unity of the divine and the human.[55] Yet, Gregory's response does not simply focus upon the moment of Christ's passion, but also offers an account of the divinity's presence in the man Jesus from the very moment of conception—a presence that remains during the separation of Christ's body and soul at death, and in his resurrection.[56]

The importance of the role of the Holy Spirit's anointing in Luke 1:35 is thus brought to the fore in this context as Gregory now identifies the original moment when the man Jesus of Nazareth 'becomes' Lord and Christ—not at his post-resurrection glorification by the Spirit, but at his conception. In a statement that both recalls and simultaneously subverts Apolinarius' parallel account of Christ's conception in *corp. et div.*, Gregory outlines the process of ordinary human generation in the following terms: '[h]uman nature (ἡ ἀνθρωπίνη φύσις) . . . has its individual existence (ὑπόστασιν) by virtue of an intellectual soul being combined with a body'.[57] This combination is based on some 'material originating principle (ὑλικῆς)', which is acted upon by a 'life-giving power' (ζωοποιός τις δύναμις).[58] However, in the unique case of Christ's generation, Gregory explains, alluding to Luke 1:35, that the life-giving power is the Holy Spirit. Therefore:

The power of the Most High exercises itself in the same way in respect of the Virgin. It implants itself immaterially, through the life-giving Spirit (διὰ

---

[54] *GNO* III/1.223.11–12.
[55] *GNO* III/1.223.13.
[56] *GNO* III/1.223.14; Orton, 243.
[57] *GNO* III/1.223.14–17; Orton, 243.
[58] *GNO* III/1.223.18; 23–24; Orton, 244.

116   TRINITY, CHRISTOLOGY, AND PNEUMATOLOGY

τοῦ ζωοποιοῦντος πνεύματος), into the undefiled body and makes the material of the flesh from the purity of the Virgin, taking up from the Virgin's body a contribution towards the one who was formed (ποιησαμένη). And so is created the truly New Man (ὁ καινὸς ὡς ἀληθῶς ἄνθρωπος), who first and alone received his individual existence (ὑποστάσεως) in this fashion.[59]

The divine power is said to have 'pervaded (διηκούσης) the whole of his [i.e. Christ's] compound nature'.[60] Thus, 'the divine nature (θεία φύσις) came to dwell in an appropriate way (καταλλήλως) in the soul and the body, and was made one with both through the union (ἓν πρὸς ἑκάτερον γενομένη διὰ τῆς ἀνακράσεως)'.[61] Gregory proceeds to note that it is the same 'divine power' (τῆς θείας δυνάμεως) and its 'life-giving activity' (τὴν ζωοποιὸν . . . ἐνέργειαν), presumably a reference to the Holy Spirit, that remains present to Christ's body and soul after his death and is raised with him. Therefore, 'the divinity (θεότης), which right from the beginning (ἐξ ἀρχῆς) was mixed in (ἐγκραθεῖσα) with both body and soul and remains with it forever, is raised up in the resurrection of him who died'.[62] Gregory cites Luke 1:35 a final time in showing how the presence of 'the divine power' and its 'life-giving activity' to Christ's body and soul throughout the entire period of his death is directly mirrored by the presence of the divine power and the Holy Spirit at his conception.

Thus, it is Christ who is said to have been 'raised from the dead', he who both is Christ and becomes Christ. He is Christ by virtue of the kingdom that he had before all ages (κατὰ τὴν προαιώνιον); he becomes Christ when the angels brought to the shepherds 'good news of great joy that will be to all people' at the time of the birth of the Saviour, who scripture says is 'the Christ, the Lord'. He is properly so called on the basis of the words of Gabriel, that 'the Holy Spirit will come upon' the Virgin and that 'the power of the Most High will overshadow' her. *So he who is born is properly called Christ and Lord*: Lord, through the power of the Most High, and Christ, *through the Spirit who anointed him* (διὰ τὸ πνεῦμα τῆς χρίσεως). It was not he who is before time (ὁ προαιώνιος) who was anointed (χρίεται) at that time, but the one of whom the scripture says, 'You are my son; today

---

[59] *GNO* III/1.223.26–31; Orton, 244.
[60] *GNO* III/1.224.2–3; Orton, 244.
[61] *GNO* III/1.224.18–19; Orton, 245.
[62] *GNO* III/1.225.12; Orton, 246.

(σήμερον) I have begotten you'. The word 'today' signifies *the midpoint* (τὸ μέσον) between the two divisions of time (τῶν δύο τοῦ χρόνου τμημάτων), *past and future*.[63]

Invoking yet a third use of the Spirit's anointing motif to counter Apolinarius' objection of a divisive christology, we see that it is the moment of conception, whereupon the divine nature and Christ's body and soul are completely and indissolubly united, that Gregory now explicitly identifies as Christ's anointing by the Holy Spirit. This is why it can be said not only that 'Christ' is born but also that 'Christ' has been raised from the dead—for, the Holy Spirit's anointing has remained present to Christ's constitutive elements from the moment of conception and right throughout the entire period of death.

Thus, in *Apoll.*, Gregory speaks three times of Christ's anointing: first in relation to eternity (cf. Ps. 44[45]:6–7), second with reference to the post-passion glorification (cf. Acts 2:36/John 17:5), and third with respect to the 'midpoint' of time, corresponding to his conception (cf. Luke 1:35). Gregory's final reference to the anointing by the Spirit at the 'midpoint' is crucial to his response to Apolinarius. On the one hand, it offers a Spirit-based account of the unity of Christ that rivals the Laodicean's own. But, furthermore, it serves to 'close the gap' between the other two anointings, showing that there is not a moment in either Christ's eternity or his earthly career that ever stands removed from the Spirit's anointing; there is never a time when he is not anointed by the Spirit, and so, in Gregory's words, 'he who is never unanointed must necessarily always be the Christ' (ὁ δὲ μηδέποτε ἄχριστος, ἀεὶ πάντως Χριστός).[64]

Thus, for Gregory, the anointing of the Spirit establishes maximal continuity between the identity of the eternal and the incarnate Christ without collapsing the distinction between eternity and economy, as Apolinarius' Spirit-based account of Christ's unity threatens to do. In making this move Gregory has offered a more definitive answer to the question of Jesus of Nazareth's identity *before* and even *during* the passion, which his exposition of Acts 2:36 in *Eun.* III left somewhat in doubt. Even before his post-resurrection flesh has been glorified by the Spirit, Gregory can say that the one who is born of Mary has *already become Christ* at conception by the

---

[63] *GNO* III/1.225.14–27; Orton, 246, my italics.
[64] *GNO* III/1.221.2; Orton, 240.

118   TRINITY, CHRISTOLOGY, AND PNEUMATOLOGY

same Spirit's anointing, an interpretation of Luke 1:35 in light of his exegesis of Ps. 44(45):6–7 and Acts 2:36/John 17:5. Therefore, whatever the post-resurrection glorification of Jesus' flesh implies about Christ's earthly life in the economy, it cannot mean that there was a momentary division in the identity of the subject of the incarnation at any time before the resurrection. This account, I suggest, is now a more satisfying response to Apolinarius' accusation that 'the orthodox', with whom Gregory identifies, hold a divisive christology that results in 'two Christs and two Lords' or a 'Quaternity'.[65] In view of what I have argued above, Gregory has thereby offered a virtual point-by-point refutation of Apolinarius' Spirit-based account of Christ's unity found in *corp. et div.*

Beyond the *Antirrheticus adversus Apolinarium*: The Unity of Christ, the Spirit, and the Church

Had Gregory's use of the anointing motif in a christological mode remained a one-off occurrence, confined solely to *Apoll.*, it might well be argued that the Spirit's anointing does not perform the kind of significant work in Gregory's christology that the present chapter claims it does. However, looking beyond Gregory's anti-Apollinarian treatise, we see that he invokes the role of the Spirit on at least two more occasions, which builds upon his christological use of the anointing motif in *Apoll.* and thus underscores its fundamental importance to him. In *hom. in 1 Cor. 15:28* he appeals to the Spirit to illustrate once again the unity of the divine and human in Christ, this time with direct implications for ecclesial unity.[66] Hence, quoting from John 17:22—'The glory that you have given to me I have given them'—he identifies 'glory' with the Holy Spirit breathed upon the disciples, and by which Christ 'united' (ἐνωθῆναι) them 'in the unity of the Spirit' (ᾗ ἑνότητι τοῦ πνεύματος).

---

[65] Cf. Grelier, *L'Argumentation de Grégoire de Nysse contre Apolinaire de Laodicée*, 688–697. Whereas Grelier speaks only of two anointings, I have pointed out the Gregory's crucial third use of the anointing motif. See also Hélène Grelier, 'Comment décrire l'humanité du Christ sans introduire une quaternité en dieu? La controverse de 2008 Grégoire de Nysse contre Apolinaire de Laodicée', in *Gregory of Nyssa: The Minor Treatises on Trinitarian Theology and Apollinarism, Proceedings of the 11th International Colloquium on Gregory of Nyssa (Tübingen, 17–20 September)*, ed. Volker Henning Drecoll and Margitta Berghaus (Leiden: Brill, 2011), 541–556.

[66] Daniélou dates the work to post-385, Downing to the time of *Eun.* I and *Refutatio confessionis Eunomii*, roughly between 380 and 383 at the earliest. See Maraval, BDGN 155. My analysis suggests that *hom. in 1 Cor. 15:28* post-dates *Apoll.*, though not by much, and was possibly written in the same year (c. 383).

Further, citing John 17:5—'Glorify me with the glory that I had in the beginning in your presence before the world existed'—he identifies the Spirit once again as the 'glory' by which Christ has the glory of the Father. Thus, says Gregory, it was necessary for Christ's flesh (σάρξ), through mixture (ἀνακράσεως), to become what the Word is through the Spirit. Then, paraphrasing John 17:22—'I have given them the glory that you gave me, that they may be one as we are one'—Gregory notes that the 'glory' given to Christ by the Father was given to the disciples so they could be united to Christ, and through him to the Father.[67]

Gregory does not of course explicitly refer to 'anointing', but this is not problematic since, as the similar quotation of John 17:5 in *Apoll.* makes clear, the anointing and the glory of the Spirit can be taken to speak of one and the same reality.[68] As in his anti-Apollinarian treatise, Gregory's notion of the transformation of Christ's flesh is pneumatologically oriented in *hom. in 1 Cor. 15:28.* That is, the flesh assumed by Christ becomes transformed into what the Word is by receiving the eternal glory of the Spirit. Evidently, the reception of the Spirit's glory by the flesh is firmly fixed in his thought as his preferred way of expressing the final transformative event in the dynamic unity of the divine and human in Christ. Since Gregory invokes the Spirit's glory as a condition for the unity of Christ, it is therefore natural also to posit the reception of the Spirit's glory as the condition for church unity among Christ's members with one another, and ultimately with the Father. The concept of 'glory' has migrated a short step from being a christological category to being an ecclesial one. Gregory's gloss on the original wording of John 17:22 is illuminating. Through the Spirit (i.e. 'glory'), the human members of the church are united to the divinity of Christ and by virtue of this unity are united to the Father.

There is, then, a strong analogy in Gregory's thought between the unity of the human and the divine via the Spirit in the case of Christ himself, and that of the human members of the church with God via the same Spirit. A second key reference to a Spirit-based christology is found in the final homily of *hom. in Cant.* The perspective from *hom. in 1 Cor. 15:28* is recapitulated there to suit the immediate context of interpreting the Song of Songs, though a full discussion is delayed until Chapter 8.

---

[67] Cf. *GNO* III/2 21.23–22.16.
[68] *GNO* III/1.222.1–7; Orton, 241.

Conclusion

I initially set out to question what role Gregory assigns the Spirit in his account of the transformation of Christ in *Apoll.* Whereas Gregory had once exploited the anointing argument to express the unity of the Spirit with the Son and the Father in his confrontation with the Macedonians, in *Apoll.* he appears to augment his earlier trinitarian use of the motif to serve a christological purpose as the situation demands. The ever-present anointing of the Spirit now counts as a necessary condition for the 'static' unity of divinity and humanity in Gregory's christology. It functions for him as the exact correlate, without any of the perceived negative consequences, to Apolinarius' notion that the Spirit unites the divinity and humanity in Christ by standing in the place of the human mind. Hence, to deny the Spirit's anointing of Christ either in eternity, or at any moment in Christ's earthly career, or in the post-passion transformation, according to Gregory's perspective, would be to introduce a rupture between the divine and human within the economy, and thus to leave the central problem of 'two Christs and two Lords' yet unresolved. For Gregory, the Spirit's anointing is not only the ground for 'static' unity *prior to the passion* but also the ground for the 'dynamic' unity of the divinity and humanity in Christ, since it is the anointing of the one and the same Spirit that transforms and glorifies Christ's human flesh *after the passion* with the eternal divine glory.[69]

Not only does Gregory's Spirit-based christology help to resolve the problem of 'two Christs and two Lords'; it also helps to resolve the charge of theological incoherence in *Eun.* III that I identified in Chapter 3. From the perspective of *Apoll.* and *hom. in 1 Cor. 15:28*, humanity's union with God through the unified activity of the Trinity is now seen to be *coherently* grounded in the same trinitarian unity of activity found in the case of the incarnate Christ who is the 'first-fruit' of the 'common lump' of humanity's sanctification. Incidentally, this is a picture of christological transformation that I argued in Chapter 2 could already be subtly discerned in Gregory's reference to John 17:5 in *Maced.* to mark the incarnate Christ's 're-entry' into the 'circular' exchange of trinitarian glory through the glorification of the Spirit. Furthermore, Gregory's Spirit-based christology is found to be properly 'Nicene' in the sense that it no longer truncates the Spirit's activity from

---

[69] Cf. Zachhuber, 'Gregory of Nyssa, Contra Eunomium III 4', 329: 'The unity of divine and human in Christ, Gregory believes cannot simply be considered in static terms, but has a dynamic dimension as well'.

SPIRIT-BASED CHRISTOLOGY 121

the economy of salvation, which would compromise the essential unity of the trinitarian persons.

Looking back to my analysis in Chapter 3, a question mark still looms over the problematic incoherence of *Eun.* III, which arises from Gregory's failure to assign any role to the Holy Spirit in Gregory's christology of transformation. What explanation might be offered for such a glaring inconsistency in Gregory's thought given that there are already strong hints of a Spirit-based account of Christ's post-passion transformation in the earlier work, *Maced*? This is the question upon which I focus in the following chapter by subjecting some of the more elusive christological texts in *Eun.* III that refer to 'pneuma' and 'anointing' to closer scrutiny.

5

Tracing the Spirit
Christology in *Contra Eunomium* III Reconsidered

Introduction

As I demonstrated in the previous chapter, Gregory articulated his Spirit-based christology in *Apoll.* (*c.* 383) in direct refutation of the Spirit-based account of Christ's unity propounded by Apolinarius in *corp. et div.* In *hom. in 1 Cor. 15:28*, Gregory shows that this Spirit-based christology has direct implications for the transformation and union with God of the rest of humanity. Indeed, Christ's post-passion transformation into union with the divinity is analogous to humanity's own transformation by the Spirit. Clearly, Gregory's Spirit-based christology documented in *Apoll.* and *hom. in 1 Cor. 15:28* differs significantly from the one articulated in *Eun.* III, which has no direct recourse to pneumatology. Curiously, however, there appears to be a direct correlation between the *difference* in Gregory's two christological accounts and the *incoherence* I identified in Chapter 3 arising from his disjointed account of humanity's and Christ's transformation. To be more precise, it appears that Gregory's Spirit-based christology of *Apoll.* just so happens to resolve the problem of incoherence between Christ's and humanity's transformation in *Eun.* III. Could this be merely a coincidence? If Gregory formulates his Spirit-based christology solely in response to the specific issues that pertain to the anti-Apollinarian context, then why does it appear to resolve inconsistencies evident in the anti-Eunomian context?

Perhaps the most straightforward explanation for the differences in Gregory's christological accounts is that his christology undergoes 'development' between the writing of *Eun.* III and *Apoll.*, motivated precisely by a desire to resolve inconsistencies in his thought about which he only gradually becomes aware. However, this explanation is complicated by the fact that Gregory's reference to John 17:5 in *Maced.*, a work likely to have been written prior to *Eun.* III, already gestures toward the Spirit-based christology found in *Apoll.* and *hom. in 1 Cor. 15:28* as I already hinted at in Chapter 2.

Christ, the Spirit, and Human Transformation in Gregory of Nyssa's In Canticum Canticorum. Alexander L. Abecina, Oxford University Press. © Oxford University Press 2024. DOI: 10.1093/oso/9780197745946.003.0006

In the present chapter I explore an alternative possibility by employing a method of abductive reasoning, or inference to the best explanation. That is, I propose as an explanatory hypothesis that Gregory in fact already held a Spirit-based christology when he wrote *Eun.* III but had pragmatic reasons for concealing it. I then test this hypothesis by marshalling relevant textual evidence and assessing it against a set of well-defined criteria.

Clarification of this issue is germane to my overarching goal of examining the systematic coherence of Gregory's doctrinal claims. If the incoherence identified in *Eun.* III results from a calculated theological trade-off on Gregory's part, then it need not count as a strike against the claim of doctrinal coherence, all things considered. Second, clarification of this issue has a direct bearing on whether one interprets the presence of Spirit-based christology and its implications for ordinary human transformation in the ascetical context of *hom. in Cant.* as a development in Gregory's doctrinal theology or as a restatement of ideas that are already deeply embedded within the structure of his thought. Whether one agrees with the argument I offer here, it presents a case that a straightforward narrative of development in Gregory's christology between *Eun.* III and *Apoll.* does not easily fit the textual data.

Spirit-based Christology in *ad Eustathium, de sancta trinitate*?

Before I attempt to reframe the christology of the *Eun.* III, it is important to undertake a preliminary analysis of *Trin.*, an earlier work written probably around 381 to defend the 'dignity' of the Holy Spirit against the Macedonians, who demoted the status of the Spirit relative to the Father and the Son.[1] I will investigate Gregory's use of the 'anointing argument' in this work and suggest that there are indications he may have already held a Spirit-based theory of Christ's unity at the time it was written.

Toward the conclusion of *Trin.*, Gregory formulates an anointing argument for the dignity of the Holy Spirit, which I outline in alphabetized sections (*A–E*) for ease of reference:

---

[1] *GNO* III/1.3–16; cf Radde-Gallwitz, 'Gregory of Nyssa's Pneumatology in Context', 259–285.

124 TRINITY, CHRISTOLOGY, AND PNEUMATOLOGY

A. For consider: the name of kingship denotes all dignity, and *our God*, it says, *is King from everlasting* (cf. Ps. 73[74]:12). But the Son, who possesses *all that the Father has* (cf. John 16:15), is himself proclaimed king by Holy Scripture (cf. John 18:36).

B. Now the divine *scripture* says that the Holy Spirit is the anointing (χρῖσμα) of the Only-begotten, intimating the dignity of the Spirit by a metaphor from the terms commonly used here below. For in ancient times, the symbol of this dignity (σύμβολον ἦν τῆς ἀξίας) for those who were being advanced to kingship was the anointing (χρῖσμα) bestowed on them. Once this took place there was a change thereafter from the private humble estate (ἀπὸ τῆς ἰδιωτικῆς ταπεινότητος) to the pre-eminence of rule, and he who was deemed worthy of this grace received after his anointing (χρῖσιν) another name, being called, instead of an ordinary man (κοινοῦ ἀνθρώπου), the Lord's anointed (cf. 1 Sam. 16:6; Ps. 2[3]:2).

C. For this reason, in order that the dignity of the Holy Spirit might be more clearly manifest to human beings, he was named by the scripture as the symbol of kingship, that is, *anointing*, from which we are taught that the Holy Spirit shares in the glory and the kingship of the Only-begotten Son of God.

D. For just as in Israel it was not permitted to enter upon the kingship without the bestowal of anointing beforehand, so the Word, by a metaphor of the names in use among us indicates the equality of power, showing that not even the kingship of the Son is assumed without the dignity of the Holy Spirit. Wherefore he is properly called Christ, since the name furnishes proof of his inseparable and unshakeable conjunction with the Holy Spirit.

E. If, therefore, *the Only-begotten God* (cf. John 1:18) is the Christ, and the Holy Spirit is his anointing, and the title of Anointed indicates his kingly authority, and the anointing is the symbol of his kingship, then the Holy Spirit also shares in his dignity.[2]

The argument is straightforward enough. In section *A* Gregory notes that the status of 'kingship' denotes 'dignity'. Scripture ascribes the status of 'king' to both Father and the Son, and so presumably both share equal 'dignity'. Gregory proceeds in *B* to point out that scripture also identifies the Holy

[2] *GNO* III/1.15.17–16.3; Silvas, 244–245.

Spirit as the 'anointing' of the Son, and since 'anointing' is a symbol of a king's 'dignity', the Spirit can be said in *C* to share in the 'glory' and 'kingdom' of the Son. In *D* Gregory argues that since the Son is always anointed by the Spirit, he is properly called 'Christ', a title that is not applied in the present context to the incarnate Christ in the economy but signifies the *eternal* Son's essential inseparability from the Spirit. Thus, in *E* Gregory sums up the argument by claiming the Holy Spirit shares the 'dignity' of the Son.

The curious inclusion of *B*, and in particular Gregory's explanation of the term 'anointing', warrants further discussion. First, it is not at all clear what Gregory means when he says that scripture teaches that the Spirit is the anointing of the Only-begotten Son. If Acts 10:38 is the background for this claim—'God anointed Jesus of Nazareth with the Holy Spirit'—it is not immediately obvious how this verse has been interpreted given that Gregory has the *eternal* anointing of the Son in view rather than that of the incarnate Jesus. Indeed, the argument would fall flat if the Spirit's 'dignity' were conditional upon Jesus' anointing in the economy. Furthermore, Gregory attempts to justify the crucial but by no means self-evident claim that 'anointing' implies 'dignity'. This connection between 'anointing' and 'dignity' rests entirely on the basis of an *earthly analogy*, namely the anointing of an ordinary man to kingship as documented in scripture. Gregory means to say that if earthly 'anointing' is capable of changing the status of an 'ordinary man' to the exalted status of 'the anointed of the Lord', then the 'anointing' itself must in some sense possess an exalted 'dignity'. It is this kind of dignity that the Holy Spirit is said to have *intrinsically* by virtue of being the 'anointing' of the Only-begotten Son.[3]

Gregory was without doubt convinced of the persuasiveness of his anointing argument. Yet, it must be judged rather problematic insofar as it requires the reader to make a monumental analogical leap from the earthly context to the theological one, where the crucial reference to the exaltation of *a man* from low to high status upon which the whole analogy rests suddenly and inexplicably drops out of the picture. Further, Gregory's analogical transposition comes dangerously close to implying that the Only-begotten Son underwent a change of status by the Spirit's anointing, analogous to the ascent of an earthly king. As I shall show below, Gregory identifies this as a 'Eunomian' teaching and repudiates it explicitly in the *Eun.* III, as we have

---

[3] Cf. Similar concept in *perf.*, although there is no reference to the Holy Spirit: *GNO* VIII/1.177.1–2; Woods Callahan, 97–98.

126 TRINITY, CHRISTOLOGY, AND PNEUMATOLOGY

already seen. But then why, we might ask, does he include such a risky and an apparently 'pro-Eunomian' analogy of the earthly king's anointing at all? Why not leave it out altogether as he does, for instance, when deploying the virtually identical anointing argument in *Maced.*, a work written against the Macedonians probably slightly later than *Trin.*? There the anointing argument takes the following simplified form:

> how will one confess Christ if he does not understand the anointing together with him who is anointed? It says, 'This one God anointed in the Holy Spirit' (cf. Acts 10:38). Well then, those who would destroy the Spirit's glory and rank him down with the subordinate nature must tell us what the anointing symbolizes (τίνος σύμβολόν ἐστιν ἡ χρίσις). *Is it not kingship? Well?* (οὐχὶ τῆς βασιλείας; τί δαί); Do they not believe that the Only-Begotten is king by nature? They won't deny it unless they have covered their heart once for all with the Jewish veil. So, if the Son is king by nature, and anointing is a symbol of kingship (βασιλείας δὲ σύμβολόν ἐστι τὸ χρίσμα), what does the argument indicate to you through this line of reasoning? That the anointing isn't something estranged from the one who is king by nature, and that the Spirit isn't ranked with the Holy Trinity as something foreign and alien. The Son is indeed king, and the living, substantial, and subsisting kingship is the Holy Spirit, in which the Only-Begotten Christ, the king of beings, is anointed.[4]

We see that Gregory still needed to establish the crucial main point from analogy *B* in *Trin.*, the notion that 'anointing' is a 'symbol of the kingship', in order for his argument to work. Yet, he no longer offers any justification for this via the analogy of the anointing of Israel's kings. Rather, the point is simply *asserted* by the posing of two rhetorical questions—*Is it not kingship? Well?*—while the burden of showing that this is *not* the case is now placed on his opponents. This, we may say, is a compacted version of the anointing argument from *Trin.*, where the part corresponding to *B* has been reduced to merely one line, possibly because Gregory realized its limitations and potentially controversial implications. On the one hand, this contraction comes at a cost to Gregory, for in the absence of an explicit scriptural analogy the anointing argument now begs the question. There is simply no reason to accept his argument in the absence of any reference to the anointing ritual in

---

[4] *GNO* III/1.102.16–29; Radde-Gallwitz, 282, my italics.

Israel's monarchy. On the other hand, it has the advantage of avoiding completely the 'pro-Eunomian' view that the Only-begotten Son advanced to the status of a king via anointing.

I will offer an explanatory theory about the presence of *B* in *Trin.* as well as its diminished presence in *Maced.* momentarily, but first, to undertake a brief theological thought experiment, it seems that Gregory's anointing argument for the Holy Spirit's 'dignity' in *Trin.* can be strengthened with very little effort by the inclusion of just one additional proposition consequent upon *B*, which I shall call β:

> β. The flesh of the 'private citizen', Jesus of Nazareth, was anointed by the Holy Spirit and was thereby transformed to share in the highest 'dignity' of the Only-begotten Son of God.

If, according to analogy *B*, 'anointing' symbolizes a 'dignity' capable of changing a 'private citizen' to the status of 'the anointed of the Lord', then, according to proposition β, the 'anointing' of Jesus' flesh by the Holy Spirit must symbolize a 'dignity' intrinsic to the Spirit that is at the same time equal to the 'dignity' of the Only-begotten Son. For this fact alone is able to *explain* the 'dignifying' of Jesus' earthly flesh with the same 'dignity' as the eternal Only-begotten Son.

The inclusion of proposition β would strengthen Gregory's original anointing argument for the Holy Spirit's 'dignity' since it extends analogy *B* to its natural, logical conclusion and therefore does not require the reader to make such a large a conceptual leap from earthly analogy to theological reality. Furthermore, it removes the 'Eunomian' implication that the eternal, Only-begotten Son was elevated to his dignified status (i.e. that the Son was 'made' Lord and Christ in the Eunomian sense, and which Gregory explicitly repudiates in *Eun.* III). At the same time, proposition β reinforces points *C–E* regarding the sharing of 'dignity' between Christ and the Spirit *in eternity* by mirroring this same unity of 'dignity' from the perspective of *the economy.* Coincidentally, proposition β just so happens to be a key element in the second stage of Gregory's Spirit-based christology found in *Apoll.*, as I outlined in Chapter 4. Consequently, it is possible to *derive* this stronger version of the anointing argument for the 'dignity' of the Holy Spirit directly from Gregory's Spirit-based christology.

While I arrived at proposition β as part of a constructive theological exercise in strengthening Gregory's original anointing argument in *Trin.* (*c.* 381),

128 TRINITY, CHRISTOLOGY, AND PNEUMATOLOGY

given that one can directly derive β from Gregory's Spirit-based christology in *Apoll.* (*c.* 383), it is reasonable to ask whether he may have in fact already been cognizant of proposition β at the time that he wrote *Trin.* I take it that if Gregory was cognizant of proposition β at that time, then he most likely also *assented* to β for the simple reasons that (a) assent to β only strengthens his anointing argument, and (b) dissent from β, while advancing point D of the anointing argument, entails that the post-resurrection Jesus does not fully share the identity of the Only-begotten Son who, as 'Christ', is eternally anointed by the Spirit. In other words, to advance D and dissent from β in Gregory's theological milieu is to concede the Eunomian (and Apollinarian) point that he teaches the existence of 'two Christs and two Lords', one human and the other divine. I cannot discern any plausible scenario in which someone of Gregory's theological acumen advances points B and D while being cognizant of proposition β and yet dissents from β.

In my analysis of *Eun.* III below I will provide what I take to be strong evidence that Gregory was indeed cognizant of and hence assented to β when he wrote *Trin.* Yet, even without such textual evidence, we might still be convinced that, on the basis of Gregory's theological milieu alone, it would be highly implausible to suppose that he could posit analogy B without being cognizant of the fact that analogy B implies proposition β. Andrew Radde-Gallwitz has shown that Gregory was directly influenced by the use of the anointing theme, which developed within the earlier 'anti-Eunomian tradition' that Gregory inherited. Epiphanius, who was part of the anti-Eunomian tradition, in the *haer.*, taught that the Holy Spirit anointed *the incarnate Christ* and thereby manifested the unity of the Trinity.[5] Epiphanius writes, 'But the Father would not have anointed *Christ's human nature*, which had been united in one Godhead with the divine Word, with a creature. However, since the Trinity is one, three Perfects, one Godhead, this needed to be done for the Son in the dispensation of the incarnation, so that the Trinity, completely glorified in all things, would be observed to be <one>'.[6] In addition, Gregory's own brother, Basil of Caesarea, taught that Christ's anointing by the Spirit *in his humanity* established Christ's essential inseparability from the Spirit.[7] Therefore, Basil claims, 'From the outset, he [i.e. the Spirit] was

---

[5] Radde-Gallwitz, 'Gregory of Nyssa's Pneumatology in Context', 270.

[6] *haer.* 69.56.11; Frank Williams, trans., *The Panarion of Epiphanius of Salamis: Books II and III, Sects 47–80, De fide*, Nag Hammadi and Manichaean Studies 36 (Leiden: Brill, 1994), 384.

[7] Radde-Gallwtiz, 'Gregory of Nyssa's Pneumatology in Context', 272.

TRACING THE SPIRIT 129

present to the very flesh of the Lord, since he was anointing (χρῖσμα), and his inseparable companion.[8]

But, perhaps most importantly, the Pseudo-Athanasian author of *On the Incarnation and Against the Arians*, who belonged to this tradition and whom several commentators observe had a direct influence on Gregory, claimed, 'it [i.e. Christ's humanity] is anointed into the kingdom of heaven, so that it might reign along with him who emptied himself for its sake and who assumed it through the form of a slave.'[9] Here we have in the Pseudo-Athanasian author a statement that very closely approximates my formulation of proposition β, though he does not explicitly identify anointing as the Holy Spirit. Had this author encountered Gregory's analogy B in the context of an anointing argument, I surmise he would have instantly understood it to be an analogy applying to exaltation of *the incarnate Christ*. It is not a stretch of the imagination to suppose that Gregory thought likewise.

I conclude from this brief survey of the anti-Eunomian tradition that Gregory would have to be largely ignorant of the theological perspectives of his day on the anointing of Jesus in the economy, including the views of his own brother Basil, not to mention ignorant of the straightforward logical entailments of his own anointing argument, to posit analogy B as justification for his anointing argument for the Spirit's 'dignity' without being cognizant of and hence assenting to β—a scenario that I find improbable.

If we allow for the moment Gregory's assent to proposition β at the time of writing *Trin.*, why did he not in fact produce β in his anointing argument? I suggest the reason is largely pragmatic. While β can be used to strengthen Gregory's argument for the 'dignity' of the Spirit as I have shown, to convince Eustathius or one's Macedonian opponents of the truth of β would require the rather elaborate and extensive exegesis of such passages as Ps. 44(45):6–7, Acts 2:36, John 17:5, and Luke 1:35, which we find only in the lengthy discourse of *Apoll.* While omitting this exegesis leaves Gregory's argument prone to the accusation of question begging, to include it in such a brief treatise as *Trin.* would have the equally undesirable effect of raising a catena of thorny issues not directly pertinent to the discussion at hand.

What Gregory offers in *Trin.*, I suggest, is a kind of compromise—an anointing argument that presupposes the truth of β, but is weakened by

[8] Basil of Caesarea, *Spir.* 16.39.
[9] Radde-Gallwitz, 'Gregory of Nyssa's Pneumatology in Context', 270; cf. Hübner, *Die Einheit*, 116–125, 269–324; cf. Zachhuber, *Human Nature*, 198.

130 TRINITY, CHRISTOLOGY, AND PNEUMATOLOGY

excluding the explicit demonstration of β. Nevertheless, the argument has every chance of succeeding if Gregory's rhetorical prowess is sufficient to convince the reader to flex his analogical imagination. My tentative suggestion that Gregory offers a truncated argument that deliberately refrains from explicating β in *Trin.* is supported by the earlier observation that the cognate anointing argument in *Maced.* appears to have deliberately truncated analogy B from *Trin.* even further. In other words, Gregory may be seen to become progressively more confident in his ability to persuade his reader that the Holy Spirit qua 'anointing' is the symbol of the dignity of Son's kingship on the strength of rhetorical force alone without having to offer full-blown exegetical justification for it.

If this account has any claim to historical plausibility, and Gregory indeed knew of and hence assented to proposition β, it reveals the provocative possibility that he already held a Spirit-based christology when writing *Trin.*, which informed the construction of analogy B of his anointing argument for the Holy Spirit's 'dignity'. Yet, my argument runs ahead of itself. Everything I have suggested so far remains a working hypothesis awaiting further confirmation or falsification. It is with a view to confirming this hypothesis with more concrete textual evidence that I turn now to *Eun.* III.

Tracing the Spirit in *Contra Eunomium* III

As I showed in Chapter 3, Gregory wrote *Eun.* III around 382 in direct response to Eunomius of Cyzicus' *Apologia Apologiae*. We recall that one of Gregory's tasks in Parts 3 and 4 of the work was to defend against the accusation that Basil of Caesarea taught the existence of 'two Christs and two Lords'. Much of this defence revolved around the exegesis of Acts 2:36— 'God has made him both Lord and Christ, this Jesus whom you crucified'. I outlined above how Gregory utilized the 'anointing argument' to respond to Apolinarius' similar objection in *Apoll.* Importantly, his exegesis of Acts 2:36 in *Eun.* III is *never* explicitly grounded in the anointing argument. Indeed, one searches the work in vain for any explicit reference to the Holy Spirit's anointing.

As a result, the historian of Christian theology may be tempted to postulate a 'development' in Gregory's christology that takes place between the writing of *Eun.* III (*c.* 382) and *Apoll.* (*c.* 383). One might speculate that *Eun.* III represents Gregory's christology still 'under construction', awaiting to emerge 'fully formed' the following year after he is forced to rethink the shortcomings of his earlier attempt from the vantage point of a new polemical setting. This hypothetical narrative is, of course, plausible. Yet, establishing such a hypothesis is not without a number of difficulties, both textual and contextual. Let us assume for the sake of argument that Gregory did in fact hold a Spirit-based christology of the kind that we find in *Apoll.* at the time of writing *Eun.* III. Should we expect him to offer a full-blown exposition of his Spirit-based christology within the anti-Eunomian context? Since the persuasiveness of such an account would depend entirely upon one's assent to the Holy Spirit's equality of 'dignity' and 'glory' with the Father and the Son, which Apolinarius is likely to have held but Eunomius did not, I suggest we should expect *not*. To advance a Spirit-based christology in the Eunomian context would be not only useless but self-defeating.

We should therefore be cautious not to infer too hastily from an absence of explicit references to the Holy Spirit's anointing in *Eun.* III that Gregory did not already hold a Spirit-based christology. In fact, it makes sense that Gregory would be inclined voluntarily to tame his characteristic predilection for the 'anointing argument' in delivering his account of Christ's unity in *Eun.* III. As Andrew Radde-Gallwitz notes, Gregory never applies the Spirit's anointing theme to 'the incarnate economy of Christ' in any of his works except those 'where the Spirit's own dignity is not being disputed: *In illud: tunc et ipse filius, Against Apollinarius,* and the final homily *On the Song of Songs*.[10]

Therefore, I postulate two criteria that, if satisfied by *Eun.* III, will substantiate my suggestion that Gregory already held a Spirit-based christology at the time he wrote the anti-Eunomian work, but probably concealed it. We would require Gregory's account of Christ's unity in *Eun.* III to show:

i. a strong resemblance to the Spirit-based christology in *Apoll.*, minus explicit references to the Holy Spirit's anointing; and

ii. *probable traces* of a Spirit-based christology, where a sample text from *Eun.* III counts as:

    a. a *null trace* if its appearance in *Eun.* III is not explained by Gregory's assent to proposition β;

    b. a *possible trace* if its appearance in *Eun.* III is explained by Gregory's assent to proposition β, but does not occur in the context of an argument for Christ's unity;

---

[10] Radde-Gallwitz, *Doctrinal Works*, 75.

132 TRINITY, CHRISTOLOGY, AND PNEUMATOLOGY

    c. a *probable trace* if its appearance in *Eun.* III is explained by Gregory's assent to proposition β, and occurs in the context of an argument for Christ's unity; and

    d. a *certain trace* if its appearance in *Eun.* III is explained by Gregory's assent to proposition β, and it occurs in the context of an argument for Christ's unity and makes explicit reference to Jesus' anointing by the Holy Spirit.[11]

A word of clarification is called for regarding how these two criteria will be used to support my argument. First, criterion (i) must be satisfied to ensure that my suggestion that Gregory has *concealed* a Spirit-based christology is plausible. By the same token, this means that criterion (ii.d) will not be satisfied. My argument is not that Gregory abandons his Spirit-based christology in *Eun.* III, but rather retains its essential features beneath a veil. I take the satisfaction of criterion (i) and the corresponding failure to satisfy criterion (ii.d) to be self-evident upon a straightforward comparative reading of *Eun.* III and *Apoll.* Second, criterion (ii.a–e) takes its cue from my earlier analysis of *Trin.* in which I argued that Gregory's use of analogy *B* implies his assent to proposition β. In this case analogy *B* counts as what I have in criterion (ii.b) labelled a *possible trace* of a Spirit-based theory of Christ's unity since *B* is explained by Gregory's assent to proposition β but does not occur in the context of an argument for Christ's unity. I will not attempt to show that *Eun.* III yields any *possible traces* of a Spirit-based theory of Christ's unity since, even if this were the case, *possible traces* are in my judgment too weak to form any solid conclusions. Therefore, I will test only for the stronger case of *probable traces*.

One last example may help to further illustrate how I shall use criteria (ii.a–e) as well as the significance of criteria (ii.a) (the *null trace*) to support my argument. Suppose we consider the following passage in *Eun.* III.

F. by mingling (ἀνακράσει) with the divine, the mortal nature is renewed to match the dominant element, and shares the power of the deity, as if one might say that the drop of vinegar mingled (ἐμμιχθεῖσαν) with the ocean is

---

[11] I hold that X explains Y if X causes one to understand Y. If Y stands for the appearance of a particular sample text in *Eun.* III and X stands for Gregory's assenting to proposition β, then X explains Y if Gregory's assenting to proposition β causes one to understand the appearance of the textual sample in *Eun.* III. A recent defence of this view may be found in Daniel A. Wilkenfeld, 'Functional Explaining: A New Approach to the Philosophy of Explanation', *Synthese*, 191/14 (September 2014), 3367–3391.

TRACING THE SPIRIT   133

made into sea by the mixing, because the natural quality of this liquid no longer remains in the infinity of the dominant element.[12]

In this passage Gregory responds to the accusation that he teaches the existence of 'two Christs and two Lords" by describing the post-passion transformation of Jesus' flesh by the divinity using the analogy of the radical change undergone by a drop of vinegar mingled with the ocean. The passage has precipitated an ongoing discussion about the philosophical theory behind Gregory's conception of mixture in the present context and within his christology more broadly. Some detect here the presence of an Aristotelian theory of mixture that claims the proposition α, while others see the presence of a Stoic theory of mixture which claims the proposition σ:

α. if a small drop of one liquid is added to a much larger volume of a second liquid, then the form of the lesser liquid dissolves and becomes part of the total volume of the larger liquid;

σ. if a small drop of one liquid is added to a much larger volume of a second liquid, then the two mutually coextend throughout each other without being destroyed.

We can think of the scholarly discussion as an attempt to answer the question: does either the proposition α or the proposition σ explain analogy F? If so, then we might say that since analogy F is explicitly about mixing, it counts as a *probable trace* (rather than merely a *possible* one) of Gregory's assent to propositions α or σ and therefore to an Aristotelian or Stoic theory of mixture. Importantly, I take it that analogy F can never be explained by Gregory's assent to proposition β, and so F satisfies criterion (ii.a) as a *null trace* of a Spirit-based christology. Readers who are inclined to disagree with my argument that Gregory already held a Spirit-based christology when he wrote *Eun.* III will need to defend the hypothesis that *Eun.* III only satisfies criteria (ii.a), and hence yields nothing except a *null trace* in its entirety. My own analysis will attempt to disprove this 'null hypothesis'. This is the kind of reasoning I wish to employ when I ask whether there are passages in the *Eun.* III that are explained by Gregory's assent to β and hence count as a *probable trace* of a Spirit-based theory of Christ's unity.

---

[12] *GNO* II.132.27–133.4; Hall III, 121.

134 TRINITY, CHRISTOLOGY, AND PNEUMATOLOGY

Let us now, therefore, consider the following example from *Eun.* III (already briefly discussed in Chapter 4) that immediately precedes analogy *F*, which I will argue satisfies criteria (ii.c) as a *probable trace* of a Spirit-based christology. We recall that the passage occurs in the context of Christ's unity, specifically Gregory's defence against the accusation of teaching the existence of 'two Christs and two Lords', one divine and the other human. Gregory formulates a πνεῦμα-based analogy relating to the post-passion transformation of Christ's flesh into union with the divinity of the Only-begotten Son:

G. Just as *air* (πνεῦμα) is not retained by water, when, pulled downward (συγκατασπασθέν) by some heavy object (τῶν βαρυτέρων), it is taken down into the depth of the water, but flows upward to what is akin to it, and the water is often lifted up by the upward flow of the air (τοῦ πνεύματος), forming a convex shape with a rather thin (λεπτῇ) and membranous surface on the aerial sphere (τῷ ἀερώδει κύκλῳ), so when after the passion *the true life* (ἀληθινῆς ζωῆς) contained in the flesh flows back up to its own self, the flesh (σαρκί) containing it is borne up with it, driven upward from corruption to incorruption by the divine immortality.[13]

I will show below that several features of this πνεῦμα-based analogy G resonate with the notion of the ὄχημα-πνεῦμα or 'vehicle of the soul' in Neoplatonist philosophy with which Gregory was certainly familiar. First, however, it is important to note the parallelism Gregory draws between the πνεῦμα that is submerged and that flows back up to what is akin to it and the 'true life' (ἀληθινῆς ζωῆς). Just as πνεῦμα transforms water into a 'thin' (λεπτῇ) surface in the air by its upward flow, so too the ἀληθινῆς ζωῆς, by which Gregory indicates *the divine element*, acts as the agent transforming the flesh of Christ into unity with the Only-begotten Son. That Christ's flesh could be transformed into unity with God *by anything other than the divinity* would of course be a severe blunder on Gregory's part. As a result, Gregory invests πνεῦμα with a divine agency, and it is quite natural to conclude from this that he has the Holy Spirit in view as the agent transforming Christ's flesh into unity with God.

We might be further persuaded of this by the fact that Gregory has a penchant for formulating πνεῦμα-based analogies to illustrate the action of the Holy Spirit in several of his other works. In the *De deitate filii et spiritus sancti*

---

[13] *GNO* II.131.22–133.7; Hall III, 120–121.

TRACING THE SPIRIT 135

Gregory comments upon the gospel prohibition against pouring new wine into old wineskins (cf. Matt. 9:17). He notes that the newly pressed wine is, due to fermentation, 'full of spirit' (πνεύματος πλήρης ἐστί) and that this is analogous to 'the teaching about the Holy Spirit' and those who are 'fervid with the Spirit' (Τῷ πνεύματι ζέοντες), which those 'grown old with disbelief do not contain'.[14] In Homily 5 of *hom. in Cant.*, Gregory uses the analogy of the spring-time πνεῦμα, which melts away the winter frost to describe the Holy Spirit's action in restoring the idolater to new life.[15] Again, in Homily 12, Gregory compares the Holy Spirit's action of empowering the human mind to understand the Scriptures to the power of πνεῦμα by which a ship sets sail.[16] Similarly, in *Pss. titt.*, Gregory notes, '[David] says the grace of the Spirit is a breeze (αὔραν δὲ λέγει τὴν τοῦ πνεύματος χάριν) which by intellectual sails brings the soul to the divine harbour'.[17] In Homily 11 Gregory offers a πνεῦμα-based analogy that closely mirrors analogy G from *Eun.* III, which I again suggest has strong Neoplatonist undertones:

> Consider how air (πνεῦμα) that comes along with water out of the earth does not stay at the bottom of the pool but becomes a bubble (πομφόλυξ) and makes it way up to what is akin to it; and only when it has got to the surface of the water and is mingled with the air (καταμιχθῇ πρὸς τὸν ἀερα) does its upward course come to halt. Something like this happens also to the soul in search of things divine. When she stretches herself out from things below toward the knowledge of things on high, once she has grasped the marvels produced by God's workings, she cannot for a while progress further by her busy search for knowledge, but is filled with wonder and worships the One (τὸν ... μόνον) who is known to exist only through the things that his activity (ἐνεργεῖ) brings about.[18]

The analogy is, to be sure, not christologically oriented in the same way as analogy G from *Eun.* III, but rather serves to illustrate the noetic limits placed on the human soul in its search for God. Just as the upward course

[14] *GNO* X/2.119.1–8.
[15] *GNO* VI.147.15–148.6.
[16] *GNO* VI.341.13–342.8.
[17] Jacobus A. McDonough, S.J., and Paulus Alexander, eds., *Inscriptiones Psalmorum, In Sextum Psalmum, In Ecclesiasten Homiliae, GNO* V (Leiden: Brill, 1962), 60.18–20; Ronald E. Heine, trans., *Gregory of Nyssa's Treatise on the Inscriptions of the Psalms: Introduction, Translation and Notes*, Oxford Early Christian Studies (Oxford: Oxford University Press, 1995), 115.
[18] *GNO* VI.334.9–335.1.

136   TRINITY, CHRISTOLOGY, AND PNEUMATOLOGY

of the bubble filled with πνεῦμα comes to a halt upon reaching the water's surface, so too does the soul's knowledge of God terminate on God's 'activity' manifested in created things, such that the divine nature remains ineffable. While at no point does Gregory make it explicit that πνεῦμα stands for the Holy Spirit, such a reading would be wholly consonant with Gregory's usage of πνεῦμα-based analogies throughout *hom. in Cant.*, as I pointed out above.[19]

A particularly revealing πνεῦμα-based analogy is found in *virg.* in relation to the ascent and illumination of the human soul by the Holy Spirit. In this example, Gregory makes explicit reference to the Neoplatonist notion of the ὄχημα-πνεῦμα or 'vehicle of the soul', which I suggested underlies analogy G from *Eun.* III. I take the Neoplatonist philosopher and eventual bishop of Ptolemais, Synesius of Cyrene (*c.* 393–414), as an example of how this notion of the 'vehicle' functions in relation to human transformation and then offer a comparison with Gregory's use of it.[20] In the *De insomniis*,[21] Synesius taught that πνεῦμα was an intermediary, quasi-material substance between body and soul, which he also called the 'first body of the soul', 'divine body', and 'pneumatic soul'.[22] This πνεῦμα, he says, is the soul's 'first and proper vehicle (ὄχημα)' borrowed from the astral spheres during the soul's first descent from the One.[23] Alluding to Plato's allegory of the chariot in the *Phaedrus*,[24] Synesius taught that a soul must strive to re-ascend and thus return the borrowed πνεῦμα to the celestial sphere by a process of regaining its 'wings', thereby dissolving itself into aether along with the material elements of fire and air which accreted to it upon its descent.[25] For Synesius a good soul makes πνεῦμα 'aetheric' (ἀπαιθεροῦται) and 'light' (λεπτύνεται), the

---

[19] We need not be troubled that Gregory uses the same bubble analogy for both Christ in *Eun.* III and the ordinary human soul in *Cant.* For as I will show in Part II, Gregory posits an analogy between Christ's post-passion transformation and that of humanity.

[20] Cf. Robert Christian Kissling, 'The ΟΧΗΜΑ-ΠΝΕΥΜΑ of the Neo-Platonists and the De insomniis of Synesius of Cyrene', *The American Journal of Philology*, 43/4 (1922), 318–330; Abraham P. Bos, 'The "Vehicle of the Soul" and the Debate over the Origin of this Concept', *Philologus*, 151/1 (2007), 31–50; Ilinca Tanaseanu-Döbler, 'Synesius and the Pneumatic Vehicle of the Soul in Early Neoplatonism', in *On Prophecy, Dreams and Human Imagination: Synesius, De insomniis, Scripta Antiquitatis ad Ethicam Religionemque pertinentia XXIV*, ed. Donald A. Russell and Heinz-Günther Nesselrath (Tübingen: Mohr Siebeck, 2014), 25–156.

[21] *insomn*, 137D; Donald A. Russell and Heinz-Günther Nesselrath, eds., *On Prophecy, Dreams and Human Imagination: Synesius, De insomniis*, Scripta Antiquitatis ad Ethicam Religionemque pertinentia XXIV (Tübingen: Mohr Siebeck, 2014), 25.

[22] *insomn*, 137D; Russell, 25.

[23] *insomn*, 137A; Russell, 23.

[24] *Phaedrus*, 246 A–D; Ioannes Burnet, ed., *Platonis Opera*, Tomus II, Tetralogius III–IV Continens, Oxford Classical Texts (Oxford: Oxford University Press, 1900).

[25] *insomn*, 138A; Russell, 25.

TRACING THE SPIRIT   137

same term Gregory used to describe the watery membrane in analogy *G* of *Eun.* III. A good soul makes πνεῦμα 'warm and dry', while a bad soul renders πνεῦμα 'heavy and earthlike' as well as 'moist'.[26] Thus, using the language of being 'pulled down' (συγκατασπασθέν) by a 'heavy object' (τῶν βαρυτέρων) found also in Gregory's analogy *G*, Synesius states:

> the natural thing is for a soul once grafted on to <the pneuma> to go along with it, pull it or be pulled by it, but in any case to stay with it till it returns to the place whence it came. So also *the pneuma*, loaded with evil, drags down with itself (συγκατασπᾷ) any soul that has let herself be weighed down (βαρυνθῆναι) by it.[27]

By contrast, the soul may ascend with the πνεῦμα, together with some of the lighter material elements of the body (i.e. fire and air), which Synesius describes as taking a *spherical shape* to match the spherical heavens, a feature reminiscent of the transformation of the thin spherical membrane of Gregory's analogy *G* in *Eun.* III. Therefore:

> perhaps also inferior things (i.e. lighter material elements)—if they do not resist the activity of the soul, but go along with it pliantly and obediently, and even allow the middle nature to pass undistracted under the leadership of the first—will become etherealized and carried upwards with it, if not the whole way, then at least far enough to pass through the height of the elements and have a taste of the world of total light (τοῦ ἀμφιφαοῦς). For as the Oracle says, it has a part in this; that is to say, it is in a certain status in the spherical <body> (τοῦ κυκλικοῦ).[28]

The views of Synesius on the 'vehicle of the soul' were widely shared by other Neoplatonists, such as Plotinus, Porphyry, Iamblichus, Proclus, and Hierocles, albeit each with their own emphases and points of difference. The notion was also taken up by Christian theologians such as Origen and Didymus the Blind.[29]

---

[26] *insomn*, 137A; 137D; 140D; Russell 23, 25, and 31.

[27] *insomn*, 138C; Russell, 27.

[28] *insomn*, 141B; Russell, 31.

[29] Andrew Smith, *Porphyry's Place in the Neoplatonic Tradition: A Study in Post-Plotinian Neoplatonism* (The Hague: M. Nijhoff, 1974), 152–158; cf. Mark J. Edwards, 'Origen's Two Resurrections', *Journal of Theological Studies*, 46/2 (1995), 502–518; cf. H. S. Schibli, 'Hierocles of Alexandria and the Vehicle of the Soul', *Hermes*, 121/1 (1993), 109–117; cf. H. S. Schibli, 'Origen, Didymus, and the Vehicle of the Soul', in *Origeniana Quinta: Historica, Text and Method, Biblica,*

138   TRINITY, CHRISTOLOGY, AND PNEUMATOLOGY

As alluded to very briefly in Chapter 1, in *virg.* Gregory adapted and transformed this Neoplatonist notion of the ὄχημα-πνεῦμα to develop his own πνεῦμα-based analogy depicting the Holy Spirit's action in elevating the soul toward God. With reference to the phenomenon of shooting stars, he observes:

> the philosophers say they [i.e. shooting stars] are nothing else than air (ἢ ἀέρα) poured into the aethereal region (τὸν αἰθέριον) by the force of the winds (πνευμάτων), and they say that the firelike trail is traced in the sky when the wind (τοῦ πνεύματος) is enflamed in the aether (τοῦ αἰθέρος)— just as this earthly air (ἀήρ), when it is forced upwards by the wind (τοῦ πνεύματος), becomes illuminated, being changed in the purity of the ae-ther (τοῦ αἰθέρος), so the mind of man, when, after leaving this muddy and dusty life, it is purified through the power of the Spirit (ἐν τῇ δυνάμει τοῦ πνεύματος), becomes illuminated, and it is mixed (ἐμμιχθῇ) with the true and lofty purity, and it glows and is filled with rays and becomes light in ac-cordance with the promise of the Lord who declared that the just will shine like the sun.[30]

Importantly, the analogy of the shooting stars comes immediately after Gregory's reference to the Neoplatonist notion of the 'vehicle of the soul', which he says is empowered by the Holy Spirit:

> How could anyone fly up to heaven unless, equipped with heavenly wings (πτερωθεὶς τῷ οὐρανίῳ πτερῷ), he be borne upwards because of his lofty way of life? Who is so removed from the mysteries of the Gospel, that he does not know that *there is one vehicle for the human soul* (ἓν ὄχημα τῇ ἀνθρωπίνη ψυχῇ) for the journey to the heavens, and that is by likening itself to the cowering dove whose wings (τὰς πτέρυγας) the prophet David longed for. It is customary for Scripture to use this symbol in referring to the power of the Spirit (τὴν τοῦ πνεύματος δύναμιν).[31]

Philosophica, Theologica, Origenism and Later Developments: Papers of the 5th International Origen Congress, Boston College, 14–18 August 1989, ed. Robert J. Daly (Leuven: Peeters, 1992), 381–391; cf. John F. Finamore, *Iamblichus and the Theory of the Vehicle of the Soul*, American Classical Studies 14 (Chico, CA: Scholars Press, 1985); cf. E. R. Dodds, *Proclus: The Elements of Theology*, 2nd ed. (Oxford: Clarendon Press, 1963), 313–321.

[30] *GNO* VIII/1.295.1–13; Woods Callahan, 40–41.
[31] *GNO* VIII/1.294.8–16; Woods Callahan, 40.

We see that Gregory has co-opted the standard vocabulary and ascent narrative of the Neoplatonist teaching on the 'vehicle of the soul'. Unlike Synesius, his explicit reference to the vehicle does not refer to πνεῦμα as an intermediary substance. Rather, the 'vehicle' is for Gregory the 'lofty way of life', which has been empowered by the 'wings' of the Holy Spirit, here adapting the Platonic imagery of the *Phaedrus* in his own way.[32]

It is reasonable, therefore, to conclude that just as Gregory has used Neoplatonist terminology and imagery in *virg.*, adapting it for his own purposes when speaking of the Holy Spirit's action on the virgin ascetic, he adapts the same Neoplatonic language and imagery in analogy G of *Eun.* III, making πνεῦμα stand in parallel with ἀληθινῆς ζωῆς, and hence investing it with divine status as the agent transforming Christ's flesh into unity with the divinity of the Only-begotten Son. This, together with Gregory's strong predilection for πνεῦμα-based analogies to depict the Holy Spirit's action, leads me to judge that analogy G satisfies criterion (ii.c) as a *probable trace* since (a) its reference to πνεῦμα likely has the Holy Spirit in view though in concealed form, (b) it is explained by Gregory's assent to proposition β, and (c) it occurs in the context of an argument for Christ's unity.

I leave this example to the side for the time being to analyse what I judge to be a comparatively much stronger case for a passage found in *Eun.* III (briefly discussed in Chapter 3), which I will argue satisfies criterion (ii.c). We recall that the passage occurs in the context of Gregory's response to Eunomius' claim, based on his reading of Acts 2:36, that the term 'made (i.e. Lord and Christ)' applies to the 'pre-temporal being'.[33] For the sake of argument, Gregory momentarily concedes the point to Eunomius and then proceeds to show that even if this were truly the case, one still cannot conclude from this anything about the Word's 'essential being' (τὴν οὐσίαν).[34] If, as Eunomius argues, it is the Only-begotten Son who is 'made' Lord and Christ, then this 'making' is merely analogous, says Gregory, to David's transition from that rank of 'private citizen' to that of king via 'anointing':

H.   [it is] rather like the story about David, which says that, being son of Jesse and in charge of the sheep, he was anointed (ἐχρίσθη) king, when the

---

[32] Gregory refers to the vehicle of the soul several times in his works. Cf. *Inscr.*, GNO V.42.9; 42.23–24; Heine 99–100; cf. *ascens.*, GNO IX.325.7–10; cf. *An. et res.*, Andreas Spira, ed., *De anima et resurrectione, Post mortem editoris praefationem accurate composuit Ekkehardus Mühlenberg*, GNO III/3 (Leiden: Brill, 2014), 29.8.

[33] GNO II.155.5; Hall III, 134.

[34] GNO II.157.1; Hall III, 135.

140 TRINITY, CHRISTOLOGY, AND PNEUMATOLOGY

anointing (χρίσεως) did not at that time make him a man, but retaining the nature (φύσιν) he already had, he was changed (μετατιθείσης) from a private citizen (ἐξ ἰδιώτου) into a king.[35]

Gregory's point is that even if one concedes that Acts 2:36 refers to 'the one who was in the beginning' (i.e. the eternal Word) rather than the 'the man' Jesus, one still cannot infer from it anything about the Word's 'being'. This is because 'lordship' is not a title of 'being' but of 'authority', while the title 'Christ' indicates 'kingship' and not 'nature'.[36] Gregory then shifts his argument from a *hypothetical* mode of reasoning to one that reflects his actual position on this matter: scripture teaches that it is the *human nature*, not the divine nature, that 'advances' to exalted status after the passion:

Whose mind is so infantile that he thinks the divinity advances toward perfection? Is it not reasonable to think such a thing *of the human nature* (τῆς ἀνθρωπίνης φύσεως), when the gospel text attests his growth (αὔξησιν) as a human being: 'Jesus advanced', it says, 'in stature, wisdom and grace' (cf. Luke 2:52). Which then is it more reasonable to suppose is meant by the apostle's word [i.e. the Apostle Peter's], that the God who is in the beginning became Lord by advancement (προκοπήν), or that *the lowly status of human nature was taken up by its fellowship with the divine into the highest dignity* (εἰς τὸ ὕψος τῆς ἀξίας)? . . . If it were religiously correct in the case of the transcendent nature to say that it has become something by advancement, in the way a king is made from a private citizen (ἐξ ἰδιώτου), the exalted from the humble (ἐκ ταπεινοῦ) (cf. 1 Sam. 16:13), and the master from the slave, it might perhaps be right to relate the saying of Peter to the divine being of the Only-begotten; but since the divinity, whatever it may be believed to be, is always the same, too high for any promotion and incapable of any diminution, *it is absolutely necessary to apply the thought to the human element* . . . Thus came about that ineffable mixture (μίξις) and combination, as human littleness was mingled (ἀνακραθείσης) with divine greatness.[37]

---

[35] *GNO* II.157.26; Hall III, 135.

[36] *GNO* II.157.3–6; Hall III, 135.

[37] *GNO* II.157.8–158.28; Hall III, 135–6. Cf. *ep.* 3, Silvas, 128.16. Johannes Zachhuber, 'Gregory of Nyssa, Contra Eunomium III 4', 332, takes Gregory's reference to Christ's 'advancement' (προκοπήν), drawn from Luke 2:52, as an indication of Gregory's interest in 'the moral and religious improvement Jesus underwent throughout his earthly life' and hence the 'gradual divinisation of humanity in Christ'. Zachhuber connects this notion to Gregory's ascetical writings, where Christ is upheld as the

The crucial point here is that Gregory's reference to Jesus' 'advancement' to the 'highest dignity' is conceptually linked to Jesus' 'anointing' in analogy *H*. Gregory has clearly recognized that the anointing of a 'private citizen', in this case David (cf. 1 Sam. 16:13), to the exalted status of a king functions as a direct analogy for the post-passion exaltation of the man Jesus of Nazareth to the elevated status of 'Lord and Christ' in unity with the Only-begotten Son. This, we might say, is Gregory's 'anointing argument' not for the 'dignity' of the Spirit as we find in the anti-Macedonian literature, but for the post-passion 'dignity' of *the man Jesus Christ*. That Gregory makes this connection here between 'anointing' and Jesus' exaltation to unity with God further strengthens my earlier argument that he already understood this to be the

moral exemplar of ascetic virtue. He notes that Gregory will later renege this view in *ep. 3* in an apparently 'humiliating recantation'.

The difficulty with this particular reading arises from Zachhuber's claim that Gregory's reference to 'advancement' from Luke 2:52 moves 'a step beyond the exegesis of Acts 2:36' when a closer reading of the text shows that Gregory's appeal to the notion of Christ's advancement in Luke 2:52 is in fact dictated by the interpretation of the Acts verse. This explains why Gregory places Luke's concept of Christ's 'advancement' on the lips of the Apostle Peter. Thus, it appears that Gregory's sole motive for turning to Luke 2:52 is that he requires a scriptural 'proof text' for his main argument that what is elevated to the status of 'Christ' and 'Lord' is not the divine nature but Christ's *human nature*. In other words, according to Gregory, if the gospel (of Luke) confirms that it is Jesus' *human nature* that advanced in 'knowledge, wisdom, and stature' during his earthly career (i.e. Luke 2:52), then it is entirely fitting likewise to view *the human* rather than divine nature as the element that is elevated from the status of 'private citizen' to 'Christ' after the passion, although not by a kind of moral, ascetic progress, but by his 'anointing' to the 'highest dignity', as per analogy *H*.

On this score, Radde-Gallwitz (2018), 173–174 is correct to note that 'Gregory's use of the verse [i.e. Luke 2:52] in *Against Eunomius* 3.4 is subtle . . . the verse functions as a kind of confirmation of the appropriateness of the language of advancement for Christ. Given that the verb is used for Jesus' growth in wisdom, stature, and favor, and given that these are functions of his humanity rather than his divinity, it is not unreasonable to think of changes in that nature as such'. See also Radde-Gallwitz, *Doctrinal Works*, 197, 209, who is otherwise sympathetic with Zachhuber. It is easy to see, however, how Gregory's appeal to Luke 2:52 in *Eun.* III could be taken the wrong way to imply that the humanity of Christ advanced to the dignity of Lordship through some kind of sequence (ἀκολουθίαν), though this was not Gregory's original intent.

Gregory's comments on Luke 2:52 in *ep. 3* therefore need not be read as a 'recantation' but rather as setting the record straight for those who may have misunderstood and therefore took issue with Gregory's subtle use of that verse in *Eun.* III. Nevertheless, it is perhaps worth asking why Gregory should appeal to Luke 2:52 to substantiate his claim that it was the *humanity* rather than the divinity that 'advanced' to the highest dignity rather than the much more relevant and useful (albeit pneumatologically loaded) texts, such as John 17:5 and Acts 10:38 to which he refers in the anti-Macedonian works. Was it because citing these latter verses would have been counter-productive in the present context?

There is still, however, one instance where Gregory unambiguously gives Luke 2:52 an ascetical interpretation. This occurs in Homily 3 of *hom. in Cant*: 'For the child who was born for us—Jesus, who within those who receive him progresses (προκόπτων) in a variety of ways in wisdom and stature and grace (cf. Luke 2:52) . . . He is manifested in a character that fits the ability of the one who takes him in, either as babe (νηπιάζων) or as making progress (προκόπτων) or as being perfected (τελειούμενος)' (cf. *GNO* VI.96.7–13; Norris II.107). Here, however, Gregory's allegorical reading serves only to show how one's capacity to receive Christ within the soul varies according to *one's own* spiritual maturity. It suggests nothing about moral progress in the life of the incarnate Christ himself. See Johannes Zachhuber, 'Gregory of Nyssa, Contra Eunomium III 4', 332.

142   TRINITY, CHRISTOLOGY, AND PNEUMATOLOGY

case when he wrote the virtually identical analogy *B* of *Trin.* about one year earlier. Hence, we gain even greater support for my earlier claim that Gregory already assented to proposition *β* at that time.

One may of course wish to remain sceptical, positing perhaps that Gregory only arrived at analogy *H* after a sudden flash of insight at the point of writing *Eun.* III Part 4, either by finally following through on the implications of analogy *B* that until then had eluded him, or perhaps even in complete ignorance of his earlier formulation of analogy *B*! Either way, the sceptical view requires a counter-explanation for how, in the context of formulating analogy *B* about the Holy Spirit's anointing of Christ in *Trin.*, Gregory could fail to be cognizant that proposition *β* is consequent upon that analogy given the prevalence of views regarding Jesus' anointing by the Holy Spirit *in the economy* within the anti-Eunomian tradition, and yet arrive at the view in *Eun.* III that Jesus is anointed *in the economy* to the status of 'Christ' and 'Lord' possibly within the very same year, presumably having been influenced by the same anti-Eunomian tradition. I can think of no plausible scenario in which the sceptical stance provides a better explanation of the textual data than the one I have offered.

Hence, I take it as secure that Gregory already held a Spirit-based account of Christ's unity when he wrote *Trin.* And this strengthens support for my contention that in formulating his 'anointing argument' for the 'dignity' of the Holy Spirit in *Trin.*, Gregory did so by adapting a pre-existing 'anointing argument' for the 'dignity' of the resurrected Jesus, constructing analogy *B* from his underlying assent to proposition *β*, but convincing his readership of it chiefly through rhetorical force rather than through a demonstration via detailed scriptural exegesis of the kind that we only find in *Apoll.*

With this in mind, we are in a better position to interpret Gregory's use of the anointing analogy in the present context of *Eun.* III Part 4 in a new light. Since references to 'anointing' in Gregory's corpus typically evoke the role of the Holy Spirit, and since this is quite clearly the case in his use of analogy *B* in *Trin.*, then we have every reason to believe that analogy *H* in *Eun.* III, which is virtually identical to analogy *B*, also has the Holy Spirit in view. To deny this would force us to concede a most remarkable inconsistency in Gregory's thought, arising perhaps from a most worrying case of theological amnesia. That Gregory stops short of explicitly identifying Jesus' 'anointing' to the status of 'Lord and Christ' as the activity of the Holy Spirit is not evidence that Gregory suffers from a memory lapse about his own pneumatology, but is best explained by his need to adapt to the anti-Eunomian context, where references to the Holy Spirit's anointing of Christ *in the economy* are counter-productive to the cause of advancing a pro-Nicene christology. Hence, I contend that Gregory's reference to the anointing of Jesus to the status of Lord and Christ in analogy *H* of *Eun.* III satisfies criterion (ii.c), as a clear example of a *probable trace* of a Spirit-based theory of Christ's unity.

I am now permitted to allow my analysis of analogy *H* to illuminate my earlier suggestion that the πνεῦμα-based analogy *G* satisfies criterion (ii.c). If analogy *H* counts as a relatively 'strong' example of a *probable trace* of a Spirit-based christology then we gain greater justification for also accepting the comparatively 'weaker' example of analogy G as a *probable trace* of a Spirit-based christology. That is, the 'weaker' case (analogy *G*) no longer counts as a stand-alone example, but is corroborated by the 'stronger' example (analogy *H*). Given three instances of mutually corroborating evidence (analogies *B*, *G*, and *H*), it is reasonable to conclude that Gregory already held a Spirit-based account of Christ's unity at the time he wrote *Eun.* III that he concealed for strategic, pragmatic reasons.

Conclusion

There are two viable ways we can interpret the textual data I have explored in this chapter. On the one hand, we may view Gregory undergoing a development of thought via a steady accretion of new ideas between the writing of *Trin.* and *Apoll.* According to this view, in *Trin.* (*c.* 381) Gregory formulates his anointing argument for the Holy Spirit's dignity for the first time. There, he posits analogy *B* to establish the view that the Holy Spirit qua 'anointing' is a symbol of the Only-begotten Son's 'kingship' and thus shares equal 'dignity' with the Only-begotten Son and the Father. He does so oblivious to the fact that the anti-Eunomian tradition, of which he is an heir, would readily recognize analogy *B* as a fitting analogy of Christ's anointing by the Spirit *in the economy*. It is only upon writing *Eun.* III (*c.* 382) that it dawns upon Gregory that analogy *H*, which is virtually identical to analogy *B*, can serve to illustrate the post-passion transformation of Jesus' flesh through anointing. Importantly, in this hypothetical reconstruction, Gregory has not yet realized that the application of analogy *H* to the christological context is suggestive of the Holy Spirit's action, even though this is precisely what the cognate analogy *B* serves to illustrate in *Trin.* Neither does he yet realize that his πνεῦμα-based analogy in *Eun.* III for Jesus' post-resurrection transformation

144 TRINITY, CHRISTOLOGY, AND PNEUMATOLOGY

into unity with the divinity of the Only-begotten Son implies the Holy Spirit's activity, even though πνεῦμα-based analogies regularly imply precisely this in both his earlier and later writings. Finally, when preparing to write *Apoll.* (*c.* 383), Gregory discovers that the solution he has been looking for to the problem of Christ's unity was right under his nose the whole time—the post-passion anointing of Jesus to the status of 'Lord and Christ' was actually the action of the Holy Spirit's anointing! With this new insight, Gregory proceeds to formulate his Spirit-based christology.

In this chapter I have provided ample argumentation to suggest that this theory of development-by-accretion is highly problematic. We make best sense of the absence of explicit references to the Spirit's anointing in *Eun.* III as a consequence of Gregory's deliberate and strategic accommodation to the ani-Eunomian context where such references would be self-defeating. That there occur two *probable traces* of a Spirit-based christology in *Eun.* III is best explained by a pre-existing commitment to a Spirit-based christology, which we have strong justification for assuming Gregory held as early as the writing of *Trin.*, likely having been influenced by the anti-Eunomian tradition that he imbided. Since the anointing argument in *Trin.* is justified by analogy *B*, which naturally entails proposition *β*, it is likely that Gregory's anointing argument for the Holy Spirit's dignity in *Trin.* is derived from his Spirit-based christology, rather than the other way around.

This comes with direct implications for how the historical theologian must now engage the christology of *Eun.* III. I suggest that the theory of Christ's unity in *Eun.* III is now to be taken as a 'defective' account of Gregory's christology in certain respects, not because it falls short of the later Chalcedonian formula,[38] nor because Gregory lacked the requisite theological insights at the time, but because Gregory himself has purposely made it so for pragmatic reasons. It is a 'defective' work *in the strictly delimited sense* that Gregory omits certain key features of his more authentic and original position on Christ's unity, which has direct recourse to the role of the Spirit. At the same time, the 'defective' quality of *Eun.* III (Parts 3 and 4) demonstrates Gregory's genius, for in it we observe the working of a theologian prepared to 'truncate' a thoroughgoing trinitarian, Spirit-based account of Christ's unity for the sake of strategically advancing a pro-Nicene position, all the while retaining

---

[38] Cf. Brian E. Daley, 'Divine Transcendence and Human Transformation: Gregory of Nyssa's Anti-Apolinarian Christology', *Modern Theology*, 18 (2002a), 497–506; ' "Heavenly Man" and "Eternal Christ": Apolinarius and Gregory of Nyssa on the Personal Identity of the Savior', *Journal of Early Christian Studies*, 10 (2002b), 469–488.

the essence of that account in veiled guise—a veil removed only by turning to the Spirit, to use one of Gregory's frequently cited biblical passages. Thus, Gregory's account of the unity of Christ in *Eun.* III cannot be regarded *prima facie* as his definitive stance.

It is nevertheless an exemplary case of what might be called a 'subset' Christology—that is, a specialized christological discourse wherein the unity of Christ's two natures is theorized in terms of the union of the divine and human natures in a single subject, while suspending references to the Holy Spirit as the agent who elevates *the human nature* in 'rank' and 'dignity' in relation to the divine nature. Further, it is a 'subset' discourse inasmuch as the choice to bracket out references to the Spirit has the effect of distancing christology from trinitarian theology.

Confirmation of the explanatory hypothesis offered in this chapter is further strengthened by the fact that it not only explains the difference in Gregory's accounts of Christ's unity between *Eun.* III and *Apoll.* in light of Gregory's use of the anointing argument in *Trin.* and other relevant textual evidence, but it also offers a straightforward explanation for why the Spirit-based christology of *Apoll.* happens to resolve the incoherence between Gregory's account of human transformation and the transformation of the 'the man' Jesus of Nazareth in *Eun.* III, which I identified in Chapter 3. Supposing the hypothesis of the present chapter is correct, Gregory's Spirit-based christology resolves the incoherence precisely because his calculated decision to 'truncate' his Spirit-based christology in *Eun.* III is what caused the incoherence in the first place.

Let us take stock now of Gregory's account of human transformation and union with God in relation to the basic interconnecting structure of trinitarian, christological, and pneumatological thought that has emerged from my literary-historical analysis here in Part I. According to Gregory, it is impossible for weak and fallen human beings to be united to Christ in 'spiritual marriage' unless strengthened by the life-giving power of the Holy Spirit. Reception of the Spirit occurs through the free choice to be baptized, whereupon one is empowered in heart, mind, and soul to live the post-baptismal life of virtue, leading from union with Christ through the Spirit up to the beatific vision of God. Gregory is adamant that, in baptism and throughout the post-baptismal life, the Holy Spirit completes the unified activity of all three trinitarian persons that 'flows' *from* the Father, *through* the Son, *in* the Spirit.'

Indeed, to separate the activity of the Spirit from the joint activity of the Father and the Son, not only at baptism but within the whole cosmos, is to

146 TRINITY, CHRISTOLOGY, AND PNEUMATOLOGY

deny the essential unity of the trinitarian persons and to disturb the basis for cosmic order and teleology. Just as there is a *descending* movement of saving activity to humanity from the Father, Son, and Spirit, so Gregory speaks of a corresponding *ascending* movement from humanity through the Spirit, and the Son to the Father so as to behold and to ultimately be joined to the eternal exchange of 'glory' within the Trinity. Baptism therefore initiates a transformational movement of humanity from the domain in which trinitarian activity can be articulated in terms of a 'linear' mode of transmission to the domain of inclusion into the trinitarian life depicted by a 'circular' exchange of glorification.

According to Gregory, this dynamic transformation of humanity is grounded in the incarnation of Christ. To freely choose to imitate Christ's own baptism in the Jordan as the 'first-fruit' of the 'common lump' regenerated by the Spirit is at the very same time to receive the unified saving activity of Father, Son, and Spirit. Further, while the human and divine natures are united in the single subject of the Son, their 'static' unity is by the anointing of the Spirit from the very moment of Christ's conception through to his death. The Spirit's anointing also actualizes the 'dynamic' unity of Christ's two natures *after the passion*, whereupon Christ's human flesh is transformed, elevated to the highest rank and dignity, and ultimately united with the eternal glory of the divinity of the Son by the glory of the Spirit, and through this into union with the Father.[39] The incarnate Christ is therefore the prototype of humanity's transformation and union with God via the unified activity of Father, Son, and Spirit. Thus, as with Christ the 'first-fruit', so too the whole body of Christ, that is the church, may undergo transformation and union with the divine Son through the glory of the Spirit, and through the Son be united to the eternal glory of God.

Without claiming to have exhaustively captured the entirety of Gregory's thought in all its specific details, I submit that the outline offered here encapsulates the essential structure of Gregory's account of human transformation and union with God grounded in (i) the unified activity of the Trinity and (ii) the incarnation of Christ, expressed in terms of a Spirit-based

---

[39] As echoed by Beeley, 'Gregory of Nyssa's Christological Exegesis', 106: 'Structurally speaking, it [i.e. Gregory's christology] operates with a two-stage model that moves from a dualist scheme prior to Christ's resurrection, shifting to a kind of unitive picture afterward'. Beeley agrees with Anthony Meredith, 'Contra Eunomium III 3', in *Jesus Christ in St Gregory of Nyssa's Theology: Minutes of the Ninth International Conference on St Gregory of Nyssa (Athens, 7–12 September 2000)*, ed. Elias D. Moutsoulas (Athens: Eptalafos, 2005), 169–170, who speaks similarly of Gregory moving from a 'diophysite' to a 'unitary' model.

christology, prior to writing *hom. in Cant*. It is, so my analysis has suggested, a structure of thought that is largely coherent in a number of senses. First, there is a *narrative* coherence to the overarching structure insofar as it is integrally grounded in events that temporally unfold in a sequential and teleological order within the economy of salvation. Second, there is a *confessional* coherence to the structure consequent upon Gregory's commitment to 'Nicene faith' and a corresponding set of theological judgments that are consciously and consistently anti-Macedonian, anti-Eunomian, and anti-Apollinarian. Third, there is a high degree of internal 'systematic' or *logical* coherence: what is logically entailed by Gregory's trinitarian claims is largely satisfied by his christology since what is logically entailed by his christological claims is largely satisfied by his pneumatology. To omit certain key features from this structure would be to introduce logical incoherence. These three aspects of coherence—the narrative, the confessional, and the logical—are mutually conditioning and contribute to the overall coherence of the structure.

It is appropriate to speak of this structure as Gregory's coherent account of the *objective* reality of human transformation and union with God in the specific sense that it captures Gregory's view of human transformation and union from the perspective of the divine initiative in the economy of salvation in a mode largely detached from the *subjective experience* of such transformation and union. Yet, it is quite evident that this account of *objective* reality is incomplete without a corresponding account of the *subjective* aspect since, as Gregory points out especially in his earliest work *virg*., human transformation and union with God also depend upon a subjective *love* for God with the whole heart, in fulfilment of the Great Command.

It is clear that if such an account of human transformation and union from the *subjective* perspective is to preserve the narrative, confessional, and logical coherence of Gregory's account of the *objective* reality, then it too must be grounded in (i) the unified activity of the Trinity and (ii) the incarnation of Christ, expressed in terms of a Spirit-based christology. Indeed, to offer an account of the *subjective* reality of human transformation and union with God that is *not* grounded in points (i) and (ii), but rather, say, only in the ethical-ascetical choice to imitate Christ's moral example alone, is, by Gregory's own standards, to deny the essential unity of the trinitarian persons. Does Gregory offer a coherent account of the *subjective* experience of transformation and union? I suggest that he does in *hom. in Cant*. by means of his exegesis of the Song of Songs. The demonstration of this claim will occupy my focus in Part II.

PART II
ANALYSIS OF *IN CANTICUM CANTICORUM* (*c.* 391)

I have shown in the Introduction that *hom. in Cant.* is probably Gregory of Nyssa's final written work. Composed probably sometime between 391 and 395,[1] it consists of fifteen homilies on the Song of Songs, the basic content of which Gregory originally preached to 'the assembly of the church'.[2] Thus, J. Warren Smith issues an important reminder that the homilies must be viewed first and foremost not as a treatise on 'mysticism' intended for spiritual elites, but as a 'Lenten sermon series' aimed at inspiring a pure and single-minded love in preparation for the upcoming Easter celebration.[3] Upon the request for a copy of these sermons by Olympias, a young widow of considerable wealth who dedicated her life to asceticism and serving the poor, Gregory consulted notes (σημείωσις) that were taken during his preaching and these were subsequently 'fashioned in the form of homilies in which the interpretation of the words followed the order of the text'.[4] It is uncertain whether Olympias received a copy of the final form of edited homilies that has now been bequeathed to us, or a slightly shorter version, possibly consisting of only the first twelve homilies, which Gregory only later expanded to include Homilies 13, 14, and 15, as suggested by Hermann Dörries.[5] In any case, there can be little doubt that Gregory had a direct hand in shaping the 'final form' of the homilies as a coherent collection.

---

[1] Daniélou (1966) dates the work to 'after 390'; Cahill (1981) between 391 and 394; Dünzl (1993) 30–33 to after 39. Cited from Maraval, BDGN 158.

[2] *GNO* VI.13.9–11; Norris II.13; cf. Canévet, *Grégoire de Nysse et l'herméneutique biblique*, 127–131.

[3] Smith, *Passion and Paradise*, 218; On 'mysticism' in Gregory's homilies, see C. W. MacLeod, 'Allegory and Mysticism in Origen and Gregory of Nyssa', *Journal of Theological Studies*, 22/2 (1971), 362–379.

[4] *GNO* VI.13.11–14; Norris II, 13.

[5] Norris II, xxii; cf. Hermann Dörries, 'Griechentum und Christentum bei Gregor von Nyssa: Zu H. Langerbecks Edition des Hohelied-Kommentar in der Leiden Gregor-Ausgabe', *Theologische*

150 ANALYSIS OF *IN CANTICUM CANTICORUM* (*c*. 391)

Gregory's exegesis of the Song of Songs is especially concerned with the *skopos* and *akolouthia* of the scriptural text, an approach to interpretation that has precedent in numerous Christian figures such as Origen and Eusebius of Caesarea, but also notably in Neoplatonic philosophers such as Iamblichus and Proclus.[6] *Skopos* refers to a text's higher literary 'aim', while *akolouthia* refers to the 'logical sequence' of ideas and topics that either lie within the text itself, or may emerge from the process of interpreting the text. The *skopos* and *akolouthia* of the Song of Songs are, for Gregory, therefore integrally related, and together they reveal to the reader, in an unfolding logical sequence, the reality of the transformation and union of created, finite, and fallen humanity with the uncreated, infinite, and incomprehensible God.

This 'reality' revealed in the Song of Songs is two-sided. On the one hand, the Song gives an account of the *objective* reality of human transformation and union with God, prophetically revealed through the inspired author Solomon, and played out in the interaction between the two main figures of the Bride and the Bridegroom of the Song. Yet, Gregory clearly intends that, through a *subjective* process of contemplating and interpreting the Song of Songs rightly (θεωρίας),[7] the *objective* reality depicted therein may actually become a *subjective* reality for the reader. In the words of Morwenna Ludlow, Gregory's reading of scripture is a 'sacramental reading which relates God's salvation-history to the history of the reader'.[8] And Norris Jr. states, 'readers of the Song may themselves, through their comprehension of it, be brought along as *actual participants* in the Song's narration of the exemplary soul's progress in knowledge and love of God . . . to understand it fully is *to be involved with the reality of which it speaks*'.[9] For Gregory, this 'actual participation' in the Song's narrative is not a mere fiction, but is of a metaphysical or ontological order. To advance in one's knowledge and love of God is, for Gregory, to advance in ontological union with God.

Literaturzeitung, 88 (1963), 572–573; The hypothesis rejected by Franz Dünzl, *Braut und Bräutigam*, Beiträge zur Geschichte der Biblischen Exegese 32 (Tübingen: Mohr Siebeck, 1993), 19–22.

[6] Heine, *Inscriptions of the Psalms*, 29–49, argues that Gregory follows Iamblichus' exegetical method by attending to *skopos* and *genos*. Gregory does not refer to *skopos* explicitly in *hom. in Cant.*, yet it seems apparent that the concept is important to his exegesis; cf. Ludlow, *Universal Salvation*, 28–30.

[7] *GNO* VI.3.4; Norris II, 3.

[8] Morwenna Ludlow, 'Theology and Allegory: Origen and Gregory of Nyssa on the Unity and Diversity of Scripture', *International Journal of Systematic Theology*, 4/1 (2002), 82.

[9] *GNO* VI; Norris II, xlv, my italics.

ANALYSIS OF *IN CANTICUM CANTICORUM* (*c.* 391)   151

It is clear, however, that not just *any* reading of the Song of Songs is sufficient for actualizing this state of affairs, since errant readings are possible. Rather, a true discernment of the Song's *skopos* and *akolouthia* requires, for Gregory, a 'turning' (ἀναστέφειν) of its words and a 'discernment' (θεωρίας) of its deeper meaning, a practice we have already seen him employ in his exegesis of Proverbs 8 in *Eun*. III. Such a 'turning' or 'discernment' is not possible, as we saw with Proverbs 8, unless the subjectivity of the *reader* of scripture is aligned with that of the *author* of the Song (Solomon) via the shared illumination of the Holy Spirit. Citing 2 Cor. 3:6—'The letter kills but the Spirit gives life'—Gregory says that the Holy Spirit 'transposes a meaning (μετατιθήσι) that is incongruous and discordant into a more divine sense'.[10] Only through the Spirit, therefore, is the Song of Songs effective for making the *objective* reality of human transformation and union with God a *subjective* reality for the reader. Built into Gregory's understanding of rightly reading the Song, therefore, is the notion that union with God is a result of the activity of the Spirit. Importantly, the right reading of the Song of Songs under the illumination of the Spirit is not simply a 'noetic' process narrowly conceived, but engages the whole person—heart, mind, body, and soul. In this way, it involves what Martin Laird has called an 'education of desire' and a pedagogy of the soul's 'noetic-erotic movement' progressively away from attachment to flesh and material things and toward God.[11]

Part II questions whether and to what degree Gregory's account of the transformative *subjective process* attached to reading and comprehending the higher meaning of the Song of Songs resonates and ultimately coheres with Gregory's doctrinal understanding of the *objective* reality of union with God outlined in Part I. A minimal number of conditions would need to be satisfied. First, it must be coherent with Gregory's claim that *baptism* is the occasion upon which one receives illumination by the Spirit and is set on the

---

[10] *GNO* VI.7.12–16; Norris II, 7.

[11] Martin Laird, 'Under Solomon's Tutelage: The Education of Desire in the Homilies on the Song of Songs', *Modern Theology*, 18/4 (2002), 509; So, Giulio Maspero, 'The *In Canticum* in Gregory's Theology: Introduction and Gliederung', in *Gregory of Nyssa: In Canticum Canticorum: Analytical and Supporting Studies. Proceedings of the 13th International Colloquium on Gregory of Nyssa (Rome, 17–20 September 2014)*, Supplements to Vigiliae Christianae 150, ed. Giulio Maspero, Miguel Brugarolas, and Ilaria Vigorelli (Leiden: Brill, 2018), 49: '*In Canticum* does not seek a merely noetic result' but is concerned with humanity's ontological perfection'; Cf. Morwenna Ludlow, *Art, Craft and Theology in Fourth Century Christian Authors* (Oxford: Oxford University Press, 2020), 96, on Gregory's deliberate use of *ekphrasis* (esp. Homily 5) to 'stimulate the audience's imaginative and emotional participation in the speaker's words'; cf. Ludlow, *Universal Salvation*, 62–63; cf. Medi Ann Volpe, *Rethinking Christian Identity: Doctrine and Discipleship*, Challenges in Contemporary Theology (Chichester: Wiley-Blackwell, 2013), 196–221.

152 ANALYSIS OF *IN CANTICUM CANTICORUM* (*c.* 391)

transformative path of union with God. Further, this *subjective process* must be coherent with the claim that the Spirit received at baptism acts in unity with the Father and the Son to join humanity to the Son and through the Son to the 'circular' exchange of trinitarian glory. Finally, this *subjective process* attached to the reading of the Song of Songs must be grounded in Gregory's Spirit-based christology.

There is of course no necessity for Gregory to be consistent in all or indeed any of these details. Nevertheless, it will be clear that if coherence exists between Gregory's accounts of the *subjective* reality and the *objective* reality of human transformation and union with God, then the doctrinal framework outlined in Part I must emerge organically from the very *subjective process* of reading the Song of Songs itself. An examination of this claim is undertaken in Chapters 6–8 through a detailed analysis of *hom. in Cant.*

6

The Baptismal Exegesis of the Song of Songs

Introduction

In Chapter 1, I showed in my analysis of *virg.* that Gregory understood 'spiritual marriage' with Christ to be possible only for weak and fallen human beings through the life-giving power of the Spirit, which he expressed in terms of a baptismal exegesis of scripture. In Chapter 2, I showed that Gregory's notion of the reception of the Spirit at baptism is integral to his arguments for the essential unity of the Trinity based on trinitarian unity of activity. This chapter focuses upon Homilies 1, 2, and 3 of *hom. in Cant.* and analyses how Gregory understood the *subjective* reality of the soul's spiritual marriage with Christ in terms of the topics explored in Chapters 1 and 2, namely the role of the Spirit, trinitarian unity of activity, and baptismal exegesis.

Homily 1 (Song 1:1–4)

Baptismal Exegesis

Gregory begins Homily 1 by setting the scene for a marriage between his readers and Christ, which he says will be brought to fulfilment via the reading of the Song of Songs. Those awaiting such a marriage, says Gregory, have taken off the 'old humanity' like a filthy 'garment' (περιβόλαιον) (cf. Col. 3:9) and are now clothed with the 'lightsome raiment' (ἱμάτια) of the Lord, having 'put on' (ἐνδυσάμενοι) Jesus Christ (cf. Gal 3:27).[1] The noetic and moral transformation that accompanies the donning of this 'holy' attire, he says, readies one to encounter the 'mystical vision' of the Song of Songs, whereby

[1] *GNO* VI.24.14–16; Norris II, 15.

Christ, the Spirit, and Human Transformation in Gregory of Nyssa's In Canticum Canticorum. Alexander L. Abecina, Oxford University Press. © Oxford University Press 2024. DOI: 10.1093/oso/9780197745946.003.0007

154 ANALYSIS OF *IN CANTICUM CANTICORUM* (*c.* 391)

'the soul is in a certain manner led as a bride toward a *spiritual* (πνευματικήν) marriage with God'.[2] We have encountered just this nexus of concepts already in the present study, in such texts as *virg.* and *bapt. Chr.*, in direct connection with Gregory's theology of baptism. Gregory, we may already infer from this introduction to Homily 1, has already begun to undertake a baptismal exegesis of the Song of Songs. By this I mean the use of the language, imagery, and inner logic of his baptismal theology, according to which humanity is transformed and brought into union with God through the unified activity of Father, Son, and Spirit, to creatively illuminate the meaning of the scriptural text.[3]

Gregory's references in this homily to both the Great Command (cf. Mark 12:30) and Jesus' sixth beatitude (cf. Matt 5:8) offer a further clue that he is preparing to undertake a baptismal exegesis of the Song. As I showed in Chapter 1, Gregory alluded in *virg.* to these very scriptural references to specify the preconditions for marriage with Christ, which he showed could only be brought about by the life-giving power of the Spirit, couched in baptismal terms. In Homily 1, Gregory's discussion of the Bride's spiritual marriage with Christ is likewise presented in terms of one who 'loves [God], with his whole heart (καρδίας) and soul (ψυχῆς) and power (δυνάμεως)' (cf. Mark 12:30).[4] The Great Command to love God with the 'whole heart and power' (ἐξ ὅλης καρδίας τε καὶ δυνάμεως) continues also to underlie Gregory's reference to marriage as 'the human soul's mingling (ἀνάκρασις) with the divine'.[5] Before he concludes this homily, Gregory will refer to the Great Command for yet a third time in relation to the 'more perfect of soul' who enters spiritually into the Bridegroom's 'chamber'.[6] Importantly, by alluding to the sixth beatitude (cf. Matt 5:8), Gregory insists that the human mind (διάνοιαν) may be initiated (μυσταγωγεῖ) into the 'divine bridal chamber' only after the soul's desire for God's true Beauty has 'purified the heart' (ἐκκαθάρας τὴν καρδίαν).[7] In appealing to these scriptural passages, it appears that Gregory

---

[2] *GNO* VI.25.14–15; Norris II, 15.

[3] Cf. Dünzl, *Braut und Bräutigam*, 29; Contra Canévet, *Grégoire de Nysse et l'herméneutique biblique*, 276, who suggests that Gregory alludes to pre-baptismal chrismation; Cf. Jean Daniélou, 'Chrismation prébaptismale et divinité de l'Esprit chez Grégoire de Nysse', *Recherches de Science Religieuse*, 56 (1968), 177–198.

[4] *GNO* VI.16.10–11; Norris II, 17.

[5] *GNO* VI.22.19–23.8; Norris II, 25; cf. Miguel Brugarolas, 'Theological Remarks on Gregory of Nyssa's Christological Language of "Mixture"', *Studia Patristica*, 84 (2017), 39–58; cf. Sarah Coakley, '"Mingling" in Gregory of Nyssa's Christology: A Reconsideration', in *Who Is Jesus Christ for Us Today? Pathways to Contemporary Christology (a Festschrift for Michael Welker)*, ed. Andreas Schuele and Günter Thomas (Louisville, KY: Westminster/John Knox, 2009), 72–84.

[6] *GNO* VI.38.20–22; Norris II, 43.

[7] *GNO* VI.22.13–17; Norris II, 23.

BAPTISMAL EXEGESIS OF THE SONG OF SONGS   155

seeks to employ a baptismal exegesis of the Song not merely to offer an account of the *objective* reality of the soul's transformation and union with God, but rather to prepare the way for the reader's own experience of the *subjective* reality of this transformation and union within the 'noetic-erotic' depths of their whole person.

Pneumatic Language, Pneumatology, and Purified Desire

If Gregory's references to spiritual marriage and putting on the 'new clothing' of Christ, together with allusions to the Great Command and the sixth beatitude, are guided by what I am calling baptismal exegesis, we should expect this, based on my analysis of his works in Part I, to be accompanied by prominent references to the advent of the Holy Spirit. We observe that Gregory indeed gestures toward the pneumatological dimension of the soul's mingling with the divine, though only very subtly at first, by invoking what I defined in Chapter 1 as pneumatic language, here drawing upon the classic Pauline opposition between 'flesh' and 'spirit'. Gregory has already invoked pneumatic language from the very opening of Homily 1 by describing the soul's marriage to Christ as πνευματικήν.[8] Now, alluding twice to 1 Cor. 6:17—'but he who is joined to the Lord is one spirit with him'—a scriptural passage also used in *virg.* to describe the marriage of the virgin to Christ under the rubric of baptism, he speaks of the soul that 'once joined (κολληθείς) to the Lord may become one spirit (πνεῦμα ἕν) through being mingled (ἀνακράσεως) with that which is inviolate and impassible, having become purified thought rather than heavy flesh'.[9]

Notably, Gregory's present reference to 1 Cor. 6:17 and becoming 'one spirit' is illuminated by a later reference to becoming 'one spirit' in the final Homily 15 via an allusion to Eph. 4:3–4, where it occurs in direct connection with his discussion of the Holy Spirit as the agent unifying the church to Christ as his body.[10] As I argued in Chapter 1, we ought not to suppose that Gregory is ever casual in his deployment of pneumatic language given its contested use in the doctrinal debates of his day. Rather, his use of such

---

[8] *GNO* VI.25.14–15; Norris II, 15.
[9] *GNO* VI.23.3–6; 24.20–25.1; Norris II, 25; 27.
[10] *GNO* VI.468.11–12; Norris II, 497.

156 ANALYSIS OF *IN CANTICUM CANTICORUM* (*c.* 391)

language, especially in relation to 1 Cor. 6:17, is pneumatologically laden, as appears to be the case in Homily 1.

Gregory's appeal to pneumatology becomes much more explicit as he deploys pneumatic language further, portraying the reader of the Song of Songs as one 'ascending the spiritual (πνευματικόν) mountain' of Moses, as depicted in the Exodus narrative (cf. Ex. 19:10–14).[11] This ascent he also describes as being initiated (μυσταγωγουμένοις) into 'the spiritual mountain of the knowledge of God' (τῷ πνευματικῷ τῆς θεογνωσίας ὄρει).[12] Importantly, Gregory elaborates upon this 'spiritual mountain' imagery in relation to the 'fire' of the Lord mentioned at Exodus 19:18.[13] The God whom Moses meets on the mountain is thus said to be one who 'burns every material thing *with fire*' (τῷ πυρί).[14] This fire from God, in turn, finds a direct correlate in the human faculty of desire (ἐπιθυμητικόν), since it too may be said to be 'set on fire' (ἀναφλέξας).[15] The fiery passion of erotic human love (ἐρωτικὸν πάθος) therefore functions, for Gregory, as a figure of guidance for the soul to love (ἐρᾶν) the 'inaccessible beauty of the divine nature'.[16] However, unlike natural human desire that is normally enflamed with passion for material things, a purified desire for God turns fiery material passion into impassibility and quells every bodily disposition. Paradoxically, therefore, it is possible for *the mind* (διάνοιαν) to 'boil' with an erotic love for God (ζέειν ἐρωτικῶς), and yet Gregory points out this can only be actualized by the Spirit (μόνῳ τῷ πνεύματι) who he identifies as that 'fire' that the Lord came to 'cast upon the earth' (cf. Luke 12:49).[17]

This reading of 'fire' as the Holy Spirit in the present context is repeated in Gregory's identical reference to this same casting down of 'fire' by the Lord later in Homily 10. There, and by reasonable inference also in the present passage, Gregory interprets Ex. 19:18 in light of Jesus' saying in Luke 12:49, which he reads as foreshadowing the events of Pentecost outlined in Acts 2:3: 'and we know that the fire is the Holy Spirit that the Lord came to cast

[11] *GNO* VI.25.13; Norris II, 27.

[12] *GNO* VI.26.2; Norris II, 27; a similar phrase occurs in *v. Mos.*, *GNO* VII/1.82.1; Malherbe and Ferguson, 91.

[13] Τὸ δὲ ὄρος τὸ Σινὰ ἐκαπνίζετο ὅλον διὰ τὸ καταβεβηκέναι ἐπ᾽ αὐτὸ τὸν Θεὸν ἐν πυρί (Ex. 19:18 LXX).

[14] *GNO* VI.26.9–10; Norris II, 29, my italics.

[15] *GNO* VI.21.16; Norris II, 23.

[16] *GNO* VI.27.7–10; Norris II, 29.

[17] *GNO* VI.27.5–15; Norris II, 29. 'Anyone instructed in the Scriptures surely knows that instead of "Spirit" Scripture often thinks of it and designates it as "fire"'. Cf. *v. Mos.*, *GNO* VII/1.67.2–4; Malherbe and Ferguson, 79.

upon the earth (cf. Luke 12:49) and that was shared among the disciples in the form of tongues (cf. Acts 2:3)'.[18]

The Baptismal 'Kiss'

Thus far we have several indications that Gregory deliberately employs what I am calling a baptismal exegesis of the Song of Songs, marked by the imagery of being clothed, together with a gradual transition from fairly subtle use of pneumatic language toward more explicit references to the Holy Spirit's transforming activity in terms of a desire-inducing fire. It seems that the one essential feature that remains to confirm this claim is a more concrete reference to baptism itself. I suggest that this is precisely what we witness in Gregory's exposition of the line 'Let him kiss me with the kisses of his mouth' (cf. Song 1:2a), a passage dense with references to the Spirit, who mediates the encounter between Bride and Bridegroom as he 'flows' from the Bridegroom as though life-giving water from a fount. The language used to interpret this line of the Song is, as we shall see, strikingly similar to what was observed in *bapt. diff.*, where Jesus is portrayed as the baptismal 'fount' from whom one drinks as the Spirit descends like fire.[19] Thus, Norris Jr. correctly suggests that Gregory's portrayal of the 'kiss' as the 'first gift of grace' (τῆς πρώτης χάριτος) that makes one worthy of the 'first-fruits of the Spirit' (τῇ ἀπαρχῇ τοῦ πνεύματος) is 'symbolic of baptism'.[20] Gregory states:

> The bride Moses kissed the Bridegroom in the same way as the virgin in the song who says *Let him kiss me with the kisses of his mouth* (cf. Song 1:2), and through the mouth to mouth converse (ὁμιλίας) accorded him by God (as the Scripture testifies), he became more intensely desirous (ἐπιθυμίᾳ) of such kisses after these theophanies, praying to see the object of his yearning (του ποθούμενον) as if he had never glimpsed him. In the same way, all of the others in whom the divine desire (ὁ θεῖος πόθος) was deeply lodged

---

[18] *GNO* VI.295.13–15; Norris II, 311.

[19] Cf. *GNO* X/2.361.2.

[20] Norris II, 43 n.27, commenting on *hom. in Cant.*, *GNO* VI.40.8–9. J. Warren Smith, 'Becoming Men, Not Stones: Epektasis in Gregory of Nyssa's Homilies on the Song of Songs', in *Gregory of Nyssa: In Canticum Canticorum: Analytical and Supporting Studies. Proceedings of the 13th International Colloquium on Gregory of Nyssa (Rome, 17–20 September 2014)*, Supplements to Vigiliae Christianae 150, ed. Giulio Maspero, Miguel Brugarolas, and Ilaria Vigorelli (Leiden: Brill, 2018), 344, follows Norris: 'the "more perfect" represented by the young maiden who has received the kiss of grace are the newly baptized'.

158 ANALYSIS OF *IN CANTICUM CANTICORUM* (*c.* 391)

never ceased from desire (τῆς ἐπιθυμίας); everything that came to them from God for the enjoyment of the object of yearning (τοῦ ποθουμένου) they made into the material and fuel for a more ardent desire (ἐπιθυμίας). And just as now the soul that is joined (συναπτομένη) to God is not satiated by her enjoyment of him, so too the more abundantly she is filled up with his beauty, the more vehemently her longings (πόθοις) abound. For since the words (τὰ ῥήματα) of the Bridegroom are 'Spirit and Life' (πνεῦμά ἐστι καὶ ζωή ἐστι) (cf. John 6:63) and everyone who is joined (κολλώμενος) to the Spirit becomes spirit (cf. 1 Cor. 6:17; John 3:6) while everyone who is attached to Life (ὁ τῇ ζωῇ συναπτόμενος) 'passes from death to life' (cf. John 5:24), according to the Lord's word, it follows that the virgin soul longs (ποθεῖ) to approach the fount of the spiritual life (τῇ πηγῇ τῆς πνευματικῆς ζωῆς). And that fount is the mouth of the Bridegroom, whence 'the words (τὰ ῥήματα) of eternal life' (cf. John 6:68) as they gush forth fill the mouth that is drawn to it, just as the prophet does when drawing the Spirit (ἕλκων τὸ πνεῦμα) through his mouth. Since, then, it is necessary for the one who draws drink from the fount to fix mouth to mouth and the fount is the Lord who says, 'If anyone thirst, let him come to me and drink' (cf. John 7:37), it follows that the soul, thirsty as she is, will bring her own mouth to the mouth that pours out life (τῷ τὴν ζωὴν πηγάζοντι), saying 'let him kiss me with the kisses of his mouth'.[21]

The passage needs to be read as a direct continuation of Gregory's exposition of the ascent of Moses upon the 'spiritual mountain'. Here, Gregory compares Moses' encounter with the Bridegroom to his readers' own encounter with the Bridegroom via the Song of Songs. Moses' 'mouth to mouth' interaction with the Bridegroom is described first of all as 'conversation' or 'instruction' (ὁμιλίας) and hence naturally involves an issuing of 'words' (τὰ ῥήματα). Yet, Gregory's allusion to John 6:63 reveals that the 'words' received by the Bride from the Bridegroom are in fact 'Spirit' and 'Life'.

That Gregory has the Holy Spirit in view with his reference to John 6:63 rather than a merely generic notion of 'spirit' is supported by his comments in *Eun.* III regarding the inspiration of the words of scripture by the Holy Spirit. In the course of his debate with Eunomius over the meaning of 2 Cor. 3:17— 'The Lord is the Spirit'—Gregory notes that scripture consists of 'the words of the Holy Spirit' (τοῦ πνεύματός εἰσι τοῦ ἁγίου φωναί).[22] On this basis,

---

[21] *GNO* VI.31.8–33.1; Norris II, 33 and 35.
[22] *GNO* II.164.26–27; Hall III, 139.

he is able to make sense of Paul's teaching that, by turning from the dead letter of scripture to the Spirit, one apprehends a 'Lord who is the lifegiving Spirit', to which Gregory immediately adds further justification by quoting John 6:63: 'the sublime Gospel says, "The words which I speak are Spirit and Life"'.[23] Gregory's allusion to John 6:63 in *Eun.* III clearly has the Holy Spirit in view, and he appears to be making a similar point about the Spirit in *hom. in Cant.* to express the nature of Bride's reception of the life-giving 'words' of the Bridegroom. The Holy Spirit's activity of 'giving life' is therefore not peripheral but rather *essential* to the initial encounter between Bride and Bridegroom. Offering a gloss on 1 Cor. 6:17, probably via a conjunction with John 3:6, the 'kiss' is now understood in terms of being 'joined to the Spirit', who acts as intermediary and cause of the Bride's becoming 'spirit' herself.

That this whole encounter is couched in terms of baptism is demonstrated by Gregory's reference to John 7:37, which features prominently throughout *hom. in Cant.* The verse facilitates the mixing of metaphors as Gregory now pictures the flow of 'words' as the life-giving water of the Spirit issuing from the 'fount' of the Bridegroom. The same verse is quoted, for instance, in *bapt. Chr.* as an exhortation to receive the 'drink' of the Spirit from Christ at baptism, while the same image, as I have already noted, also features prominently in *bapt. diff.*[24] It is not a stretch of the imagination, therefore, to see Gregory directly drawing upon his 'linear' model of the single and unbroken transmission of 'life-giving power' from the Father, through the Son, and in the Spirit, to depict the baptismal 'kiss' between Bride and Bridegroom. To be sure, explicit reference to the Father is absent (a general feature of *hom. in Cant.* on the whole), as is the technical ἐκ—διά—ἐν phrasing. Nevertheless, in this passage, Gregory retains a very strong sense of unified activity of Christ (as Bridegroom) and the Spirit, as well as ordered differentiation of trinitarian persons, which the technical language of the 'linear' baptismal model was intended to safeguard.

---

[23] *GNO* II.165.17–22; Hall III, 140. So Martin Laird, *Gregory of Nyssa and the Grasp of Faith: Union, Knowledge and Divine Presence* (Oxford: Oxford University Press, 2004), 139: 'Gregory has subtly identified the words of the Bridegroom with the Holy Spirit', though I would contest the claim to subtlety; cf. Canévet, *Grégoire de Nysse et l'herméneutique biblique*, 326.

[24] Cf. *GNO* IX.235.19–20; NPNF II/5.523; *GNO* X/2.361.2.

160 ANALYSIS OF *IN CANTICUM CANTICORUM* (*c.* 391)

Power, Activity, and the Spiritual Senses

The application of a baptismal exegesis to Homily 1 would, I suggest, still be incomplete without the kinds of references to the post-baptismal transformation in virtue that we find, for instance, in *bapt. Chr.* and *Maced.* Gregory sets up this connection to the virtuous life, first by explaining the difference between God's 'power' and his 'activity', and then by explaining how human spiritual perception at the level of the divine activity may lead to the soul's 'noetic-erotic' transformation and perfection.

The distinction between divine 'power' and 'activity' is derived from Gregory's interpretation of the lines 'Let us love your breasts more than wine' (cf. Song 1:2) and 'The king brought me into his treasure house' (cf. Song 1:4b). According to Gregory, the 'treasure house' (θησαυρόν) of the Bridegroom's 'heart' stands for the hidden and ineffable 'power of the Godhead' (τῆς θεότητος δύναμιν).[25] Meanwhile, Gregory speaks of the Bridegroom's 'breasts', through which God suckles the 'life' (ζωήν) of each individual, and which lie nearby the treasure house of the 'heart', as the 'beneficent activities (τὰς ἀγαθὰς . . . ἐνεργείας) of the divine Power (τῆς θείας δυνάμεως)'.[26]

For Gregory, 'power' and 'activity' function as technical philosophical terms. In Hellenistic philosophy, they typically belong to the *nature-power-activity* triad, designed to articulate the manner in which a nature's capacity to act is distinctly manifested.[27] In Homily 1 the power-activity framework is employed, on the one hand, to underscore and safeguard the ineffability of God. Yet, while the framework can be used to emphasize the *difference* between power and activity, it also serves to emphasize fundamental *unity* between them. Thus, while Gregory appeals to the power-activity framework to uphold divine transcendence, it also provides him with the metaphysical framework for articulating a theory of the soul's capacity to 'sense' divine *activity* by which it may be led into deeper union with, though never complete apprehension of, the divine *power*.

Standing behind these two main uses of the power-activity framework in *hom. in Cant.* is Gregory's prior usage of it in his more polemical works to

---

[25] *GNO* VI.33.16–18; Norris II, 35.

[26] *GNO* VI.33.12–21; Norris II, 35.

[27] Barnes, *Power of God*, 13: 'Gregory understands δύναμις as the capacity to act that is distinctive to a specific existent and that manifests that nature of that existent'; cf. Pottier, *Dieu et le Christ selon Grégoire de Nysse*, 107–142.

BAPTISMAL EXEGESIS OF THE SONG OF SONGS   161

argue for trinitarian unity of persons. As Barnes notes, Gregory maintains that if the Father and Son manifest the same 'power' they share the same 'nature'.[28] Further, Barnes observes that when pneumatology is the focus of discussion, Gregory favours the more conventional attribution of 'activity' (ἐνεργεία) to the Spirit rather than 'power', which is typically associated with the Son.[29] Nevertheless, in the *pneumatological* context, Gregory's concept of 'activity' plays a similar role to 'power' in the *christological* context.[30] Thus, if the Son and the Spirit manifest the same 'activity', then by implication they share the same 'power' and hence the same 'nature'. When the *nature- power- activity* scheme is employed in *hom. in Cant.*, therefore, it is especially suited to communicating the unity of Christ and the Spirit at the level of 'activity', and by implication their ultimate unity at the level of 'power' and 'nature'.

With the technical distinction between divine 'power' and 'activity' in place, Gregory is now able to introduce into Homily 1 the related notion of a 'more divine' mode of perception (αἴσθησις), by which the soul is able to 'sense' divine *activity*, although not the ineffable divine *power* itself.[31] For instance, Gregory identifies a spiritual sense of 'taste' at the level of divine *activity* that perceives the spiritual milk of the divine 'breast'. Further, elaborating upon the touching of lips involved in the baptismal 'kiss', he posits a kind of 'touch' at the level of divine *activity* that 'makes contact' with the Word (ἡ ἁπτομένη τοῦ λόγοῦ), further described as an incorporeal and intelligible 'touching' (ἐπαφήσεως)'.[32] It is important to bear in mind, therefore, that the nature-power-activity distinction is presupposed as a metaphysical framework throughout *hom. in Cant.* wherever Gregory speaks of the soul's spiritual senses (e.g. touch, smell, taste, sight, hearing), even when the nature-power-activity framework is not explicitly invoked.

---

[28] Barnes, *Power of God*, 13.

[29] Barnes, *Power of God*, 16–17, 296–307.

[30] Cf. Barnes, *Power of God*, 296, commenting on *Ad Ablabium*: 'in specific arguments for the Holy Spirit that parallel earlier arguments for the Son, *activity* appears in the former where *power* appeared in the latter'.

[31] *GNO* VI.34.2–5; Norris II, 35, 37.

[32] *GNO* VI.34.11–14; Norris II, 37; cf. Hans Boersma, 'Saving Bodies: Anagogical Transposition in St. Gregory of Nyssa's Commentary on the Song of Songs', *Ex Audito*, 26 (2010), 177–178. So in *Eun.* II, 'Human thought . . . reaches out and touches (θιγγάνει) the unapproachable and sublime nature'; cf. *GNO* I.265.28–31; Hall II, 89.

162 ANALYSIS OF *IN CANTICUM CANTICORUM* (*c.* 391)

Post-baptismal Virtue and the Unified Activity of Christ and the Spirit

While the notion of spiritual 'touch' appears oriented primarily to the encounter between the Bride and the activity of the Word, Gregory indicates that spiritual 'smell' is oriented toward the Bride's encounter with Christ through the activity of the Holy Spirit. Thus, just as there is a spiritual sense of touch, '[i]n the same way, too, the scent (ὀσμή) of the divine perfumes (μύρων) is not a scent (ὀσμή) in the nostrils but pertains to a certain intelligible and immaterial faculty that inhales (συνεφελκομένης) the fragrance (εὐωδίαν) of Christ (cf. 2 Cor. 2:15) by drawing in the Spirit (τῇ τοῦ πνεύματος ὁλκῇ)'.[33] The implication is that one encounters Christ via spiritual *touch*, but only through the Spirit via spiritual *smell*.[34] The particular ordering of the spiritual senses of touch and smell is important here, and it reflects something of Gregory's anti-Sabellian notion of differentiated, *taxis* of the unified trinitarian activity in his baptismal theology.

An important background text that helps to clarify Gregory's notions of the spiritual sense of smell and its connection to the unified activity of Christ and the Spirit in Homily 1, and indeed throughout *hom. in Cant.*, is found in *Eun.* III Part 6. Gregory responds to Eunomius' claims about the begetting of the Son by the Father using the analogy of perfume and fragrance. In the process, according to Michel Barnes, he offers 'the definitive pro-Nicene exegesis of Heb 1,3 [*sic*]'.[35] Central to this exegesis is his taxonomy outlining four different ways that things derive from a cause (ἐξ αἰτίας): from 'material and art', 'material and nature', 'material emission' (ὑλικῆς ἀπορροίας), and a fourth 'where the cause is immaterial and incorporeal, while the begetting

---

[33] *GNO* VI.34.15–18; Norris II, 37.

[34] Cf. Canévet, *Dieu et le Christ selon Grégoire de Nysse*, 327–328; A similar perspective on the unity of the spiritual senses of touch and smell is found in *Maced.*, where Gregory argues that 'whosoever is to touch (ἄπτεσθαι) the Son by faith (διὰ τῆς πίστεως) must needs first encounter (προεντυγχάνειν) the perfume (τῷ μύρῳ) in the very act of touching (διὰ τῆς ἀφῆς); there is no part of him devoid of the Holy Spirit'. *GNO* III/1.103.1–10. While Gregory is most explicit about the spiritual sense of *touch* in this quote, Susan Ashbrook Harvey convincingly argues that the sense of *smell* is also directly implied by the 'encounter' here. Thus, commenting upon this text, Harvey, *Scenting Salvation: Ancient Christianity and the Olfactory Imagination* (Oakland: University of California Press, 2015), 21, states: 'I would also stress that Gregory's analogy is a functionally *olfactory* one, although the passage does not identify the model by its scent. Because the discussion explores Christ's divine anointment with the Holy Spirit, and because that image itself conflates Old Testament passages of priestly anointment with fragrant holy oil, the consideration of ointment in the analogy includes the ritual ointment's perfume. The sense would link with the pervasive image of the Holy Spirit as an invisible but perceptible fragrance for when scented oil has been absorbed into the skin it is the fragrance that is most immediately apparent'.

[35] Barnes, 'Contra Eunomium III 6', 370.

BAPTISMAL EXEGESIS OF THE SONG OF SONGS 163

is visible and corporeal.'[36] Regarding the third type of cause (i.e. material emission), Gregory uses the example of scents and perfumes. He states that this cause denotes cases where the original remains as it is, while what flows (ῥέον) from it is considered in itself, such as with the sun and its ray, a torch and its light, or scents and perfumes and their odour.[37]

According to Gregory, while none of these causes can be applied to the divine nature in a straightforwardly literal sense, we may, by analogy, form ideas of God from them,[38] though one must not include the 'corporeal implications of the words'.[39] Thus, Gregory points to the third cause of generation, 'material emission' (ὑλικῆς ἀπορροίας), as particularly apt to describe the divine mode of the Father's begetting of the Son. Here he cites an example of such generation that alludes to Song 1:3a, namely the 'odour of perfume' (ὀσμὴν μύρου).[40] According to Gregory, 'breath' does not imply the exhaling of matter, nor 'odour' the conversion (μετάστασιν) of perfume into vapour, nor 'radiance' the pouring out through rays of the substance of the sun, but rather that one exists from the other with no interval (διαστήματος) intervening between the Father and the one derived from him.[41] Gregory concludes from these analogies that the Son possesses a being (οὐσία) that is not alienated (οὐκ ἀπεξενωμένη) or broken off (ἀπερρωγυίᾳ) from its source in the Father.[42] His argument concludes on his exegesis of Heb. 1:3, which states that the Son is the 'radiance of glory', and to Song 1:3, which Gregory reads *christologically*, as referring to the Son as the 'odour of perfume'.[43]

In Homily 1, it appears that Gregory uses the 'material emission' mode of causation to a similar end as in *Eun.* III Part 6. However, the point is *not* to establish the inseparability of the Son and the Father at the level of 'being' (οὐσία), but rather to establish the inseparable unity of *Christ and the Spirit* at the level of divine *activity* (ἐνέργεια) within the economy. According to Gregory's technical philosophical framework, this implies a unity of Christ and the Spirit at the level of a single divine *power* and ultimately at the level of *nature*.

---

[36] *GNO* II.196.26–28; Hall III, 158.
[37] *GNO* II.196.28; Hall III, 158.
[38] *GNO* II.197.32–33; Hall III, 159.
[39] *GNO* II.198.34; Hall III, 159.
[40] *GNO* II.199.37; Hall III, 160.
[41] *GNO* II.199–200.39; Hall III, 160.
[42] *GNO* II.200.40; Hall III, 161.
[43] *GNO* II.202.46; Hall III, 162. There is a similar discussion in *Eun.* I, *GNO* I.87.12–13; Hall I, 110.

164   ANALYSIS OF *IN CANTICUM CANTICORUM* (*c.* 391)

The notion of spiritual senses, in connection with the fundamental inseparability of Christ and the Spirit at the level of divine *activity*, now offers a basis for Gregory's teaching on the soul's growing maturity in post-baptismal virtue. First, he notes that the superior 'perfumed ointments' (cf. Song 1:3a) relate to the incomparable 'Virtue itself' of God.[44] That God's 'name' is 'a perfumed ointment emptied out' (cf. Song 1:3a) suggests for Gregory that the 'divine power' cannot be contained by human thought or word.[45] Rather, human language can at best 'refer to some slight trace (βραχεῖαν) of the divine perfume (τοῦ θείου μύρου) that the whole creation imitates within itself (ἐν ἑαυτῇ)'.[46] Thus, for Gregory, human knowledge of God can be likened to the experience of smelling a perfume vessel that has been emptied out upon the created order. Humanity may *only guess* about the nature of the perfume itself (αὐτὸ τὸ μύρον) based on the faint vapour (ἀτμῶν) that is left behind.[47]

This manner of conceiving of the absolute Virtue of God in terms of the fragrance of perfumed ointments emptied out into the created order forms the relevant background for understanding Gregory's comments on those who are said to be 'more mature' in their advancement in virtue. Whereas the less mature have had their love for the Bridegroom merely *awakened* by the fragrance of the perfume, the 'more perfect soul' is likened to the one whom the Song says has already been brought into the king's 'treasure house' (cf. Song 1:4a) after having sensed this very same fragrance.[48] Therefore, commenting on the line 'The king brought me into his treasure house' (cf. Song 1:4a), he says:

> the soul that has desired (ποθήσασα) to touch (ἐφαψαμένη) the Good with the tips of her lips . . . cries out . . . that by the 'first-fruit of the Spirit' (τῇ ἀπαρχῇ τοῦ πνεύματος) (cf. Rom. 8:23)—of which she was made worthy by a 'kiss' (cf. Song 1:2)—she may . . . search 'the depths of God' (cf. 1 Cor. 2:10) and, like Paul, see (as he says) invisible things and hear unspeakable words (cf. 2 Cor. 12:2–4).[49]

The passage thus recalls the entire episode on the 'spiritual mountain' where the *baptismal* 'kiss' (cf. Song 1:2) takes place. Gregory's explicit references

[44] *GNO* VI.36.7; Norris II, 39.
[45] *GNO* VI.36.12–14; Norris II, 39.
[46] *GNO* VI.37.18–38.2; Norris II, 41.
[47] *GNO* VI.37.7–11; Norris II, 41.
[48] *GNO* VI.39.19; Norris II, 43.
[49] *GNO* VI.40.2–12; Norris II, 43.

to the spiritual senses of 'smell', 'touch', 'sight', and 'hearing' indicate that his exegesis of the Song continues firmly to operate within the *nature-power-activity* framework, and it is clear that this, just like his exposition of Moses' encounter with God, is cast in emphatically trinitarian and baptismal terms. Thus, not only is the soul 'awakened' to the virtuous life by the 'smell' of the divine the fragrance of Christ by inhaling the Spirit, but, once one has reached the 'treasure house' by advancing in spiritual maturity, it is by the same Spirit who joins one to Christ via the initial baptismal 'kiss' that one continues to desire to search the depths of God (cf. 1 Cor. 2:10).[50]

Homily 2 (Song 1:5–8)

Baptismal Illumination

My analysis of Homily 1 has shown that Gregory employs baptismal exegesis in his interpretation of Song 1:1–4. Given this emphasis on baptism, there is a curious absence of references to baptismal illumination. As he says in *or. catech.*, 'baptism' (βάπτισμα), 'illumination' (φώτισμα), and 'regeneration' (παλιγγενεσίαν) are all interchangeable terms that capture a different aspect of the one same reality.[51] We find, however, that the theme of illumination pervades Homily 2, a feature I suggest is best explained by Gregory's deliberate continuation of baptismal exegesis of the previous homily. While the saving efficacy of baptism is, for Gregory, grounded in trinitarian unity of activity, it is nonetheless true that the spiritual illumination of the baptized was traditionally attributed to the Holy Spirit, though of course not independently of the activity of Father and the Son.[52] As I showed in Chapters 1 and 5, in *virg.* Gregory spoke of the virgin's 'spiritual marriage' with Christ as only being possible through the life-giving power of the Spirit received at baptism, which uplifts the soul to be illuminated in the 'aetherial' realm. In *bapt. Chr.*, the post-baptismal life of virtue is depicted through the use of light imagery. We must be attuned to this baptismal framework for the soul's illumination,

---

[50] Gregory routinely upholds the connection between the Holy Spirit and searching the 'depths of God'; cf. *v. Mos*: GNO VII/1.66.22–67.2; 91.2–4; 108.10–11; Malherbe and Ferguson, 80, 98, 110.

[51] Ekkehard Mühlenberg, ed., *Oratio Catechetica*, GNO III/4 (Leiden: Brill, 1996), 82.2–5; Rowan A. Greer, trans., 'Concerning Perfection', in *One Path for All: Gregory of Nyssa on the Christian Life and Human Destiny*, assisted by J. Warren Smith (Eugene, OR: Cascade, 2015), 134.

[52] Cf. Laird, *Grasp of Faith*, 190–197; 190 n.68: 'Gregory follows the other Cappadocians in associating the Holy Spirit with light'.

166 ANALYSIS OF *IN CANTICUM CANTICORUM* (*c.* 391)

just as Gregory's listening congregation and his eventual readership would have been, if we are fully to appreciate the presence of pneumatology and trinitarian theology in Homily 2.

The central theme of light is introduced via Gregory's comparison of the text of the Song of Songs to the tent of witness of the Exodus narrative (cf. Ex. 40:34), having an 'exterior' corresponding to the Song's words, and an 'interior' that corresponds to the divine reality of God toward whom the words draw the reader. Thus, says Gregory, 'The things that belong to the interior . . . are a Person of many lights' who is the 'true Lampstand' and 'true Ark'.[53] The ability to read the text this way, and hence to draw near to God, he argues, requires the proper spiritual preparation. For, just as the law of Moses required the priest to be cleansed before entering the Holy of Holies, so one must 'wash' (πλύνῃ) the 'garment' (ἱματίον) of one's conscience through obedience to the 'law of the Spirit (ὁ τοῦ πνεύματος νόμος)' (cf. Rom. 8:2).[54] This is not merely a throw-away line, but a signpost alerting the listener-reader to pneumatological and baptismal elements that shall feature throughout the homily.

Illumination by Christ and the Spirit

Gregory proceeds to comment on the words spoken by the Bride to her maidens: 'I am dark and beautiful, O daughters of Jerusalem, as the tents of Kedar, as the curtains of Solomon' (cf. Song 1:5). Employing once again the metaphor of being 'clothed' (ἐπιβάλλοντος), which facilitated his baptismal exegesis in Homily 1, the Bride speaks of the Bridegroom's 'philanthropy' (φιλανθρωπίαν) in the incarnation, whereby her sin, represented by 'darkness' (μελανία), is transferred to the Bridegroom in exchange for his 'purity' and 'beauty' (τὸ κάλλος).[55] Since human transformation is conceived as a transition *out of darkness*, Gregory will come to express being clothed in Christ's beauty in terms of divine illumination.

Crucially, Gregory's notion of being adorned with Christ's lightsome raiment is expressed in terms of Christ indwelling the soul in association with baptism. First, commenting on Song 1:5, Gregory sees the Bride speaking to her maidens, declaring that they will become the 'curtains' of Solomon's

[53] *GNO* VI.44.16–17; Norris II, 49.
[54] *GNO* VI.45.11–12; Norris II, 49.
[55] *GNO* VI.46.6–13; Norris II, 51.

BAPTISMAL EXEGESIS OF THE SONG OF SONGS   167

temple when King Solomon 'dwells within' (ἐνοικήσαντος).[56] Gregory claims
to find support for this reading of the indwelling of Christ under the figure
of 'Solomon' in Romans, where Paul establishes the love of God for us on
the ground that, when we were sinners and 'dark', God made us full of light
(φωτοειδεῖς) by shining (ἐπιλάμψαι) his grace upon us (cf. Rom. 5:1–8).[57]
With the coming of this light, the Bride's life is transformed into 'luminous
grace' (μορφὴ πρὸς τὴν φωτεινὴν χάριν).[58]

The connection between Christ's indwelling and baptism is established
via Gregory's immediate citation of 1 Tim. 1:14 and the account found
there of Paul's own transformation. Gregory understood the apostle to have
taught that Christ came 'to make dark ones bright (λαμπρούς)' and to 'shine
like stars' (λάμπειν ὡς φωστῆρας) by the 'laver of rebirth' (τῷ λουτρῷ τῆς
παλιγγενεσίας) through the washing of darkness with water.[59] The Spirit's
agency is not directly mentioned here, though this is hardly necessary. That
Gregory understood the power of baptismal regeneration and illumination
to come from the Holy Spirit is demonstrated, for example, in *Eun*. I. Hence,
rebutting his Eunomian opponents, he asks, 'why do they believe in the Holy
Spirit…? How can they after their mortal birth be born again (ἀναγεννῶνται)
by baptism, when on their view even the power (δυνάμεως) that gives them
rebirth (ἀναγεννώσης) does not by nature possess indefectibility and self-
sufficiency'.[60] The immediate implication of Gregory's comment on baptism
is that the illumination of the Bride is brought about not only by Christ's
indwelling as 'Solomon' but also by the Spirit's regenerative power, a sign of
the unified activity of Christ and the Spirit.

Baptism, Pneumatology, and the Restoration of Humanity

Since the removal of the darkness of sin is brought about by baptismal illumination, Gregory naturally conceives of humanity's fall into sin as a falling
away from an original state of divine brightness. It is against this background
that he interprets the lines 'Do not gaze at me, for I have been made dark, because the sun has looked askance at me' (cf. Song 1:6).[61] While human nature

[56] *GNO* VI.47.16–17; Norris II, 53.
[57] *GNO* VI.48.3–14; Norris II, 53.
[58] *GNO* VI.48.13; Norris II, 53.
[59] *GNO* VI.48.15–49.4; Norris II, 53.
[60] *GNO* I.111.21–112.3; Hall I, 125.
[61] *GNO* VI.50.16; Norris II, 55.

168 ANALYSIS OF *IN CANTICUM CANTICORUM* (*c.* 391)

came into existence as a copy of the true light, temptation and trial, by their 'fiery heat', destroyed 'the shoot' of humanity while it was still without root (cf. Matt 13:3–23; Luke 8:5–15).[62] Gregory must reassure his readers that the 'sun', which is typically a *positive* symbol of God's divine light, rightly functions here now as a *negative* symbol of temptation. Thus, he identifies several scriptural passages indicating how the church receives divine protection from the fiery 'sun' that darkens. For instance, the Psalm teaches that the Lord protects from the burning sun (cf. Ps. 120[121]:6), while Isaiah speaks of 'daughters' being lifted 'on shoulders' (ἐπ᾿ ὤμων) and 'children' (παῖδας) carried on 'covered vehicles' (λαμπήναις), thus needing protection from 'sunshades' (σκιαδείοις) (cf. Isa. 49:22; 60:4; 66:20).[63]

It is quite telling, however, that Gregory not only justifies the use of the 'sun' as a negative symbol here, but also uses the scriptural verses he has just cited as an opportunity to illustrate the post-baptismal life in the power of the Spirit. Thus, for Gregory, these very same scriptural passages simultaneously supply images of 'the virtuous life' (τὸν ἐν ἀρετῇ . . . βίον) of those who are as 'newborn' children (ἀρτιγενές), and of 'the soul that is being led to God *as a bride*' (τὴν τῷ θεῷ νυμφοστολουμένην ψυχήν).[64] Most importantly, the obscure reference to the 'covered vehicle' (λαμπήνην) is said to refer to 'the shining grace of the enlightenment' (τὴν ἐκλαμπτικὴν τοῦ φωτίσματος χάριν) by means of which we become 'children' (παῖδες) that are carried from earth to the 'heavenly life' (πρὸς τὴν οὐρανίαν ζωήν).[65] Norris Jr. rightly remarks, 'This is no doubt an allusion to baptism, for which φωτισμός . . . was a traditional designation'.[66]

Although Norris notes that the reference to λαμπήνη (literally a covered chariot) is 'obscure', I suggest we make best sense of it as being synonymous with the ὄχημα (chariot, vehicle) to which Gregory refers in several other writings to represent the virtuous form of life that ascends heavenward, empowered by the Holy Spirit, as I discussed in Chapter 5. That the role of the Holy Spirit in offering protection from temptation is not far from Gregory's discussion of baptismal enlightenment is apparent from his reference in this section to 'the cloud of the Spirit (τῇ νεφέλῃ τοῦ πνεύματος), which the Lord would spread out for such souls to serve them as a shelter (σκέπην)'.[67]

---

[62] *GNO* VI.51.11–19; Norris II, 57.
[63] *GNO* VI.51.19–52.10; Norris II, 59.
[64] *GNO* VI.52.11–15; Norris II, 59, my italics.
[65] *GNO* VI 52.17–53.2; Norris II, 59; cf. Timothy P. McConnell, *Illumination in Basil of Caesarea's Doctrine of the Holy Spirit* (Minneapolis, MN: Fortress Press, 2016), 9–69.
[66] Norris II, 59 n.18.
[67] *GNO* VI.53.5–7; Norris II, 59.

BAPTISMAL EXEGESIS OF THE SONG OF SONGS   169

Thus, while the 'sun' of temptation led to the darkening of humanity's original brightness, Gregory employs a baptismal exegesis of Song 1:6b to also show that baptismal rebirth and illumination through the Spirit restores humanity's original brightness, protects from temptation, and thus unites one's soul to Christ in spiritual marriage.

The exegesis of Song 1:6b regarding humanity's fall into sin leads to further elaboration on the theme of divine illumination. Naturally, Gregory identifies the 'vineyard' with the paradisal garden of Genesis.[68] Thus, he highlights a feature of the Genesis narrative that sees the human being cast out of the garden and made 'a dweller in the place of the setting sun' (τῶν δυσμῶν) after having been removed from 'the sunrise' (τῆς ἀνατολῆς) (cf. Gen 3:24).[69] Yet, this casting out is viewed against the broader horizon of the eventual overcoming of darkness by the rising of divine light. Gregory points out that scripture teaches that when the light has shined in the darkness, the darkness will be transformed (μεταποιηθῇ) into brightness and the dark one may become beautiful again.[70] Therefore, the 'vineyard' of Song 1:6b stands for the site of humanity's return to the original godlikeness of the paradisal state—a return to the state of the one who 'at the beginning shone with the true Light'.[71] Because of God's love, the Bride can exclaim that she has become 'full of light (φωτοειδής)'.[72] The 'fruit' of this vineyard is then identified as 'purity' (καθαρότης) that is 'ripe and gleaming' (λαμπρός) and whose appearance is 'a shining like the sun's' (ὁ ἡλάξων).[73]

As I showed in my analysis of Gregory's baptismal exegesis of Gen. 2–3 in *virg.*, he views the Holy Spirit as a chief agent in humanity's return to the original, paradisal state of godlikeness, expressed in terms of the restoration of the divine image. Gregory's emphasis upon the Bride's illumination as a return to the original lustrous state would suggest that the same baptismal theology and pneumatology is in operation in the present homily. There is confirmation of this when, referring to the fruitful 'vineyard', he says, '[t]he abundant leaves, shaken delicately against the branches by the gentle wind (τῷ ἠρεμαίῳ πνεύματι), are the manifold adornment of the divine virtues, which belong to those who are sprouting together by the Spirit (τῶν συναναθαλλόντων τῷ πνεύματι)'.[74]

---

[68] *GNO* VI.57.10; Norris II, 63.
[69] *GNO* VI.57.11–13; Norris II, 63; cf. Gen. 3:24.
[70] *GNO* VI.57.15; Norris II, 65.
[71] *GNO* VI.60.1–2; Norris II, 67.
[72] *GNO* VI.60.18–20; Norris II, 67.
[73] *GNO* VI.60.6–8; Norris II, 67.
[74] *GNO* VI.60.11–14; Norris II, 67.

The Spirit as 'Drink' Poured from Christ's Side

The trinitarian dimension of Gregory's baptismal exegesis becomes ever more apparent as he proceeds to comment on the line 'Speak to me, you whom my soul loves, where do you pasture your flock, where do you rest them at the noontide?' (cf. Song 1:7). Taking Jesus' Parable of the Lost Sheep (cf. Luke 15:3–7) to speak of the incarnation, he identifies Christ with the 'Good Shepherd' (cf. John 10:11) who took 'the whole human nature' (πᾶσα ἡ ἀνθρωπίνη φύσις) as one flock of sheep upon his shoulders.[75] Yet, Gregory is intent to show that the saving effect of Christ's assumption of human nature is inseparable from the activity of the Spirit. Hence, presenting a series of allusions to the 'divine waters' of John's gospel for 'those who thirst' (τοῖς διψῶσι) (cf. John 7:37), Christ is depicted as the fountain from whom the flock of 'sheep' that is humanity drinks and thus receives eternal life. The Bride is said to run to 'the Fountain' (τὴν πηγήν) to draw in 'the divine drink' (τοῦ θείου πόματος) and become a spring 'welling up to eternal life' (cf. John 4:14). Further, evoking the baptismal 'kiss' (cf. Song 1:2), previously described as a 'mouth to mouth' encounter (στόμα κατὰ στόμα) in Homily 1, the Bride is said to drink from Christ's pierced side that was given a 'mouth' (ἀναστομώσαντος) by the spear (cf. John 19:34), and thus takes 'rest at midday' in the 'unshadowed light' (ἐν τῷ ἀσκίῳ φωτί).[76]

The allusion to John 4:14 is important for identifying the essential role of the Spirit in Gregory's understanding of Christ's incarnation. In *Eun.* III Part 8, Gregory cites John 4:14, stating that the one who has received the 'grace' of the Holy Spirit will become a spring *welling up to eternal life* (cf. John 4:14).[77] In Homily 5 of *hom. in Cant.*, Gregory identifies the Holy Spirit as the warm wind that melts the one frozen by idolatry into water *welling up into eternal life* (cf. John 4:14).[78] While the Spirit is identified as 'grace' in the former passage, and as 'wind' in the latter, in both passages Gregory clearly views the Spirit as the agent who causes one to well up as water leading to eternal life. We ought to conclude that, in Homily 2, Gregory cites John 4:14 with a similar purpose to speak of the Holy Spirit as the 'drink' that pours from Christ's side at the cross (cf. John 19:34), causing eternal life to be given to 'the whole of human nature'. Thus, even in the union of the whole of human

---

[75] *GNO* VI.61.8–9; Norris II, 69.
[76] *GNO* VI.62.1–10; Norris II, 69.
[77] *GNO* II.246.15–17; Hall III, 191.
[78] *GNO* VI.147.18–148.3; Norris II, 161.

BAPTISMAL EXEGESIS OF THE SONG OF SONGS 171

nature to Christ, humanity is not saved independently of the life-giving activity of the Spirit. Already we see here a glimpse of Gregory's Spirit-based christology working in tandem with his baptismal exegesis.[79]

Importantly, Gregory introduces the terms 'son of the light' (υἱὸς φωτός) and 'son of the day' (υἱὸς ἡμέρας), a reference to 1 Thess. 5:5, to refer to those 'sheep' who have truly entered this noonday rest of Song 1:7.[80] The phrases 'son of the light' and 'son of the day' are baptismal phrases that connote adoption as sons of God by the Holy Spirit, as demonstrated by Gregory's use of these phrases in *perf.* There he states, 'Through his birth from above (τῆς ἄνωθεν γεννήσεως), and through His making us 'children of the day and children of light' (cf. 1 Thess. 5:5) born 'of water and the Spirit (δι' ὕδατος καὶ πνεύματος) (cf. John 3:5) . . . He himself acts as our guide in this birth in the water of the Jordan, drawing the grace of the Spirit upon the first-fruit of our nature.[81] The allusion to 1 Thess. 5:5 in the present context of the illumination of baptism (φωτισμός) not only harks back to his earlier reference in this homily to the 'newborn' protected from the 'sun' by the shade of the Spirit, but foreshadows several more substantive comments Gregory will make later in Homily 10 that are explicitly about the Holy Spirit, in whom human persons are adopted as 'sons of light' and 'sons of day'.

Homily 3 (Song 1:9–14)

Transformation through Baptismal Waters

According to Gregory, Song 1:1–8 expounded in Homilies 1 and 2 functions as a 'preface' (προοιμίοις) to what follows. The opening two lections are therefore likened to the mere glow that occurs 'before the dawn' (αὐγῇ). It is 'not a pure light (καθαρὸν φῶς)', he says, 'but light's preface' (ἀλλά φωτός ἐστι προοίμιον) that is meant to point to the 'sunrise of the true light'.[82] This interpretive move is determined by the fact that the present lection (i.e. Song 1:9–14) is spoken in the voice not of the Bride but of the Bridegroom himself. Thus, Gregory intensifies the light imagery prominent in Homily 2 as the

[79] Maspero views the fontal imagery as a reference to Father and the Son, rather than Christ and the Spirit. Cf. Maspero, 'The *In Canticum* in Gregory's Theology', 34–35.
[80] *GNO* VI.62.13–14; Norris II, 69.
[81] *perf., GNO* VIII/1.202.3–5; Woods Callahan II, 114, slightly modified.
[82] *GNO* VI.70.13–20; Norris II, 79.

172 ANALYSIS OF *IN CANTICUM CANTICORUM* (*c*. 391)

voice of the Bridegroom 'like a sun's orb rises up and eclipses with the light of its rays all the brightness of the stars that shone earlier and of the glistening dawn'.[83] This 'sunrise' of the Bridegroom's direct speech is described as 'a participation (μετουσία) in the Godhead itself (τῆς θεότητός)' and 'a fellowship (κοινωνίαν) with the undefiled power (τῆς ἀκηράτου δυνάμεως)'.[84]

Gregory will return to this sun-ray imagery momentarily when commenting upon Christ's indwelling within the Bride in terms of the power-activity distinction. First, however, via an exposition of the line 'I have likened you, my close one, to my horse among the chariots of Pharaoh' (cf. Song 1:9), he introduces the notion that such indwelling is conditional upon the Bride's prior purification by virtue. Naturally, Gregory takes this verse as a reference to the Exodus narrative, yet since the original narrative makes no reference to any 'horse', he reasons, on the basis of Hab. 3:8, that it stands for 'the invisible power' (ἀόρατος δύναμις) of the 'the angelic host'.[85] The Bride of the Song may come to be likened to this angelic cavalry only if she runs 'the race of virtue', which makes her fit to accept the Word as her rider.[86] Therefore, one cannot become like the 'horse' unless one is liberated by 'the water of the mystery' (διὰ τοῦ μυστικοῦ ὕδατος . . . ἐλευθερούμενος) and leaves behind in the water every sin and evil and rises up 'purified'.[87] Here, we see Gregory once again employing a baptismal exegesis of the Song in continuity with the baptismal exegesis of Homilies 1 and 2.[88] Gregory indicates that while Christ's indwelling is dependent upon the acquisition of virtue, the virtuous life is itself conditional upon baptism.

The Spiritual Senses and the Unified Activity of Christ and the Spirit

Despite the initial cleansing in baptismal waters, the Bride is still not ready, argues Gregory, to be indwelt by the king. First, the Bride must be adorned with 'likenesses of gold' (cf. Song 1:11), which stand for *instruction* about the 'ineffable nature' (τῆς ἀρρήτου φύσεως) of God.[89] Since God's nature

[83] *GNO* VI.70.20–71.3; Norris II, 79.
[84] *GNO* VI.71.5–8; Norris II, 79.
[85] *GNO* VI.74.9–13; Norris II, 83.
[86] *GNO* VI.76.16–17; Norris II, 85.
[87] *GNO* VI.7.2–8; Norris II, 87.
[88] Norris, 87 n.9, notes the water in Homily 3 'is plainly the water of baptism, of which the Red Sea is a type'; cf. Dünzl, *Braut und Bräutigam*, 77.
[89] *GNO* VI.85.16; Norris II, 95.

BAPTISMAL EXEGESIS OF THE SONG OF SONGS   173

'transcends the mind's grasp', Gregory indicates that the soul 'must bring the nature that transcends all intellect within herself by faith alone'.[90] The paradoxical notion of intimate communion with a God who is by nature ineffable motivates Gregory's following discussion of 'faith' in relation to the human spiritual senses, a topic already introduced in Homily 1. Even after the Bride has received instruction about God's 'ineffable nature', the Bridegroom is still not manifested to her 'eyes', but his presence is mediated by an ensemble of other sensory faculties:

> she *touches* (ἐφάπτεται) the one she seeks through her sense of *smell* (ὀσφραντικῆς αἰσθήσεως), as if by her power of *smell* she recognized the distinctive quality of some *color*, and she says that she recognizes his *scent* (τὴν ὀσμήν) by means of the *fragrance* of a perfume (τῇ εὐωδίᾳ τοῦ μύρου) whose name is *spikenard* (νάρδος) (cf. Song 1:12b).[91]

This appeal to the spiritual senses in turn alerts us to the fact that Gregory is invoking the framework already introduced in Homily 1, although now it is the first and third terms of the standard *nature-power-activity* triad that are emphasized. This philosophical framework is used to navigate further the paradox of God, who indwells the soul yet remains wholly ineffable.

Thus, when the Bride states, 'My spikenard gave off his scent' (cf. Song 1:12), Gregory takes this to mean that the Bride senses in *her own* perfume (διὰ τῆς εὐπνοίας τοῦ ἐμου μύρου) the fragrance of the Bridegroom himself (τὴν αὐτου ἐκεινου εὐδωίαν τῇ αἰσθήσει)'.[92] Furthermore, it means that the 'fragrance' (εὐωδία) of the incomprehensible being is 'blended within us (ἐν ἡμῖν)' by the virtues and imitates (μιμουμένη) that which is by nature (τῇ φύσει) the Undefiled, Good, Incorruptible, and Unchangeable. In short, the virtue of the Bride imitates the true Virtue (τὴν ἀληθινὴν ἀρετήν) of God.[93] Gregory suggests that as the Bride draws near to the Bridegroom, it is his *activity* and not his *nature* that becomes diffused within her. In this way, the soul that has drawn near to the Bridegroom may turn her spiritual senses 'inwardly' upon herself in order to encounter the Bridegroom, but only at the level of divine *activity* blended within the soul, which imitates the unapproachable divine *nature*.

---

[90] *GNO* VI.87.5–8; Norris II, 97; cf. Laird, *Grasp of Faith*, 86.
[91] *GNO* VI.88.13–17; Norris II, 99, my italics.
[92] *GNO* VI.89.3–7; Norris II, 99.
[93] *GNO* VI.89.19–80.2; Norris II, 99 and 101.

174 ANALYSIS OF *IN CANTICUM CANTICORUM* (*c.* 391)

The same nature-activity framework is then applied to the analogy of the sun and its rays with which Gregory introduced the present homily. Therefore, the virtuous person cannot look directly upon the Word just as one cannot look directly at the sun. Yet, says Gregory, he sees 'the sun within himself' (ἐν ἑαυτῷ) like a mirror, since the rays (ἀκτῖνες) of divine Virtue shine (ἐλλάμπουσαι) upon the purified life and make the Invisible visible and the Incomprehensible comprehensible'.[94] Thus, just as human beings do not have direct visual perception of the Sun, but only of the sun's rays, by analogy one cannot have a direct spiritual perception of God's *nature*, but only of his *activity*, which may be manifested within the soul as virtue imitating divine Virtue.[95]

So far, a selection of different sensory analogies have been used to speak of a *single reality* of human encounter with God. Hence, Gregory states, 'it is one and the same thing to speak of rays of the sun (ἀκτῖνας . . . ἡλίου) or emanations of virtue (τῆς ἀρετῆς ἀπορροίας) or aromatic fragrances (τὰς ἀρωματικὰς εὐωδίας) [i.e. of perfume]. For no matter which of these we adopt to express the point of our text, all of them give rise to a single notion'.[96] What, we might ask, accounts for Gregory's imaginative conflation of fragrance, light, and virtue language in Homily 3? On the surface, they are all linked to the concept of the 'material emission' mode of causation I discussed in my analysis of Homily 1. Yet, as I showed earlier, the 'material emission' model of causation serves to illustrate Gregory's deeper point about the ultimate *unity* of all divine activity with a single divine power and nature. This means that even though the Song of Songs may speak of multiple divine activities correlated to different spiritual senses under a plurality of analogies of 'material emission', these activities are all inseparable, being fundamentally united under a single notion since they all derive from one divine *power* and *nature*.[97]

This point is crucial to understanding Gregory's comments in this homily on Christ's indwelling of the soul together with the Holy Spirit. As we saw in Homily 1, spiritual *smell* is oriented toward the Bride's encounter with Christ

[94] *GNO* VI.90.10–16; Norris II, 101.
[95] Cf. Lenka Karfíková, 'The Metaphor of the Mirror in Platonic Tradition and Gregory's Homilies on the Song of Songs', in *Gregory of Nyssa: In Canticum Canticorum: Analytical and Supporting Studies. Proceedings of the 13th International Colloquium on Gregory of Nyssa (Rome, 17–20 September 2014)*, Supplements to Vigiliae Christianae 150, ed. Giulio Maspero, Miguel Brugarolas, and Ilaria Vigorelli (Leiden: Brill, 2018), 265–287.
[96] *GNO* VI.90.16–19; Norris II, 101.
[97] Precisely this point is made by Gregory in *ep. 5* (*GNO* VIII/2.78.26–79.6).

BAPTISMAL EXEGESIS OF THE SONG OF SONGS 175

through the activity of the Holy Spirit. In his first explicit reference to the Holy Spirit in Homily 3, Gregory presents a similar idea:

> knowledge of the Good that transcends every intellect comes to us through the virtues, even as it is possible through some image (εἰκονος) to get a glimpse (ἀναλογίσασθαι) of the archetypal Beauty. So it was with the Bride Paul. He imitated (μιμούμενος) the Bridegroom by *his* virtues and inscribes within himself the unapproachable Beauty by means of their fragrance (εὐώδους), and out of the fruits of the Spirit (ἔκ τε τῶν καρπῶν τοῦ πνεύματος)—love and joy and peace and the like (cf. Gal. 5:22–23)—he blended this *spikenard* (τὴν νάρδον). Hence he said that he was 'the fragrance of Christ' (Χριστοῦ εὐωδίαν) (cf. 2 Cor. 2:15), capturing within himself the scent (ἐν ἑαυτῷ ὀσφραινόμενος) of that transcendent and unapproachable Grace and providing himself for others to have a part according to their ability, as though he were an incense (θυμίαμα).[98]

The appeal to the spiritual senses means we must again assume the *nature-power-activity* framework is operative even though it is not mentioned explicitly. That is, while Gregory has already acknowledged Christ to be Virtue according to his 'nature', Paul *imitates* Christ by means of the 'emanations of virtues' within himself at the level of *activity*. Yet, at the very same time, Gregory conceives of the virtues in terms of the olfactory sense vis-à-vis the 'fragrance of Christ' (cf. 2 Cor. 2:15). These virtues he associates with 'love and joy and peace' and hence simultaneously with the 'spikenard' blended from the 'fruits of the Spirit' (cf. Gal. 5:22–23). What appears to underlie this passage is a notion identical to that which Gregory introduced in Homily 1 whereby one 'inhales' the fragrance of Christ but only by drawing in the Spirit (τῇ τοῦ πνεύματος ὀλκῇ).[99] Hence, Gregory has portrayed Paul as a site of the intimate, unified, yet differentiated activity of Christ and the Spirit such that he can be said to be an imitator of the unapproachable beauty and grace of the divine nature.

---

[98] *GNO* VI.91.3–11; Norris II, 101; Verna E. F. Harrison, *Grace and Human Freedom According to St. Gregory of Nyssa*, Studies in the Bible and Early Christianity Volume 30 (New York: Edwin Mellen Press, 1992a), 99–107; cf. Gabriel Horn, 'L'Amour Divin', *Revue d'ascetique et mystique*, 6 (1925), 378–389.

[99] *GNO* VI.34.15–18.

176 ANALYSIS OF *IN CANTICUM CANTICORUM* (*c.* 391)

Baptismal Exegesis of Christ's Anointing by 'Spikenard'

Given that Gregory understood the Bride's (i.e. Paul's) 'spikenard' to be blended from the fruits of the Holy Spirit, which then emanate the 'fragrance of Christ' *for others* around him, we thereby gain insight into his immediately following interpretation of the Bride's 'spikenard' (cf. Song 1:12b) in connection with the perfume poured on Jesus' head in Matt. 26:6–13 (cf. //Mark 14:3–9//John 12:1–8). It is helpful to begin with Origen of Alexandria's interpretation of this line from the Song, which bears important similarities to Gregory's.[100]

In *Cant.*, Origen drew a parallel between Song 1:12b and the anointing of Jesus' *feet* (cf. John 12:3) rather than of his head. He took the 'Mary' who anointed Jesus' feet to stand for the church, arguing that Mary's ointment was originally 'scentless' (*quae prius odorem non dederat*).[101] Only *after* she anointed Jesus' feet and wiped them with her hair is she said to receive the ointment back, now steeped with the fragrance of the virtue of Christ's body (*ad semet ipsam unguentum ex qualitate ac uirtute corporis eius*).[102] Importantly, the odour that then fills the whole house is identified by Origen as the 'grace' of the Holy Spirit (*et recipiens ex hoc gratiam Spiritus Sancti*).[103] We have, therefore, a clear precedent in Origen for the pneumatological exegesis of this episode in the gospel and in the Song.

Origen's pneumatological interpretation appears to have influenced Gregory, though he adds his own emphases in basic agreement with the baptismal exegesis he has already undertaken in Homilies 1–3. First, he believes that the Song of Songs and the gospel accounts appear to teach that 'the spikenard' (νάρδος) in the gospel is akin (συγγενές) to the perfume (μύρον) of the Bride.[104] Beginning with the plain sense of the scripture, he interprets the woman's action as 'foreshadow[ing] with the perfume (διὰ τοῦ μύρου) the mystery of the death (τὸ τοῦ θανάτου μυστήριον)', just as Jesus states, 'She has prepared me for burial' (cf. Matt. 26:12). He proceeds to suggest that the house that is 'filled with fragrance (τῆς εὐωδίας)' can be understood to stand for the 'entire cosmos', which similarly absorbs the 'perfume's scent' (ἡ ὀσμή) through the preaching of the gospel.[105] Therefore, drawing an analogy

---

[100] Cf. Canévet, *Grégoire de Nysse et l'herméneutique biblique*, 278–279.
[101] *Cant.* 278. 9.1; Lawson, 160.
[102] *Cant.* 278. 9.3; Lawson, 160.
[103] *Cant.* 280. 9, 5; Lawson, 161.
[104] *GNO* VI.92.8–13; Norris II, 103.
[105] *GNO* VI.92.16–93.3; Norris II, 103.

BAPTISMAL EXEGESIS OF THE SONG OF SONGS   177

between the gospel account and the Song of Songs, Gregory suggests, 'in the Song of Songs, the spikenard (νάρδος) conveys to the Bride the scent (ὀσμήν) of the Bridegroom, while in the Gospel the fragrance (ἡ εὐωδία) that then filled the house becomes the anointing (χρῖσμα) of the whole *body* of the church (τοῦ σώματος τῆς ἐκκλησίας) in the whole cosmos'.[106]

Crucially, Gregory's interpretation of Matt. 26:6–13 in light of Song 1:12b is framed in terms of Christ's 'burial' (cf. Matt. 26:12) to which he refers using baptismal language as the 'mystery of death'.[107] That baptism is most certainly in the background of Gregory's exegesis is confirmed by his sudden and curious reference to the 'fragrance' (ἡ εὐωδία) that fills the house *not* as Origen's 'grace' but as the 'anointing' (χρῖσμα) of the whole church. On one other occasion in *hom. in Cant.* (cf. Homily 12), Gregory associates 'anointing' with the Holy Spirit,[108] while in other works the term is often associated with the Holy Spirit's activity, as is notably the case in his deployment of the 'anointing argument' in the anti-Macedonian works, in *Apoll.* and in *hom. in 1 Cor. 15:28*.[109] It follows that Gregory's exegesis of Matt. 26:6–13 reinforces the point he made earlier about the exemplary apostle Paul. Just as Paul emitted the 'fragrance of Christ' to others through the blending of the 'fruits of the Spirit', so too the church, as Christ's body baptismally anointed by the Spirit, performs this same function in the whole cosmos. The implication of Gregory's exegesis, therefore, is that the Christian church, just like Paul, becomes a site for the unified activity of Christ and the Spirit in the world. This, in turn, agrees with Gregory's notion, uncovered in Chapter 2, that trinitarian unity of activity is a basic causal and teleological principle operative within the entire cosmic order.

That Gregory's interpretation of Matt. 26:6–13 in Homily 3 is an instance of baptismal exegesis is confirmed by his interpretation of Song 3:6 in Homily 6 regarding the line 'Who is this coming up from the wilderness, like tree trunks of smoke, myrrh being burnt and frankincense, from all the powders of the perfumer?'. There he notes that myrrh is used to prepare for burial, while frankincense is for honouring the divine.[110] Thus, the one who seeks to

---

[106] *GNO* VI.93.4–8; Norris II, 103.

[107] In *ep. 24* baptism is the 'mystery of salvation'; cf. *GNO* VIII/2.75.8–9.

[108] *GNO* VI.364.15–17; Norris II, 385.

[109] So Manabu Akiyama, 'Johannine Eschatology of the In Canticum', in *Gregory of Nyssa's Mystical Eschatology*, Studia Patristica CI, ed. Giulio Maspero, Miguel Brugarolas, and Ilaria Vigorelli (Leuven: Peeters, 2021), 155 notes: 'We could recognize here an allusion of Gregory to the ecclesiastic practice: in the Byzantine rite, indeed, the confirmation or χρῖσμα is administered together with baptism'.

[110] *GNO* VI.189.1–4; Norris II, 201.

178   ANALYSIS OF *IN CANTICUM CANTICORUM* (*c.* 391)

honour God, says Gregory, must 'first become myrrh . . . having been buried together with the one who submitted to death', a clear reference to baptism (cf. Rom. 6:3–4; Col. 2:12).[111] This 'myrrh', Gregory then proceeds to note, is 'that myrrh which was used to prepare the Lord for burial', importantly citing again Matt. 26:12 to support this baptismal reading. Immediately following, he quite fittingly interprets the 'powders of the perfumer' (cf. Song 3:6) *pneumatologically* such that the one who inhales these powders 'becomes sweet smelling because having been anointed he has become full of the Spirit (τοῦ μεμυρισμένου πνεύματος πλήρης γενόμενος)'.[112] Thus, in Homily 6, as in his exegesis of Song 1:12b in Homily 3, Gregory observes a clear baptismal and hence *pneumatological* significance in Jesus' proleptic preparation for burial with myrrh in Matt. 26:6–13.

Unified Activity of Christ and the Spirit

Evidently, Gregory's reference to 'anointing' (χρῖσμα) in Homily 3, which I suggest is a probable allusion to baptismal anointing by the Holy Spirit, is echoed in his exegesis of the immediately following line of the Song, 'My kinsman is for me an oil of myrrh (στακτῆς), he shall lie between my breasts' (cf. Song 1:13). Gregory likens this practice to wives who use some 'aromatic herb' (ἄρωμα) concealed within their clothing to make their bodies seem pleasing to their husbands by its 'sweet aroma' (τῇ τοῦ ἀρώματος εὐπνοίᾳ).[113] The practice of the 'noble-minded' virgin, however, takes 'the bundle' of myrrh to be 'the Lord himself' (αὐτὸς ὁ κύριος), who lies in the 'conscience' (συνειδήσεως), dwelling in her 'very heart' (αὐτῇ μου τῇ καρδίᾳ), and gives the body a sweet smell (τὴν εὐοσμίαν).[114] Elaborating further upon the physiology of the heart, Gregory is eager to point out that it lies anatomically 'between the breasts', that it is 'a source of heat (θερμοῦ) within us' and, by being 'heated by the heart's fire' (ἔνθερμά . . . τῷ πυρὶ τῆς καρδίας), that all the limbs of our body are kept 'alive' (ζωτίκα).[115] Each one of these details is then directly related to the unified activity of Christ and the Spirit:

---

[111] *GNO* VI.189.4–10; Norris II, 203.
[112] *GNO* VI.189.13–15; Norris II, 203; cf. *GNO* VI.34.15–18; *GNO* VI.34.15–18.
[113] *GNO* VI.94.4–5; Norris II, 105.
[114] *GNO* VI.94.7–12; Norris II, 105.
[115] *GNO* VI.94.12–19; Norris II, 105.

BAPTISMAL EXEGESIS OF THE SONG OF SONGS   179

When, then, she has accepted the fragrance (εὐωδίαν) of the Lord (cf. 2 Cor. 2:15) within her ruling part (ἡγεμονικῷ) and has made her heart a container for such incense, she accustoms all the several pursuits of her life, like the limbs of some body, to boil by the Spirit (ζέειν . . . τῷ . . . πνεύματι) that spreads from her heart, and no lawlessness chills the love (ἀγάπην) of God in any member of her body.[116]

While it is 'the Lord himself' who is said to be taken into the Bride's 'heart' acting as a container for the fragrant 'myrrh', Gregory says it is the Holy Spirit, acting as though it were 'the heart's fire' that boils the 'perfume', who actively enlivens love for God in every aspect of the Bride's life. The analogy that Gregory has formed here harks back to Homily 1, and his identification of the 'fire' cast down by the Lord on the 'spiritual mountain' as the Holy Spirit. He spoke there of loving the divine beauty of God through the 'mind' (τὴν διάνοιαν) that 'boils' with love, but 'only by the Spirit' (μόνῳ τῷ πνεύματι), because it is heated by that 'fire' that the Lord came to 'cast upon the earth'. In Homily 3, it is not the mind per se, but rather the conscience, heart, and *hegemonikon* that are in view, yet here again we see Gregory emphasizing the joint activity of Christ and the Spirit in actualizing the Bride's *subjective* experience of love for God by which she is transformed in the depths of her whole person.

Conclusion

I have shown in this chapter that Gregory consistently employs a baptismal exegesis of Song 1:1–14 throughout Homilies 1–3. As with his exegesis of Genesis 1–2 in *virg.*, this approach to interpreting the Song does not so much have in view a literal baptismal ritual as it does an account of human transformation and union with God in terms of the inner logic of Gregory's baptismal doctrine. Gregory's interpretive strategy invites his reader continually to undergo a kind of 'baptism' analogous to actual baptism in the depths of their person—heart, mind, body, and soul—in the very act of reading and comprehending the deeper meaning of the Song of Songs. My claim that Gregory undertakes 'baptismal exegesis' in Homilies 1–3 (and indeed throughout all of *hom. in Cant.*) is given strong support by J. Warren

[116] *GNO* VI.94.19–95.3; Norris II, 105.

180 ANALYSIS OF *IN CANTICUM CANTICORUM* (*c.* 391)

Smith's suggestion that Gregory's homilies comprise a Lenten sermon series. If the co-incidence of Epiphany with the traditional date of Christ's baptism marked a popular occasion for one's enrolment as a candidate for baptism, while Easter marked the occasion of baptism itself, then the period of Lent was ideally suited for extensive preaching on the baptismal theme.

Crucial to this baptismal exegesis is the metaphysical distinction Gregory draws among God's nature, power, and activity. This supplies Gregory with the technical framework necessary to uphold the essential unity of trinitarian persons in a single *power* and *nature*, and yet to allow for ordered differentiation in their unified *activity* within the economy of salvation. Further, this distinction is especially suited to the exegesis of the Song's rich use of sensory language since it forms a basis for a theory of the soul's spiritual senses, and thus for an account of human transformation and union with God from the perspective of 'noetic-erotic' *subjective* experience. It will, as I shall show in Chapter 7, endow this subjective transformative experience with its uniquely 'epektatic' character. I suggest that on the basis of Gregory's deliberate baptismal exegesis of the Song of Songs in Homilies 1–3 we already gain a sense in which he is developing an account of the *subjective* reality of human transformation and union with God that coheres with his doctrinal account of that *objective* reality. On this basis, Homilies 1–3 may now provide a hermeneutical touchstone for the remainder of my analysis of *hom. in Cant.*

7

Advancement and Ascent

The Unified Activity of Christ and the Spirit

Introduction

In this Chapter I analyse Homilies 4, 5, 8, 9, 10, 11, and 12 of *hom. in Cant.* These homilies build upon Gregory's baptismal exegesis in Homilies 1–3 by interpreting the Song of Songs in light of the continued transformation of the Bride by the unified activity of Christ and the Spirit. As I showed in my analysis of *Maced.*, Gregory claimed that the 'downward' transmission of life *from* the Father, *through* the Son, and *in* the Holy Spirit at baptism has a corresponding 'upward' movement in the reverse order, whereby the baptized may come to 'behold' and, hence, actually be 'joined' to the eternal 'glory' of the Trinity. The homilies analysed in this chapter trace this 'ascent' of the Bride to union with Christ through the Spirit as a further outworking of Gregory's baptismal exegesis. The themes covered here include Gregory's notions of the soul's perpetual 'epektatic' purification and transformation into likeness to the Spirit, culminating in participation in divine 'glory'. That Gregory conceives of this 'ascent' as an 'advancement' (προκοπή) suggests it is analogous to Jesus' own postpassion 'advancement' into unity with the Only-begotten Son by the Spirit's 'anointing', as discussed in Chapters 3, 4, and 5.

Homily 4 (Song 1:15–27)

Purification and Advancement to Christ via the Spirit

Human nature, says Gregory, was in the beginning 'golden' and 'gleaming' (λάμπουσα) because of its 'likeness' to God, but became darkened by turning to evil.[1] In this condition, restoration to its original lustre cannot come about,

---

[1] *GNO* VI.100.16–18; Norris II, 113.

Christ, the Spirit, and Human Transformation in Gregory of Nyssa's In Canticum Canticorum. Alexander L. Abecina, Oxford University Press. © Oxford University Press 2024. DOI: 10.1093/oso/9780197745946.003.0008

182 ANALYSIS OF *IN CANTICUM CANTICORUM* (*c.* 391)

he suggests, unless, like gold, the human soul undergoes repeated purification as if in fire. Therefore, Gregory observes that the Bride of the Song of Songs undergoes several phases of purification. At the first stage she comes to be identified with the 'handsome form of the horse' (cf. Song 1:9), but in light of Song 1:15a—'Behold, you are beautiful, my close one'—she comes to be identified as the 'close one', having reached a second stage of purification. Importantly, Gregory describes each stage of Bride's purification as an upward 'ascent' (ἄνοδος) that is at the same time an 'advancement' (προκοπήν) of the soul toward God.[2] That the Holy Spirit, already identified with purifying 'fire' in Homily 1, is essential to Gregory's notion of the soul's Christ-like 'advancement' toward God will become a major theme of Homily 4 and subsequent homilies.

The Bride's second stage of purification is described in terms of the human capacity to choose between virtue and vice, where Gregory notes that humans 'take on the shape (συσχηματίζεσθαι) of whatever we want (ἄν ἐθέλῃ)'.[3] In other words, human persons are like a mirror reflecting the image of that which they elect to draw near. According to Gregory, the human person is 'transformed' in accordance with its choices, and in this way is 'likened to a mirror. If it looks upon gold, gold it appears, and by way of reflection it gives off the beams of that substance (τὰς ταύτης αὐγὰς τῆς ὕλης)'.[4] Thus, by choosing to come close to the 'archetypal Beauty' who is the Bridegroom, the Bride becomes beautiful herself 'informed like a mirror' by the Bridegroom's appearance.[5] Gregory employed the analogy of the 'mirror' already in Homily 3 in relation to the *nature-power-activity* framework, and it is evident that a similar use of the analogy is operative here.

While Gregory's initial comparison of 'the close one' to a 'mirror' depicts the encounter between the Bride and the activity of the Bridegroom, his following comments on Song 1:15b—'Behold, you are beautiful: your eyes are doves'—indicate that this encounter is inseparable from a corresponding activity of the Holy Spirit. First, he appeals to the physical phenomenon of seeing the image of faces in the pupils that look upon someone. Gregory says, 'people receive in themselves the likeness of whatever they gaze upon intently', and in this manner the eyes of the Bride take the 'image (εἶδος) of a dove'.[6] Naturally, in light of the gospel accounts of Christ's baptism (cf.

---

[2] *GNO* VI.115.3–4; Norris II, 129.
[3] *GNO* VI.103.15–16; Norris II, 115.
[4] *GNO* VI.104.4–6; Norris II, 115.
[5] *GNO* VI.104.1–2; Norris II, 115.
[6] *GNO* VI.105.10–16; Norris II, 117.

ADVANCEMENT AND ASCENT   183

Matt. 3:16//Mark 1:10//Luke 3:22; John 1:32), the 'dove' is identified as the Holy Spirit, and Gregory proceeds to allude to several Pauline passages that speak of life in the Spirit in distinction to that characterized by the fleshly (σαρκικός) and the merely psychic (ψυχικός) (cf. 1 Cor. 15:44–46).[7] Thus, if one no longer gazes upon 'flesh and blood' but looks to 'the spiritual life' (πρὸς τὸν πνευματικὸν βίον), 'lives by the Spirit', 'walks by the Spirit' (cf. Gal. 5:25), and becomes 'wholly spiritual' (ὅλος δι' ὅλου πνευματικός), then this soul has in its eyes the 'shape of the dove', and the 'imprint of the spiritual life' (τὸν χαρακτῆρα τῆς πνευματικῆς ζωῆς) is beheld in the soul.[8]

Gregory does not employ the analogy of the mirror in commenting on Song 1:15b, though the notion of receiving the 'imprint' (τὸν χαρακτῆρα) of the spiritual life on the soul and, a little later, receiving the 'imprint of the dove' (τοῦ τῆς περιστερᾶς χαρακτῆρος) functions in virtually the same way.[9] We also note here the very dense concentration of pneumatic language, including Gregory's references to the term 'the spiritual life', which he first used in Homily 1 in the context of the baptismal 'kiss'.[10] Clearly, Gregory's use of these terms is heavily laden with pneumatology. Thus, for Gregory, the Bridegroom declares the Bride to be beautiful, not only because her soul radiates *his own* beauty by choosing to draw near to him, but also because the eye of her soul and the whole manner of her life bear the imprint of the Holy Spirit.

Seeing the Beauty of God in Christ with the Eyes of the Spirit

That the Bride draws close with the eyes *already* affected by the prior imprint of the Spirit is also important for Gregory. Thus, he points out, 'for the first time, the virgin gazes upon the form of the Bridegroom, now, that is, that

[7] Gregory's dispute with Apolinarius' tripartite anthropology, which divided the human person into body, soul, and spirit (cf. 1 Thes. 5:23), prompted him to explain the differences among lives that are fleshly, psychic, and spiritual. Regarding the interpretation of 1 Cor. 14:45, the 'first Adam' is described only as a 'living soul' because he sinned, while the incarnate Christ is called life-giving 'spirit' because he did not sin (cf. Orton, 118). Later on, Gregory notes that Paul distinguishes between the 'person of soul' (cf. 1 Cor.15:45) who is said to be halfway between the 'person of flesh' and the 'person of spirit' (cf. 1 Cor. 3:1). Thus, the 'person of flesh' is weighed down by the burden of the body, the 'person of spirit' keeps their thought fixed on sublime matters, and the 'person of soul' displays features both fleshly and spiritual (cf. Orton, 221). Furthermore, a 'person of spirit' is one whose 'mode of life tends towards things above' (cf. Orton, 222).

[8] *GNO* VI.105.17–106.4; Norris II, 117.

[9] *GNO* VI.106.5–6; Norris II, 117.

[10] Cf. *GNO* VI.32.12.

184 ANALYSIS OF *IN CANTICUM CANTICORUM* (*c.* 391)

she has the dove in her eyes (for "No one can say, 'Jesus is Lord!' except by the Holy Spirit") (cf. 1 Cor. 12:3)'.[11] Unlike Origen, who took the reference to the eyes like 'doves' of Song 1:15 to point to the Bride's ability to understand the 'spirit' *of the scriptures* via the Holy Spirit, Gregory's citation of 1 Cor. 12:3 facilitates the emphatically anti-Macedonian and anti-Eunomian point that having the Spirit's imprint in the eye of the soul is a *precondition* for beholding the Beauty of the Bridegroom.[12] Gregory's association of the Spirit with the eye of the soul evokes Hellenistic theories, such as those found among Stoics and Galen, regarding of the role of vital or psychic *pneuma* (described as luminous and light-like) in ordinary human visual perception.[13] Perhaps Gregory's idea is that the divine Pneuma is necessary for seeing Christ as 'Lord', just as vital or psychic pneuma is, according to some philosophical theories, necessary for visualizing everyday objects.

Whatever the case may be, the appeal to the Spirit is especially important in view of Christ's incarnation, since Gregory argues that Christ's human body veils the divinity from human spiritual perception. For Gregory, Christ had to come 'in the shadow by our bed' (cf. Song 1:16), that is, 'shaded by the garment of a body' since mortal and perishable humanity cannot see the face of God and live (cf. Ex. 33:20). It is necessary, therefore, for the sake of fallen humanity's preservation, that the incarnate 'body' of Christ 'mediates' (ἐμεσίτευσεν) between 'the Light' of God and 'us who live in darkness'.[14] Only with eyes receptive of the Spirit, however, is the Bride capable of seeing the Bridegroom for who he truly is, 'the very essence of the Beautiful' (τοῦ καλοῦ ἡ οὐσία).[15] The underlying anti-Macedonian tenor of this Homily gives rise to a subtle and complex interplay in Gregory's thought between the notions of humanity's fallenness, the necessity for the pure divinity of Christ to be 'shaded' in the form of the incarnate human body, and the need to have the Spirit in the eye of the soul in order to declare Jesus, veiled in human flesh, as 'Lord'.

The same pattern of seeing God via eyes purified by the Spirit is reiterated later in Homily 4. Gregory identifies the first 'stage' of the Bride's

[11] *GNO* VI.106.7–11; Norris II, 117.

[12] For other citations of 1 Cor. 12:3, cf. *Eun.* I, *GNO* I.180.4–6; Hall I, 168; *fid.*, *GNO* III/1.67.22–23; *Maced.*, *GNO* III/1.98.27–28; 114;4–5; *Steph. 1*, *GNO* X/2.91.6–7.

[13] Cf. Katerina Ierodiakonou, 'On Galen's Theory of Vision', *Bulletin of the Institute of Classical Studies*, Supplement 114, Philosophical Themes in Galen (2014), 239ff; cf. D. C. Lindberg, *Theories of Vision from Al-Kindi to Kepler* (Chicago: University of Chicago Press, 1976), 1–17.

[14] *GNO* VI.108.7–10; Norris II, 119.

[15] *GNO* VI.106.17–107.4; Norris II, 119.

advancement as being made like the 'horse' (cf. Song 1:9), the second as the soul becoming the 'close one' (cf. Song 1:15) having the eyes made like doves, and now the third as the Bride brought ever closer, no longer as the 'close one', but as 'sister' of the Master (cf. Song 2:2).[16] Here, he has in mind *adoption* as brothers, sisters, and mothers (i.e. family) of God. That Gregory understands this third stage of 'ascent' and 'advancement' (προκοπήν) in the Bride's purification *pneumatologically* is made explicit by his reference to the Pauline notion of adoption by the Holy Spirit (cf. Rom. 8:15). Thus, 'she has been adopted by "the Spirit of Sonship" into this kinship'.[17]

This is the second time in *hom. in Cant.* that Gregory has referred to human transformation in terms of the Pauline notion of adoption as children. In Homily 2, the link between adoption and the activity of the Spirit was somewhat subtle, but here is explicit. Importantly, given that the subject is 'adoption', the Bride does not now look to the Bridegroom, but with the eyes of the Spirit is said to behold 'the Father'.[18] Thus, at each stage of the Bride's progressive purification depicted so far in the Song of Songs, the Holy Spirit's activity alongside Christ's has been crucial for Gregory. Not only does the Bride become an adopted 'sister' who beholds the Father by the Spirit, but she becomes a 'horse' only through baptismal water, and becomes a 'close one' who looks upon Christ by receiving the imprint of the Spirit.

Excursus: Sarah Coakley on Romans 8 and the 'Incorporative' Model of the Trinity

I have already mentioned briefly in the Introduction Sarah Coakley's comments on Homily 4, especially as it relates to Gregory's allusion to Rom. 8:15, but her views repay closer investigation. In *God, Sexuality and the Self*, Coakley contrasts two kinds of trinitarian models derived from the New Testament that are given varying articulations in early Christianity. The first of these is denoted 'incorporative' or 'reflexive' since 'in it the Holy Spirit is perceived as the primary means of incorporation into the trinitarian life of God, constantly and "reflexively" at work in believers in the circle of response to the Father's call'.[19] The second model is denoted 'linear' since the 'primary

[16] *GNO* VI.115.4–8; Norris II, 129.
[17] *GNO* VI.115:12–16; Norris II, 129.
[18] *GNO* VI.115:13; Norris II, 129.
[19] Sarah Coakley, *God, Sexuality and the Self: An Essay 'On the Trinity'* (Cambridge: Cambridge University Press, 2013), 111.

186 ANALYSIS OF *IN CANTICUM CANTICORUM* (*c.* 391)

focus is given to the Father-Son relationship, and the Holy Spirit becomes the secondary purveyor of that relationship to the church'. She sees this model embedded specifically in John's gospel.[20] The scriptural roots of the incorporative-reflexive model, argues Coakley, are located chiefly in Romans 8 'with its description of the cooperative action of the praying Christian with the energizing promptings of the Holy Spirit'. Perceptively, she notes that with regard to the incorporation of creation into the life of the Son, Romans 8:15–16 assigns both logical and experiential priority to the Spirit.[21]

For Coakley, Gregory of Nyssa, like the other Cappadocians, understood inclusion into the Trinity in terms 'characteristically more explicitly "linear"'.[22] Yet, in her *Modern Theology* article, as we have seen, Coakley also notes that in Homily 4 of *hom. in Cant.*, Gregory offers a 'reflection on the *incorporative* theme of Romans 8'.[23] And in Coakley's follow-up work she offers further comment on Homily 4, observing that '[i]nstead of the Spirit inviting one into the *taxis* of the three-in-one one on a linear or "chain" model of ascent . . . in the *Song* commentary we get something inspired much more directly by the *reflexive*, dialectical, *incorporation* suggested by Rm 8.14–27 [*sic*]'.[24] Arriving at a new insight after the publication of *God, Sexuality and the Self*, Coakley states, 'Gregory's *Song* commentary represents, I now see, a final assimilation and expression by him of what I call the *Romans 8* model, worked out with unusual freedom and originality'.[25]

Coakley is right to observe the presence of two 'trinitarian models' in Gregory's thought, which I have discussed in Chapter 2. However, while she recognizes that the difference between the two models is not an absolute one *according to the New Testament* sources,[26] she does not explain how they might be connected in Gregory's own thought. Indeed, as I have already pointed out, Coakley seems to suggest the incorporative-reflexive model is, for Gregory, something of a radical departure from the linear type—what I called in my Introduction a '*discontinuous* development'. By contrast, I argue for a more plausible explanation, more firmly rooted in several of Gregory's writings.

---

[20] Coakley, *God, Sexuality and the Self*, 101, 111 n.12.
[21] Coakley, *God, Sexuality and the Self*, 112.
[22] Coakley, *God, Sexuality and the Self*, 138.
[23] Coakley, 'Re-Thinking Gregory of Nyssa', 439, my italics.
[24] Coakley, 'Spiritual Ascent and Trinitarian Orthodoxy', 367, my italics.
[25] Coakley, 'Spiritual Ascent and Trinitarian Orthodoxy', 367 n.32.
[26] Coakley, 'Spiritual Ascent and Trinitarian Orthodoxy', 111 n.12.

ADVANCEMENT AND ASCENT   187

As argued in Chapter 2, from as early as the composition of *Maced.* there is strong evidence that Gregory already understood the 'linear' baptismal-trinitarian model as the appropriate way to describe *the initiating phase* of divine descent and Christian ascent—one that is *always destined* to be and in certain ways *already is* incorporated into that eschatological reality described by the 'circular' trinitarian model. Considered together as they ought to be, Gregory's 'linear' scheme is no less incorporative than the 'circular' scheme, in Coakley's sense. The basis for the relationship between these two models, as I have argued in preceding chapters, is not the Spirit's promptings of the praying Christian, but rather the incarnate Christ himself vis-à-vis his own baptism in the Jordan as 'first-fruit', and the subsequent post-passion transformation and incorporation of his flesh into the intra-trinitarian circle of glorification by the 'anointing' of the Spirit. This would have been an impossible synthesis for Gregory without recourse to the 'anointing argument', which he learned from the anti-Eunomian tradition.

To anticipate the argument of Chapter 8, so far as concerns the literary structure of *hom. in Cant.*, Homilies 13, 14, and 15 mark a clear transition point in Gregory's exegesis of the Song of Songs from the 'linear' model to the 'circular' one, essentially as a recapitulation of the baptismal argument already articulated in *Maced.*, which I analysed in Chapter 2. As we would expect, there are precursors to his climactic comments on the 'circular' model throughout *hom. in Cant.*, especially in Homilies 7, 8, and 9, as we shall see.

Second, while Coakley rightly identifies Romans 8 as a key source for what she calls the 'incorporative' model in *hom. in Cant.*, I suggest that she makes it do too much of the heavy lifting. Gregory does not cite Romans 8 to the same effect anywhere else in his corpus. Rather, it seems that for Gregory the key text supporting the incorporative *trinitarian* model is in fact John's gospel, specifically John 17:5 and John 17:22–23 as discussed previously (though it needs to be recognized that there is a strong connection with the incorporative *christological* model of Acts 2:36). As I have shown in Chapters 2 and 4, these passages are cited multiple times in Gregory's corpus, and often in connection with the 'incorporative' model. Gregory cites them not only in support of his contention that Christ's flesh was incorporated into the intra-trinitarian 'glory' by the Spirit's anointing, but also in support of the view that the church too is incorporated into this same 'circular' glory by an analogical process. The verses are worth quoting for the purposes of my forthcoming argument:

188 ANALYSIS OF *IN CANTICUM CANTICORUM* (*c.* 391)

> John 17:5—And now, Father, glorify me in your presence with the *glory* I had with you before the world began.

> John 17:22–23—I have given them the *glory* that you gave me, that they may be one as we are one—I in them and you in me—so that they may be brought to complete unity.

I suggest that the 'incorporative' significance of Romans 8 is, for Gregory, largely guided by the more prominent 'incorporative' use of what we might now call the John 17 model. Consider, for example, Romans 8:16–17:

> The Spirit himself testifies with our spirit that we are God's children. Now if we are children, then we are heirs—heirs of God and co-heirs with Christ, if indeed we share in his sufferings in order that we *may also share in his glory*.

There are obvious resonances between the Johannine and Pauline passages cited, not only in their trinitarian structure (recall, Gregory reads 'glory' pneumatologically in John 17), but crucially in their common references to sharing in Christ's 'glory'. It is not surprising, therefore, that Gregory conflates two of these passages in Homily 7 (to be discussed at length in Chapter 8), specifically with regard to the Bride's identification through baptism with Christ's death and resurrection into the 'glory' he had with the Father and the Spirit. Thus:

> and [Christ] was restored again to the glory proper to the divinity, which he possessed from the beginning, before the cosmos existed (cf. John 17:5) . . . the one who suffers with him will be fully glorified with him (cf. Rom. 8:17).[27]

The dovetailing of Romans 8 and John 17 in *hom. in Cant.* lends support to my contention that, *pace* Coakley, Gregory's incorporative use of Romans 8 in *hom. in Cant.* does *not* mark a new insight for Gregory but, rather, a recapitulation of earlier trinitarian and Spirit-based christological thought.

---

[27] *GNO* VI.242.14–19; 243.19; Norris II, 253; 255.

Homily 5 (Song 2:8–17)

The Spirit and the Coming of the Incarnate Christ

The unceasing nature of the Bride's 'ascent' toward the Bridegroom continues to be a central theme in Homily 5. Gregory opens by noting how the present lection (i.e. Song 2:8–17) 'evoke[s] a desire (ἐπιθυμίαν) for the contemplation of transcendent goods' yet our soul grieves with the 'despair of our grasping the Incomprehensible'.[28] This is because the soul realizes that even though it has been purified 'through love' (δι' ἀγάπης) and has been exalted in her 'participation in the Good' (τὴν τοῦ ἀγαθοῦ μετουσίαν), she has still not 'laid hold of what she seeks'.[29] Interpreting the line 'The voice of my kinsman' (cf. Song 2:8a), he claims the Bride has only but 'a reference to the "voice" of the One who is desired', which creates a 'plausible conviction' but not yet 'assurance'.[30]

Despite the Bride's lack of certainty, Gregory adopts a hopeful stance regarding her spiritual advancement stemming from his interpretation of the line 'Behold, he is coming' (cf. Song 2:8), which, for Gregory, speaks of the incarnation of Christ as the final fulfilment of prophecy. Thus, 'these expressions look forward to the economy of the divine Word, made known to us in the gospel, announced beforehand by the prophets but revealed through God's manifestation in the flesh'.[31] Furthermore, the line 'Behold, he stands behind our wall, looking through the windows, peeping through the lattices' (cf. Song 2:9) is also about the prophecy concerning Christ's incarnation. For Gregory, the 'windows' stand for the prophets, who are said to 'bring in the light (τὸ φῶς εἰσάγοντας)', while the 'lattices' are identified as the 'law's injunctions'.[32]

Thus, through the law and the prophets 'the beam of the true Light (ἡ αὐγὴ τοῦ ἀληθινοῦ φωτός) steals into the interior. After that, however, comes the Light's perfect illumination (ἡ τελεία τοῦ φωτὸς ἔλλαμψις), when, by its mingling (συνανακράσεως) with our nature, the true Light shows itself to those who are in darkness and the shadow of death' (cf. Ps. 23[24]:4, LXX).[33] Here, the beams refer to the 'beams (αἱ αὐγαι) of the prophetic and legal *ideas*'

---

[28] *GNO* VI.137.4–8; Norris II, 151.
[29] *GNO* VI.137.8–10; Norris II, 151.
[30] *GNO* VI.138.8–12; Norris II, 151.
[31] *GNO* VI.140.9–10; Norris II, 153.
[32] *GNO* VI.144.19–145.5; Norris II, 157.
[33] *GNO* VI.145.5–9; Norris II, 159.

190 ANALYSIS OF *IN CANTICUM CANTICORUM* (*c.* 391)

(νοημάτων) that 'illumine the soul' (ἀλλάμπουσαι τῇ ψυχῇ) and 'induce a desire (ἐπιθυμίαν) to see the sun in open air'.[34] Gregory's reference to the 'mingling' of the true light with our nature, such that it becomes illumined and desires to see God, is clearly focused on Christ's incarnation.

While Gregory begins with the coming of Christ as the fulfilment of prophecy, he instinctively proceeds to relate the event of the incarnation to the corresponding advent of the Spirit. Therefore, the Song's reference to 'the winter is past' (cf. Song 2:11) marks the changing of seasons from the 'winter' that stands for the fallen state of man. In this state of wintery frozenness, 'human nature cannot be changed for the better because it is frozen stiff by the chill of idolatry'.[35] Gregory then applies the same notion introduced in Homily 4, that we adopt the form of that upon which we look, spelling out now both its positive and negative implications. Thus, 'just as those who look upon the true Godhead (πρὸς τὴν ἀληθινὴν θεότητα) take to themselves the characteristics of the divine nature (τὰ τῆς θείας φύσεως ἰδιώματα), so too the person who is devoted to the vanity of idols is transformed into the stone he looks upon and becomes other than human'.[36]

At this point, Gregory adds to the *incarnational* perspective with which he introduces the homily an accompanying *pneumatological* perspective on humanity's rescue from the harsh winter of idolatry. Therefore, the 'Sun of Righteousness' is said to rise and bring 'the spring of the Spirit' (τοῦ μεσημβρινοῦ πνεύματος). The person 'warmed' (διαθερμανείς) by the Spirit and heated (ὑποθαλφθείς) by the ray of the Word again becomes water that 'springs up to eternal life' (εἰς ζωὴν αἰώνιον) (cf. John 4:14). For, says Gregory, citing Ps. 147(148):7, 'His Spirit will blow, and the waters will flow'.[37]

Once again, we see that Gregory's christological exegesis occurs in direct parallel with a pneumatological exegesis of the Song of Songs. The coming of Christ, as the 'rising sun' in spring, *simultaneously* brings the Spirit, as the warm air of the 'spring wind'.[38] Thus, it is by the unity of activity of Christ and the Spirit that humanity is transformed from its likeness to the idols, precisely as we saw in Homily 4. The reference to John 4:14 is a passage to which Gregory has already alluded in Homily 2, and it thus reinforces the point made there in relation to Christ's crucifixion, whereupon the spear that

---

[34] *GNO* VI.145.6–9; Norris II, 159.
[35] *GNO* VI.147.5–8; Norris II, 159 and 161.
[36] *GNO* VI.147.11–14; Norris II, 159 and 161.
[37] *GNO* VI.147.18–148.3; Norris II, 161.
[38] The exegesis is no doubt influenced by Gregory's own experience of springtime in Cappadocia. Cf. *ep.* 12.

ADVANCEMENT AND ASCENT 191

pierces Christ's side releases the flow of the Spirit as 'drink' that gives eternal life to all human nature.[39]

Epektasis and Pneumatology

Gregory's interest in pneumatology is further accentuated by his interpretation of the line 'Arise! Come! My close one, my beauty, my dove' (cf. Song 2:14), which he interprets as a call to the Bride to 'virtue', to 'transformation', and to come 'close to the light'.[40] His interpretation here is not too dissimilar to the one given in Homily 4. Again, he employs the analogy of the mirror receiving the 'impression' of a beautiful form to explain how human nature becomes 'beautiful' (καλόν) and is 'formed by the image' of that to which it draws near.[41]

> When, therefore, it has drawn close to the Light, it becomes light, and in this light the beautiful form of the dove is imaged (ἐνεικονίζεται)—and the dove I am talking about is the one whose form (εἶδος) makes known the presence of the Holy Spirit.[42]

The *nature-power-activity* framework appears also to underlie Gregory's notion of 'light' coming from 'Light'. Meanwhile, the analogy of a 'mirror' that Gregory applied earlier to the Bride's encounter *with Christ* now applies instead to *the Holy Spirit*. The 'archetypal Beauty' that Gregory says is reflected in the mirror of human nature is not so much that of the Father or Son, but the beauty of the Spirit.

Reflecting further on the Spirit, Gregory comments upon the Song's rather curious repetition of the line 'Come, rise up, my close one, my beauty, my dove' (cf. Song 2:10), which leads to a lengthy discussion on human participation in the infinity of the divine nature. Gregory speaks of the 'eternal nature', which 'runs out to infinity and beyond all limit', is 'beyond all infinity', and 'stands unlimited in goodness'.[43] Therefore, as it 'draws the human soul to participation (μετουσίαν) in itself, it always surpasses that which participates

---

[39] See the reference to this in Homily 2. Gregory interprets John 4:14 pneumatologically in *Eun.* III, *GNO* II.246.15–17.

[40] *GNO* VI.148.20–151.2; Norris II, 161 and 163.

[41] *GNO* VI.150.9–13; Norris II, 163.

[42] *GNO* VI.150.18–151.2; Norris II, 163.

[43] *GNO* VI.157.14–21; Norris II, 171.

192   ANALYSIS OF *IN CANTICUM CANTICORUM* (*c.* 391)

in it to the same degree . . . the being that ever more and more participates (μετεχούσης) in it discovers that it is always surpassed to the same extent'.[44] This is a classic exposition of what has come to be known as Gregory's notion of *epektasis*—the infinite, unceasing spiritual 'ascent' of the soul to God.[45] What is most interesting for our purposes, however, is the manner in which Gregory incorporates pneumatology into his understanding of human transformation through participation in the infinite God. The Bride's becoming like the dove is but only one step in this infinite process of becoming more *dove-like*. Hence, Gregory recalls that even after the Word summons the Bride to draw near to the Light so as to be given the form of the dove (τὸ εἶδος τῆς περιστερᾶς), her 'desire' (ἐπιθυμίαν) continues to increase 'in proportion to her advancement (προκοπῆς)' toward that Light, which is always 'beyond her'.[46]

Gregory further emphasizes this pneumatological framing of infinite participation in God in terms of an unceasing transformation in 'glory'. Thus, he relates the teaching of 2 Cor. 3:18—'be transformed from glory to glory'—to the *epektatic* transformation of the Bride 'from dove-likeness to dove-likeness', so to speak. According to Gregory, just as 'glory is always being received', so too the dove becomes 'a dove again (περιστερὰν . . . πάλιν) by being transformed (μεταμορφώσεως) for the better'.[47] The original context of 2 Cor. 3:18 is important to consider, for there transformation in 'glory' is understood explicitly in terms of the Holy Spirit. Gregory appears to have followed the Pauline association of the Lord's 'glory' with the Spirit by preaching on the soul's *epektatic* journey of union with the Bridegroom in emphatically pneumatological terms. There is already here an important recollection of Gregory's appeal to 'glory' as a pneumatological category in earlier anti-Macedonian works as well as a foreshadowing of references to

---

[44] *GNO* VI.158.12–19; Norris II, 171.

[45] The literature on *epektasis* is extensive; cf. entry and bibliography in Mateo-Seco, BDGN, 263–268; Classically, Jean Daniélou, *Platonisme et théologie mystique: Essai sur la doctrine spirituelle de saint Grégoire de Nysse* (Paris: Aubier, 1954), 291–307. More recently, see especially Jessica Scott, 'A Theological Exploration of the Shape of Life and Death in Dialogue with the Biographical Works of Gregory of Nyssa' (PhD diss., University of Cambridge, 2021), https://doi.org/10.17863/CAM.75286; Michael Motia, *Imitations of Infinity: Gregory of Nyssa and the Transformation of Mimesis* (Philadelphia: University of Pennsylvania Press, 2022), especially chapter 5; Michael Motia, 'Three Ways to Imitate Paul in Late Antiquity: Ekstasis, Ekphrasis, Epektasis', *Harvard Theological Review*, 144/1 (2021), 96–117; cf. Ramelli (2018); cf. Smith (2018); cf. Smith (2004), 104–125; cf. Paul M. Blowers, 'Maximum the Confessor, Gregory of Nyssa, and the Concept of "Perpetual Progress"', *Vigiliae Christianae*, 46 (1992), 151–171; cf. Canévet, *Grégoire de Nysse et l'herméneutique biblique*, 253–254.

[46] *GNO* VI.158.19–159.11; Norris II, 171.

[47] *GNO* VI.160.1–9; Norris II, 173.

ADVANCEMENT AND ASCENT   193

'glory' and pneumatology in later Homilies (especially Homilies 7, 8, and 9), culminating in Homily 15, where Gregory will comment extensively on the incorporation of the Bride into the 'circular' exchange of 'glory' within the Trinity.

The notion of *epektasis* features in many of Gregory's works, but it is in *hom. in Cant.* that he gives it his most sustained attention. Scholarly analyses of *epektasis* have for a long time recognized its centrality to Gregory's thought, where it is standardly summarized as the finite soul's 'continual stretching out' toward the infinite God. The term itself is derived from Gregory's frequent appeal to Paul's statement in Phil 3:13—'this one thing I do: forgetting what lies behind and straining forward (ἐπεκτεινόμενος) to what lies ahead'.[48]

Heine argues that Gregory's notion of *epektasis* aims to solve the problem of satiety or boredom (κόρος), which Origen suggested led to the fall of the heavenly spirits.[49] Importantly, the term ἐπεκτείνω is closely related to the idea of 'tension' (τόνος, τείνω), which we saw in Chapter 1 is used by Gregory in *virg.* and *hom. in Cant.* to denote the soul's 'good tension', which coincides with its strength. The usage is not unique to Gregory, for Anna Silvas has observed the link between the soul's 'tension' (τόνος) and its 'stretching' (τείνω) in Basil of Caesarea's own notion of *epektasis*, and that Gregory followed his elder brother's lead.[50] Thus, in the *Shorter Rule* 211, Basil notes that the measure of love for God is 'to be ever stretching the soul (τὸ . . . ἀεὶ τὴν ψύχην ἐπεκτείνεσθαι) beyond its power (ὑπερ δύναμιν) towards the will of God'.[51] Importantly, citing Basil's *Letter 233*, Silvas explicitly identifies the importance of pneumatology for Basil's notion of *epektatic* progress, noting 'the Spirit as the protagonist of our progress, gradually curing the coarseness and opacity of our spiritual senses to divine realities in the measure that the *noos* is receptive to his [i.e. the Spirit's] influences'.[52]

Thus, argues Silvas, 'when he [i.e. Basil] delivered his teaching on *tonos* to Gregory, Basil's theology of the life of Christ was already disposed to

---

[48] *GNO* VI.39.13; 119.16; 173.15; 291.17; 352.10; 366.15; 443.9.

[49] R. E. Heine, *Perfection in the Virtuous Life*, 71–97.

[50] Anna M. Silvas, 'A Paradosis of Mystical Theology between Basil the Great and Gregory of Nyssa', in *Gregory of Nyssa's Mystical Eschatology*, Studia Patristica CI, ed. Giulio Maspero, Miguel Brugarolas, and Ilaria Vigorelli (Leuven: Peeters, 2021), 52–53.

[51] Silvas, 'A Paradosis of Mystical Theology', 53.

[52] Silvas (2021), 'A Paradosis of Mystical Theology', 57–58; Cf. *Letter 233*: 'But the intellect that is melded with the divinity of the Spirit (ὁ μέντοι τῇ θεότητι τοῦ Πνεύματος ἀνακραθεὶς) is already initiated into view of the great things contemplated, and observes the divine beauties, but only to the extent that grace allows and its constitution admits'.

194 ANALYSIS OF *IN CANTICUM CANTICORUM* (*c.* 391)

the greatly expanded use that Gregory would make of it later.[53] I briefly commented in Chapter 1 upon the central role the Stoics assigned to *pneuma* in giving the soul 'good tension', with which Gregory's own usage resonates, although in an explicitly pneumatological register. As we have seen in the present chapter, Gregory's notion of the soul's continual *epektatic* 'tension', which he shares in common with Basil, is, likewise, inseparable from the activity of the Holy Spirit.

These observations regarding the Spirit's essential role in *epektasis*, in both Basil and Gregory, would assist in redirecting and rebalancing recent scholarly analyses of the concept.[54] Further, they complement the widely cited 1970 study by Marguerite Harl regarding Gregory's use of 2 Cor. 3:18, which convincingly argues that Gregory's teaching on *epektasis* is shaped by earlier liturgical tradition, with especially strong connections to baptism.[55]

Nourished by Christ and the Spirit

Just as we have witnessed previously, Gregory's exegesis moves instinctively from a focus on Christ in the incarnation to the activity of the Holy Spirit, as evidenced again by his exegesis of the line 'My beloved is mine and I am his; he feeds his flock among the lilies, until the day dawns and the shadows depart' (cf. Song 2:16). Once more, Gregory portrays the Bridegroom as 'the Good Shepherd' (cf. John 10:11–18) who 'nourishes (τρέφει) his sheep not with 'grass' but with 'pure lilies' (καθαροῖς κρίνοις)'.[56] The image is not too dissimilar to the image in Homily 2 of the Good Shepherd who carries the 'flock' of the whole human nature on his shoulders, while nourishing this flock by the 'divine drink' that flows from the 'mouth' of his pierced side. In the present context, the 'lily' with which the Good Shepherd nourishes the sheep of humanity is none other than the Holy Spirit, here associated with 'fragrance', in line with Gregory's custom in the previous homilies. Therefore:

---

[53] Silvas, 'A Paradosis of Mystical Theology', 58.

[54] Cf. Motia (2021); Motia (2022); Ramelli (2018); Theodoros Alexopoulos, 'Das unendliche Sichausstrecken (Epektasis) zum Guten bei Gregor von Nyssa und Plotin. Eine vergleichende Untersuchung', *Zeitschrift für Antikes Christentum*, 10 (2007), 303–312; Louth (2007), 87–88; Smith (2004), 202.

[55] Marguerite Harl, 'From Glory to Glory: L'interprétation de II Cor. 3, 18b par Grégoire de Nysse et la liturgie baptismale', in *Kyriakon: Festschrift Johannes Quasten*, vol. 2, ed. Patrick Granfield and Josef A. Jungmann (Münster: Aschendorff, 1970), 732–733.

[56] *GNO* VI.168.14–169.1; Norris II, 181.

But if a person becomes spirit by being born of the Spirit (cf. John 3:6), that person will no more graze upon the life of grass. His nourishment (τροφή) will be the Spirit, which is signified by the purity of the sweet scent (εὐπνοια) of the lily (τοῦ κρίνου). Therefore that person too will be a lily (κρίνον), pure and sweet-scented (εὔπνουν), once he has been changed into the nature (φύσιν) of that which nourishes him.[57]

Once more, we see unity of activity of Christ and the Spirit in the transformation of the Bride at the very same time that we observe Gregory's Spirit-based christology influencing the approach to exegesis. Christ, as the 'Good Shepherd', feeds his sheep (i.e. all human nature) with the nourishment of the Spirit, while the Spirit is the agent who ever purifies the soul and thus unites the Bride to Christ in her *epektatic* ascent. Further, Gregory's interpretation of John 3:6 suggests that to become 'spirit' by being 'born of the Spirit' (and, hence, to become the 'lily' by feeding on the pure-sweet 'Lily' that is the Spirit) is precisely what it means to be fed by Christ. While there is unity of activity between Christ and the Spirit, there is also *differentiated order*, such that the one activity does not just collapse into identity with the other.

The reference to the 'day' of Song 2:16 subsequently also refers to the Holy Spirit. Thus, 'This Spirit is that day (ἡμέρα) that is poured (διαχεομένη)—or rather breathed (διαπνέουσα)—out by the radiance (ταῖς ἀκτῖσιν) . . . They [i.e. those nourished by the Spirit] will look toward the true ground of the being of things, having become "sons of light" (υἱοὶ φωτός) and "sons of the day" (υἱοὶ ἡμέρας) (cf. 1 Thess. 5:5)'.[58] As in *perf.* and Homily 2, Gregory has interpreted 1 Thess. 5:5 and the associated subject of 'adoption' in pneumatological terms. The whole passage, however, falls under the broader context of being fed by the 'shepherd' who is Christ and therefore further underscores Christ's unity of activity with the Spirit in transforming the Bride's spiritual vision.

[57] *GNO* VI.169.6–10; Norris II, 181.
[58] *GNO* VI.169.11–170.9; Norris II, 181.

Homilies 8 and 9 (Song 4:8–15)

Burial and Resurrection with Christ through the Spirit

In this section I shall take the analysis of Homilies 8 and Homily 9 together as they draw from the same lection (i.e. Song 4:8–15). Evidently, Gregory's preaching of Homily 8 was cut short at Song 4:9, and he presumably resumed his interpretation of Song 4:10–15 with Homily 9 later that day or the next. From a literary-rhetorical viewpoint, it is worth bearing in mind that these homilies stand in fundamental continuity with theological themes that are first introduced in Homily 7, which I shall discuss in Chapter 8.

Gregory opens Homily 8 by again commenting on the soul's 'ascent' (ἀναβάσεως), noting that while the pure in heart 'see' God according to what they are capable of seeing (cf. Matt. 5:8), the human mind cannot completely apprehend the Godhead: 'the infinity and incomprehensibility of the Godhead remains beyond all direct apprehension'.[59] The soul's desire never rests content, but always journeys higher toward the infinite. It is against this background that Gregory interprets the opening line 'Come away (Δεῦρο ἀπό) from frankincense, my bride, come away from frankincense' (cf. Song 4:8a) in light of John 7:37—'If anyone thirst, let him come to me to drink'. Since, in John 7:37, Christ is said to set 'no limit' upon one's thirst or urge to come to him, nor any 'limit' on the *enjoyment* of drinking from him, Gregory interprets the call to the Bride to 'come away from frankincense' as a summons to 'mount up to a desire for that which lies beyond (τῶν ὑπερκειμένων)'.[60] He proceeds, therefore, to link this further ascent of the Bride to the upward ascent initiated by her baptism. Importantly, his 'epektatic' interpretation of the Bride's post-baptismal advancement 'away from frankincense' stands in direct continuity with Homily 7 (to be analysed in Chapter 8), where Gregory reflects upon the Bride who accompanies the Bridegroom to the 'mountain of myrrh' (cf. Song 4:6) through identification with his *death* in baptism. Yet, after having ascended the 'mountain of myrrh', the Bride goes even further on with him to 'the hill of frankincense' (cf. Song 4:6) through baptismal identification with his *resurrection*, whereupon she is exalted to 'communion with Godhead'.[61]

---

[59] *GNO* VI.246.8–12; Norris II, 259.
[60] *GNO* VI.249.9–10; Norris II, 263.
[61] *GNO* VI.249.11–16; Norris II, 263.

The pneumatological element of the Bride's further advancement *away from* 'frankincense' is evident in Gregory's exegesis of Song 4:8b—'Come and pass through from the beginning of faith, from the peak of Sanir and Hermon'. For Gregory, this line signifies the 'mystery of the birth from above (τῆς ἄνωθεν γεννήσεως)' given that the mountain peaks of Sanir and Hermon are said to be the source of the springs of the Jordan.[62] On this score he states, 'the stream that flows out of these springs is for us the beginning of our being remade (μεταποιήσεως) for existence at the level of the divine (πρὸς τὸ θεῖον)'.[63] Further, he speaks of fallen humanity being 'brought, by the Jordan, and the myrrh and the frankincense (cf. Song 4:6)' to a state of 'walking on high with God'.[64] Finally, he speaks also of 'the mysteries made known to us at the Jordan'.[65]

These various baptismally loaded references to the Jordan River must have been intended to direct the attention of Gregory's listeners and readers to Jesus' own baptism and the descent of the Holy Spirit upon him, despite the fact this event is never explicitly spelled out in the present homily. Gregory's exegesis of Song 4:8b therefore has the ring of one of his Epiphany sermons. Consonant with those sermons, Gregory communicates here the underlying logic that the Bride's union with the divine through baptism traces its origins to the baptism in the Jordan of Christ, who, as 'first-fruit' of those regenerated by the Spirit, is the basis for the rest of humanity's transformation by the same Spirit. Here too, we see that Gregory envisages this baptismal restoration of humanity to which Song 4:8b points as the unified activity of Christ and the Spirit.

Baptism and Transformation in Trinitarian Glory

As I previously indicated, Homily 8 appears to be cut short at Gregory's preaching on Song 4:9, yet he continues the baptismal train of thought in Homily 9 by referring from the very outset to those who 'have been raised with Christ' (i.e. through baptism; cf. Col. 2:12).[66] Importantly, he says these ones will one day appear with Christ 'in glory' (cf. Col. 3:1–4), which for

---

[62] *GNO* VI.250.9–10; Norris II, 263.
[63] *GNO* VI.250.11–12; Norris II, 263.
[64] *GNO* VI.251.13–15; Norris II, 265.
[65] *GNO* V.251.18–20; Norris II, 265.
[66] *GNO* VI.262.1–2; Norris II, 277.

198 ANALYSIS OF *IN CANTICUM CANTICORUM* (*c.* 391)

Gregory is synonymous with being 'transformed into a more divine state of being'.[67] Furthermore, invoking his customary pneumatic language, one's appearing with Christ 'in glory' is just to have 'come apart from flesh and blood and been transformed into a spiritual nature (εἰς δὲ τὴν πνευματικὴν μεταστοιχειωθέντες φύσιν)'.[68]

The invocation of the category of divine 'glory', together with the use of pneumatic language here, alerts us to Gregory's pneumatology in this section, facilitated by his baptismal exegesis of Song 4:12–14, where emphasis is placed upon *both* identification with Christ's death *and* resurrection birth by the Spirit. Thus, he notes that the reference to the Bride as both 'sister' and 'bride' (cf. Song 4:12) indicates that she has first been 'renewed for virginity by the birth from above (τῆς ἄνωθεν γεννήσεως)' and then made more perfect in her advancement to perfection.[69] Toward the end of the homily, after a lengthy commentary on the Bride's perpetual progress in virtue, via his exegesis of Song 4:12–14a, Gregory returns to the subject of human participation in divine 'glory', once again in baptismal terms.

The give-away sign that pneumatology and Spirit-based christology are at the forefront of his exegesis, especially when read in continuity with Gregory's allusion to John 17:5 in the preceding Homily 7, is the claim that 'no one becomes *a participant* (κοινωνός) *in the glory of God* (τῆς τοῦ θεοῦ ... δόξης) without first being conformed to the likeness of death' (cf. Rom. 6:5;Phil. 3:10, 21).[70] Commenting on Song 4:14—'myrrh, aloe with all the finest perfumes'—Gregory notes that 'myrrh', 'aloe', and 'the finest perfumes' refer to a 'sharing in burial' with Christ.[71] Meanwhile, that the Bride then becomes 'a spring of water that is living and that flows from frankincense' in the very next line of the Song (cf. Song 4:15) is interpreted pneumatologically and is said by Gregory to bring the Bride 'to her greatest height':

> As to these things, we know from the Scriptures that they pertain to the life-giving nature (περὶ ζωοποιοῦ μεμαθήκαμεν φύσεως), since on the one hand the prophecy says, in the very person of God (ἐκ προσώπου τοῦ θεοῦ), 'They have deserted me, the fountain of living waters (πηγὴν ὕδατος

---

[67] *GNO* VI.262.9–11; Norris II, 277.
[68] *GNO* VI.262.20–22; Norris II, 279.
[69] *GNO* VI.263.14–19; Norris II, 279.
[70] *GNO* VI.290.6; Norris II, 305.
[71] *GNO* VI.290.6–7; Norris II, 305 and 307. The link to baptism is noted by Françoise Vinel, 'The Key Eschatological Role of the Song of Songs', in *Gregory of Nyssa's Mystical Eschatology*, Studia Patristica CI, ed. Giulio Maspero, Miguel Brugarolas, and Ilaria Vigorelli (Leuven: Peeters, 2021), 90.

ζῶντος)' (cf. Jer. 2:13); and then, on the other hand, the Lord says to the Samaritan woman, 'If you knew the gift of God and who it is saying to you, "Give me a drink", you would ask him, and he would give you living water (ὕδωρ ζῶν)' (cf. John 4:10)—not to mention, 'If anyone is thirsty, let him come to me and drink; for those who believe in me, as the Scripture says, "Rivers of water shall flow from their hearts". Now this he said concerning the Spirit, whom those who believe in him were going to receive' (cf. John 7:37–39). Everywhere, then, it is the divine nature (τῆς θείας φύσεως) that is understood when living water (ζῶντος ὕδατος) is mentioned, and here in our text the truthful witness of the Word constitutes the Bride a well of living water (ὕδατος ζῶντος), the direction of whose flow is from frankincense.[72]

The passage is very dense, but the trinitarian focus is clear nonetheless. Gregory intends to show that the 'living water' of Song 4:15 refers to the 'life-giving nature' and 'divine nature' of God. The references to John 4:10 and John 7:37–39 indicate, at the same time, that the 'living water' is, in emphatically anti-Macedonian and anti-Eunomian terms, also a reference to the Holy Spirit. That the bride is also a 'spring of living water' means that she imitates God by virtue of her imitation of both Christ and the Spirit. For, as Gregory goes on to note, 'she has been made like to the archetypal Beauty (τὸ ἀρχέτυπον κάλλος)—for by the fountain, the Fount is exactly imitated; by her life, the Life; by her water, the Water'.[73]

We see that Homily 8 and Homily 9 form something of a homiletical-literary unit, 'enclosed' we might say by references to John 7:37, and are hence underpinned by references to baptism, pneumatology, and the church's future participation in trinitarian 'glory'. With these motifs Gregory stresses the unity of Christ's and the Spirit's activity in the transformation of the Bride, such that by her unceasing desire for the Bridegroom she imitates in her very self Christ, the Spirit and the archetypal Beauty of God. The stress on the Spirit's divinity strongly resonates with Gregory's baptismal argument for the unity of the trinitarian person in *ep. 5*, *ep. 24*, *Maced.*, and *bapt. Chr.*

---

[72] *GNO* VI.292.9–293.3; Norris II, 309; Laird, *Grasp of Faith*, 98–99, suggests that 'John does not specify the nature of the living water, but Gregory does . . . the divine nature itself'. Yet, John does specify the living water is *the Holy Spirit* who is subsequently, in anti-Macedonian/anti-Eunomian terms, of the divine nature.

[73] *GNO* VI.293.8–13; Norris II, 309.

200 ANALYSIS OF *IN CANTICUM CANTICORUM* (*c.* 391)

Homily 10 (Song 4:16–5:2a)

The Mind Ruled by the Spirit

Gregory's introduction to this homily calls for the 'guidance on the part of the Holy Spirit', likening the interpretation of the Song of Songs to beholding celestial beauty. Here he invokes the language of lights, comparing the Song of Songs' transcendent teachings to the 'sparklings and shinings' (μαρμαρυγαί τε καὶ λαμπηδόνες) of the stars.[74] Nevertheless, he says it is possible to understand these exalted teachings with the assistance of the Holy Spirit. Therefore, referring to Elijah's assumption to heaven (cf. 4 Kgdms. 2:11), Gregory claims that one's understanding may be 'seized up in a fiery chariot' (τῷ πυρίνῳ ἅρματι) and carried toward the beauty of the heavens, such that divine thought and spiritual words (πνευματικῶν λογίων) flash about our souls.[75] For Gregory, who alludes to Luke 12:49 and Acts 2:3, 'the fire' to which Elijah's chariot points is none other than 'the Holy Spirit that the Lord came to cast upon the earth and that was shared among the disciples in the form of tongues (γλωσσῶν)'. Not only does this interpretation of 4 Kgdms. 2:11, Luke 12:49, and Acts 2:3 foreshadow further important references to the Spirit in this homily, but, as I pointed out in Chapter 6, it clarifies the pneumatological tenor of Gregory's earlier reference to the 'fire which the Lord came to cast upon the earth' in Homily 1 in the context of the Bride's ascent of the 'spiritual mountain' of Moses.

Gregory proceeds to assign the title of 'Queen' to the Bride since she 'rules the minds of the two winds (τῶν δύο ἀνέμων)', the 'north wind' and the 'south wind' of Song 4:16—'Away, north wind, and come, south wind!'. He interprets this verse in light of the Roman centurion's command in the gospel, whereby one servant is sent away and another is summoned in his stead (cf. Matt. 8:10). Thus, Song 4:16 is said to illustrate 'the basic truth' that contraries such as 'darkness and light' that have nothing 'in common' (cf. 2 Cor. 6:14) cannot occupy the same place.[76] By introducing the topic of 'light' in conjunction with the original subject of 'wind', Gregory has now set up the appropriate 'pneumatic categories' to preach on the transforming activity of the Holy Spirit.

---

[74] *GNO* VI.295.6–7; Norris II, 311.
[75] *GNO* VI.295.13–15; Norris II, 311.
[76] *GNO* VI.298.1–2; Norris II, 315.

ADVANCEMENT AND ASCENT   201

Thus, immediately he states, 'when darkness departs it is strictly necessary that light be visible in its place, and when evil has gone away, that good be introduced in its stead—and once this has been accomplished, that "the mind of the flesh" (τὸ φρόνημα τῆς σαρκός) (cf. Rom. 8:7; 7:23) no longer rebel against the Spirit (ἀνταίπειν τῷ πνεύματι) . . . but that instead it becomes available for every appropriate service, rendered obedient and submissive by the lordship of the Spirit (τῇ δυναστείᾳ τοῦ πνεύματος)'.[77] Here, Gregory has aligned 'flesh' with 'darkness' and 'the Spirit' with 'light'.

Appealing to Eph. 6:14–15, Gregory now refers to the mind receptive of the Holy Spirit as 'the soldier of virtue', and, as such, it is no longer submissive to the flesh but to the Spirit. Therefore, 'the soldier of virtue' replaces the 'mercenary allied with evil' and is now armed with 'the sword of the Spirit' (τοῦ πνεύματος), 'the helmet of salvation', and 'the shield of faith'—ready and bearing within himself the whole spiritual panoply (τὴν πνευματικὴν πανοπλίαν)' (cf. Eph. 6:14–15).[78] It follows that the mind that is submissive to the Spirit becomes, for Gregory, the lord and ruler over the body, so that the body and mind *in joint operation* with the Spirit can now achieve virtue. While, on the one hand, the Bride's achievement of virtue comes about by bringing the body into submission to *the mind* like a slave before its 'ruler' (κρατοῦντος),[79] for Gregory, the mind, which is itself prone to the darkness of the 'flesh', is unable to command the body toward virtue unless it too is brought into submission to the Spirit.

Once again, we see just how crucial is the activity of the Holy Spirit for Gregory's understanding of human transformation in the life of virtue, which leads to union with the Bridegroom. As I discussed in Chapter 1 regarding his use of 'pneumatic language', it appears that what Gregory identifies as 'mind' in this section he elsewhere calls 'spirit', that is, the mind that has been borne of, and is in fellowship with, the Holy Spirit.[80]

Transformation by the Spirit of Pentecost

For Gregory, then, the 'north wind' (cf. Song 4:16) is an evil force identified as the 'Prince of the power of darkness'.[81] The exegesis of this verse is somewhat

[77] *GNO* VI.298.3–9; Norris II, 315.
[78] *GNO* VI.298.11–16; Norris II, 315.
[79] *GNO* VI.298.10–21; Norris II, 315.
[80] Cf. *GNO* II.161.3.
[81] *GNO* VI.392.12; Norris II, 317.

202 ANALYSIS OF *IN CANTICUM CANTICORUM* (*c.* 391)

convoluted. Citing Prov. 27:16 for proof, Gregory notes the 'north wind' is both 'harsh' and 'on the righthand side'. This means that the person upon whom it blows must be *heading west*, toward the darkness and wintery cold of the setting sun, and hence *away from the east*, which stands for rising sun and warmth of Christ. Thus, Prov. 27:16 in turn informs Gregory's exegesis of the line 'Come, O south wind, blow through my garden, and let my fragrances be made to flow' (cf. Song 4:16), where Gregory continues to speak of the transformative activity of the Holy Spirit, now with a focus upon the church:

> So it is a good thing that the voice of the Queen, in tones of authority, should send him packing, summoning to her presence the warm and ever bright noontide wind (τὸ μεσημβρινὸν πνεῦμα τὸ θερμόν). This wind, which makes the pleasant streams (τρυφῆς ῥέει) of the springtime thaw flow forth, she calls 'south', and she says, 'Come, O south wind, blow (διάπνευσον) through my garden, and let my fragrances be made to flow' (cf. Song 4:16), so that with that 'mighty blast' (τῇ βιαίᾳ πνοῇ)—just as we hear it happened for the disciples (cf. Acts 2:2)—you may fall upon the ensouled plants and move God's plantation to bring forth fragrances (τῶν ἀρωμάτων), and prepare them, as you pour out the sweet savor (εὐωδίαν) of the doctrines, to let sweet-smelling prophecy (εὐώδη προφητείαν) and the saving teachings of the faith flow from their mouths freely in every type of tongue (γλώσσης) (cf. Acts 2:4). In this way the hundred and twenty disciples who have been planted in the house of God (cf. Acts 1:15ff) will put forth, by the help of the 'blast' of such a south wind (τῇ πνοῇ) (cf. Acts 2:2), the blossom of teaching through tongues (τὴν διὰ τῶν γλωσσῶν διδασκαλίαν).[82]

Here, Gregory has interpreted the Song in light of the events of the coming of the Holy Spirit in the upper room at Pentecost, as recounted in Acts. The Apostle Paul is, once again, upheld as an exemplar of one who issues such fragrances of the Spirit. Therefore, alluding to 2 Cor. 2:15:

> The great Paul was himself such a river of fragrances (ἀρωμάτων) issuing (ῥέων) from the garden of the church by the Spirit (δία τοῦ πνεύματος), and his stream (ῥεῖθρον) was the sweet fragrance of Christ (Χριστοῦ εὐωδία) (cf. 2 Cor. 2:15); and the same can be said of John, of Luke, of Matthew, of Mark, and of all the others, the noble plants of the Bride's garden. Breathed

[82] *GNO* VI.301.7–19; Norris II, 319.

through (διαπνευσθέντες) by that bright (τῷ φωτεινῷ) noonday wind, they became fountains of aromas (πηγαὶ ἀρωμάτων), bursting with the fragrance of the Gospels.[83]

The passage is reminiscent of Homily 3 and Gregory's description there of Paul as one emitting the fragrance of the Spirit, having drawn near to Christ. As I argued, in that same homily Gregory also viewed the 'anointed' body of Christ that is the church in much the same light. Here, in Homily 10, we see Gregory reiterating the basically identical notion—the church, through the unified activity of Christ and the Spirit working within her 'garden', becomes a source of good news to others.

As Gregory comes to interpret the remainder of the lection (cf. Song 5:1–2a), the strong pneumatological focus with which he began the first half of the homily recedes momentarily to the background. The emphasis then shifts to an interpretation of the Song in terms of Christ the 'kinsman' coming down to his 'garden' to 'eat the fruit of his fruit trees' (cf. Song 5:1). He notes that since Christ's 'food' is to do the will of his Father (cf. John 4:34), and the Father's will is that 'all people should be saved' (cf. 1 Tim. 2:4), then Song 5:1 means that Christ comes down to bring 'salvation' to the church.[84] The strong emphasis on the Father's will is counterbalanced by Gregory's interpretation of 'fruit' as representing the human faculty of choice (προαίρεσις), which entrusts itself *of its own accord* to God, who 'plucks' such fruit.

Importantly, however, the pneumatological aspect has not completely disappeared from view as Gregory reminds his reader once again that the virtuous and fruitful garden of the church upon which Christ descends to bring salvation is that 'through which the south wind [i.e. the Holy Spirit] has blown'.[85] The second half of the homily must therefore be read in continuity with the first. At the closing of the homily, then, Gregory has constructed an image of the church as a body constituted of souls, once frozen in darkness and the chill of evil, but now, with the same Spirit that came upon the disciples at Pentecost flourishes with the fruit of virtue, ripe for salvation by Christ. The joint activity of Christ and the Spirit once again animates Gregory's exegesis on the transformation of the church and her union with God.

---

[83] *GNO* VI.302.13–303.2; Norris II, 319.
[84] *GNO* VI.303.14–304.3; Norris II, 321.
[85] *GNO* VI.305.5–7; Norris II, 321.

204 ANALYSIS OF *IN CANTICUM CANTICORUM* (*c.* 391)

Homily 12 (Song 5:5–7)

The Choice to Be 'Buried with Christ'

The theme of mortification and vivification of the body and soul dominates Homily 12, and it is in this light that Gregory interprets the opening line of the lection, 'I rose up to open to my kinsman; my hands dropped myrrh, my fingers choice myrrh' (cf. Song 5:5). He points out that the only way the living Word 'comes within us' (ἐν ἡμῖν) is through 'incorruptibility and holiness'.[86] For Gregory, such 'dwelling with him' (συνοικίζοντα) happens 'if one removes the cover of the flesh by mortifying one's earthly members (cf. Col. 3:5)', thus opening the door to the Word who 'makes the soul his home (εἰσοικίζεται)'.[87]

Two main factors are fundamental in this initial act of mortifying the flesh. The first, argues Gregory, is identification with Christ *through baptism*, and the second is that such baptism is *voluntary*. Thus, continuing to interpret Song 5:5, Gregory claims, 'by these words she [i.e. the Bride] states the way in which the door is opened to the Bridegroom: "I have risen up by being 'buried with him through baptism into his death'" (cf. Col. 2:12; Rom. 6:4), for resurrection does not become actual if it is not preceded by voluntary death (τῆς ἑκουσίου νεκρότητος)'.[88] A similar notion has already featured prominently in Homilies 8 and 9 in light of Gregory's exegesis of the meaning of 'myrrh' and 'frankincense' (cf. Song 4:8).[89]

Having emphasized the role of choice in his introductory remarks, Gregory reiterates this point several more times throughout the first half of Homily 12. Thus, he speaks of 'the mortification of bodily passions that comes about through choice (ἐκ προαιρέσεως) that originates in oneself'.[90] Further, '[t]he myrrh [which stands for mortification] (cf. Song 5:5) was not placed on my [i.e. the Bride's] hands by another agent, but flowed from my [i.e. the Bride's] own choice (προαιρέσεως)'.[91] Gregory elaborates further upon human choice in view of the 'dual nature' (διπλῆς ... τῆς φύσεως) of man. On the one hand, our 'fine and intelligent and light' aspect 'has a native

---

[86] *GNO* VI.342.12–15; Norris II, 363.
[87] *GNO* VI.342.15–343.1; Norris II, 363.
[88] *GNO* VI.343.3–10; Norris II, 363.
[89] Gregory stresses the voluntary nature of baptism as a necessary imitation of Christ's own voluntary death in *Apoll.*; cf. *GNO* III/1.226.29–31.
[90] *GNO* VI.343.16–344.3; Norris II, 363.
[91] *GNO* VI.344.9–13; Norris II, 365.

course upwards', while the 'coarse and material and heavy' has a motion that 'ever flows downwards'.[92] Gregory argues that it is only by 'our power of choice (προαίρεσις) and self-governance (αὐτεξούσιος), which is stationed *in the middle* (μέση) between these' that one can overcome the natural tendency to be dragged 'downwards' and so give the 'spoils of victory' (τὰ νικητήρια) to the 'upward' course.[93]

Similarly, Gregory takes the good and wicked servants in Jesus' parable of the master's household (cf. Matt. 24:45–51) each to represent 'our faculty of choice' (προαίρεσις).[94] The good servant is praised for putting to death the adversaries, while the wicked servant who delivers strikes (πληγαῖς) on God's household is condemned 'for in truth a strike (πληγή) marks the flourishing of vice (τῆς κακίας) over against the virtues (τῶν ἀρετῶν)'.[95] The interpretation of the parable is most intriguing given that Gregory will attach a *positive* meaning to being stricken by God in the second half of the homily. For the time being, the sole focus of Gregory's exegesis of the Song remains fixed on foregrounding the power of human choice to identify with Christ in baptism.

Choice, Faith, and Works

Once the central role of human choice to be 'buried' with Christ in baptism has been established, Gregory proceeds to question how it is that 'death raises us up from death'.[96] This marks a significant turning point in the homily as Gregory attends to the subject of the soul's 'post-baptismal' vivification and *epektatic* 'advancement' toward God.[97] First, alluding to the narrative of Genesis, Gregory makes a point of showing how thoroughly death has become mingled (καταμιχθέντος) with human nature, such that humanity is now 'enfolded' by a 'dead form of existence' and 'deprived of immortality'. However, via a traditional christophanic interpretation of Hab. 3:2,[98]

[92] *GNO* VI.345.11–17; Norris II, 365.
[93] *GNO* VI.345.17–346.2; Norris II, 365.
[94] *GNO* VI.346.5; Norris II, 365.
[95] *GNO* VI.346.10–11; Norris II, 367.
[96] *GNO* VI.347.15; Norris II, 367.
[97] Cf. *GNO* VI.369.23; Hall III, 389.
[98] Gregory appears to be influenced by Eusebius of Caesarea's reading of Hab. 3:2 in *d.e.* 6.15. Ivar A. Heikel, *Eusebius Werke, Band 6: Die Demonstratio evangelica*, Die griechischen christlichen Schriftsteller 23 (Leipzig: Hinrichs, 1913), 269–270. Cf. Bogdan G. Bucur, 'A Blind Spot in the Study of Fourth-Century Christian Theology: The Christological Exegesis of Theophanies', *Journal of Theological Studies*, 69/2 (2018), 596 n.26; cf. Bogdan G. Bucur and Elijah N. Mueller, 'Gregory

206 ANALYSIS OF *IN CANTICUM CANTICORUM* (*c.* 391)

Gregory demonstrates that the incarnate Christ, who stood between life and death, offers humanity the 'spoils of victory' over its present mortal existence:

> the one [i.e. Christ] who is made known '*in the midst* (μεσιτεύει) between two forms of life' (cf. Hab. 3:2) stands in between (Ἐν μέσῳ) these two kinds of life, in order that by removal of the worse he may award the spoils of victory (τὰ νικητήρια) to the one that is undefiled. So just as by dying to the true life humanity fell instead into this dead form of existence, so too when it dies to this dead and animal life, it is redirected toward life eternal.[99]

By introducing the subject of Christ's incarnation as a solution to humanity's mortality, Gregory already begins subtly to shift the focus away from the role of human choice in overcoming death toward the *divine initiative*. By referring for a second time in this homily to the 'spoils of victory' (τὰ νικητήρια) awarded to the undefiled form of life, Gregory envisages the triumphant Christ standing in the very same position that he had earlier 'placed' the human faculty of choice, that is, 'in the middle' of two opposing forms of life. This is not to diminish the role of human choice, for Gregory clearly views it as crucial, but rather to relativize its role as secondary to Christ's prior triumph over death.

The power of human choice to secure union with God is relativized even further in light of the infinite 'epektatic' ascent toward God that lies ever in front of the hopeful Bride. This motivates Gregory to explore the notion of the soul's perpetual progress in light of the tension between the roles played by the Bride's 'works' and her 'faith'. Interpreting the line 'Hands on the bar, I opened to my kinsman' (cf. Song 5:5b–6), he suggest that the 'hands' represent the Bride's 'works' (τὰ ἔργα) while the 'bar' (τοῦ κλείθρου) stands for the Bride's 'faith' (τῆς πίστεως), and concludes that 'it is by both of these—by works, I mean, and by faith—that the Word equips us with the key (ἡ κλείς) of the kingdom' (cf. Matt. 7:14).[100] However, the following line of the Song, 'My kinsman passed me by, my soul went forth at his word' (cf. Song 5:6), is immediately shown to capture the existing tension between the Bride's

Nazianzen's Reading of Habakkuk 3:2 and Its Reception: A Lesson from Byzantine Scripture Exegesis', *Pro Ecclesia*, 20/1 (2018), 86–103.
    GNO VI.351.6–13; Norris II, 371.

[99] *GNO* VI.351.6–13; Norris II, 371.
[100] *GNO* VI.353.8–11; Norris II, 373.

'works' and her 'faith', for at the very moment the Bride hoped, by her 'works', to know the Bridegroom, 'at that very instant the One she sought escaped her apprehension' even as he continues to draw the Bride to himself.[101] The Bride's hopeful longing for a face-to-face encounter with God thus imitates Moses' own theophanic experience.[102]

The rich exposition that follows concerning the human mind's total inability to rationally apprehend the transcendent God serves to illustrate the diminished role that human choice plays in the soul's ascent to God: the Bride's desire for the Bridegroom is not able, says Gregory, 'to want (θελῆσαι) all that he is, but only as much as her power of choice can intend (ὅσον βουληθῆναι ἡ προαίρεσις δύναται)'.[103] In other words, the Bride's merely *finite* power of 'choice' imposes an intrinsic limit upon her desire for the *infinite* Bridegroom with whom she can be united only by 'faith'.[104]

There are two notable interpretations of Homily 12 upon which my analysis can build. Gregory's reference to Moses' theophany is taken up by Verna Harrison,[105] who discerns three different modes of divine presence—as 'the positive fullness' in the soul, as 'the guide' who is both incomprehensibly distant but apprehensibly near, and as 'the goal of the unending journey', which is the divine essence itself.[106] While Harrison deftly teases out subtle distinctions in Gregory's thinking, greater attention to literary-historical context would result in an expansive reading that is more fully expressive of Gregory's ideas. As I will show, the literary-rhetorical shaping of Homily 12 serves as a clear example of why Radde-Gallwitz's advice ought to be heard.[107] Since theological *content* is inseparable from literary *form* and *skopos*, Harrison's observations concerning 'modes of divine presence' would be enriched by greater attention to pneumatological, and Spirit-based christological dynamics, particularly as these function as a climactic point toward which Gregory's preaching aims in Homily 12, as we will shortly see.

A similar point can be made regarding Martin Laird's analysis of Homily 12. His main interest is in Gregory's technical usage in this homily of the concept of 'faith', specifically as it functions within Gregory's well-known

---

[101] *GNO* VI.353.11–13; Norris II, 373.
[102] *GNO* VI.353.11–13; Norris II, 373.
[103] *GNO* VI.38.19–359.2; Norris II, 379.
[104] The notion of 'faith' as a technical term in Gregory discussed in Laird (2004).
[105] Harrison, *Grace and Human Freedom*, 73–85.
[106] Harrison, *Grace and Human Freedom*, 84.
[107] Radde-Gallwitz, *Doctrinal Works*, 8–9: 'each passage must be set within the part of the work in which it appears; each part must be nested within the whole work'.

208 ANALYSIS OF *IN CANTICUM CANTICORUM* (*c.* 391)

analogy of the archer. In Homily 4, Gregory notes that the tip of the archer's arrow, which stands for 'faith', has been moistened 'τῷ πνεύματι τῆς ζωῆς', which Laird notes is 'evocative both of the Holy Spirit and baptism'.[108] As Laird proceeds to analyse Gregory's discussion of the Bride's 'wounding' in terms of the archer analogy in Homily 12, he, unlike Harrison, *does* note Gregory's strong emphasis on pneumatology. Yet, while the archer analogy stands in direct continuity with the interpretation of the Bride's 'wounding', Laird makes no attempt to link Gregory's notion of 'faith' to either pneumatology or to baptism, as is strongly warranted by the use of the archer analogy in Homily 4 and, indeed, by the key baptismal and pneumatological theme that pervades Homily 12 itself.

The methodological approach undertaken in this book, which stresses the importance of literary-rhetorical analysis, helps us to see how Laird's somewhat disconnected insights into the Spirit, baptism, and faith are in fact organically and integrally connected as a unified theological vision for Gregory. Gregory's notion of 'faith' is inseparable from his broader reflection upon baptism and the unified activity of Christ and the Spirit. These aspects that underpin the Bride's seeking after the Bridegroom through 'faith' will become clearer in the next section as I explore the 'wounding' theme in more detail.

Mortification and Vivification as Unified Activity of Christ and the Spirit

While Gregory emphasized the power of human choice at the beginning of Homily 12, he now arrives at a point in the homily where this defining human capability is further relativized in light of God's infinity and humanity's finitude. It is with this in mind that Gregory now interprets the line 'the watchmen who go their round in the city found me, they struck me, they wounded me, the guards of the walls took my veil away' (cf. Song 5:7). As we shall see, Gregory interprets this line in terms of the Bride's continued 'advancement' (προκοπῆς) and 'ascent (ἀναβάσεως) to higher and nobler things', stressing the unified activity of Christ and the Spirit.

Gregory notes an ambiguity in the present lection since in the previous one (cf. Homily 1; Song 5:2b–4) the Bride had already removed her 'tunic'

---

[108] Laird, *Grasp of Faith*, 94.

ADVANCEMENT AND ASCENT 209

(τὸν χιτῶνά) (cf. Song 5:3), whereas presently she still wears the 'veil' (τὸ θέριστρον) (cf. Song 5:7). For Gregory, the ambiguity serves further to reinforce his notion of the Bride's unceasing spiritual advancement. In view of her perpetual progress in purity, it is *as if* the Bride has not yet removed her old 'tunic' but, 'even after that former stripping, finds something on her to be taken off'.[109] It is in light of these comments on the Bride's *epektatic* ascent that Gregory's reflections upon the Spirit are brought to the fore.

Thus, commenting on the line 'the watchmen who go their rounds in the city found me' (cf. Song 5:7), Gregory understands 'city' to represent the Bride's soul, while the 'watchmen' over the 'city' stand for the 'ministering spirits' (Λειτουργικὰ πνεύματα) of Heb. 1:14, sent to serve those who inherit salvation.[110] According to Song 5:7, '[the watchmen] have removed her veil (τὸ θέριστρον) by *striking and wounding* her . . . And the removal of the veil (προκαλύμματος), so that the eye, freed from what obscures it, **gazes** without interference on the Beauty it desires, is *a good thing*.[111] While the 'watchmen' represent 'ministering spirits', Gregory ultimately attributes the removal of the Bride's veil not to *them* but, rather, to the power of the Spirit (τῇ δυνάμει τοῦ πνεύματος): 'But when one turns to the Lord, the veil (κάλυμμα) is removed; and the Lord is the Spirit (cf. 2 Cor. 3:16–17)'.[112] Gregory has intentionally substituted the 'veil' (θέριστρον) of Song 5:7 with the 'veil' (κάλυμμα) of the pneumatologically weighted passage, 2 Cor. 3:16–17. This subtle substitution will allow Gregory to counter-balance his original emphasis on the role of human choice with a newfound focus on the essential role of Christ and the Spirit in vivifying the mortified flesh of the Bride.

The 'striking' and 'wounding' of the Bride therefore come to be understood in emphatically pneumatological terms. While Gregory acknowledges that the terms 'struck' and 'wounded' are 'repellent' in their ordinary sense (cf. Song 5:7), in the present context they actually refer to something nobler. This stance is justified via an appeal to Prov. 23:13–14 in addition to other Old Testament citations. Thus:

> How does Wisdom free the soul of a youth from death? What does she plan to do to prevent the youth from dying? Let us hear Wisdom herself. 'If you strike (πατάξῃς) him with a rod (ῥάβδῳ)', says she, 'he will not die (μὴ

[109] GNO VI.360.5–10; Norris II, 381.
[110] GNO VI.360.15; Norris II, 381.
[111] GNO VI.360.16–361.1; Norris II, 381; cf. Laird, *Grasp of Faith*, 95, my italics.
[112] GNO VI.361.1–4; Norris II, 381.

210 ANALYSIS OF *IN CANTICUM CANTICORUM* (*c.* 391)

ἀποθάνῃ). For you will strike (πατάξεις) him with a rod (ῥάβδῳ), and you will free his soul from death' (cf. Prov. 23:13–14). The expression *They struck me* (Ἐπάτεξάν) (cf. Song 5:7), then, appears to signify immortality, in accordance with the Word's statement: 'If you strike him with a rod (πατάξῃς τῇ ῥάπδῳ), he will not die', and 'It is not possible for the soul to be freed from death except it be struck with the rod (ἐὰν μὴ παταχθῇ)' (cf. Prov. 23:13–14). We are shown, then, by these words that it is a beautiful thing to be struck (παταχθῆναι), precisely because it is truly a beautiful thing for the soul to be freed from death. The prophet says that God too acts in this way: by killing he gives life (ζωοποιοῦντα), and by striking (πατάσσειν), heals (ἰώμενον). For it says: 'I will kill and I will make alive (ζῆν ποιήσω); I will strike (πατάξω) and I will heal (ἰάσομαι)' (cf. Deut. 32:39). That is why David said that the effect of a rod (ῥάβδου) of this sort is not affliction (πληγήν) but comfort (παράκλησιν): 'Your rod (ῥάβδος) and your staff (βακτηρία), they comfort (παρεκάλεσαν) me' (cf. Ps. 22[23]:5–6) . . . it is assuredly a good thing (ἀγαθόν) to be struck by the rod (τὸ παταχθῆναι τῇ ῥάβδῳ) that is the source of the abundance of so many good things.[113]

Gregory's positive interpretation of being 'found', 'struck', and 'wounded' is also justified by his interpretation of Ps. 88(89):21—'I *found* (εὗρον) David my servant; I *anointed* (ἔχρισα) him with my holy oil'.[114] Clearly, Gregory has correlated the typically negative actions of being 'found' (Εὕροσάν), 'struck', and 'wounded' (cf. Song 5:7) with the positive ones of being 'found' (εὗρον) and 'anointed' (cf. Ps. 88[89]:21). As we shall see, this second reference to 'anointing' in *hom. in Cant.*, much like its first occurrence in his exposition of the 'spikenard' in Homily 3,[115] not to mention its typical usage throughout his corpus, is heavily laden with pneumatology. Thus, the references to 'striking' and 'wounding' come to be understood by Gregory as the Bride's 'anointing' by the Holy Spirit through her imitation of Christ.

On this score, Gregory's appeal to Ps. 22(23):5–6 is immediately relevant, for the use of the term παράκλησις makes the link among Christ, the Holy Spirit, and the Bride absolutely concrete (cf. John 14:16, 26; 15:26; 16:7). Gregory points out that upon her 'advancement upwards' (τῆς ἐπὶ τὸ ἄνω προκοπῆς) the Bride 'felt the activity (τὴν ἐνέργειαν) of the *spiritual* rod (τῆς

[113] *GNO* VI 361.16–362.17; Norris II, 383; cf. parallels between the references to Psalm 22 (23) in Homily 12 and Gregory's sermon *ascens*, *GNO* IX/1.324.11–14.
[114] *GNO* VI.364.15–17; Norris II, 385.
[115] *GNO* VI.364.15–17.

ADVANCEMENT AND ASCENT   211

πνευματικῆς ῥάβδου)'.[116] The Bride's reference to being 'wounded' (cf. Song 5:7) is understood by Gregory to refer to 'the mark left in the depth of her being by the divine rod (διὰ τῆς θείας ῥάβδου)'.[117] Therefore, he goes on to state, 'that divine rod (ἡ θεία ῥάβδος) and comforting staff (ἡ παρακλητικὴ βακτηρία), by which a strike (πατάσσειν) works healing, is the Spirit' (cf. Deut. 32:39).[118] That these blows of the Spirit do not operate independently of Christ is evident in Gregory's reference to Gal. 6:17:

> For Paul too, who bore the marks (στιγματίας) of such strikes (τῶν . . . πληγῶν), similarly exulted in wounds (τραύμασι) of this sort when he said, 'I bear in my body the marks of Christ (Τὰ στίγματα τοῦ Χριστοῦ)' (cf. Gal. 6:17), displaying that weakness in every vice by which *the power that belongs to Christ* is brought to perfection in virtue (ἐν ἀρετῇ τελειοῦται). By these words, then, he shows us that the wound (τὸ τραῦμα) too is an admirable thing (καλόν). It occasions the stripping off of the Bride's veil (τοῦ θερίστρου) (cf. 2 Cor. 3:16), so that the soul's beauty is revealed once her covering no longer obscures it.[119]

The pneumatological exegesis of Song 5:5–7 continues to influence the remainder of Gregory's homily as he reflects further on the meaning of the 'strike' that the Bride has received. It is understood not only in terms of the mortification of the flesh, but pertains to the Bride becoming a wellspring of the Holy Spirit herself, in *imitation* of Christ. Therefore, in the context of her unceasing journey of ascent toward the Bridegroom, Gregory designates the Bride a 'wellspring of living water' in reference to John 7:37–39, a passage that has consistently been of key significance to Gregory's pneumatological exegesis throughout his homilies, most notably at the conclusion of Homily 9.[120] Further, citing Ps. 77(78):20, Gregory claims that the Bride 'receives the strike (πατάσσουσαν) of the rod (ῥάβδον). She imitates (μιμεται) the rock of which the prophet says: "He struck (Ἐπάταξε) the rock, and waters gushed out (ἐρρύησαν)"' and on this same note he adds, 'she was struck (πατασσομένη) just as the precipice was struck by Moses (cf. Num. 20:10–13), in order that she too, like it (ὁμοιότητα), might gush forth (πηγάσῃ), for those who are

---

[116] *GNO* VI.365.10–13; Norris II, 385.
[117] *GNO* VI.365.11–12; Norris II, 385.
[118] *GNO* VI.365.17–18; Norris II, 385; Cf. Psalm 22 (23):4 LXX—ἡ ῥάβδος σου καὶ ἡ βακτηρία σου αὐταί με παρεκάλεσαν.
[119] *GNO* VI.366.2–6; Norris II, 385.
[120] *GNO* VI.367.4–5; Norris II, 387.

212 ANALYSIS OF *IN CANTICUM CANTICORUM* (*c.* 391)

thirsty, the Word who poured water forth (ἀνομβρήσαντα) from his wound (πληγῆς)' (cf. John 19:34).[121]

Here, Gregory evokes once again, as in Homily 2, the image of Christ as Good Shepherd pierced on the cross, from whose side the Spirit flows as the divine drink that gives eternal life to his sheep.[122] Just as the Spirit pours forth from Christ's pierced side, so too the Bride 'anointed' by the Spirit's 'striking' and 'wounding' now imitates the 'stricken' and 'wounded' Christ (himself 'wounded' by the same Spirit, presumably) by 'gushing forth' the life-giving Spirit to others.

Excursus: Baptismal Exegesis in the 'Middle Homilies'

In this chapter I have emphasized Gregory's depiction of the Bride's advancement and ascent by the unified activity of Christ and the Spirit, with attention given to drawing out the pneumatological aspect. It may be asked whether the kind of baptismal exegesis that Gregory employs in Homilies 1–3 has receded into the background in the middle homilies. As a first response, we need to recognize that while *hom. in Cant.* consists of fifteen individual homilies, Gregory intended them to be heard or read in sequence. There is, therefore, a narrative arc of sorts that runs throughout the homilies, structured both by the narrative arc of the Song of Songs itself, and by the trinitarian and Spirit-based christological underpinnings of Gregory's exegetical approach. Thus, even if baptismal exegesis were to recede to the background in the middle homilies, we have every reason to suppose that Gregory's account of the Bride's advancement and ascent by the Spirit is yet grounded and propelled by the baptismal reality depicted in the opening three homilies.

Nevertheless, it is the case that baptismal exegesis continues to animate Gregory's interpretation of the Song even in the middle homilies. In the following I shall briefly recapitulate the many instances of baptismal exegesis in Homilies 4–12. The density of such references across these homilies is indicative of Gregory's intent to portray the Bride's ascent in emphatically baptismal terms. Thus, we recall from the present chapter Gregory's identification in Homily 4 of the 'dove' as the Holy Spirit, a connection that is only intelligible in light of Christ's baptism in the Jordan. That one can see Christ

---

[121] *GNO* VI.367.13–368.1; Norris II, 387.
[122] Cf. *GNO* VI.62.1–10.

only with the eyes of the Spirit is, of course, a key baptismal argument for the dignity of the Spirit based on 1 Cor. 12:3, which Gregory advances in *Maced.*, as noted in Chapter 2. In Homily 5, Gregory's depictions of 'springs' and 'flowing waters' in connection with John 4:14 are suggestive not only of pneumatology but also of baptism. So too is the allusion to John 3:6 in this same homily, as suggested by similar allusions in *virg.* as well as Homily 2 and Homily 15 of *hom. in Cant.*[123] Gregory's reference to 2 Cor. 3:18 not only is pneumatologically charged, but also, as Marguerite Harl has shown, draws from a long patristic tradition associating this verse with baptismal liturgy.[124] And we may also add to this list Gregory's reference to 'adoption' as 'sons' by the Spirit, which is clearly a baptismal notion in *bapt. Chr.* as I showed in Chapter 2. In Homily 8, Gregory's interpretation of 'myrrh' and 'frankincense' in terms of identification with Christ's death and resurrection is clearly baptismal. This coheres with Gregory's references to the Jordan River, and hence indirectly to Christ's baptism, in this same homily. Homily 9 stands in direct continuity with the baptismal theme of Homily 8 via the notion of being 'buried' and 'raised with Christ' in baptism unto glory (cf. Rom. 6:4; Col. 2:12). The baptismal connotation therefore coheres with Gregory's following emphasis on water imagery, specifically in connection with John 7:37–39. Homily 12 repeats the baptismal theme prevalent in Homilies 8 and 9 by alluding once again to Rom. 6:4 and Col. 2:12 on baptismal identification with Christ.

I have omitted the analysis of Homily 6 and Homily 7 from the study of 'middle homilies' in the present Chapter as they are analysed in Chapter 6 and Chapter 8, respectively. In Homily 6, I have already briefly noted that Gregory refers to mortification of the flesh by being buried together with Christ. Again, Rom. 6:4 and Col. 2:12 appear to stand behind this exegesis and are therefore accurately described as baptismal in tenor. As I shall show, Gregory employs baptismal exegesis in Homily 7 in several parts: by commenting on the 'rebirth' of the church, by depicting the church as 'adopted' in pneumatological terms, and especially by exploring the mortification and vivification of the church, which climaxes in strongly baptismal terms in Homilies 8 and 9.

This leaves only Homily 11 to comment upon. Ideally, an analysis of this homily would be included in Chapter 6 owing to its overt use of baptismal

---

[123] Cf. *GNO* VIII/1.304.21–305.6; *GNO* VI.32.9; *GNO* VI.468.10–13.
[124] Harl (1970).

214 ANALYSIS OF *IN CANTICUM CANTICORUM* (*c.* 391)

exegesis, though I have refrained from this so as to analyse the homilies in sequence where possible. Homily 11 stands out as especially important for Gregory's baptismal exegesis since he makes the connection with *literal baptism* beyond a shadow of a doubt. Commenting on the line 'I have removed my tunic. How shall I put it on? I have washed my feet. How shall I soil them?' (cf. Song 5: 3), Gregory comments:

> These are the ways in which she opened a way into her soul for the Word, having rent the veil of her heart, that is, the flesh. When I say 'flesh', what I mean is 'the old humanity' (cf. Col. 3:9), which the apostle commands to be stripped off and put aside by those who are going to wash off the filth of the soul's feet in the bath of the Word.[125]

Norris notes, 'Clearly in this whole passage Gregory has baptism, the beginning of the Christian way, in his mind, not only as a washing but as a "putting off" of one identity and the assumption of a new identity'.[126] Commenting on the same verse of the Song, Gregory speaks of the Bride being 'renewed through the rebirth from above' (διὰ τῆς ἄνωθεν γεννήσεως) and being clothed with light (φωτοειδές).[127] A little later on, Gregory comments on the washing of the Bride's feet (cf. Song 5: 3), and here the link to baptism becomes undeniable. Thus, 'You perceive clearly, then, what these words convey: that she who has once and for all, *through baptism* (διὰ τοῦ βαπτίσματος), taken off her sandals . . . for it is the proper business of *the baptizer* (τοῦ βαπτίζοντος) to loose the thongs of those wearing sandals, . . . has had her feet washed'.[128] The passage provides an important hermeneutical key for Gregory's baptismal exegesis not only in Homily 11, but throughout *hom. in Cant.* It suggests that his repeated allusions to baptism throughout the work are the result of a basic inclination to view the whole life course of Christian spiritual formation through the lens of an actual baptismal ritual.

We can conclude, therefore, that while the 'middle homilies' trace the Bride's advancement and ascent by the unified activity of Christ and the Spirit, baptismal exegesis remains essential to Gregory's interpretation of the Bride's progress. This reinforces my claim that Gregory intends the

---

[125] *GNO* VI.327.18–328.; Norris II, 347.
[126] Norris II, 347 n.24.
[127] *GNO* VI.328.14–15; 328.20; Norris II, 347, 349.
[128] *GNO* VI.331.3–10; Norris II, 351.

baptismal theme of Homilies 1–3 to continue on throughout the narrative arc of the 'middle homilies'. We should thus expect to find baptismal exegesis to be a prominent feature in the climax of this narrative arc in the remaining Homilies 13, 14, and 15.

Conclusion

The focus of this chapter has been Gregory's understanding of the 'advancement' and 'ascent' of the soul in terms of the unified activity of Christ and the Spirit. In Homily 4 Gregory shows that the soul must undergo repeated stages of purification, just as gold is purified by fire. Such purification is achieved not only by drawing near to Christ the Bridegroom in order to reflect his image in the 'mirror' of the soul, but also by looking upon the Spirit so as to receive his impression upon the eye of the soul. Only by receiving the form of the Spirit in this way is the soul no longer threatened by the pure holiness of divine light, but is enabled to see the transcendent beauty of God once veiled by Christ's body. That the Spirit is essential to humanity's vision of the divine light veiled in the incarnate Christ indicates Gregory's thoroughly anti-Macedonian and anti-Eunomian understanding of the soul's 'advancement' and 'ascent'.

Homily 5 is framed in terms of the fulfilment of prophecy in Christ's incarnation, by which humanity is rescued from idolatry. While Christ's coming is compared to the rising of the springtime sun, this event is fundamentally inseparable from the accompanying advent of the warm springtime wind of the Spirit who, likewise, acts to cure humanity frozen in idolatry. Gregory's emphasis on 'epektasis' in this homily is, similarly, grounded not only in a christological core but also in a pneumatological core. The soul's advancement 'from glory to glory' is synonymous with its unceasing transformation into the 'dove', which symbolizes the Spirit. Yet, Gregory informs us that the Spirit that empowers the soul's *epektatic* ascent is none other than the same Spirit by whom Christ the 'Good Shepherd', who united himself to 'the sheep' of the whole human nature in the incarnation, nourishes his flock.

I showed that Homilies 8 and 9 form a literary unit, enclosed by references to John 7:37. This enframes the prominent baptismal theme of these two homilies, where Christ's own baptism in the Jordan, resulting in 'the birth from above', is an especially important theme. Gregory appears in this homily to be recapitulating the structure of thought prominent in his Epiphany

216 ANALYSIS OF *IN CANTICUM CANTICORUM* (*c.* 391)

sermons, where Christ, as 'first-fruit' of the 'common lump' of humanity's salvation, receives regeneration by the Spirit. Homilies 8 and 9 culminate in Gregory's reflections on the bride's transformation in trinitarian 'glory' as she becomes a well of 'living water' imitating Father, Son, and Spirit. In this way, yet to be shown in Chapter 8, these two homilies complete a train of thought commenced in Homily 7 regarding the transformation of the Bride in divine 'glory', in imitation of Christ's own post-resurrection transformation in 'glory'.

In Homily 10, Gregory places a strong emphasis on the transformation of the Bride's mind by the Spirit, such that both body and mind may attain virtue. Further, this transformative process is likened to the birth of the church at Pentecost. Gregory likens the church, in this regenerated state, to a garden producing fruit by the Spirit upon which Christ descends to bring salvation.

Finally, in Homily 12, Gregory focuses on the soul's 'advancement' and 'ascent' in terms of mortification and vivification. Whereas there is an indispensable role to be played by human choice in baptismal identification with Christ's death and resurrection, the finitude of one's capacity to choose means it is ultimately incapable of achieving the desired union with God, who is infinite. The power of human choice, great and necessary though it is for Gregory, is relativized in light of humanity's need for the mortifying and vivifying activity of the Spirit given by Christ.

My analysis of these homilies further reinforces the fact that Gregory is interested in a baptismal exegesis of the Song of Songs. To read the Song the right way is *subjectively* to experience a kind of 'baptism' by which the whole human person, through imitation of Christ, is progressively transformed toward union with God. Whereas Gregory's baptismal exegesis in Homilies 1– 3 served to depict the Bride's *initial* encounter with the Bridegroom through the Spirit, the homilies belonging to the middle section of *hom. in Cant.* analysed in this chapter are especially interested in tracing the Bride's subsequent and unceasing 'advancement' and 'ascent' by the same unified activity of Christ and the Spirit that featured in the first three homilies.

In this way, the Bride's perpetual, *epekatic* progress is analogous, though not exactly identical, to the incarnate Christ's own 'advancement' to the rank of 'Lord' after the passion through the Spirit's anointing. This progressive ascent, by which the Spirit incorporates one into the 'glory' of God, closely mirrors the 'ascent narrative' of *Maced.*, analysed in Chapter 2. According to that narrative, ascent toward God occurs through a movement of humanity in the Spirit, to Christ, and finally to the Father, which culminates in beholding the 'circular' intra-trinitarian exchange of 'glory'. The climax of this ascent will be the subject of the next and final chapter as I turn now to analyse Homilies 13, 14, and 15 of *hom. in Cant.*

8
Christ's Pneumatic Body in the Glory of the Trinity

Introduction

As I showed in Chapter 2, Gregory advanced two 'models' of trinitarian unity in *Maced.*—the 'linear' and the 'circular'. These two models, I suggested, are integrally connected, for it is according to the trinitarian unity of activity at baptism that characterizes the 'linear' model that humanity may be transformed and thereby come to be joined to the 'circular' exchange of intra-trinitarian glory. I argued that Gregory's passing reference to John 17:5 in *Maced.* gestures toward the view that he understood the definitive point of transition *within the economy of salvation* from the 'linear' and 'circular' model to have prototypically occurred in the post-passion glorification of the incarnate Christ's flesh into union with the divinity of the Only-begotton Son, and through *this* union to the Father, by the Spirit's 'anointing'. This claim, I submit, has been fully vindicated by my analysis in Chapter 4 of Gregory's further references to John 17:5 in the context of (a) his Spirit-based account of the unity of Christ in *Apoll.* and (b) the eschatological unity of the church as the body of Christ in the Spirit's 'glory', which Gregory expounds in *hom. in 1 Cor. 15:28*. And this claim is further substantiated by the argument I advanced in Chapter 5, that Gregory already held a Spirit-based christology (and thus probably a Spirit-based *ecclesiology*) at the time he wrote *Maced.*

In the present chapter, I advance the argument that this basic theological outlook underpins Gregory's exegesis of Homilies 13, 14, and 15 of *hom. in Cant.* That is, while the earlier homilies appear to draw from the 'linear' scheme to depict the *subjective* reality of a *descending* transmission of trinitarian unity of activity from God to humanity and a corresponding *ascending* advancement of humanity to God, we may discern a clear transition to the 'circular' model that occurs in the final three homilies. On this note, Gregory will stress the unity of the 'common lump' of the church as the 'pneumatic body' of Christ, who is the 'first-fruit'. This culminates in Gregory's account

Christ, the Spirit, and Human Transformation in Gregory of Nyssa's In Canticum Canticorum. Alexander L. Abecina, Oxford University Press. © Oxford University Press 2024. DOI: 10.1093/oso/9780197745946.003.0009

CHRIST'S PNEUMATIC BODY   219

of the eschatological unity of the church in the 'circular' glory of the Trinity. Thus, in Homilies 13, 14, and 15, Gregory grounds the *subjective* reality of human transformation and ultimate union with God in the unified activity of the Trinity and Spirit-based christology.

Before undertaking this analysis, however, I shall begin with an investigation of Homily 7, in which several of the ideas that feature in Homilies 13, 14, and 15 are already foreshadowed. Beginning with Homily 7 allows me to show that the Spirit-based ecclesiology that Gregory develops in the final three homilies is already anticipated at the midway point of *hom. in Cant.* and thus reveals the deeper intentionality and logical substructure that steers his exegesis of the Song of Songs.

Homily 7 (Song 3:9–4:7a)

Christ's Pneumatic Body

Homily 7 opens with Gregory's commentary on the line 'King Solomon made himself a palanquin' (cf. Song 3:9). Naturally, Gregory takes 'Solomon' to be 'a type of the true King', Christ.[1] Yet, it is not only Christ that Gregory has in view but also the Holy Spirit, for just as Solomon built the temple, so, Gregory notes, Christ built the 'holy temple' of the church that is 'joined together' (συναρμοσθέντας) in 'the unity (τη ἑνότητι) of the faith' and 'bond (συνδέσμῳ) of peace' such that it has 'become the dwelling place (κατοικητήριον) of God in the Spirit (cf. Eph. 2:22; 4:3–4).'[2] The Song's reference to the 'palanquin' (cf. Song 3:9) is therefore said to signify the church, and Gregory will proceed to discuss its meaning in relation to the activity of both Christ and the Spirit.

The inclusion of 'wood' among the 'gold and silver and scarlet and gemstones' (cf. Song 3:10) from which the 'palanquin' of the church is constructed piques Gregory's interest for, according to Paul, 'wood' will be destroyed in the fire (πυρός) of judgment (cf. 1 Cor. 3:10–15).[3] Gregory makes sense of the negative connotation of 'wood' by reasoning that sinful human beings, who have been made 'wooden' (τοῦ ξύλου) in the likeness of

[1] *GNO* VI.201.3–4; Norris II, 215.
[2] *GNO* VI.202.7–9; Norris II, 215.
[3] *GNO* VI.207.18–208.4; Norris II, 219.

220 ANALYSIS OF *IN CANTICUM CANTICORUM* (c. 391)

the 'tree' (ξύλινα) of the knowledge of good and evil (cf. Gen. 2:9 LXX), may change themselves into 'gold or silver or some other precious thing (cf. Song 3:10) . . . on the basis of its own capacity for choice (προαιρέσεως)'.[4] Yet, as in Homily 12, Gregory relativizes the human capacity for 'choice' by situating it in terms of baptismal 'regeneration' (παλιγγενεσίας) that 'changes' (μεταστοιχειώσας) wood into the lustrous nature of silver and gold.[5] Not surprisingly, therefore, Gregory makes an immediate link between this baptismal regeneration and the gifts of the Holy Spirit bestowed upon the 'palanquin' that stands for the church:

> the apostle says that God measured the gifts of the Holy Spirit to each individual and gives to one the gift of prophecy according to the proportion of faith, while to another he gives some other function, according as each has the natural disposition and the ability to receive grace—either becoming an eye of the body of the church, or being assigned the role of a hand, or supplying support in the place of a foot (cf. 1 Cor. 12:7–31). In the same way, one person becomes, in the structure of the *palanquin* (cf. Song 3:9), a post, another becomes the seat, while another becomes the part where the head is (called backrest), and some, further, are meant for the interior . . . the beauty contrived for each part is different and appropriate.[6]

What we witness here, I suggest, is yet another example of Gregory's baptismal exegesis, where the 'palanquin' stands for the transformation of humanity into the body of Christ, that is the church, through baptismal regeneration and the illumination of the Spirit. Christ's body, we might say, is conceived in Homily 7 as a baptized and hence *pneumatic* body. As we shall see, the church is, for Gregory, a pneumatic body analogously to Christ's pneumatic body, glorified by the Spirit after the passion.

Since Song 4:1–5 concerns the praise of various parts of the Bride's body, Gregory interprets these in terms of the pneumatologically charged passage 1 Corinthians 12, showcasing a knowledge of physiology reminiscent of his reflections in *De hominis opificio*. Of the seven members of the Bride's body that are praised in Song 4:1–5—eyes, hair, teeth, lips, cheek, neck, and breasts—four are particularly important with respect to the Holy Spirit's presence. The first is the 'eye' (cf. Song 4:1), which, he suggests, stands for

---

[4] *GNO* VI.208.17–18; Norris II, 221.
[5] *GNO* VI.208.16–20; Norris II, 221.
[6] *GNO* VI.209.21–210.12; Norris II, 221 and 223.

the 'noblest members' who are 'assigned to lead the people'.[7] The role of the 'eye' is to recognize God and thereby fulfil the Great Command to 'love our true friend with all our heart and soul and strength' (cf. Mark 12:30).[8] Therefore, beginning with a comment on the line 'Your eyes are doves outside your veil' (cf. Song 4:1), Gregory notes that 'purity' is the native characteristic of doves.[9] Then, recalling his previous exegesis on the 'eye' of Song 1:15 in Homily 4, whereby one is said to take on 'the form' (τὴν μορφήν) of that which is gazed upon as though one were a 'mirror', he suggests that those who have 'eyelike authority' in the church may come to acquire a 'spiritual life' (ὁ πνευματικός . . . βίος) by gazing upon nothing 'material' (ὑλῶδες) or 'corporeal' (σωματικόν). In this way, those who lead the church in purity have lives that take the form of the pure dove, who is the Holy Spirit.[10]

Gregory's use of the term πνευματικός in his discussion of the 'eye' to describe the one whose form of life 'is shaped in conformity to the grace of the Holy Spirit' (τὸ πρὸς τὴν τοῦ πνεύματος τοῦ ἁγίου χάριν μεμορφῶσθαι αὐτῶν τῆς ζωῆς τὸ εἶδος) helps to clarify his further use of pneumatic language in his subsequent discussion of the 'teeth' of Christ's body (cf. Song 4:2). These, he says, refer to 'teachers' in the church who are able to 'grind the divine mysteries up small . . . so that spiritual nourishment (τὴν πνευματικὴν ταύτην τροφήν) can more easily be taken into the church's body'.[11] In particular, the 'teeth' are able to take the old covenant law and render it 'spiritual' (πνευματικόν) since 'the law is spiritual' (πνευματικός) (cf. Rom. 7:14). To be sure, Gregory does not refer to the Holy Spirit explicitly with regard to the church's 'teeth', but in light of Gregory's use of pneumatic language so far in this homily, within *hom. in Cant.* as a whole, and within his corpus more broadly (as I discussed at length in Chapter 1), the Holy Spirit is clearly in view with respect to the function of the 'teeth' to provide spiritual nourishment to Christ's body.

The third member of the church with respect to which the Spirit plays a prominent role is the 'neck', which Gregory comments upon in relation to the line 'your neck is like a tower of David' (cf. Song 4:4). He draws significance from the way the human neck assists in *breathing*. Therefore, he points out that the neck contains the 'windpipe' (τράχηλος), which functions as

---

[7] *GNO* VI.216.17–18; Norris II, 227.
[8] *GNO* VI.218.2–4; Norris II, 229.
[9] *GNO* VI.218.15; Norris II, 229.
[10] *GNO* VI.219.1–5; Norris II, 231.
[11] *GNO* VI.225.19–23; Norris II, 235 and 237.

222 ANALYSIS OF *IN CANTICUM CANTICORUM* (*c.* 391)

a receptacle of 'the breath' (τοῦ πνεύματος) that comes from outside and rushes in, dwells in us (ἡμῖν εἰσοικιζομένου), and kindles the fire within the heart (δι' οὗ τὸ ἐγκάρδιον πῦρ) to fulfil its natural 'activity' (ἐνέργειαν).[12] Furthermore, he notes that beneath the windpipe is where the voice is produced by means of the 'exhaled breath' (πνεύματι).[13] While Gregory notes that the neck bears 'the true head' who is Christ, it must do so by being 'receptive of the Spirit' (τοῦ πνεύματός), which sets the heart on 'fire' (πυροειδῆ) and 'warms it' (ἐκθερμαίνοντος), thus enabling it to serve as an instrument of intelligible speech that articulates the 'motions of the heart' (τὰ τῆς καρδίας κινήματα). The neck receptive of the Spirit thus produces a 'constant flow of nourishment' (ἐπιρρεούσης γὰρ ἀεὶ τῆς τροφῆς) through its teaching, which strengthens the body of the church and sustains it in being.[14] Previously we have seen Gregory speak of the Spirit residing in the heart, where it warms love for God through the whole body (cf. Homily 3). Here, we see a similar teaching, now applied to the ecclesial setting. Building further upon his earlier interpretation in Homily 5 of the 'lily' that provides sweet scented 'nourishment', the Spirit, which now resides in the heart of the church, gives 'nourishment' through the neck to the whole body of Christ. It is important also to note the synergy that exists between the 'neck' and the 'teeth' insofar as both provide spiritual nourishment via the activity of the Spirit to the whole body of the church through teaching.

The fourth 'member' that Gregory connects closely to the Holy Spirit is the 'breasts' with regard to the line 'Your breasts are like two twin fawns that feed among the lilies, until the day breathes (διαπνεύσῃ) and the shadows are moved' (cf. Song 4:5–6). He observes that since the 'light' (τοῦ φωτός) has already 'dawned' (διαλάμψαντος) in this part of the Song, then all things are 'illumined' (καταυγασθῇ) by the 'day' (ἡμέρας), which 'breathes out light (διαπνεούσης τὸ φῶς) where it will (ὅπου θέλει)'.[15] Gregory's rather unusual expression 'breathes out light' (διαπνεούσης τὸ φῶς) is a phrase he has already employed in Homily 5 in relation to those nourished by the Holy Spirit.[16] The pneumatological point toward which Gregory has been driving is now made explicit. Those familiar with the gospel, says Gregory, know that Song 4:6 is actually about the Holy Spirit, who breathes 'where it wills' (ὅπου

---

[12] *GNO* VI.233.23–234.3; Norris II, 245.
[13] *GNO* VI.234.7–11; Norris II, 245.
[14] *GNO* VI.234.11–236.4; Norris II, 245, 247.
[15] *GNO* VI.239.8–10; Norris II, 249.
[16] Cf. *GNO* VI.169.11–170.9; Norris II, 181.

βούλεται) (cf. John 3:8) and 'enlightens' (φῶς ἐμποιοῦν) those in whom he is 'born' (ἐγγένηται) as 'sons of light' (υἱοὶ φωτός) and 'sons of the day' (υἱοὶ ἡμέρας) (cf. 1 Thess. 5:5). Thus, the 'light' and 'day' are said to be none other than the Holy Spirit, who banishes the darkness.[17] Once again, Gregory draws upon the Pauline teaching on adoption as sons as a mode of human transformation through the Spirit. His statement here further consolidates his similar teaching in Homily 5 and makes explicit the pneumatological import of his reference to 1 Thess. 5:5 in Homily 2.[18]

The Post-resurrection Glorification of Christ's Body

With his discussion of Song 4:5–6, Gregory has now characterized the body of Christ as a *pneumatic body*—one that is shaped, nourished, and ultimately united by the activity of the Holy Spirit nourishing all its members. This is just to be expected given Gregory's earlier allusions in this homily to Paul's emphatic teaching on ecclesial unity in the Spirit in the letter to the Ephesians. Yet, Gregory's focus on the *essential* role of the Spirit in giving birth to and unifying the church as Christ's body has not ended here. In his concluding remarks on Song 4:6–7, Gregory comments upon *the whole body* of the church and ties this to a discussion about the post-resurrection transformation of the body of the incarnate Christ in the eternal 'glory' of God. Thus, the Bridegroom praises the Bride's 'whole body' (ὁλοσώματον) since 'through death he destroyed him who has the power of death (cf. Heb. 2:14) and was brought up again to the glory proper to the Godhead (πάλιν ἐπαναγάγῃ ἑαυτὸν πρὸς τὴν ἰδίαν δόξαν τῆς θεότητος), which he possessed from the beginning (ἀπ' ἀρχῆς), before the cosmos existed (cf. John 17:5)'.[19]

For Gregory, the reference to John 17:5, while brief, is nevertheless crucial for understanding his interpretive intent in this homily (as well as Homilies 8 and 9), for it immediately recalls his references to this same verse in *Maced.*, *Apoll.*, and *hom. in 1 Cor. 15:28*, where it marks the post-resurrection transformation of the incarnate Christ's flesh into unity with the divinity of the Son, and through the Son with the Father, in the 'glory' of the Spirit. To this present reference to John 17:5 Gregory adds a comment on the Song's

[17] *GNO* VI.239.11–240.5; Norris II, 251.
[18] Cf. *GNO* VI.62.13–14; Norris II, 69.
[19] *GNO* VI.242.17–19; Norris II, 253.

224 ANALYSIS OF *IN CANTICUM CANTICORUM* (*c.* 391)

reference to the 'mountain of myrrh' and 'hill of frankincense' (cf. Song 4:6–7), where 'myrrh' is said to stand for Christ's 'suffering', while 'frankincense' stands for Christ's restoration to 'the glory of the Godhead' (τὴν δόξαν τῆς θεότητος).[20] Gregory indicates that the praise attributed *to Christ* in his post-resurrection transformation and glorification may also be transferred, via identification with Christ and his suffering, to *Christ's pneumatic body*, the church. Thus, says Gregory, 'the one who suffers with him [i.e. Christ] will be fully glorified with him (συνδοξάζεται πάντως)' just as 'the one who has once for all entered into the divine glory (ἐν τῷ θεεία δόξῃ) (cf. John 17:5) becomes all beautiful'.[21]

The crucial question is *how* does Gregory envisage the transfer of benefits from Christ's glorified body to the church's glorified body taking place? To be sure, while Gregory has characterized the church as Christ's *pneumatic body*, he refers neither to the essential role of the Holy Spirit's activity in glorifying Christ's resurrected body into union with the Trinity, nor in the transferral of these benefits to the church in the present context of Homily 7. However, this is evidently due to the very deliberate homiletical-literary shaping of theology in Gregory's homilies. As my previous analysis in Chapter 7 suggests, Gregory in fact intentionally delays his reference to the Spirit's activity in *glorifying* the church as the pneumatic body of Christ until the immediately following Homilies 8 and 9. There, as I showed in the previous chapter, the subject of 'the glory of God' continues to be explored in the emphatically baptismal terms of dying and rising with Christ, culminating in an image of the glorified body of the church as a 'well' and 'river' that runs deep with the life-giving waters of the Holy Spirit, in imitation of the Trinity. From this vantage point, the theological-literary substructure of Homilies 7, 8, and 9 appears to be closely patterned after the Spirit-based christology of *Apoll.* and the Spirit-based ecclesiology of *hom. in 1 Cor. 15:28*, as discussed in Chapter 4.

We observe in Homily 7 something similar to the absence of overt references to the Holy Spirit's post-passion anointing of Christ in 'glory' in *Eun.* III. Such references need not be stated explicitly for the attentive reader to discern, upon a more holistic reading of Gregory's corpus, the Spirit-based christology (and corresponding Spirit-based ecclesiology) that lies just beneath the surface of the text. In any case, it appears that Gregory ultimately reserves his fullest exposition of the meaning of John 17:5 and the theme of

---

[20] *GNO* VI.243.2; Norris II, 253.
[21] *GNO* VI.243.19–21; Norris II, 255.

CHRIST'S PNEUMATIC BODY 225

Christ's transformation in the Spirit's glory for the climactic exegesis of Song 6:1–9 in Homily 15, as I will discuss momentarily.

Excursus: Christ's Pneumatic Body in *Hom. in 1 Cor. 15:28*

Before I analyse Homilies 13, 14, and 15, it is perhaps helpful to provide one further piece of background to Gregory's exegesis of those homilies with reference to *hom. in 1 Cor. 15:28*, which I commented upon only briefly in Chapter 4.[22] In this work, Gregory offers an interpretation of 1 Cor. 15:28— 'Then the Son will be subjected to the one who put all things in subjection under him'—refuting those who take this verse to refer to the subjection, and hence *subordination*, of the Only-begotten Son to the Father. The treatise also makes significant reference to Christ as 'first-fruit' of humanity's eschatological union with God who will become 'all in all'. As we shall see, 1 Cor. 15:28 and the 'first-fruit' motif will feature prominently in Homilies 13, 14, and 15 of *hom. in Cant.*

After pointing out that the term 'subjection' carries a variety of different senses in scripture, Gregory proceeds to inquire into the specific sense that 'subjection' takes when applied to the Son in 1 Cor. 15:28. He is certain that since subjection implies mutability, yet the Son is immutable, then the controversial term cannot apply to the Son according to his being the 'power' of God.[23] Nevertheless, Gregory readily acknowledges that this term in 1 Cor. 15:28 does indeed apply to the Son, though only in some *temporal* sense since Paul speaks of this event happening 'at the end of the future consummation of the universe'.[24] The exegetical dilemma with which Gregory must grapple, therefore, is how the *temporal* subjection of the Son to the Father is to be properly understood.

Gregory's strategy is to interpret 1 Cor. 15:28 against its broader thematic context, which he takes to be the eschatological resurrection of the dead. Thus, he notes that humanity may be resurrected with Christ, 'For as in Adam all die so also in Christ will all be made alive' (cf. 1 Cor. 15:22).[25] While the Only-begotten Son came to exist in the mortal human nature, from this 'mixture' there subsisted a 'first-fruit of the common lump' (ἀπαρχή τις τοῦ

[22] Cf. Boulnois 'Le cercle des glorifications', 36–38; cf. Maspero, *Trinity and Man*, 187–191.
[23] *GNO* III/2.7.4–14; Greer, 119–120.
[24] *GNO* III/2.9.9–11; Greer, 121.
[25] *GNO* III/2.13.11–13; Greer, 123.

226 ANALYSIS OF *IN CANTICUM CANTICORUM* (*c.* 391)

κοινοῦ φυράματος) (cf. Rom. 11:16), that is, 'the man according to Christ' (ὁ κατὰ Χριστὸν ἄνθρωπος) through whom humanity (τὸ ἀνθρώπινον) is assimilated to divinity. Thus, in *him*, says Gregory, began the annihilation of sin, death, and evil.[26] Gregory points out that those who imitate Christ by withdrawing from evil will become like him who was himself 'first-fruit of those fallen asleep' (cf. 1 Cor. 15:20) and 'firstborn from the dead' (cf. Col. 1:18).[27]

This notion of Christ as 'first-fruit', which I explored in Chapter 2, in turn serves to clarify the meaning of 'subjection' in 1 Cor. 15:28. Hence, says Gregory, when evil is destroyed, it is necessary to subject all things to God, who rules over all. Crucially, this 'subjection' does not refer to the Son *simpliciter*, but rather to all those incorporated into the Son's body, that is, *the church.* By 'imitating the first-fruit' (μίμησιν τῆς ἀπαρχῆς), 'the whole batch of our nature' (ὅλον τὸ φύραμα τῆς φύσεως) (cf. Rom. 11:16) that is mixed with it and made one with 'the conjoined body' (τὸ συνεχὲς σῶμα) will be governed by the 'good alone' such that the subjection of the Son takes place '*through us*' (δι' ἡμῶν) and '*in us*' (ἐν ἡμῖν), that is, Christ's 'body' (cf. 1 Cor. 12).[28]

Importantly, the church's 'subjection' to God coincides, for Gregory, with the cosmological event of God's becoming 'all in all' (cf. 1 Cor. 15:28) since, at that point, evil will have been completely destroyed. Furthermore, he claims that when God becomes 'all in all', the church will come to 'have' God, where 'having God' (τὸ ἔχειν τὸν θεόν) is 'being united to God' (ἐνωθῆναι θεῷ) as 'members of the same body' (cf. Eph. 3:6) in the 'unity of the faith' (cf. Eph. 4:13).[29] Citing John 17:21, Christ is therefore understood as the mediator, 'by uniting all people to himself and through himself to the Father'.[30]

Gregory's argument clearly begins with a focus on Christ and the Father, and yet, while continuing to comment on John 17:21, he shifts his focus away from Christ as 'mediator' to identify the Holy Spirit as the bond of unity amongst the individual members of Christ's body. In this manner, Gregory follows through on the soteriological implications of the Spirit-based christology articulated in *Apoll.*, as I intimated in my brief analysis of *hom. in 1 Cor. 15:28* in Chapter 4. Just as the man assumed in the economy is united to

---

[26] GNO III/2.14.10–19; Greer, 124.
[27] GNO III/2.15.5–14; Greer, 124.
[28] GNO III/2.16.13–22; Greer, 125.
[29] GNO III/2.18.14–18; Greer, 126.
[30] GNO III/2.21.15–19; Greer, 128.

the divinity of the Son of God by the Spirit's anointing, so too is Christ's *ecclesial body* now united to the Son of God via the same Spirit, and through the Son to the heavenly Father.

In this sense, Gregory views the Holy Spirit's activity as essential, not peripheral, to the eschatological overcoming of evil in the 'common lump', of which Christ is the 'first-fruit'. Hence, quoting from John 17:22—'The glory that you have given to me I have given them'—he identifies 'glory' with the Holy Spirit breathed upon the disciples, and by which he 'united' (ἐνωθῆναι) them 'in the unity of the Spirit' (τῇ ἑνότητι τοῦ πνεύματος).[31] Further, citing the all-important verse, John 17:5—'Glorify me with the glory that I had in the beginning in your presence before the world existed'—he identifies the Spirit once again as the 'glory' by which Christ has the glory of the Father. It was necessary, says Gregory, for Christ's flesh (σάρξ), through mixture (ἀνακράσεως), to become what the Word is through the Spirit. Paraphrasing John 17:22—'I have given them the glory that you gave me, that they may be one as we are one'—Gregory notes that the 'glory' given to Christ by the Father was given to the disciples so they could be united with Christ, and through him to the Father.[32]

We see, therefore, that just as is the case in Gregory's account of Spirit-based christology in *Apoll.*, the Holy Spirit's activity plays an *essential* rather than subsidiary or peripheral role in his understanding of the resurrection of humanity from the dead, the 'subjection' of the church as Christ's body to God, and hence to God finally becoming 'all in all' in his eschatological triumph over evil (cf. 1 Cor. 15:28). Gregory conceives of human salvation now from an *eschatological* and *cosmological* vantage point, as inclusion into Christ's *pneumatic body* by the 'glory' of the Spirit. This, it seems, is the natural outworking of the *cosmic* principle of trinitarian unity of activity to which I alluded in Chapter 2, the 'first-fruit' concept, and Gregory's Spirit-based christology mutually operating as a cohesive exegetical framework. While baptism is not mentioned explicitly, Gregory's language of needing to withdraw from evil in imitation of Christ the 'first-fruit' is immediately evocative of both the baptism ritual and the post-baptismal life of virtue.

---

[31] *GNO* III/2.22.3–4; Greer, 128.
[32] *GNO* III/2.21.23–22.16; Greer, 128.

228 ANALYSIS OF *IN CANTICUM CANTICORUM* (*c.* 391)

Homilies 13, 14, and 15 (Song 5:8–6:9)

Christ's Pneumatic Body in Trinitarian Glory

Returning now to *hom. in Cant.*, we see that Gregory's view of salvation as inclusion into Christ's pneumatic body appears to undergird his exegesis of the Song of Songs in Homilies 13, 14, and 15. As I shall show, Gregory's exegesis of these three homilies recapitulates the (Spirit-based) christological exegesis of Song 3:9–4:15 in Homilies 7, 8, and 9 and of the contested term 'subjection' of 1 Cor. 15:28 in *hom. in 1 Cor. 15:28.*

Homily 13 begins with a commentary on the Bride's oath in the line 'I have adjured you, O daughters of Jerusalem, by the powers and virtues of the field' (cf. Song 5:8). After establishing that 'the field' stands allegorically for 'the cosmos', Gregory identifies the 'powers' and 'virtues' of the cosmos as two things that bring humanity to 'close affinity' with God: 'the truthfulness of one's idea of that which is (τῆς περὶ τὸ ὄντως)' regarding God, and 'pure thinking' that banishes the disorder of the soul. According to Gregory, the person who lives by 'these two ways' is fit to 'become a dwelling place of the One who resides within him' and hence 'to see the one we desire' (cf. Matt 5:8), namely Christ.[33]

Since a major theme of the preceding Homily 12 is the removal of the Bride's 'veil', Gregory continues in the present homily to comment on the Bride, who having had her 'veil' *removed by the power of the Spirit*, now 'looks toward the truth [i.e. the Bridegroom] with the uncovered eye of the soul'.[34] Here, he notes that the incarnate Christ upon whom the Bride looks is 'in one respect created (κτιστόν) and in another respect uncreated (ἄκτιστον)', and thus one must properly distinguish between the eternal Logos and the one manifested in the flesh.[35] On the basis of this dual-aspect christology, he points out that the uncreated aspect of Christ is 'completely incapable of being grasped' by the mind and is 'unutterable' in words. However, what is manifested for us through the flesh can be known to some degree.[36] Hence, it is the *human* aspect, rather than the divine, which the Bride is said to describe in this section of the Song.

---

[33] *GNO* VI.376.8–377.20; Norris II, 397.
[34] *GNO* VI.380.12; Norris II, 401.
[35] *GNO* VI.380.20–381.13; Norris II, 401.
[36] *GNO* VI.381.10–16; Norris II, 403.

CHRIST'S PNEUMATIC BODY 229

Yet, drawing upon the familiar notion of Christ as the 'first-fruit' of the rest of humanity's sanctification, Gregory seamlessly transitions from a discussion about Christ's incarnate flesh to the body of the church:

> since he once for all, through the first-fruit (τῆς ἀπαρχῆς), drew to himself the mortal nature of flesh (τὴν ἐπίκηρον τῆς σαρκὸς φύσιν), which he took on by means of an uncorrupted virginity (cf. Luke 1:35), he ever sanctifies the common lump of that nature (τὸ κοινὸν τῆς φύσεως φύραμα) through its first fruit (τῇ ἀπαρχῇ) (cf. Rom. 11:16), nourishing his body (σῶμα), the church, in the persons of those who are united to him in the participation of the mystery (ἑνουμένων αὐτῷ κατὰ κοινωνίαν τοῦ μυστηρίου); and those members that are grafted into him through faith he fits into the common body (τῷ κοινῷ σώματι), and he fashions a comely whole by fitly and appropriately assigning believers to roles as eyes and mouth and hands and the other members (cf. 1 Cor. 12).[37]

Zachhuber's suggestion that Gregory's statement about being 'united to him [i.e. Christ] in the participation of the mystery' is a reference to the Eucharist may be better understood as a reference to baptism given the pervasiveness of the baptismal theme throughout *hom. in Cant.* and in Homilies 13 and 15 especially.[38] The baptismal theme will resurface momentarily, but for now Gregory's main point is to establish the idea that to look upon the church is, in a very real sense, to look upon Christ himself. In this way, he is permitted to draw an important analogy between the cosmos and the church. Just as one can discern the divine Wisdom in the created cosmos, so too can one discern God by looking upon 'the cosmos that is the church', which has been 'renewed by the birth from above', again probably a reference to baptismal regeneration by the Spirit.[39] Thus, just as one can look upon the perceptible cosmos and grasp invisible Beauty and Wisdom through the visible, so too the person who looks upon the new cosmos (τὸν καινὸν τοῦτον κόσμον) created in the church via the Spirit sees within it the eschatological event of

---

[37] *GNO* VI.381.19–382.6; Norris II, 403.

[38] Cf. Everett Ferguson, 'Theology of Baptism in the In Canticum Canticorum of Gregory of Nyssa', in *Gregory of Nyssa: In Canticum Canticorum: Analytical and Supporting Studies. Proceedings of the 13th International Colloquium on Gregory of Nyssa (Rome, 17–20 September 2014)*, Supplements to Vigiliae Christianae 150, ed. Giulio Maspero, Miguel Brugarolas, and Ilaria Vigorelli (Leiden: Brill, 2018), 263; cf. also Gregory's reference to baptism as the 'mystery' in *hom. in Cant.*, *GNO* VI.7.2–8 and *Maced.*, *GNO* III/1.101.14–16.

[39] *GNO* VI.385.5; Norris II, 405.

230 ANALYSIS OF *IN CANTICUM CANTICORUM* (*c.* 391)

God 'who is and is "becoming all in all" (cf. 1 Cor. 15:28)'.[40] Here, we start to glimpse how Gregory's exegesis is guided by virtually identical themes and concerns that influenced his exegesis of 1 Cor. 15:28 in *hom. in 1 Cor. 15:28*.

By what means, therefore, is the Bride of the Song able to reveal the Bridegroom to the virgin 'daughters of Jerusalem' with whom she converses (cf. Song 5:8)? In short, she does so by describing *his body*, the church. Gregory proceeds to comment on the individual members of Christ's body. As in Homily 7 and *hom. in 1 Cor. 15:28*, Gregory will stress that Christ's body is a *pneumatic body*.

First, he identifies the 'head' of the church as Christ himself (cf. Song 5:11), though importantly this is to be understood as a reference to Christ 'the man' (ἄνθρωπον), not to 'the Deity in its eternity (τὸ ἀίδιον τῆς θεότητος)'.[41] Gregory's focus thus remains upon Christ under the aspect of 'first-fruit of the common lump (τὴν ἀπαρχὴν τοῦ κοινοῦ φυράματος)' and 'first-fruits of our entire nature'.[42] In addition to Christ according to his 'deity' and his 'humanity', however, Gregory also shows a clear interest in commenting upon the Holy Spirit's presence, just as he did in Homily 7. Thus, the 'locks' of hair (cf. Song 5:11), which refer to the apostles of the church, contribute to the beauty of Christ the 'head', as they are 'tossed about by the breeze of the Spirit (τῇ τοῦ πνεύματος αὔρᾳ)'.[43]

The 'eyes' also receive especial attention with respect to the Spirit since, according to Song 5:11, they are 'as doves by full pools of waters, washed in milk, sitting by full pools of waters'. Gregory understands the 'eyes' shaped as 'doves' to be a reference to the 'teachers of truth' within the church who live by, and walk in, the Spirit (cf. Gal. 5:25).[44] Here, the baptismal theme recurs once more as Gregory identifies the 'dove' with the form that descended upon the water of the Jordan, highlighting once again Christ baptized as the 'first-fruit' of the whole church sanctified by the Spirit.[45] There are clear echoes here, therefore, of *perf.* and *bapt. Chr.*, where the Holy Spirit's descent upon Christ in the Jordan as the 'first-fruit' of salvation sanctifies the rest of the 'common lump' of humanity. At the conclusion of Homily 13, then, Gregory has portrayed the church as the 'common lump', sanctified by Christ as the 'first-fruit', though this is inseparable for him from the presence of the Spirit,

---

[40] *GNO* VI.385.22–386.9; Norris II, 407.
[41] *GNO* VI.391.8; Norris II, 413.
[42] *GNO* VI.390.22–391.12; Norris II, 413.
[43] *GNO* VI.393.2–5; Norris II, 415.
[44] *GNO* VI.395.2–5; Norris II, 417.
[45] *GNO* VI.395.3–8; Norris II, 417.

CHRIST'S PNEUMATIC BODY 231

through whom God is becoming 'all in all' (cf. 1 Cor. 15:28). As in *hom. in 1 Cor. 15:28*, it appears that Gregory portrays the salvation of the 'common lump' of humanity in terms of membership in Christ's *pneumatic body*, with clear cosmological overtones.

This same strategy for interpreting the Song of Songs continues in Homily 14. That is, by looking upon the beauty of the *pneumatic body* that is the church, Gregory argues one may discern the beauty of *Christ*. In this homily he covers six members of the body (cf. Song 5:13–16)—the jaw, the lips, the hands, the heart, the throat, and the legs—three of which are directly related to the Spirit. Thus, the homily begins with a reflection on the meaning of the 'jaw' (cf. Song 5:13), which Gregory takes to be a reference to those who are ready to chew upon the 'more solid food' of spiritual teaching, and which he then proceeds to connect to his earlier observation about the 'eyes' in Homily 13. For Gregory the 'eye' that sits by the pool of the 'spiritual waters' (τῶν πνευματικῶν ὑδάτων) must become washed in order to be likened to the 'innocent dove' so that 'it may make all those who constitute the body of the church participants in its own good things'.[46] In the same way, 'it is appropriate for the "jaws" to be praised along with *them* [i.e. the 'eyes'], for their job is to grind small the food by which the body's nature and power are preserved'.[47] By this he means teaching the 'open statement of the truth' (cf. 2 Cor. 4:2).[48]

In establishing this direct connection between 'eye' and 'jaw' Gregory expounds upon the Holy Spirit that jointly operates between them. Hence, there follows further commentary on the line 'his jaws are like bowls of spices pouring forth perfumes' (cf. Song 5:13). The pneumatological aspect of the 'spices' is elaborated in relation the Apostle Paul, who, according to Gregory, was one such 'bowl' of 'spice'. At his 'baptism' the 'scales' were cast from his eyes together with 'the flesh'. Thus, Paul became a 'a child of the Holy Spirit' (cf. Acts 9:17) bringing within himself 'the divine drink (τὸ θεῖον ποτόν)' (cf. John 7:37–39) and becoming the 'sweet fragrance (εὐωδίας) of Christ' (cf. 2 Cor. 2:15) he poured it out, like a perfumer (μυρεψῶν).[49] Identifying the Spirit, yet again, with 'the divine drink' and the 'fragrance of Christ', Paul functions as a symbol of the corporate 'jaw' of the church, depicted as

---

[46] *GNO* VI.400.9–15; Norris II, 423.
[47] *GNO* VI.401.4–9; Norris II, 425.
[48] *GNO* VI.402.22–403.1; Norris II, 427.
[49] *GNO* VI.403.2–11; Norris II, 427.

232 ANALYSIS OF *IN CANTICUM CANTICORUM* (c. 391)

a source of nourishment to the ecclesial body through the unified activity of Christ and the Spirit.

Gregory then comments on the line 'His belly (κοιλία) is an ivory tablet on a sapphire stone' (cf. Song 5:14) and seeks to understand what this says about the 'belly' of the church. Identifying it with the 'the purity of the heart' (cf. Matt. 5:8),[50] Gregory cites other scriptural passages in support of this reading, but his ultimate justification comes from John's gospel, noting that those who believe in Christ will have 'rivers of living water' flowing from his 'belly' (κοιλίας) (cf. John 7:37–38). Thus, the 'belly' stands for 'the pure heart' (cf. Matt. 5:8) upon which God's law is written not with 'ink' but rather with 'the Spirit of the living God' (cf. 2 Cor. 3:3).[51]

Finally, Gregory views the 'throat' (cf. Song 5:16) and the 'breath that comes from the windpipe' in terms of the Holy Spirit. He claims the term 'throat' signifies the servants and interpreters of the Word, in whom Christ speaks. At the same time, he observes that the prophets, who handed their organs of speech to the Spirit within them (αὐτοῖς πνεύματι), became 'sweetness' as they poured forth the divine words from their throat.[52]

At the conclusion of Homily 14 it is evident that Gregory has sought to portray the church not only as the body *of Christ*, but as Christ's *pneumatic body*, animated and enlivened throughout by the Holy Spirit. That Christ is the 'first-fruit' of the 'common lump' of the sanctified humanity that is the church cannot be separated in Gregory's thought from the necessary and essential activity of the Holy Spirit that unites the church to Christ, the first-fruit, just as I argued in Chapter 2.

The exegesis of the Song of Songs in Homily 15, the final and climactic homily of *hom. in Cant.*, stands in fundamental continuity with the exegetical strategy of Homilies 13 and 14. It brings to completion Gregory's exposition of the view first articulated in *hom. in 1 Cor. 15:28*, that salvation is eschatological membership in Christ's pneumatic body. Since Christ's body is conceptualized as a 'micro-cosmos', Gregory portrays this membership in thoroughly cosmological terms. While the eschatological framing was already flagged by Gregory's first reference to 1 Cor. 15:28 in Homily 13,[53] it becomes ever more pronounced in his present interpretation of Song 6:1 in terms of Christ's future coming in 'glory':

[50] *GNO* VI.413.15–16; Norris II, 439.
[51] *GNO* VI.414.10–18; Norris II, 439; 441.
[52] *GNO* VI.425.11–13; Norris II, 451.
[53] Cf. *GNO* VI.385.22–386.9.

CHRIST'S PNEUMATIC BODY 233

They [i.e. the maidens of Song 5:8] may . . . once they have been taught where he turns his regard, may so station themselves that his glory (τὴν δόξαν) may be revealed to them as well—that glory whose epiphany is the salvation of those who behold it.[54]

Initially, Gregory foregrounds *Christ's* condescension to humanity in the incarnation and his being 'mingled with flesh and blood'.[55] Yet, his focus on Christ's incarnation and mingling with humanity transitions gradually to a focus on the Holy Spirit, beginning with his interpretation of the line 'Turn your eyes away from that which stands over against me, for they give me wings' (cf. Song 6:5). Citing an array of scriptural passages that refer to God's 'wings' (cf. Ps. 16[17]:8; Ps. 90[91]:4; Deut. 32:11; Matt. 23:37),[56] he concludes that scripture declares that 'wings' are associated with 'the divine nature' (περὶ τὴν θείαν φύσιν).[57] Furthermore, since human beings were created 'after the image and likeness of God', Gregory states that humanity itself was originally constituted 'with wings' (ἐν ταῖς πτέρυξιν) in 'likeness to the divine'.[58] However, humanity was robbed of its 'wings' due to the 'impulse toward evil', and, therefore, God's grace needed to be manifested in order to illuminate (φωτίζουσα) humanity that it may grow wings again (πτεροφυήσωμεν).[59]

The references to 'wings' and (baptismal) 'illumination' are obviously pneumatologically laden, and they clearly hark back to Gregory's use of this motif in his very first work, *virg.*, as I discussed in Chapter 1. The connection to the Holy Spirit is only gradually made explicit, however, beginning with Gregory's exposition of the line 'There are sixty queens and eighty concubines and young maidens without number. One is my dove, my perfect one, the only one that belongs to her mother, the elect of the one who bore her' (cf. Song 6:8–9). For Gregory, this line of the Song of Songs suggests that different groups of people will progress along the path to restoration in different ways. What accounts for their differences is their 'proper dignity (ἀξίαν)' based upon the 'choices' they have made.[60] While both the 'queens' and the 'concubines' are said to become 'one body with the Word (σύσσωμοι

54 *GNO* VI.435.2–8; Norris II, 463.
55 *GNO* VI.443.11; Norris II, 471.
56 *GNO* VI.447.2–448.5; Norris II, 475.
57 *GNO* VI.447.13–15; Norris II, 475.
58 *GNO* VI.448.5–449.3; Norris II, 475.
59 *GNO* VI.449.1–3; Norris II, 475.
60 *GNO* VI.449.4–460.2; Norris II, 489.

234 ANALYSIS OF *IN CANTICUM CANTICORUM* (*c.* 391)

τῷ λόγῳ)', only the former group, whose dispositions are shaped by 'love', are 'mingled together (ἀνακραθεῖσαι) with God's purity' and thus 'share in his kingship (κονωνίαν τῆς βασιλείας)'. The 'concubines', however, who 'work the good out of fear and not love', do not share in his 'dignity' (κοινωνὸς τῆς ἀξίας).[61]

We must recall that the categories of 'kingship' and 'dignity' that Gregory has introduced in this section of the homily are central to his pneumatology, and indeed also to his Spirit-based christology. In *Maced.*, Gregory argued that while the Only-begotten Son is 'king by nature', the Holy Spirit, understood as 'anointing', is the Son's 'kingship' (βασιλεία).[62] Furthermore, he claims, 'the dignity (ἀξιώματι) of kingship (βασιλείας) is the Holy Spirit, in which the Son is anointed'.[63] Finally, on the inseparable unity of the Spirit and Christ, he states that 'kingship (βασιλεία) is always understood together with the king' (βασιλέως).[64] We have also observed the cognate argument in *Trin.*, as I discussed in Chapter 5. Gregory's introduction of the categories of 'kingship' and 'dignity' in Homily 15 are thus not only pneumatologically but also christologically laden.

This is, of course, to be expected if, as I suggest, the exegesis of Song 6:1–9 is grounded in Gregory's account of the union of divine and human natures in Christ—or, in other words, his Spirit-based christology.[65] These references to 'kingship' and dignity' are intended to anticipate Gregory's upcoming comments on yet a third category, the all-important one of 'glory', which we have seen also functions as a key pneumatological-christological term throughout his corpus.

Gregory first explains the reference to the number 'sixty' (cf. Song 6:8) in terms of the six commandments implied in Matt. 25:35–36, whereupon he proposes 'six commandments whose observance readies *kingship* (ἡ βασιλεία)' for the 'queens'.[66] By reading Matt. 25:35–36 in conjunction with Jesus' parable of the 'faithful servant' who multiplies his talent by 'ten' and hence 'enters into the joy' of his Lord (cf. Matt. 25:14–30), Gregory

---

[61] *GNO* VI.461.10–462.6; Norris II, 491; it appears that Gregory is making a distinction between the baptized and the non-baptized.

[62] *GNO* III/1.102.30; Radde-Gallwitz, 282.

[63] *GNO* III/1.103.28; Radde-Gallwitz, 283.

[64] *GNO* III/1.103.21–22; Radde-Gallwitz, 283; cf. also *Trin.*, *GNO* III/1.16.3–21; Silvas, 245.

[65] Echoing Sarah Coakley's perceptive comment that Gregory's 'christology' and 'Trinitarianism' are conjoined in *hom. in Cant*: 'To be knit into the Trinity by the Spirit's "adoption" and through the operation of "spiritual sense" is to be mingled with Christ'. Cf. Coakley, 'Gregory of Nyssa on Spiritual Ascent', 371.

[66] *GNO* VI.462.18–19; Norris II, 491.

CHRIST'S PNEUMATIC BODY   235

pictures the 'queen' as one who, having far exceeded her observance of God's commands, has been given 'participation in *kingship*' (κοινωνίαν ἡ βασιλεία) and thus becomes a 'participant in the *kingship* of Christ' (κοινωνὸς τῆς τοῦ Χριστοῦ βασιλείας).[67] If, however, the second group of 'concubines' (cf. Song 6:8) should at some point turn their characteristic 'fear' into the same 'love' that is readily found among the 'queens',[68] Gregory suggests, a higher unity within the church would be attained.

With the key pneumatological categories in place, he proceeds to comment on this ecclesial unity as incorporation into the 'circular' intra-trinitarian sharing of 'glory'. Here, his exegesis of the Song resonates with the exegesis of John 17:5 in *Maced.*, the Spirit-based christology of *Apoll.*, and the corresponding Spirit-based ecclesiology in *hom. in 1 Cor. 15:28*. Moreover, it echoes Gregory's earlier reference to John 17:5 and Spirit-based christology in Homily 7 and the subsequent inclusion of the Bride in trinitarian 'glory' in Homilies 8 and 9:

'That they may all be one, even as you, Father, are in me and I in you, that they also may be one with us' (cf. John 17:21). Now that which holds this unity together is glory, and no one who looks into the matter will deny that 'glory' means Holy Spirit, if account is taken of the Lord's words; he says, after all, 'The glory that you have given to me, I have given to them' (cf. John 17:22). For the one who truly gave the disciples glory of this order was the one who said, 'Receive the Holy Spirit' (cf. John 20:22). He who invested himself with human nature (ὁ τὴν ἀνθρωπίνην φύσιν περιβαλόμενος) received this glory before the cosmos existed, and when the human nature had been glorified by the Spirit, the further gift of the Spirit's glory was passed on to all the same kin (ἐπὶ πᾶν τὸ συγγενὲς), beginning with the disciples. That is why he said, 'The glory that you have given me, I have given them, so that they may be one, even as we are one: I in them and you in me, that they may become perfectly one' (cf. John 17:22–23). Therefore the person who has left immaturity behind, and by growing attained to mature manhood, and achieved the measure of the intelligible stature, who from being a slave and a concubine has come to share *the dignity of kingship* (τὴν τῆς βασιλείας ἀξίαν) and by impassibility and purity has become a recipient of the Spirit's glory (τῆς τοῦ πνεύματος δόξης)—this is that perfect dove

---

[67] *GNO* VI.462.9–463.18; Norris II, 493.
[68] Probably a reference to baptism.

236 ANALYSIS OF *IN CANTICUM CANTICORUM* (*c.* 391)

upon whom the Bridegroom looks as he says: 'One is my dove, my perfect one, one is she for her mother, the chosen of the one who bore her' (cf. Song 6:9).[69]

With this, Gregory's recapitulation in Homilies 13, 14, and 15 of his interpretation of 1 Cor. 15:28 in *hom. in 1 Cor. 15:28* is practically complete. Without having to mention the contested term explicitly, these three homilies depict the eschatological 'subjection' (cf. 1 Cor. 15:28) of the Son to the Father through Christ's baptized *pneumatic body*. Importantly, while he alluded to 1 Cor. 15:28 in Homily 13, his second allusion to this verse in the present homily further echoes his argument in *hom. in 1 Cor. 15:28* that the unity of Christ's body in the Spirit's 'glory' anticipates the final defeat of evil 'when . . . "God may become all in all" (cf. 1 Cor. 15)'.[70]

The event of Jesus' baptism in the Jordan, first introduced in Homily 13, is revisited here once more as Gregory explains the birth of the 'dove' by the dove's 'mother' (cf. Song 6:9). Quoting the all-important passage, John 3:6— 'that which is born of the Spirit is spirit'—he identifies the dove's 'mother' as 'the dove that flew down from heaven upon Jordan'.[71] We could gain no clearer confirmation that, for Gregory, Christ's baptism in the Jordan as 'first-fruit', upon whom the 'mother Spirit' first descends, serves as the prototypical event that births the pneumatic body of the church via the unified activity of Father, Son, and Spirit. Not only does Christ's and the church's baptism instantiate a larger cosmic principle of trinitarian unity of activity, but here, in the final homily of *hom. in Cant.*, Gregory shows that because they are grounded in one unified triune operation, both baptism and the cosmos share a common eschatological *telos*.[72] It is telling, given that Homily 1 began with the 'linear' reception of life via the unified activity of the Trinity in the baptismal 'kiss', that the resounding note upon which the final homily ends is

---

[69] *GNO* VI.467.5–468.4; Norris II, 497, slightly modified. Vinel, 'The Key Eschatological Role of the Song of Songs', 99, remarks on Gregory's exegesis of Song 6:9: 'For this verse, Gregory attaches less importance to the image of the dove, symbol of the Spirit, than to the adjective μία'. However, when read in light of the broader literary-rhetorical aims of Homilies 13–15, Gregory's notion of 'oneness' vis-à-vis Song 6:9 is completely dependent upon the unifying activity of the Spirit and his Spirit-based christology.

[70] *GNO* VI.469.6; Norris II, 497.

[71] *GNO* VI.468.10–13; Norris II, 497.

[72] Maspero, 'The *In Canticum* in Gregory's Theology', 44 notes: 'Gregory, therefore, contemplates the Church in light of Christ, and, therefore, in light of the Trinity. The perspective is not institutional, but cosmic'.

CHRIST'S PNEUMATIC BODY   237

the ultimate goal of the 'linear' baptismal dynamic—the inclusion of Christ's baptized, pneumatic body in the 'circular' exchange of trinitarian 'glory'.

Conclusion

I have demonstrated that a recurring, coherent pattern of thought underpins Gregory's exegesis of Song 3:9–4:15 in Homilies 7, 8, and 9; of 1 Cor. 15:28 in *hom. in 1 Cor. 15:28*; and of Song 5:8–6–9 in Homilies 13, 14, and 15. According to this underlying structure of thought, Gregory viewed the church as the pneumatic body of Christ, united to the Only-begotten Son, and through this union to the Father, in the 'glory' of the Holy Spirit. The final, eschatological unity of the church mirrors the final unity of the cosmos, when evil will be overcome, and God will become 'all in all'. As we can see, the notion of the church as Christ's pneumatic body is underpinned by what I have called Gregory's Spirit-based christology, the most detailed expression of which is found in *Apoll.*, though clear traces of it can be discerned in the earlier works *Trin.* and *Maced.*, and the later work *hom. in 1 Cor. 15:28*.[73] Just as Christ, by the Spirit's anointing, was the 'first-fruit' of humanity to 'advance' (προκοπή) and thus to enter into the intra-trinitarian exchange of glory after the passion, so too the 'common lump' of the church may 'advance' and 'ascend' so as to enter this 'glory' in an analogous manner, through identification with Christ's death and resurrection in baptism.

---

[73] A response to Ludlow's suggestion that Gregory's statements about the Holy Spirit's role in establishing ecclesial unity are 'rare and usually vague'; cf. Ludlow, *Universal Salvation*, 91 n.44.

Conclusion

In Part I, I undertook an analysis of a select number of Gregory's major doctrinal works written prior to *hom. in Cant.* There emerged from this analysis what I referred to as Gregory's doctrinal account of the *objective* reality of human transformation and union with God. It is objective in the specific sense that this account is grounded in events brought about by the divine initiative and activity, and can therefore be considered in a manner largely detached from the *subjective*, first-person experience of this reality. In short, I showed that Gregory based this account upon the notion of trinitarian unity of activity of Father, Son, and Spirit (especially in connection with baptismal theology) and his Spirit-based christology.

While I suggested in the conclusion to Part I that this account is largely coherent in a confessional, narrative, and logical-systematic manner, I also claimed that it called for a corresponding account from the perspective of *subjective* human experience. After all, embedded within the very account of the *objective* reality is Gregory's claim that one can only be transformed and united to God through a *desire* and *love* rooted in the very depths of the person—heart, mind, body, and soul. Thus, unless such an account of the *subjective* aspect materializes within Gregory's oeuvre, the account of the *objective* reality is radically incomplete. Further, it is clear that such an account, if it is to preserve the coherence of Gregory's thought, and indeed to safeguard it from radical incoherence, needs also to be grounded in Gregory's notion of trinitarian unity of activity and his Spirit-based christology.

The burden of Part II was to show that *hom. in Cant.* offers just this account. Thus, my analysis in Chapters 6–8 shows that Gregory sought to ignite his readers' love and desire for transformation and union with God through a *subjective process* of reading the Song of Songs likened to a kind of 'baptism', through which one 'senses' the unified activity of Father, Son, and Spirit that enflames the reader's desire and thus reorients the whole person—heart, mind, body, and soul. In this way, such a reading of the Song of Songs *subjectively* draws the reader away from present attachment to material reality as they 'advance' and 'ascend' toward the eschatological Spirit-based unity

Christ, the Spirit, and Human Transformation in Gregory of Nyssa's In Canticum Canticorum. Alexander L. Abecina, Oxford University Press. © Oxford University Press 2024. DOI: 10.1093/oso/9780197745946.003.0010

CONCLUSION 239

of Christ's 'pneumatic body'—of which Christ himself was the 'first-fruit' through his incarnation, baptism, and resurrection—and thus into the eternal exchange of Trinitarian glory in which God is and is becoming 'all in all' (cf. 1 Cor. 15:28).

This study advances contemporary scholarship on Gregory of Nyssa in several key respects. First, it draws our attention to the fact that pneumatology, a feature too often neglected or downplayed by Gregory's commentators, is not an afterthought for Gregory, but rather is at the forefront of his theology. I have shown that from his earliest work to his last, Gregory assigns a central role to pneumatology in his exhortation to spiritual marriage with Christ.

I have also offered the most comprehensive account of Gregory's Spirit-based christology to date. Gregory's well-known anti-Macedonian 'anointing argument' for the Holy Spirit's dignity is not only intrinsically bound up with, but may be regarded as a direct corollary of, his Spirit-based christology. Further, I have shown that this Spirit-based christology, rather than being an anomalous feature of Gregory's thought, is in fact the more original and authentic form of his christology.

One of the unintended outcomes of this approach is the response I offer to the influential thesis that Gregory held a dual, and ultimately irreconcilable, 'humanistic' and 'physical' soteriology. I have shown that due attention to the *essential* rather than merely peripheral role of the Spirit provides a more compelling alternative. It is no coincidence that Gregory's christological work that seems most strongly to indicate a turn to 'physical' soteriology (i.e. *Eun.* III), whereby salvation is mediated to humanity through a necessary, automatic, and impersonal process at the level of *phusis*, is precisely that which downplays the role of the Spirit, probably for strategic reasons, as I have argued. Once we appreciate that Gregory's more authentic christology is, in fact, Spirit-based, we can see that his pneumatology bridges the apparent humanistic-physical divide.

On the question of doctrine and exegesis, I have documented a more rigorous account of the relationship between the two than has been offered until now. Gregory's interpretation of the Song of Songs is firmly grounded in a body of carefully articulated trinitarian and christological doctrine that was articulated years in advance. As a result, I have specified how *hom. in Cant.* not only completes but also renders coherent Gregory's earlier doctrinal works from the perspective of *subjective* experience. The trinitarian theology and christology found in the later *exegetical* work completes the earlier

240 CONCLUSION

doctrinal works precisely by being in fundamental *continuity* rather than discontinuity with them.

Finally, without sacrificing sensitivity to historical context, my analysis presents a case for appreciating Gregory as a coherent thinker, even if he is not systematic in every detail. That Gregory's Spirit-based christology and its soteriological implications are internally consistent with his principle of trinitarian unity of activity; that his 'anointing argument' for the Holy Spirit's divine status is a direct logical corollary of his Spirit-based christology; and that his Spirit-based christology is extrapolated to form an analogous Spirit-based notion of eschatological ecclesial unity in Christ's pneumatic body, could hardly have arisen by accident. Gregory, it seems, was well aware that these doctrinal commitments formed a nexus of strongly overlapping ideas that needed to be internally consistent across a variety of works, both 'doctrinal' and 'exegetical', in order to uphold Nicene doctrine and spiritual practice.

As we turn our attention to implications raised by the present study, we begin by noting the extent to which Gregory's theology of baptism illuminates multiple facets of his writings. In 'triangulating' his understanding of Christ, the Spirit, and human transformation, I showed that baptismal theology was a major hub around which much of Gregory's reflections about these topics revolved. Nevertheless, I have only scratched the surface over a select few works. Scholars have long recognized the importance of baptism for Gregory, and while several shorter studies are available as has been noted in this book, there is currently no monograph-length investigation across Gregory's corpus. Given the degree to which baptism animated Gregory's theological imagination, a full treatment of the subject is well overdue.

Looking beyond Gregory to broader theological matters, this book contributes to the ongoing discussion about the relevance of patristic studies to contemporary systematic theology. Here, I take my cue from Lewis Ayres, who argues, '[a]t the heart of attempting to appropriate and engage pro-Nicene theological culture lies the task of asking how Christians considering their most fundamental doctrines may see the task before them as one of *contemplating the Scriptures* even as they are persuaded by many modern assumptions'.[1] For Ayres, the comprehensiveness of pro-Nicene approaches to scripture bequeaths to us an expansive 'theology of theology in all its aspects'.[2] Following the lead of pro-Nicene 'theology of theology' will

[1] Ayres, *Nicaea and Its Legacy*, 415, my italics.
[2] Ayres, *Nicaea and Its Legacy*, 415.

CONCLUSION   241

therefore allow us to see how 'theology is fundamentally a contemplation of Scripture', where scripture serves as the primary source for articulating the credal faith and vision of life within the Trinity.[3]

Thus, while the present work falls within the domain of historical theology, it nonetheless commends *hom. in Cant.* as a work worthy of the systematic theologian's attention. Gregory's homilies on the Song of Songs exemplify a patristic 'theology of theology' in the sense defined by Ayres. Systematic theologians who understand the need for their own patterns of attention to remain focused upon the patristic modes of thought in which their theological categories originally sprang can therefore look to Gregory's interpretation of the Song of Songs as a model performance of the contemplation of scripture as the primary source of fundamental christological and trinitarian doctrine.

On a related note, this book complements recent systematic theological interest in the subject of Spirit christology, viewed by its proponents as a necessary corrective to the 'Logos-centric' nature of conciliar christology.[4] While there is an awareness of the need to retrace the roots of Spirit christology in patristic thinkers, their retrieval of early Christian thought carves out only the basic contours. For those who seek a more nuanced engagement with the intersection of pneumatological and christological thought among early Christians, the account of Gregory's Spirit-based christology outlined in this book may now be considered a touchstone for further investigation. The degree to which contemporary accounts of Spirit christology are a recovery of earlier forms can only be properly assessed when more sophisticated analyses of patristic thought become available. Building off the present book, therefore, one could easily imagine an investigation on pneumatology in 'Antiochene' and 'Alexandrian' christologies of the fourth century as a novel way to revisit, with new eyes, the similarities and differences between their christological approaches. The additional payoff of such an enquiry, for patristics specialists, is that it would reopen the vault on the neglected area of Antiochene christologies, which Johannes Zachhuber has recently identified as an urgent desideratum in patristic studies.[5]

---

[3] Ayres, *Nicaea and Its Legacy*, 416–417.

[4] Cf. Ralph Del Colle, *Christ and the Spirit: Spirit Christology in Trinitarian Perspective* (Oxford: Oxford University Press, 1994); Myk Habets, *The Anointed Son: A Trinitarian Spirit Christology*, Princeton Theological Monograph Series 129 (Eugene, OR: Wipf and Stock, 2010); Skip Jenkins, *A Spirit Christology*, Ecumenical Studies 3 (New York: Peter Lang, 2018); Frank Macchia, *Jesus the Spirit Baptizer* (Grand Rapids: Eerdmans, 2010).

[5] Johannes Zachhuber, 'Christology in the Fourth Century: A Response', in *Fourth-Century Christology in Context: A Reconsideration*, Studia Patristica CXII, Papers presented at the

242 CONCLUSION

Lastly, the analysis undertaken in this book makes a contribution to on-going scholarly discussion regarding the theological interpretation of scripture. While much has already been written on the subject in recent years, often motivated by a desire to recapture pre-modern approaches as valid alternatives to the historical-critical method,[6] the unique contribution of this study is the way in which it firmly demonstrates the connection between patristic theological interpretation of scripture and what Simeon Zahl calls 'the affective salience of doctrines'.[7] By this, Zahl means the capacity for Christian doctrines, as the 'object of our attention', to evoke and bring to awareness particular bodily affective states.[8] The tendency to separate Gregory's doctrinal works from his spiritual writings, as discussed in the Introduction to this book, has obscured the manner in which Gregory intends his doctrinal teachings to be affectively salient.[9] By showing how *hom. in Cant.* is related to his polemical works, I have also highlighted how receiving Gregory's *exegesis* of the Song, in the spirit in which he intended, is in fact to receive at the very same time Gregory's trinitarian and Spirit-based christological *doctrine* of salvation in a rhetorical-literary mode that amplifies its affective salience.

This study therefore highlights the value of turning our attention to patristic theologians like Gregory, who closely integrated their objective ontological accounts of soteriological doctrine with subjective experiences of the same doctrine. According to Zahl, '[t]heologians like Didymus, Maximus, and Augustine are representatives of a Christian thought-world that simply did not recognize the sort of clear distinction between experiential and ontological realities that is operative in so much modern theology'.[10] While Zahl

eighteenth International Conference on Patristic Studies held in Oxford 2019, ed. Miguel Brugarolas (Leuven: Peeters, 2021), 187–207.

[6] R. R. Reno, *The End of Interpretation: Reclaiming the Priority of Ecclesial Exegesis* (Grand Rapids, MI: Eerdmans, 2022); Grant Macaskill, 'Identifications, Articulations, and Proportions in Practical Theological Interpretation', *Journal of Theological Interpretation*, 14/1 (2020), 3–15; Darren Sarisky, *Reading the Bible Theologically*, Current Issues in Theology (Cambridge: Cambridge University Press, 2019); Hans Boersma, *Scripture as Real Presence: Sacramental Exegesis in the Early Church* (Grand Rapids: Baker, 2017).

[7] Simeon Zahl, 'On the Affective Salience of Doctrines', *Modern Theology*, 31/3 (July, 2015), 428–444.

[8] Zahl, 'On the Affective Salience of Doctrines', 431.

[9] However, see Volpe, *Rethinking Christian Identity*, 196; cf. Medi Ann Volpe, 'Living the Mystery: Doctrine, Intellectual Disability, and Christian Imagination', *Journal of Moral Theology*, 6/2 (2017), 87–102.

[10] Simeon Zahl, *The Holy Spirit and Christian Experience* (Oxford: Oxford University Press, 2020), 140.

cites these three patristic luminaries, Gregory of Nyssa ought to be counted among them. His writings, and especially *hom. in Cant.*, offer to contemporary theologians an exemplary 'theology of theology' that might assist not only in contemporary re-integration of doctrine and exegesis, but also the re-integration of doctrine and affect.

Bibliography of Primary Sources

I. Works by Gregory of Nyssa

A. Editions Cited

Callahan, Johannes F. *De oratione dominica, De beatitudinibus. GNO* VII/2. Leiden: Brill, 1992.

Downing, J. Kenneth, Jacobus A. McDonough S.J., and Hadwiga Hörner, eds. *Opera Domatica Minora, Pars II. GNO* III/2. Leiden: Brill, 1987.

Gebhardt, Ernestus, ed. *Sermones, Pars I. GNO* IX. Leiden: Brill, 1967.

Heil, Gunterus, Johannes P. Cavarnos, and Otto Lendle, eds. *Sermones, Pars II.* Post mortem Henrici Dörrie volume edendum curavit Friedhelm Mann. *GNO* X/2. Leiden: Brill, 1990.

Jaeger, Wernerus, ed. *Contra Eunomium Libri, Pars Prior: Liber I et II (Vulgo I et XIIB). GNO* I. Leiden: Brill, 1960.

Jaeger, Wernerus, ed. *Contra Eunomium Libra, Pars Altera: Liber III (Vulgo III–XII), Refutatio Confessionis Eunomii (Vulgo Liber II). GNO* II. Leiden: Brill, 1960.

Jaeger, Wernerus, Johannes P. Cavarnos, and Virginia Woods Callahan, eds. *Opera Ascetica. GNO* VIII/1. Leiden: Brill, 1952.

Langerbeck, Hermannus, ed. *In Canticum canticorum. GNO* VI. Leiden: Brill, 1960.

McDonough S.J., Jacobus A., and Paulus Alexander, eds. *In Inscriptiones Psalmorum, In Sextum Psalmum, In Ecclesiasten Homiliae. GNO* V. Leiden: Brill, 1962.

Mueller, Fridericus, ed. *Gregorii Nysseni Opera Dogmatica Minora, Pars I. GNO* III/1. Leiden: Brill, 1958.

Mühlenberg, Ekkehard, ed. *Epistula canonica. GNO* III/5. Leiden: Brill, 2008.

Mühlenberg, Ekkehard, ed. *Oratio Catechetica. GNO* III/4. Leiden: Brill, 1996.

Musurillo, Herbertus, ed. *De vita Moysis. GNO* VII/1. Leiden: Brill, 1964.

Pasquali, Georgio. *Gregorii Nysseni Epistulae. GNO* VIII/2. Leiden: Brill, 1959.

Spira, Andreas, ed. *De anima et resurrectione*, Post mortem editoris praefationem accurate composuit Ekkehardus Mühlenberg. *GNO* III/3. Leiden: Brill, 2014.

B. Cited English Translations

anim. et res.

Callahan, Virginia Woods, trans. 'On the Soul and the Resurrection'. In *Saint Gregory of Nyssa: Ascetical Works.* The Fathers of the Church 58. Washington, DC: Catholic University of America Press, 1967, 198–272.

Apoll.

Orton, Robin, trans. 'Refutation of the Views of Apolinarius'. In *St. Gregory of Nyssa: Anti-Apollinarian Writings.* The Fathers of the Church 131. Washington, DC: Catholic University of America Press, 2015, 89–258.

bapt. Chr.

Moore, William, and Henry Austin Wilson, trans. 'On the Baptism of Christ'. In *Nicene and Post-Nicene Fathers: Select Writings and Letters of Gregory, Bishop of Nyssa.* Nicene and Post-Nicene Fathers, series 2, volume 5. Grand Rapids: Eerdmans, 1994, 518–524.

246 BIBLIOGRAPHY

beat. 1–8

Hilda C. Graef, trans, *St. Gregory of Nyssa: The Lord's Prayer, The Beatitudes*. Ancient Christian Writers 18. Washington: Catholic University of America Press, 1954, 85–198.

Eun. I

Hall, Stuart G., trans., in Lucas F. Mateo-Seco and Juan L. Bastero, eds. *El 'Contra Eunomium I' en la producción literaria de Gregorio de Nisa*. Pamplona: Ediciones Universidad de Navarra, 1988, 35–135.

Eun. II

Hall, Stuart G., trans., in Lenka Karfíková, Scot Douglass, and Johannes Zachhuber, eds. *Gregory of Nyssa:* Contra Eunomium II. *An English Version with Supporting Studies*. Proceedings of the 10th International Colloquium on Gregory of Nyssa (Olomouc, September 15–18, 2004). Supplements to Vigiliae Christianae 82. Leiden: Brill, 2004, 59–201.

Eun. III

Hall, Stuart G. trans., in Johan Leemans and Matthieu Cassin, eds. *Gregory of Nyssa: Contra Eunomium* III. *An English Translation with Commentary and Supporting Studies*. Proceedings of the 12th International Colloquium on Gregory of Nyssa (Leuven, 14–17 September, 2010). Supplements to Vigiliae Christianae 124. Leiden: Brill, 2014, 42–233.

ep. 1–25

Silvas, Anna M. *Gregory of Nyssa: The Letters: Introduction, Translation and Commentary*, Supplements to Vigiliae Christianae 83. Leiden: Brill, 2007.

fid.

Moore, William, and Henry Austin Wilson, trans. 'On the Faith: To Simplicius'. In *Nicene and Post-Nicene Fathers: Select Writings and Letters of Gregory, Bishop of Nyssa*. Nicene and Post-Nicene Fathers, series 2, volume 5. Grand Rapids: Eerdmans, 1994, 518–524.

hom.1–15 in Cant.

Norris Jr., Richard A. *Gregory of Nyssa: Homilies on the Song of Songs*. Writings from the Greco-Roman World 13. Atlanta: SBL, 2012, 1–499.

hom. in 1 Cor. 15:28

Greer, Rowan A. trans. 'On "Then Also the Son Himself Will Be Subjected to the One Who Subjected All Things to Him" '. In *One Path for All: Gregory of Nyssa on the Christian Life and Human Destiny*, assisted by J. Warren Smith. Eugene, OR: Cascade, 2015, 118–132.

Trin.

Silvas, Anna M., ed. and trans. 'Letter to Eustathius the Physician'. In *Gregory of Nyssa: The Letters: Introduction, Translation and Commentary*. Supplements to Vigiliae Christianae 83. Brill: Leiden, 2007, 236–245.

Maced.

Radde-Galwitz, Andrew, ed. and trans. 'On the Holy Spirit against the Macedonian Spirit-Fighters'. In *The Cambridge Edition of Early Christian Writings*: Volume 1. Cambridge: Cambridge University Press, 2017, 270–293.

or. catech.

Green, Ignatius, trans. *St. Gregory of Nyssa: Catechetical Discourse: A Handbook for Catechists*. Popular Patristics Series 60. New York: St. Vladimir's Seminary Press, 2019, 60–157.

or. dom.
Graef, Hilda C., trans. *St Gregor of Nyssa: The Lord's Prayer, The Beatitudes*. Ancient Christian Writers 18. New York: Paulist Press, 1954, 21–84.
perf.
Callahan, Virginia Woods, trans. 'On Perfection'. In *Saint Gregory of Nyssa: Ascetical Works*. The Fathers of the Church 58. Washington, CD: Catholic University of America Press, 1967, 95–122.
Greer, Rowan A., trans. 'Concerning Perfection'. In *One Path for All: Gregory of Nyssa on the Christian Life and Human Destiny*, assisted by J. Warren Smith. Eugene, OR: Cascade, 2015, 24–44.
Pss. titt.
Heine, Ronald E., trans. *Gregory of Nyssa's Treatise on the Inscriptions of the Psalms: Introduction, Translation and Notes*. Oxford Early Christian Studies. Oxford: Oxford University Press, 1995, 81–213.
virg.
Callahan, Virginia Woods, trans. 'On Virginity'. In *Saint Gregory of Nyssa: Ascetical Works*. The Fathers of the Church 58. Washington, DC: Catholic University of America Press, 1967, 1–75.
v. Mos.
Malherbe, Abraham J., and Everett Ferguson, trans. *Gregory of Nyssa: The Life of Moses*. The Classics of Western Spirituality. New York: Paulist Press, 1978, 27–137.

II. Works by Other Ancient Authors

Alexander of Aphrodisias
   De mixtione
      Todd, R. B, trans. *Alexander of Aphrodisias on Stoic Physics*. PA 28. Leiden: Brill, 1976, 108–173.

Apolinarius of Laodicea
   fr. 1–171
      Lietzmann, Hans. *Apollinaris von Laodicea und seine Schule*. Tübingen: J.C.B. Mohr, 1904.
      Norris Jr., Richard A., ed. and trans. 'On the Union in Christ of the Body with the Godhead'. In *The Christological Controversy*. Sources of Early Christian Thought. Philadelphia, PA: Fortress, 1980, 103–111.
Athanasius
   Ar. 2
      Metzler, Karin and Kyriakos Savvidis, eds. *Athanasius Werke. Erster Band. Erster Teil Die Dogmatischen Schriften 2. Lieferung. Orationes I et II Contra Arianos*. Herausgegeben von der Patristischen Arbeitsstelle Bochum der Nordrhein Westfälischen Akademie der Wissenschaften unter der Leitung von Martin Tetz. Berlin: De Gruyter, 1998, 176–260.
      Newman, John Henry, trans. 'Four Discourses against the Arians'. In *Nicene and Post-Nicene Fathers* II/4, edited by Philip Schaff and Henry Wace. Peabody, MA: Hendrickson, 1994, 303–447.

248 BIBLIOGRAPHY

Basil of Caesarea
  ep. 1–366
    Deferrari, Roy J., trans. *Letters:* Volume II: *Letters 59–185.* Loeb Classical Library 215. Cambridge, MA: Harvard University Press, 1928.
  Eun 1–3
    DelCogliano, Mark, and Andrew Radde-Gallwitz, trans. *St. Basil of Caesarea: Against Eunomius.* The Fathers of the Church, volume 122. Washington, DC: Catholic University of America Press, 2011.
  Spir.
    Pruche, Benoît. *Basile de Césarée: Sur le Saint-Esprit.* Sources Chrétiennes 17 bis. 2nd ed. Paris: Éditions du Cerf, 2013.
Epiphanius of Salamis
  haer.
    Williams, Frank. trans. *The Panarion of Epiphanius of Salamis: Books II and III, Sects 47–80.* De fide, Nag Hammadi and Manichaean Studies 36. Leiden: Brill, 1994.
Eusebius of Caesarea
  d.e.
    Heikel, Ivar A. *Eusebius Werke, Band 6: Die Demonstratio evangelica.* Die griechischen christlichen Schriftsteller 23. Leipzig: Hinrichs, 1913.
Galen
  loc. aff.
    Siegel, Rudolph E., trans., *Galen on the Affected Parts: Translation from the Greek Text with Explanatory Notes.* Buffalo: New York, 1976.

Marcellus of Ancyra
  fr. 1–115
    Vinzent, Markus. *Markell von Ankyra: Die Fragmente der Brief an Julius von Rom.* Leiden: Brill, 1997.
Origen
  Cant.
    Fürst, Alfons, and Holger Strutwolf. *Der Kommentar zum Hoheleid.* Alfons Fürst and Christoph Markschies, eds. Origenes: Werke mit deutscher Übersetzung. Im Auftrag der Berlin-Brandenburgischen Akademie der Wissenschaften und der Forschungstelle Origenes der Westfälischen Wilhelms-Universität Münster. Band 9/1. Berlin: de Gruyter, 2016, 56–430.
    Lawson, R. P., trans. *The Song of Songs Commentary and Homilies.* Ancient Christian Writers 26. New York: The Newman Press, 1956, 21–263.
Plato
  Phaedrus
    Burnet, Ioannes, ed. *Platonis Opera, Tomus II, Tetralogius III–IV Continens.* Oxford Classical Texts. Oxford: Oxford Universrity Press, 1900, 227–279.
pseudo-Athanasius
  inc. et c. Ar.   *de incarnatione et contra Arianos*
    Migne, J.-P., ed. Patrologia Graeca 26, 983A–1028A.
Synesius of Cyrene
  insomn.
    Russell, Donald A., and Heinz-Günther Nesselrath, eds. *On Prophecy, Dreams and Human Imagination: Synesius, De insomniis.* Scripta Antiquitatis ad Ethicam Religionemque pertinentia XXIV. Tübingen: Mohr Siebeck, 2014, 12–59.

BIBLIOGRAPHY 249

Bibliography of Secondary Sources

Abecina, Alexander L. 'Gregory of Nyssa on Soteriology, the Cosmos and Christ's Pneumatic Body'. *International Journal of Systematic Theology* 24, 4 (2022): 460–479.

Abecina, Alexander L. 'Power in Weakness: Pneumatology in Gregory of Nyssa's *De virginitate*'. In *Studia Patristica* 115, edited by Markus Vinzent. Leuven: Peeters, 2021, 231–242.

Abecina, Alexander L. 'Tracing the Spirit: Christology in Gregory of Nyssa's *Contra Eunomium III*'. *Journal of Theological Studies* 71, 1 (2020): 212–235.

Abecina, Alexander L. 'The Unity of Christ and the Anointing of the Spirit in Gregory of Nyssa's *Antirrheticus adversus Apolinarium*'. *Modern Theology* 35, 4 (2019): 728–745.

Akiyama, Manabu. 'Johannine Eschatology of the *In Canticum*'. In *Gregory of Nyssa's Mystical Eschatology*. Studia Patristica CI, edited by Giulio Maspero, Miguel Brugarolas, and Ilaria Vigorelli. Leuven: Peeters, 2021, 151–159.

Alexopoulos, Theodoros. 'Das unendliche Sichausstrecken (Epektasis) zum Guten bei Gregor von Nyssa und Plotin. Eine vergleichende Untersuchung'. *Zeitschrift für Antikes Christentum* 10 (2007): 303–312.

Anatolios, Khaled. *Retrieving Nicaea: The Development and Meaning of Trinitarian Doctrine*. Grand Rapids, MI: Baker, 2011.

Aubineau, Michel, trans. *Traité de la Virginité: Introduction, texte critique, traduction, commentaire et index*. Sources Chretiennes 119. Paris: Éditions du Cerf, 1966.

Ayres, Lewis. 'Innovation and Ressourcement in Pro-Nicene Pneumatology'. *Augustinian Studies* 39, 2 (2008): 187–205.

Ayres, Lewis. *Nicaea and Its Legacy: An Approach to Fourth-Century Trinitarian Theology*. Oxford: Oxford University Press, 2004.

Barnes Michel René. 'Contra Eunomium III 6'. In *Gregory of Nyssa: Contra Eunomium III: An English Translation with Commentary and Supporting Studies. Proceedings of the 12th International Colloquium on Gregory of Nyssa (Leuven, 14–17 September, 2010)*, edited by Johan Leemans and Matthieu Cassin. Leiden: Brill, 2014, 369–382.

Barnes, Michel René. *The Power of God: Δύναμις in Gregory of Nyssa's Trinitarian Theology*. Washington, DC: Catholic University of America Press, 2001.

Beeley, Christopher A. 'The Early Christological Controversy: Apollinarius, Diodore, and Gregory Nazianzen'. *Vigiliae Christianae* 65 (2011): 376–407.

Beeley, Christopher A. 'Gregory of Nyssa's Christological Exegesis'. In *Exploring Gregory of Nyssa: Philosophical, Theological, and Historical Studies*, edited by Anna Marmodoro and Neil B. McLynn. Oxford: Oxford University Press, 2018, 93–109.

Beeley, Christopher A. 'The Holy Spirit in the Cappadocians: Past and Present'. *Modern Theology* 26, 1 (2010): 90–119.

Beeley, Christopher A. *The Unity of Christ: Continuity and Conflict in Patristic Tradition*. New Haven, CT: Yale University Press, 2012.

Behr, John. *The Case against Diodore and Theodore: Texts and their Contexts*. Oxford: Oxford University Press, 2011.

Blowers, Paul M. 'Maximum the Confessor, Gregory of Nyssa, and the Concept of "Perpetual Progress"'. *Vigiliae Christianae* 46 (1992): 151–171.

Boersma, Hans. *Embodiment and Virtue in Gregory of Nyssa: An Anagogical Approach*. Oxford: Oxford University Press, 2013.

Boersma, Hans. 'The Sacramental Reading of Nicene Theology: Athanasius and Gregory of Nyssa on Proverbs 8'. *Journal of Theological Interpretation* 10, 1 (2016): 1–30.

250   BIBLIOGRAPHY

Boersma, Hans. 'Saving Bodies: Anagogical Transposition in St. Gregory of Nyssa's Commentary on the Song of Songs'. *Ex Audito* 26 (2010): 168–200.

Boersma, Hans. *Scripture as Real Presence: Sacramental Exegesis in the Early Church.* Grand Rapids: Baker, 2017.

Boersma, Hans. *Seeing God: The Beatific Vision in Christian Tradition.* Grand Rapids, MI: Eerdmans, 2018.

Bos, Abraham P. 'The "Vehicle of the Soul" and the Debate over the Origin of this Concept'. *Philologus* 151, 1 (2007): 31–50.

Boulnois, Marie-Odile. 'Le cercle des glorifications mutuelles dans la Trinité selon Grégoire de Nysse: De l'innovation exégétique à la fécondité théologique'. In *Grégoire de Nysse: la Bible dans la construction de son discours*, edited by Matthieu Cassin and Hélène Grelier, Collection des Etudes Augustiniennes. Paris: Brepols, 2008, 21–40.

Brakke, David. *Demons and the Making of the Monk: Spiritual Combat in Early Christianity.* Cambridge: Cambridge University Press, 2006.

Brugarolas, Miguel. 'Anointing and Kingdom: Some Aspects of Gregory of Nyssa's Pneumatology'. In *Studia Patristica* 67, edited by Markus Vinzent. Leuven: Peeters, 2013, 113–119.

Brugarolas, Miguel. 'Christological Eschatology'. In *Gregory of Nyssa's Mystical Eschatology.* Studia Patristica 101, edited by Giulio Maspero, Miguel Brugarolas, and Ilaria Vigorelli. Leuven: Peeters, 2021, 31–46.

Brugarolas Miguel. 'The Holy Spirit as the 'Glory' of Christ: Gregory of Nyssa on John 17:22'. In *The Ecumenical Legacy of the Cappadocians*, edited Nicu Dumitrascu. New York: Palgrave MacMillan, 2015, 247–263.

Brugarolas, Miguel. 'The Incarnate Logos: Gregory of Nyssa's *In Canticum canticorum* Christological Core'. In *Gregory of Nyssa: In Canticum Canticorum: Analytical and Supporting Studies. Proceedings of the 13th International Colloquium on Gregory of Nyssa (Rome, 17-20 September 2014).* Supplements to Vigiliae Christianae 150, editged by Maspero, Giulio, Miguel Brugarolas, and Ilaria Vigorelli. Leiden: Brill, 2018, 200–232.

Brugarolas, Miguel. 'Theological Remarks on Gregory of Nyssa's Christological Language of "Mixture"'. In *Studia Patristica* 84, edited by Ilaria Ramelli. Leuven Peeters, 2017, 39–58.

Bucur, Bogdan G. 'A Blind Spot in the Study of Fourth-Century Christian Theology: The Christological Exegesis of Theophanies'. *Journal of Theological Studies* 69, 2 (2018): 588–610.

Bucur, Bogdan G., and Elijah N. Mueller. 'Gregory Nazianzen's Reading of Habakkuk 3:2 and its Reception: A Lesson from Byzantine Scripture Exegesis'. *Pro Ecclesia* 20, 1 (2018): 86–103.

Cadenhead, Raphael A. *The Body and Desire: Gregory of Nyssa's Ascetical Theology.* Oakland: University of California Press, 2018.

Cahill, J. B. 'The Date and Setting of Gregory of Nyssa's Commentary on the Song of Songs'. *Journal of Theological Studies* 32, 2 (1981): 447–460.

Canévet, M. *Grégoire de Nysse et l'herméneutique biblique: Étude des rapports entre le langage et la connaissance de Dieu.* Paris: Études Augustiniennes, 1983.

Cassin, Matthieu. *L'Écriture de la Controverse chez Grégoire de Nysse: Polémique littéraire ett exégèse dans le Contre Eunome.* Collection des Études Augustiniennes, Série Antiquité 193. Paris: Institut d'Études Augustiniennes, 2012.

Coakley, Sarah. *God, Sexuality and the Self: An Essay 'On the Trinity'.* Cambridge: Cambridge University Press, 2013.

BIBLIOGRAPHY 251

Coakley, Sarah. 'Gregory of Nyssa on Spiritual Ascent and Trinitarian Orthodoxy: A Reconsideration of the Relation between Doctrine and Askesis'. In *Gregory of Nyssa: In Canticum Canticorum: Analytical and Supporting Studies. Proceedings of the 13th International Colloquium on Gregory of Nyssa (Rome, 17–20 September 2014).* Supplements to Vigiliae Christianae 150, edited by Giulio Maspero, Miguel Brugarolas, and Ilaria Vigorelli. Leiden: Brill, 2018, 360–375.

Coakley, Sarah. '"Mingling" in Gregory of Nyssa's Christology: A Reconsideration'. In *Who Is Jesus Christ for Us Today? Pathways to Contemporary Christology (a Festschrift for Michael Welker)*, edited by Andreas Schuele and Günter Thomas. Louisville KY: Westminster/John Knox, 2009, 72–84.

Coakley, Sarah. 'Re-Thinking Gregory of Nyssa: Introduction – Gender, Trinitarian Analogies, and the Pedagogy of *The Song'. Modern Theology* 18, 4 (2002): 431–443.

Daley, Brian E. *God Visible: Patristic Christology Reconsidered.* Oxford: Oxford University Press, 2018.

Daley, Brian E. 'Divine Transcendence and Human Transformation: Gregory of Nyssa's Anti-Apolinarian Christology'. *Modern Theology* 18 (2002): 497–506.

Daley, Brian E. '"Heavenly Man" and "Eternal Christ": Apolinarius and Gregory of Nyssa on the Personal Identity of the Savior'. *Journal of Early Christian Studies* 10 (2002): 469–488.

Daniélou, Jean. *The Bible and the Liturgy.* Liturgical Studies 3. Notre Dame, IN: University of Notre Dame Press, 1956, 262–286.

Daniélou, Jean. 'Chrismation prébaptismale et divinité de l'Esprit chez Grégoire de Nysse'. *Recherches de Science Religieuse* 56 (1968): 177–198.

Daniélou, Jean. 'La chronologie des oeuvres de Grégoire de Nyssa'. In *Studia Patristica* 7, edited by F. L. Cross. Leuven: Peeters, 1966, 159–169.

Daniélou, Jean. 'La chronologie des sermons de Grégoire de Nysse'. *Revue des Sciences Religieuses* 29, 4 (1955): 346–372.

Daniélou, Jean. 'L'apocatastase chez Saint Grégoire de Nysse'. *Recherches de Science Religieuse* 30, 3 (1940): 328–347.

Daniélou, Jean. *Platonisme et théologie mystique. Essai sur la doctrine spirituelle de saint Grégoire de Nysse.* Paris: Aubier, 1954.

DelCogliano, Mark. 'Basil of Caesarea, Didymus the Blind, and the Anti-Pneumatomachian Exegesis of Amos 4:13 and John 1:3'. *Journal of Theological Studies* 61, 2 (October 2010): 644–658.

DelCogliano, Mark. 'Basil of Caesarea on Proverbs 8:22 and the Sources of Pro-Nicene Theology'. *Journal of Theological Studies* 59, 1 (April, 2008): 183–190.

Del Colle, Ralph. *Christ and the Spirit: Spirit Christology in Trinitarian Perspectve.* Oxford: Oxford University Press, 1994.

Diekamp, Franz. *De Gotteslehre des heiligen Gregory von Nyssa: Ein Beitrag zur Dogmengeschichte der patrischen Zeit.* Münster: Aschendorff, 1896.

Dodds, E. R. *Proclus: The Elements of Theology.* 2nd ed. Oxford: Clarendon Press, 1963.

Dörries, Hemann. 'Griechentum und Christentum bei Gregor von Nyssa: Zu H. Langerbecks Edition des Hohelied-Kommentar in der Leidenr Gregor-Ausgabe'. *Theologische Literaturzeitung* 88 (1963): 569–582.

Dowling, Maurice. 'Proverbs 8:22–31 in the Christology of the Early Fathers'. *Irish Biblical Studies* 24 (2002): 99–117.

Downing, J. K. 'The Treatise of Gregor of Nyssa: "In Illud: Tunc et ipse Filius." A Critical Text with Prolegomena'. PhD dissertation, Harvard University, 1947.

252 BIBLIOGRAPHY

Drecoll, Volker Henning. 'Spuren von Trinitätstheologie in den Hoheliedhomilien Gregors von Nyssa'. In *Gregory of Nyssa: In Canticum Canticorum: Analytical and Supporting Studies. Proceedings of the 13th International Colloquium on Gregory of Nyssa (Rome, 17–20 September 2014)*. Supplements to Vigiliae Christianae 150, edited by Giulio Maspero, Miguel Brugarolas, and Ilaria Vigorelli. Leiden: Brill, 2018, 180–199.

Dünzl, Franz. *Braut und Bräutigam*. Beiträge zur Geschichte der Biblischen Exegese 32. Tübingen: Mohr Siebeck, 1993.

Edwards, Mark J. 'Origen and Gregory of Nyssa on the Song of Songs'. In *Exploring Gregory of Nyssa: Philosophical, Theological, and Historical Studies*, edited by Anna Marmodoro and Neil B. McLynn. Oxford: Oxford University Press, 2018, 74–92.

Edwards, Mark J. 'Origen's Two Resurrections'. *Journal of Theological Studies* 46, 2 (1995): 502–518.

Elm, Susanna. *Virgins of God: The Making of Asceticism in Late Antiquity*. Oxford: Oxford University Press, 1994.

Ferguson, Everett. 'Exhortation to Baptism in the Cappadocians'. *Studia Patristica* 32, edited by E. A. Livingston. Leuven: Peeters, 1996, 112–120.

Ferguson, Everett. 'Preaching at Epiphany: Gregory of Nyssa and John Chrysostom on Baptism and the Church'. *Church History* 66, 1 (1997): 1–17.

Ferguson, Everett. 'Theology of Baptism in the *In Canticum Canticorum* of Gregory of Nyssa'. In *Gregory of Nyssa: In Canticum Canticorum: Analytical and Supporting Studies. Proceedings of the 13th International Colloquium on Gregory of Nyssa (Rome, 17–20 September 2014)*. Supplements to Vigiliae Christianae 150, edited by in Giulio Maspero, Miguel Brugarolas, and Ilaria Vigorelli. Leiden: Brill, 2018, 256–263.

Finamore, John F. *Iamblichus and the Theory of the Vehicle of the Soul*. American Classical Studies 14. Chico, CA: Scholars Press, 1985.

Grelier, Hélène. 'Comment décrire l'humanité du Christ sans introduire une quaternité en dieu? La controverse de 2008 Grégoire de Nysse contre Apolinaire de Laodicée'. In *Gregory of Nyssa: The Minor Treatises on Trinitarian Theology and Apollinarism, Proceedings of the 11th International Colloquium on Gregory of Nyssa (Tübingen, 17–20 September)*, edited by in Volker Henning Drecoll and Margitta Berghaus. Leiden: Brill, 2011, 541–556.

Grelier, Hélène. *L'Argumentation de Grégoire de Nysse contre Apolinaire de Laodicée: Étude littéraire et doctrinale de l'Antirrheticus adversus Apolinarium et de l'Ad Theophilum adversus apolinaristas*. Accessed January 16, 2023. http://theses.univ-lyon2.fr/docume nts/lyon2/2008/grelier_h/pdfAmont/grelier_h_these.pdf.

Gribomont, J. '*Le panégyrique de la Virginité, oevre de jeunes de Grégoire de Nysse'. Revue d'ascétique et de mystique* 43 (1967): 249–266.

Grillmeier S. J., Aloys. *Christ in Christian Tradition*: Volume 1: *From the Apostolic Ages to Chalcedon (451)*. John Bowden, trans. Westminster: John Knox, 1975.

Habets, Myk. *The Anointed Son: A Trinitarian Spirit Christology*. Princeton Theological Monograph Series 129. Eugene, OR: Wipf and Stock, 2010.

Hanson, R. P. C. *The Search for the Christian Doctrine of God: The Arian Controversy, 318–381*. Grand Rapids, MI: Baker, 2006.

Harl, Margeurite, ed. *Écriture et culture philosophique dans la pensée de Grégoire de Nysse. Actes du Colluque de Chevetogne*. Leiden: Brill, 1971.

Harl, Marguerite. 'From Glory to Glory: L'interprétation de II Cor. 3, 18b par Grégoire de Nysse et la liturgie baptismale'. In *Kyriakon: Festschrift Johannes Quasten*, Volume

BIBLIOGRAPHY 253

2, edited by Patrick Granfield and Josef A. Jungmann. Münster: Aschendorff, 1970, 730–735.

Harrison, Verna E. F. 'Allegory and Asceticism in Gregory of Nyssa'. *Semeia* 57 (1992): 113–130.

Harrison, Verna E. F. 'Gender, Generation, and Virginity in Cappadocian Theology'. *Journal of Theological Studies* 47, 1 (1996): 38–68.

Harrison, Verna E. F. *Grace and Human Freedom According to St. Gregory of Nyssa*. Studies in the Bible and Early Christianity 30. New York: Edwin Mellen Press, 1992.

Hart, Mark D. 'Gregory of Nyssa's Ironic Praise of the Celibate Life'. *Heythrop Journal* 33 (1992): 1–19.

Hart, Mark D. 'Reconciliation of Body and Soul: Gregory of Nyssa's Deeper Theology of Marriage'. *Theological Studies* 51 (1990): 450–478.

Harvey, Susan Ashbrook. *Scenting Salvation: Ancient Christianity and the Olfactory Imagination*. Oakland: University of California Press, 2015.

Haykin, Michael A. G. *The Spirit of God: The Exegesis of 1 and 2 Corinthians in the Pneumatomachian Controversy of the Fourth Century*. Leiden: Brill, 1994.

Heine, Ronald E. 'Origen on the Christological Significance of Psalm 45 (44)'. *Consensus* 23, 1 (1997): 21–37.

Heine, Ronald E. *Perfection in the Virtuous Life: A Study in the Relationship between Edification and Polemical Theology in Gregory of Nyssa's De Vita Moysis*. Cambridge, MA: Philadephia Patristic Foundation, 1975.

Holl, Karl. *Amphilochius von Ikonium in seinem Verhältniszu den grossen Kappadoziern*. Tübingen and Leipzig: Mohr (Siebeck), 1904.

Horn, Gabriel. 'L'Amour Divin'. *Revue d'ascetique et mystique* 6 (1925): 378–389.

Hübner, Reinhard M. *Die Einheit des Leibes Christi bei Gregor von Nyssa*. Philosophia Patrum 2. Leiden: Brill, 1974.

Hughes, Amy Brown. 'The Legacy of the Feminine in the Christology of Origen of Alexandria, Methodius of Olympus, and Gregory of Nyssa'. *Vigiliae Christianae* 70 (2016): 51–76.

Hupsch, Piet Hein. *The Glory of the Spirit in Gregory of Nyssa's Adversus Macedonianos: Commentary and Systematic-Theological Synthesis*. Supplements to Vigiliae Christianae 163. Leiden: Brill, 2020.

Hupsch, Piet Hein. 'Mystagogical Theology in Gregory of Nyssa's Epiphany Sermon *In diem luminum*'. In *Seeing through the Eyes of Faith. New Approaches to the Mystagogy of the Church Fathers*. Late Antique History and Religion 11, edited by Paul van Geest. Leuven: Peeters, 2016, 125–136.

Ierodiakonou, Katerina. 'On Galen's Theory of Vision'. *Bulletin of the Institute of Classical Studies*. Supplement 114: Philosophical Themes in Galen (2014): 235–247.

Jaeger, Werner. *Gregor von Nyssa's Lehre vom Heiligen Geist*. Leiden: Brill, 1966.

Jenkins, Skip. *A Spirit Christology*. Ecumenical Studies 3. New York: Peter Lang, 2018.

Karfíková, Lenka. 'The Metaphor of the Mirror in Platonic Tradition and Gregory's *Homilies on the Song of Songs*'. In *Gregory of Nyssa: In Canticum Canticorum: Analytical and Supporting Studies. Proceedings of the 13th International Colloquium on Gregory of Nyssa (Rome, 17–20 September 2014)*. Supplements to Vigiliae Christianae 150, edited by Giulio Maspero, Miguel Brugarolas, and Ilaria Vigorelli. Leiden: Brill, 2018, 265–287.

Karras, Valerie A. 'A Re-evaluation of Marriage, Celibacy, and Irony in Gregory of Nyssa's On Virginity'. *Journal of Early Christian Studies* 13, 1 (2005): 111–121.

254 BIBLIOGRAPHY

Kissling, Robert Christian. 'The ΟΧΗΜΑ-ΠΝΕΥΜΑ of the Neo-Platonists and the De insomniis of Synesius of Cyrene'. *The American Journal of Philology* 43, 4 (1922): 318–330.

Kobusch, Theo. 'The Exegesis of the *Song of Songs*: A New Type of Metaphysics in the *Homilies on the Song of Songs* by Gregory of Nyssa'. In *Gregory of Nyssa: In Canticum Canticorum: Analytical and Supporting Studies. Proceedings of the 13th International Colloquium on Gregory of Nyssa (Rome, 17–20 September 2014)*. Supplements to Vigiliae Christianae 150, edited by Giulio Maspero, Miguel Brugarolas, and Ilaria Vigorelli. Leiden: Brill, 2018, 155–169.

Laird, Martin. *Gregory of Nyssa and the Grasp of Faith: Union, Knowledge and Divine Presence*. Oxford: Oxford University Press, 2004.

Laird, Martin. 'Under Solomon's Tutelage: The Education of Desire in the *Homilies on the Song of Songs*'. *Modern Theology* 18, 4 (2002): 507–525.

Lindberg, D. C. *Theories of Vision from Al-Kindi to Kepler*. Chicago: University of Chicago Press, 1976.

Louth, Andrew. *Origins of the Christian Mystical Tradition: From Plato to Denys*. Oxford: Oxford University Press, 2007.

Ludlow, Morwenna. *Art, Craft and Theology in Fourth Century Christian Authors*. Oxford: Oxford University Press, 2020.

Ludlow, Morwenna. 'Demons, Evil, and Liminality in Cappadocian Theology'. *Journal of Early Christian Studies* 20, 2 (2012): 179–211.

Ludlow, Morwenna. *Gregory of Nyssa: Ancient and [Post]modern*. Oxford: Oxford University Press, 2007.

Ludlow, Morwenna. 'Theology and Allegory: Origen and Gregory of Nyssa on the Unity and Diversity of Scripture'. *International Journal of Systematic Theology* 4, 1 (2002): 45–66.

Ludlow, Morwenna. *Universal Salvation: Eschatology in the Thought of Gregory of Nyssa and Karl Rahner*. Oxford: Oxford University Press, 2000.

Ludlow, Morwenna. 'Useful and Beautiful: A Reading of Gregory of Nyssa's *On Virginity* and a Proposal for Understanding Early Christian Literature'. *Irish Theological Quarterly* 79, 3 (2014): 219–240.

Macaskill, Grant. 'Identifications, Articulations, and Proportions in Practical Theological Interpretation'. *Journal of Theological Interpretation* 14, 1 (2020): 3–15.

Macchia, Frank. *Jesus the Spirit Baptizer*. Grand Rapids, MI: Eerdmans, 2010.

MacLeod, C. W. 'Allegory and Mysticism in Origen and Gregory of Nyssa'. *Journal of Theological Studies* 22, 2 (1971): 362–379.

Malingrey, Anne-Marie, ed. and trans. *Jean Chrysostome, Lettres à Olympias*, 2nd ed., augmentée de la *Vie Anonyme D'Olympias: Introduction, Texte Critique, Traduction et Notes*. Sources Chréttiennes 29. Paris: Éditions du Cerf, 1968.

Maspero, Giulio. 'The *In Canticum* in Gregory's Theology: Introduction and *Gliederung*'. In *Gregory of Nyssa: In Canticum Canticorum: Analytical and Supporting Studies. Proceedings of the 13th International Colloquium on Gregory of Nyssa (Rome, 17–20 September 2014)*. Supplements to Vigiliae Christianae 150, edited by Giulio Maspero, Miguel Brugarolas, and Ilaria Vigorelli. Leiden: Brill, 2018, 3–52.

Maspero, Giulio. 'The Spirit Manifested by the Son in Cappadocian Thought'. In *Studia Patristica* 67, edited by Markus Vinzent. Leuven: Peeters, 2013, 3–12.

Maspero, Giulio. *Trinity and Man: Gregory of Nyssa's Ad Ablablium*. Supplements to Vigiliae Christianae 86. Leiden: Brill, 2007.

BIBLIOGRAPHY   255

Maspero, Giulio, Miguel Brugarolas, and Ilaria Vigorelli, eds. *Gregory of Nyssa's Mystical Eschatology*. Studia Patristica CI. Peeters: Leuven, 2021.

Mateo-Seco, Lucas F., and Giulio Maspero, eds. *The Brill Dictionary of Gregory of Nyssa*. Supplements to Vigiliae Christianae 99. Leiden: Brill, 2010.

May, Gerhard. 'Die Chronologie des Lebens und der Werke des Gregor von Nyssa'. In *Écriture et Culture Philosophique dans la Pensée de Grégoire de Nyssa. Actes du Colloque de Chevetogne (22–26 Septembre 1969)*, edited by Marguerite Harl. Leiden: Brill, 1971, 51–67.

McConnell, Timothy P. *Illumination in Basil of Caesarea's Doctrine of the Holy Spirit*. Minneapolis, MN: Fortress Press, 2016.

Meredith, Anthony. 'Contra Eunomium III 3'. In *Jesus Christ in St Gregory of Nyssa's Theology: Minutes of the Ninth International Conference on St Gregory of Nyssa (Athens, 7–12 September 2000)*, edited by Elias D. Moutsoulas. Athens: Eptalafos, 2005, 165–171.

Meredith, Anthony. 'The Pneumatology of the Cappadocian Fathers and the Council of Constantinople'. *Irish Theological Quarterly* 48, 3–4 (1981): 196–211.

Meyendorff, John. *The Byzantine Legacy in the Orthodox Church*. New York: St. Vladimir's Press, 1982.

Motia, Michael. *Imitations of Infinity: Gregory of Nyssa and the Transformation of Mimesis*. Philadelphia: University of Pennsylvania Press, 2022.

Motia, Michael. 'Three Ways to Imitate Paul in Late Antiquity: Ekstasis, Ekphrasis, Epektasis'. *Harvard Theological Review* 144, 1 (2021): 96–117.

Moutsalas, Elias D. 'La Pneumatologie du *Contra Eunomium I*'. In *Gregory of Nyssa: Contra Eunomium I: An English Translation with Supporting Studies*. Supplements to Vigiliae Christianae 148, edited by in Miguel Brugarolas. Leiden: Brill, 2018, 557–568.

Nawar, Tamer. 'The Stoic Theory of the Soul'. In *The Routledge Handbook of Hellenistic Philosophy*, edited by Kelly Arenson. New York: Routledge, 2020, 148–159.

Orton, Robin. 'Struggling with Christology: Apolinarius of Laodicea and St Gregory of Nyssa'. *Vox Patrum* 37 (2017): 243–251.

Orton, Robin. '"A Very Bad Book"? Another Look at St Gregory of Nyssa's *Answer to Apolinarius*'. In *Studia Patristica* 72, edited by A. Brent, M. Ludlow, and M. Vinzent. Leuven: Peeters, 2014, 171–189.

Panczová, Helena. '"The Bridegroom Descended to His Garden and the Garden Blossomed Again": Images of the Incarnation in the *Homilies on the Song of Songs* by Gregory of Nyssa'. In *Gregory of Nyssa: In Canticum Canticorum: Analytical and Supporting Studies. Proceedings of the 13th International Colloquium on Gregory of Nyssa (Rome, 17–20 September 2014)*. Supplements to Vigiliae Christianae 150, edited by Giulio Maspero, Miguel Brugarolas, and Ilaria Vigorelli. Leiden: Brill, 2018, 485–497.

Parvis, Sara. 'Christology in the Early Arian Controversy: The Exegetical War'. In *Christology and Scripture: Interdisciplinary Perspectives*, edited by Andrew T. Lincoln and Angus Paddison. London: T&T Clark, 2008, 120–137.

Pottier, Bernard. *Dieu et le Christ selon Grégoire de Nysse: Etude systématique de 'Contre Eunome' avec traduction inédite des extraites d'Eunome*. Ouvertures 12. Paris: cultur et verité, 1994.

Radde-Gallwitz. Andrew. *Basil of Caesarea, Gregory of Nyssa, and the Transformation of Divine Simplicity*. Oxford: Oxford University Press, 2009.

Radde-Gallwitz, Andrew, ed. *The Cambridge Edition of Early Christian Writings*: Volume 1: *God*. Cambridge: Cambridge University Press, 2017.

256 BIBLIOGRAPHY

Radde-Gallwitz, Andrew. 'Contra Eunomium III'. In *Gregory of Nyssa: Contra Eunomium III: An English Translation with Commentary and Supporting Studies: Proceedings of the 12th International Colloquium on Gregory of Nyssa (Leuven, 14–17 September 2010)*. Supplements to Vigiliae Christianae 124, edited by Johan Leemans and Matthieu Cassin. Leiden: Brill, 2014, 293–312.

Radde-Gallwitz, Andrew. *Gregory of Nyssa's Doctrinal Works: A Literary Study*. Oxford: Oxford University Press, 2018.

Radde-Gallwitz, Andrew. 'Gregory of Nyssa's Pneumatology in Context: The Spirit as Anointing and the History of Trinitarian Controversies'. *Journal of Early Christian Studies* 19, 2 (2011): 259–285.

Ramelli, Ilaria. 'Apokatastasis and Epektasis in *Cant* and Origen'. In *Gregory of Nyssa: In Canticum Canticorum: Analytical and Supporting Studies. Proceedings of the 13th International Colloquium on Gregory of Nyssa (Rome, 17–20 September 2014)*. Supplements to Vigiliae Christianae 150, edited by Giulio Maspero, Miguel Brugarolas, and Ilaria Vigorelli. Leiden: Brill, 2018, 312–339.

Ramelli, Ilaria. 'Baptism in Gregory of Nyssa's Theology and Its Orientation to Eschatology'. In *Ablution, Initiation, and Baptism: Late Antiquity, Judaism, and Early Christianity*. Beihefte zur Zeitschrift für die neutestamentliche Wissenschaft und die Kunde der älteren Kirche, edited by in David Hellholm, Tor Vegge, Øyvind Norderval, and Christer Hellholm. Berlin: De Gruyter, 2011, 1205–1231.

Reno, R. R. *The End of Interpretation: Reclaiming the Priority of Ecclesial Exegesis*. Grand Rapids, MI: Eerdmans, 2022.

Sarisky, Darren. *Reading the Bible Theologically*. Current Issues in Theology. Cambridge: Cambridge University Press, 2019.

Scarborough, Jason M. 'Asceticism as Ideology: Gregory of Nyssa's *De virginitate*'. *Union Seminary Quarterly Review* 57 (2003): 131–150.

Schibli, H. S. 'Hierocles of Alexandria and the Vehicle of the Soul'. *Hermes* 121, 1 (1993): 109–117.

Schibli, H. S. 'Origen, Didymus, and the Vehicle of the Soul'. In *Origeniana Quinta: Historica, Text and Method, Biblica, Philosophica, Theologica, Origenism and Later Developments: Papers of the 5th International Origen Congress, Boston College, 14–18 August 1989*, edited by in Robert J. Daly. Leuven: Peeters, 1992, 381–391.

Scott, Jessica. 'A Theological Exploration of the Shape of Life and Death in Dialogue with the Biographical Works of Gregory of Nyssa'. PhD dissertation, University of Cambridge, 2021. https://doi.org/10.17863/CAM.75286.

Silvas, Anna M. 'A *Paradosis* of Mystical Theology between Basil the Great and Gregory of Nyssa'. In *Gregory of Nyssa's Mystical Eschatology*. Studia Patristica CI, edited by Giulio Maspero, Miguel Brugarolas, and Ilaria Vigorelli. Leuven: Peeters, 2021, 47–58.

Smith, Andrew. *Porphyry's Place in the Neoplatonic Tradition: A Study in Post-Plotinian Neoplatonism*. The Hague: M. Nijhoff, 1974.

Smith, J. Warren. 'Becoming Men, Not Stones: *Epektasis* in Gregory of Nyssa's *Homilies on the Song of Songs*'. In *Gregory of Nyssa: In Canticum Canticorum: Analytical and Supporting Studies. Proceedings of the 13th International Colloquium on Gregory of Nyssa (Rome, 17–20 September 2014)*. Supplements to Vigiliae Christianae 150, edited by Giulio Maspero, Miguel Brugarolas, and Ilaria Vigorelli. Leiden: Brill, 2018, 340–359.

Smith, J. Warren. *Passion and Paradise: Human and Divine Emotion in the Thought of Gregory of Nyssa*. New York: Herder and Herder, 2004.

BIBLIOGRAPHY 257

Smythe, H. R. 'The Interpretation of Amos 4 13 in St. Athanasius and Didymus'. *Journal of Theological Studies* 1, 2 (October 1950): 158–168.

Spoerl, Kelly McCarthy. 'Apolinarian Christology and the Anti-Marcellan Tradition'. *Journal of Theological Studies* 45 (1994): 545–568.

Spoerl, Kelly McCarthy. 'Apolinarius and the Holy Spirit'. In *Studia Patristica* 37, edited by Maurice F. Wiles. Leuven: Peeters, 2000, 571–592.

Spoerl, Kelly McCarthy. 'Apolinarius and the Response to Early Arian Christology'. In *Studia Patristica* 26, edited by E. A. Livingstone. Leuven: Peeters, 1993, 421–427.

Staats, R. '*Basilius als lebende Mönchsregel in Gregor von Nyssa De Virginitate*'. *Vigiliae Christianae* 39 (1985): 228–255.

Steven, Luke. 'Mixture, Beauty, and the Incarnation'. In *Gregory of Nyssa: In Canticum Canticorum: Analytical and Supporting Studies. Proceedings of the 13th International Colloquium on Gregory of Nyssa (Rome, 17–20 September 2014)*. Supplements to Vigiliae Christianae 150, edited by Giulio Maspero, Miguel Brugarolas, and Ilaria Vigorelli. Leiden: Brill, 2018, 508–516.

Stewart, Columba. '*Working the Earth of the Heart': The Messalian Controversy in History, Texts, and Language to AD 431*. Oxford: Clarendon Press, 1991.

Tanaseanu-Döbler, Ilinca. 'Synesius and the Pneumatic Vehicle of the Soul in Early Neoplatonism'. In *On Prophecy, Dreams and Human Imagination: Synesius, De insomniis*. Scripta Antiquitatis ad Ethicam Religionemque pertinentia XXIV, edited by Donald A. Russell and Heinz-Günther Nesselrath. Tübingen: Mohr Siebeck, 2014, 25–156.

Tieleman, Teun. 'Wisdom and Emotion: Galen's Philosophical Position in Avoiding Distress'. In *Galen's Treatise Περὶ Ἀλυπίας (De indolentia) in Context*. Studies in Ancient Medicine 52, edited by Caroline Petit. Leiden: Brill, 2019, 199–215.

Upson-Saia, Kristi. 'Gregory of Nyssa on Virginity, Gardens, and the Enclosure of the Παράδεισος'. *Journal of Early Christian Studies* 27, 1 (Spring 2019): 99–131.

Vaggione, Richard P. *Eunomius: The Extant Works*. Oxford: Oxford University Press, 1987.

Van der Eijk, Philip. 'Galen on Soul, Mixture and Pneuma'. In *Body and Soul in Hellenistic Philosophy*, edited by Brad Inwood and James Warren. Cambridge: Cambridge University Press, 2020, 62–88.

Van der Sypt, Liesbeth. 'Are There Messalian Syneisakts in Gregory of Nyssa's De virginitate 23,4?'. In *Gregory of Nyssa: Contra Eunomium III: An English Translation with Commentary and Supporting Studies: Proceedings of the 12th International Colloquium on Gregory of Nyssa (Leuven, 14–17 September 2010)*. Supplements to Vigiliae Christianae 124, edited by Johan Leemans and Matthieu Cassin. Leiden: Brill, 2014, 704–717.

Van Parys, M. J. 'Exégèse et théologie dans les livres contre Eunome de Grégoire de Nysse: Textes scripturaires controversés et élaboration théologique'. In *Écriture et Culture Philosophique dans la Pensée de Grégoire de Nyssa*. Actes du Colloque de Chevetogne (22–26 Septembre 1969), edited by Marguerite Harl. Leiden: Brill, 1971, 169–196.

Van Parys, M. J. 'Exégèse et théologie trinitaire: Prov. 8,22 chez les Pères Cappadociens'. *Irénikon* 43 (1970): 362–379.

Veillard, Christelle. 'Soul, Pneuma, and Blood: The Stoic Conception of the Soul'. In *Body and Soul in Hellenistic Philosophy*, edited by Brad Inwood and James Warren. Cambridge: Cambridge University Press, 2020, 145–170.

258 BIBLIOGRAPHY

Vinel, Françoise. 'The Key Eschatological Role of the Song of Songs'. In *Gregory of Nyssa's Mystical Eschatology*. Studia Patristica CI, edited by Giulio Maspero, Miguel Brugarolas, and Ilaria Vigorelli. Leuven: Peeters, 2021, 79–100.

Volpe, Medi Ann. 'Living the Mystery: Doctrine, Intellectual Disability, and Christian Imagination'. *Journal of Moral Theology* 6, 2 (2017): 87–102.

Volpe, Medi Ann. *Rethinking Christian Identity: Doctrine and Discipleship*. Challenges in Contemporary Theology. Chichester: Wiley-Blackwell, 2013.

Wickham, L. R. 'Soul and Body: Christ's Omnipresence (De Tridui Spatio 290, 18–294, 13)'. In *The Easter Sermons of Gregory of Nyssa: Translation and Commentary*. PMS 9, edited by Andreas Spira and Christoph Klock. Cambridge: Philadelphia Patristic Foundation, 1981, 279–292.

Wilkenfeld, Daniel A. 'Functional Explaining: A New Approach to the Philosophy of Explanation'. *Synthese* 191, 14 (September 2014): 3367–3391.

Zachhuber, Johannes. 'Christology in the Fourirth Century: A Response'. In *Studia Patristica* 112, edited by Markus Vinzent. Leuven: Peeters, 2021, 187–207.

Zachhuber, Johannes. 'From First Fruits to the Whole Lump: The Redemption of Human Nature in Gregory's *Commentary on the Song of Songs*'. In *Gregory of Nyssa: In Canticum Canticorum: Analytical and Supporting Studies. Proceedings of the 13th International Colloquium on Gregory of Nyssa (Rome, 17–20 September 2014)*. Supplements to Vigiliae Christianae 150, edited by Johan Leemans and Matthieu Cassin. Leiden: Brill, 2018, 233–255.

Zachhuber Johannes. 'Gregory of Nyssa, Contra Eunomium III 4'. In *Gregory of Nyssa: Contra Eunomium III: An English Translation with Commentary and Supporting Studies: Proceedings of the 12th International Colloquium on Gregory of Nyssa (Leuven, 14–17 September 2010)*. Supplements to Vigiliae Christianae 124, edited by Johan Leemams and Matthieu Cassin. Leiden: Brill, 2014, 313–334.

Zachhuber, Johannes. *Human Nature in Gregory of Nyssa: Philosophical Background and Theological Significance*. Supplements to Vigiliae Christianae 46. Leiden: Brill, 2000.

Zahl, Simeon. *The Holy Spirit and Christian Experience*. Oxford: Oxford University Press, 2020.

Zahl, Simeon. 'On the Affective Salience of Doctrines'. *Modern Theology* 31, 3 (July 2015): 428–444.

Scripture Index

For the benefit of digital users, indexed terms that span two pages (e.g., 52–53) may, on occasion, appear on only one of those pages.,

Old Testament

Gen. 2-3, 53, 58, 169
Gen. 2:7, 51–52, 53–54
Gen. 2:9, 219
Gen. 2:16-17, 53
Gen. 3:1-5, 53
Gen. 3:6, 53
Gen. 3:7, 53
Gen. 3:21, 53
Gen. 3:23, 53
Gen. 3:24, 169
Gen. 4:1, 53
Gen. 4:1-2, 86
Ex. 19:10-14, 156
Ex. 19:18, 156–57
Ex. 33:20, 184
Ex. 40:34, 166
Num. 20:10-13, 211–12
Deut. 6:5, 48
Deut. 32:11, 233
Deut. 32:39, 209–11
1 Sam. 6:13, 95, 96, 97–98
1 Sam. 16:6, 124
4 Kgdms. 2:11, 200
Ps. 2(3):2, 124
Ps. 16(17):8, 233
Ps. 22(23):5-6, 209–11
Ps. 23(24):4, 189–90
Ps. 35(36):9, 60–61
Ps. 44(45):6-7, 104–9, 113–14, 117–
18, 129
Ps. 71(72):3,
Ps. 73(74):12, 124
Ps. 77(78):20, 211–12
Ps. 88(89):21, 210
Ps. 90(91):4, 233

Ps. 112(113):9, 56
Ps. 120(121):6, 167–68
Ps. 147(148):7, 190
Prov. 3:19, 82–83
Prov. 8:22, 80, 83
Prov. 8:22-25, 78–79, 81
Prov. 8:22-31, 79
Prov. 8:23-25, 84
Prov. 8:24-25, 83–84
Prov. 8:24-28, 83–84
Prov. 8:25, 84
Prov. 8:26-31, 84–85, 94
Prov. 8:27, 78–79, 81, 85
Prov. 8:28, 85
Prov. 8:31, 85
Prov. 9:1, 82–83
Prov. 23:13-14, 209–10
Prov. 27:16, 201–2
Eccl. 11:5, 63–64
Song 1:1-4, 165–66
Song 1:1-8, 171–72
Song 1:2, 157–58, 164–65
Song 1:3, 163, 164
Song 1:4, 164
Song 1:5, 166–67
Song 1:6, 167–69
Song 1:7, 170, 171
Song 1:9, 172, 182, 184–85
Song 1:9-14, 171–72
Song 1:11, 172–73
Song 1:12, 173, 176
Song 1:13, 178
Song 1:14, 179–80
Song 1:15, 181–82, 184–85, 220–21
Song 1:16, 184

260 SCRIPTURE INDEX

Song 2:2, 184–85
Song 2:8, 189
Song 2:8-17, 189
Song 2:9, 189
Song 2:11, 190
Song 2:14, 191
Song 2:16, 194, 195
Song 3:9, 219
Song 3:10, 219–20
Song 4:1, 220–21
Song 4:1-5, 220
Song 4:2, 221
Song 4:4, 221–22
Song 4:5-6, 222–23
Song 4:6, 196, 197, 223–24
Song 4:8, 196, 197, 204
Song 4:8-15, 196
Song 4:9, 196, 197–98
Song 4:10-15, 196
Song 4:12-14, 198
Song 4:14, 198
Song 4:15, 198, 199
Song 4:16, 200, 201–2
Song 5:1, 203
Song 5:1-2, 203
Song 5:3, 214
Song 5:5, 204
Song 5:5-6, 206–7
Song 5:5-7, 211–12
Song 5:7, 209–11
Song 5:8, 230, 233
Song 5:11, 230–31
Song 5:13, 230–31
Song 5:13-16, 230–31
Song 5:14, 232
Song 5:16, 232
Song 6:1, 232
Song 6:1-9, 224–25, 234
Song 6:5, 233
Song 6:8, 234–35
Song 6:8-9, 233–34
Song 6:9, 235–37
Isa. 6:10, 75
Isa. 9:5, 83–84
Isa. 49:22, 167–68
Isa. 60:4, 167–68
Isa. 66:20, 167–68
Jer. 2:13, 198–99

Amos 4:13, 36–37
Hab. 3:2, 205–6

New Testament,

Matt. 3:11, 67–68
Matt. 3:16, 182
Matt. 5:8, 49, 51, 154–55, 196, 228, 232
Matt. 6:9-13, 71
Matt. 7:14, 206–7
Matt. 8:10, 200
Matt. 9:17, 134–35
Matt. 13:3-23, 167–68
Matt. 23:37, 233
Matt. 24:45-51, 205
Matt. 25:14-30, 234–35
Matt 25:35-36, 234–35
Matt. 26:6-13, 176, 177–78
Matt. 26:12, 176–77
Matt. 28:19, 23, 29, 59
Matt. 28:19-20, 10, 59, 60–61, 62–63,
      68, 73–74
Mark 1:10, 89, 182–83
Mark 5:4, 44–45
Mark 5:1-20, 43
Mark 5:13, 43
Mark 12:30, 48, 49, 50–51, 154–
      55, 220–21
Mark 14:3-9, 176
Luke 1:35, 100, 103–4, 114–18, 129, 229
Luke 2:52, 96
Luke 3:22, 182–83
Luke 8:5-15, 167–68
Luke 10:27, 48–49
Luke 11:2, 8
Luke 11:2-4, 71
Luke 12:49, 156–57, 200
Luke 15:3-7, 170
Luke 23:46,, 94
John 1:2, 92
John 1:13, 56–57
John 1:14, 92, 100
John 1:18, 124
John 1:32, 182–83
John 3:5, 89, 171
John 3:6, 36–37, 38, 54, 58, 157–59, 195,
      212–13, 236–37
John 3:8, 222–23

SCRIPTURE INDEX 261

John 3:13, 100
John 3:15, 60–61
John 4:10, 198–99
John 4:14, 170–71, 190–91, 212–13
John 4:34, 203
John 5:21, 62
John 6:40, 60–61
John 6:63, 62, 157–59
John 7:37, 157–58, 159, 170, 196,
    199, 215–16
John 7:37-38, 232
John 7:37-39, 198–99, 211–13,
    219, 231–32
John 10:11, 170
John 10:11-18, 194
John 10:18, 94
John 12:1-8, 176
John 12:3, 176
John 12:28, 65
John 12:36, 87
John 14:16, 210–11
John 14:23, 34–35, 36
John 14:26, 210–11
John 15:26, 210–11
John 16:7, 210–11
John 16:15,
John 17, 188
John 17:4-5, 65
John 17:5, 10, 66, 76, 97, 101–2, 103–4,
    109–14, 118–19, 120–21, 122, 129,
    187, 188, 198, 223–25, 235
John 17:21, 226–27, 235–36
John 17:22, 118–19, 227, 235–36
John 17:22-23, 187, 188, 235–36
John 18:36, 124
John 19:34, 170–71
John 20:22, 235–36
Acts 1:15, 202
Acts 2:2, 202
Acts 2:3, 156–57, 200
Acts 2:4, 202
Acts 2:36,, 88, 91–92, 93, 95, 96, 97, 109–
    14, 117–18, 129, 130, 139, 140, 187
Acts 9:17, 231–32
Acts 10:38, 125
Rom. 5:1-8, 166–67
Rom. 6:4, 204, 212–13
Rom. 6:5, 198

Rom. 7:14, 53–54, 221
Rom. 7:23, 201
Rom. 8:2, 166
Rom. 8:7, 201
Rom. 8:14-27, 186
Rom. 8:15, 184–86
Rom. 8:15-16, 186
Rom. 8:16, 37, 58
Rom. 8:16-17, 188
Rom. 8:17, 188
Rom. 8:23, 71, 164
Rom. 8:29, 70, 89
Rom. 11:16, 70, 71–72, 89–90, 225–
    26, 229
1 Cor. 1:24, 104–6, 107, 109
1 Cor. 2:10, 81–82, 164
1 Cor. 3:10-15, 219–20
1 Cor. 6:17, 42, 48–49, 50–51, 56–57,
    155–56, 157–59
1 Cor. 7:32-33, 49
1 Cor. 8:6, 92
1 Cor. 12, 220–21, 226, 229
1 Cor. 12:1-11, 83–85
1 Cor. 12:3, 183–84, 212–13
1 Cor. 12:7-31, 220
1 Cor. 15, 236
1 Cor. 15:20, 70, 225–26
1 Cor. 15:22, 225–26
1 Cor. 15:28, 64, 225–27, 230–31,
    232, 236
1 Cor. 15:44-46, 182–83
1 Cor. 15:45, 100
1 Cor. 15:53, 67–68
2 Cor. 2:15, 162, 175, 179, 202, 231–32
2 Cor. 3:3, 232
2 Cor. 3:6, 151
2 Cor. 3:16, 211
2 Cor. 3:16-17, 209
2 Cor. 3:17, 37, 158–59
2 Cor. 3:18, 192–93, 212–13
2 Cor. 4:2, 231
2 Cor. 5:17, 89–90
2 Cor. 6:14, 200
2 Cor. 12:2-4, 164
Gal. 3:27, 153
Gal. 5:22, 84–85
Gal. 5:22-23, 84–85, 175
Gal. 5:25, 182–83, 230–31

262   SCRIPTURE INDEX

Gal. 6:17, 210–11
Eph. 2:22, 219
Eph. 3:6, 226
Eph. 4:3, 39
Eph. 4: 3-4, 155–56, 219
Eph. 4:13, 226
Eph. 4:22, 67–68
Eph. 5:9, 84–85
Eph. 6:14-15, 201
Phil. 1:21-23, 39–40
Phil. 2:7, 92, 93
Phil. 3:10, 198
Phil. 3:13, 193
Phil 3:21, 198
Col. 1:15, 70, 89–90
Col. 1:18, 70, 89, 225–26

Col. 2:12, 197–98, 204, 212–13
Col. 3:1-4, 197–98
Col. 3:2, 85
Col. 3:5, 204
Col. 3:9, 67–68, 153–54, 214
1 Thess. 5:5, 87, 171, 195, 222–23
1 Tim. 1:14, 167
1 Tim. 2:4,
1 Tim. 2:15, 56
1 Tim. 3:16, 29
1 Tim. 4:1-2, 42
2 Tim. 2:26, 44–45
Heb 1:3, 8, 162–63
Heb. 1:6, 70, 89
Heb. 1:14, 209
Heb. 2:4, 223

Index

For the benefit of digital users, indexed terms that span two pages (e.g., 52–53) may, on occasion, appear on only one of those pages.

adoption, 26, 27–28, 37, 68–69, 74–75, 171, 184–85, 195, 212–13, 222–23
advancement, 13, 92, 95, 96, 97–98, 140, 141–42, 164, 181–217, 218–19
affect, 1–2, 25–26, 29
    See also affective salience
affective salience (of doctrine), 242–43
allusion (to Scripture), 11–12, 34–35, 38, 40, 42, 43, 48–49, 52–53, 56–57, 59, 65, 66, 73–74, 81–82, 85, 94, 96, 112, 115, 136–37, 154–56, 158, 159, 163, 168, 170–71, 178, 185–86, 190–91, 198, 200, 202, 205–6, 212–13, 214, 223, 236
Anatolios, Khaled, 76
anointing, 11–13, 56–57, 95, 96–98, 99, 100, 102–19, 123–30, 131, 132, 139–40, 141–44, 145, 146, 176–78, 181, 187, 203, 210, 212, 216–17, 218, 224–25, 226–27, 234, 237, 239, 240
apokatastasis, 52, 53–54, 78–86, 89, 90, 169, 181–82, 223–24
Apoll., 6–7, 10, 11–12, 18–19, 20, 23, 96–97, 99–121, 122, 123, 127–28, 129, 130–31, 132, 142, 143–44, 145, 177, 218, 223–24, 226–27, 235, 237
Apolinarius of Laodicea, 99, 100–4, 122, 130–31
Apollinarians, 1–2, 93, 99–121, 122, 127–28, 146–47
arrow, 26, 36, 207–8
ascent, 13, 25–26, 27, 28, 39, 41, 50, 65, 85, 125–26, 136–37, 139, 145–46, 156, 158, 168–69, 181–217, 218–19, 237, 238–39
ascetic, asceticism, 3–4, 10, 20, 21, 33–34, 41–42, 44–46, 52, 55, 58, 71–73, 75, 123, 139, 147, 149

Athanasius, 38, 79–80, 81–82, 83, 84
Ayres, Lewis, 8–9, 240–41

bapt. Chr., 6, 7, 10, 67–75, 153–54, 160, 165–66, 199, 212–13, 230–31
bapt. diff., 6, 7, 10, 67–75
baptism, 9–10, 33–34, 36, 47, 51–52, 60–61, 62, 63–64, 66, 67–68, 72, 73–75, 76, 153–55, 157–59, 164–69, 170, 171–72, 177–78, 179–80, 185, 188, 196, 197, 199, 204, 205, 207–8, 212–14, 215, 219–20, 229–30, 231–32, 236–37
baptismal exegesis, 9–10, 13, 52–53, 54, 58, 59–61, 153–80, 181, 198, 212–15
baptismal formula, 10, 23, 29, 59, 60–61, 62–63, 68, 73–74, 76
Barnes, Michel René, 8–9, 105–6, 160–61, 162–63
Basil of Caesarea, 3–4, 6–7, 38, 59, 77, 80, 92, 93, 99, 128–29, 130, 193–94
beat. 1-8 24, 35
beauty, 49–50, 52–53, 154–55, 156, 157–58, 166, 175, 179, 182, 183–85, 191–92, 199, 200, 209, 211, 215, 220, 229–30, 231
Behr, John, 110
Brugarolas, Miguel, ix
burial, 176–78, 196–97, 198, 204–6, 212–13

Cadenhead, Raphael A., 3, 6–7, 19–20, 21, 55–56
cause, causation, 8–9, 26, 27–28, 61, 162–63, 174
choice, 42, 44, 51–52, 87, 88, 129–30, 147, 182, 203, 204–8, 209, 216, 219–20, 233–34

264 INDEX

christology:
adoption, 68–69, 70–71, 87, 90–91, 110
anointing, 95, 96–98, 104–19, 123–30,
131, 132, 139–40, 142–44, 145
baptism, 67–69, 74, 76, 89, 90–91, 94–
95, 97, 182–83, 188
conception, 11–12, 102–4, 111, 114–
18, 146
dignity, 37, 88, 127, 140, 141–42, 145,
146, 234, 235–36
divisive, 91–92, 104–5, 106,
109, 117–18
dual-aspect, 91–92, 96, 228
firstborn, 70, 89–91, 94–95, 97, 225–26
first-fruit, 69–74, 76, 89–91, 94–95, 97,
98, 120–21, 146, 187, 197, 215–16,
218–19, 225–26, 227, 229, 230–31,
232, 237, 238–39
glory, 64–65, 66–67, 76, 94, 96–97,
101–2, 103–4, 106, 111–12, 113–14,
117–19, 120–21, 124–25, 126, 163,
188, 198, 220, 223–25, 227, 228–37
kingship, 95, 96–97, 123–30, 140, 143–
44, 146, 233–36
simplicity, 104–6, 107, 108–9
Son, 86–88, 90–91
subset, 145
chronology of works, 2–7
Apoll., 6–7
bapt. Chr., 6, 7
bapt. diff., 6, 7
ep. 5, 5–6, 7
ep. 24, 5–6, 7
Eun. III, 6–7
hom. in 1 Cor. 15:28 6–7
hom. in Cant.: 4–5, 7
Maced., 5–6, 7
virg., 3, 7
v. Mos., 4–5
church, 13, 23, 24, 26, 27–28, 41–42, 84–
86, 107, 119, 146, 149, 153, 155–56,
167–68, 176–77, 185–86, 187, 199,
201–3, 213, 216, 218–37
See also pneumatic body
Coakley, Sarah, ix, 19–20, 25–26, 27,
28, 185–88
coherence (of theology), 10–11, 13, 14,
15–17, 18, 19–20, 21–22, 28–29,

72–73, 76, 98, 122, 123, 145, 146–47,
151–52, 180
cosmos, cosmology, 64–65, 72–73, 145–
46, 176–77, 188, 223, 226, 227, 228,
229–31, 232, 235–37
Council of Antioch, 5–6
Council of Constantinople, 5–6, 7, 77, 99
Council of Cyzicus, 3–4
Council of Gangra, 3–4
Council of Cyzicus, 3–4
Council of Gangra, 3–4

Daley, Brian E., 110
Daniélou, Jean, 3, 6–7
dark, darkness, 40, 51–52, 74–75, 166–69,
181–82, 184, 189–90, 200, 201–2,
203, 222–23
death, 9–10, 39–42, 44–45, 46, 47, 51–54,
56–57, 60–61, 93, 94, 105–6, 111, 115,
116, 117, 146, 176–78, 188, 189–90,
196, 198, 204, 205–6, 209–10, 212–
13, 216, 223, 225–26, 237
demons, demonic, 4, 41–46
desire, 34–35, 38–39, 40, 41, 49–50, 51,
83–84, 153–55, 156, 157–58, 164–65,
189–90, 191–92, 196, 199, 207, 209,
228, 238–39
development (of thought), 18–22, 122, 123
Christology, 130–31
circularity, 20, 21
convergent, 19–20
discontinuous, [earlier refs?] 186
divergent, 19–20, 22, 29
explanatory power, 20
long-term, 19–20, 21, 22
short-term, 20, 22
doctrine and exegesis, 22–30
Coakley, Sarah, 25–26, 27
Theologizing I and II, 25, 28–30
dove, 67–68, 71, 89, 138, 182–85, 191–93,
212–13, 215, 220–21, 230–31, 233–
34, 235–37
drink, 35, 67–68, 157–58, 159, 170–71,
194, 196, 198–99, 212, 231–32

Elijah, 200
ep. 5, 5–6, 7, 10, 23, 60–67, 68, 199
ep. 24, 5–6, 7, 10, 60–67, 68, 199

ep. 29, 6–7
epektasis, 19–20, 180, 181, 191–94, 195, 196, 205–7, 208–9, 215–16
Epiphanius of Salamis, 128–29
Epiphany (sermons), 6, 10, 67–75, 90–91, 179–80, 197
eschaton, eschatology, 55, 64, 84–86, 89, 90–91, 187, 218–19, 225–26, 227, 229–30, 232, 236–37, 238–39, 240
Eucharist, 71, 229
Eun. I, 6–7, 24–25
Eun. II, 6–7
Eun. III, 6–7, 10–11, 12–13, 18–19, 20, 77–98, 117–18, 120–21, 122–47, 158–59, 162–63, 170–71
Eunomius of Cyzicus, 6–7, 11, 12–13, 23, 37, 59, 77–98, 110, 113, 130–31, 139, 158–59, 162–63
Eustathius of Sebaste, 3–4, 60, 129
evil, 42–43, 48, 51–53, 64, 137, 172, 181–82, 201–2, 203, 219–21, 225–26, 227, 233, 236, 237
experience, 1–2, 13, 22–23, 147, 154–55, 164, 179, 180, 206–7, 216, 238, 239–40, 242–43
eye, 44, 172–73, 182–85, 212–13, 215, 220–21, 228, 229, 230–32

faith, 35, 36, 60–61, 83–84, 85, 172–73, 201, 205–8, 219, 220, 226, 229
fid., 36–37, 38
fire, 40, 50, 63, 67–68, 94, 136–37, 138, 156–57, 178, 179, 181–82, 200, 215, 219–20, 221–22
first-fruit, 10, 16–17, 69–73, 74, 76, 89–91, 94–95, 97, 146, 157–58, 164, 171, 187, 197, 215–16, 218–19, 225–26, 227, 230, 232, 236–37
See also Christology; Holy Spirit; Trinity
flesh, 10–12, 41–42, 47, 53–54, 56–57, 64–65, 66–67, 70–71, 78–80, 82–83, 84–85, 86, 89–90, 91, 93, 94–95, 97–98, 100, 101–2, 103–4, 106, 109–10, 111, 113–14, 115–16, 117–19, 120, 127, 128–29, 133, 134, 139, 143–44, 146, 151, 155, 182–83, 184, 187, 189, 197–98, 201, 204, 209, 211–12, 213, 214, 218, 223–24, 227, 228, 229, 231–32, 233

flock, 170, 194, 215
See also sheep
fount, fountain, 60–61, 67–68, 69–70, 157–58, 159, 170, 198–99, 202–3
fragrance, 162–63, 164–65, 173, 174, 175, 176–77, 179, 194, 201–3, 231–32
See also perfume
frankincense, 177–78, 196, 197, 198–99, 204, 212–13, 223–24
See also myrrh
fruits (of the Spirit), 56–57, 157, 175, 176, 177

Galen, 43, 44, 183–84
glory. *See* Christology; Holy Spirit; Trinity
gold, 172–73, 181–82, 215, 219–20
Good Shepherd, the, 170, 194, 195, 212, 215
gospel, 36–37, 83–84, 96, 138, 140, 158–59, 176–77, 189, 202–3, 222–23
grace, 65–66, 67–68, 69–70, 74–75, 89, 96, 124, 134–35, 140, 157, 166–67, 168, 170–71, 175, 176, 177, 220, 221, 233

Harl, Marguerite, 194, 212–13
Harrison, Verna, 55, 207–8
Hart, Mark D., 46–47
heart, 2, 13, 29, 42, 45–46, 47, 48–49, 50–51, 56–57, 107–8, 126, 145, 147, 151, 154–55, 160, 178, 179–80, 196, 198–99, 214, 220–22, 231, 232, 238–39
Holy Spirit
anointing, 11–13, 56–57, 104–19, 123–44, 145, 146, 176–78, 181, 187, 210, 212, 216–17, 218, 224–25, 226–27, 234, 237, 239, 240
dignity, 12–13, 37, 62–63, 68–69, 73–74, 96–97, 123–31, 142, 143–44, 212–13, 233–34, 235–36, 239
drink, 170–71
fire, 156–57
first-fruit, 72–73, 146, 157, 164, 230–31, 236–37
glory, 62–63, 65, 73–74, 96–97, 101–2, 111–12, 113–14, 118–19, 120, 124–25, 126, 130–31, 146, 187, 188, 192–93, 197–98, 215, 227, 234, 235–36

266 INDEX

Holy Spirit (*cont.*)
  kingship, 124–25, 126–27, 143–44, 234–35
  life, life-giving power, 60–61, 63–64, 71, 115, 154–55, 157–59, 170–71, 198–99, 212
  sight, 182–85, 195
hom. in 1 Cor. 15:28 6–7, 10, 64, 118–19, 120–21, 122
hom.1-15 in Cant., 1–3, 4–5, 7, 9–10, 13, 16, 17, 20, 22, 24, 25–26, 27, 28–30, 34, 36, 38, 44, 48–49, 58, 59–76, 77–78, 99, 119, 123, 134–36, 146–47, 153–80, 181–217, 218–37
horse, 172, 181–82, 184–85
human nature, 11–13, 71–73, 86–87, 88, 91, 96, 128–29, 140, 145, 167–68, 170–71, 181–82, 190–91, 194, 195, 205–6, 215, 225–26, 235–36

illumination, 9–10, 74–75, 81–82, 102–3, 136–37, 138, 151–52, 165–69, 171, 189–90, 220, 233, 240
  See also light
image, 51–52, 53, 65, 182–83, 191
imitation, 34–35, 40–41, 71–74, 75, 146, 147, 164, 173, 174, 175, 199, 206–7, 210, 211–12, 215–16, 224, 225, 226, 227
incarnation, 2, 10–12, 13, 19, 23, 34–35, 38–39, 57–58, 62, 64–65, 66–68, 70–71, 72–73, 76, 78–79, 84, 85–87, 88, 89–92, 97, 98, 99, 101, 103–4, 106, 109, 110, 112, 113–14, 117–18, 120–21, 124–25, 128–29, 131, 146–47, 166, 170–71, 184, 187, 189–91, 194, 205–6, 215, 216–17, 218, 223–24, 228, 229, 233, 238–39
incomprehensibility, 49–50, 61, 150, 173, 174, 189, 196, 207
indwelling, 36, 38–39, 166–67, 172, 173, 174–75
infinity, 94, 110, 132–33, 150, 191–93, 196, 206–7, 208–12, 216

Jordan (river), 10, 67–70, 71, 72, 76, 91, 97, 146, 171, 187, 197, 212–13, 215–16, 230–31, 236–37

kingdom, 116–17, 124–25, 129, 206–7
kiss, 157–59, 164–65, 170, 183, 236–37

Laird, Martin, 151, 207–8
law, 83–84, 166, 179, 189–90, 221, 232
light (sun, ray, beam), 44, 49, 50, 51–52, 63, 74–75, 81–82, 87, 105–6, 107, 137, 138, 153–54, 162–63, 165–69, 170, 171–72, 174, 182, 183–84, 189–92, 195, 200, 201–2, 214, 215, 222–23
lily, 194, 195, 221–22
living water, 198–99, 211–12, 215–16, 232
love, 13, 26, 36, 45–46, 47–49, 50–51, 147, 149, 150, 154–55, 160, 164, 166–67, 169, 170, 175, 179, 189, 193, 194, 220–22, 233–35, 238–39
Ludlow, Morwenna, ix, 17, 40, 150

Maced., 5–6, 7, 10, 11–13, 23, 60–67, 68, 76, 96–97, 112, 120–21, 122, 125–26, 127, 129–30, 160, 181, 187, 199, 212–13, 216–17, 218, 223–24, 234, 235, 237
Macedonians, 1–2, 5–6, 9–10, 12, 33–35, 36–37, 38, 60–61, 62–64, 73–74, 96, 112, 120, 123, 125–26, 141–42, 146–47, 164, 183–84, 192–93, 199, 215
Marcellus of Ancyra, 5–6, 78–80, 81–82, 83, 84
Maspero, Giulio, ix, 15–16
Messalianism, 3–4
mind, 2, 11–12, 13, 29, 37, 40–41, 45–46, 47, 48, 49–51, 78–79, 84, 85, 96, 99, 101, 120, 134–35, 138, 140, 145, 151, 154–55, 156, 179–80, 196, 200–1, 207, 216, 228
mingling, 27–28, 93, 110, 132–33, 140, 154–55, 189–90, 205–6, 233–34
mirror, 174, 182–83, 191, 215, 220–21
mortification, 41–42, 204–5, 208–12, 213, 216
  See also vivification
Moses, 35, 156, 157–58, 164–65, 166, 200, 206–7, 211–12
mouth, 157–58, 170, 194, 202
myrrh, 177–78, 179, 196, 197, 198, 204–5, 212–13, 223–24
  See also frankincense

INDEX 267

mystery, 23, 29, 61, 63–64, 81–84, 93, 138, 172, 176–77, 197, 221, 229–30

nature-power-activity, 8–9, 160–61, 164–65, 173, 174, 175, 180, 182, 191
neoplatonism. *See* platonism
nourishment, 24–25, 194–95, 215, 221–23

Olympias, 5, 149
or. catech., 23, 165–66
or. dom., 24
Origen of Alexandria, 137, 150, 176–77, 183–84, 193
Orton, Robin, 6–7, 104, 106, 108–9

participation, 34–35, 55, 56, 101–2, 150, 171–72, 181, 189, 191–93, 198, 199, 229–30, 234–35
Pentecost, 156–57, 201–3, 216
perf., 38, 70, 171, 195, 230–31
perfume, 162–63, 164, 173, 174, 176–78, 179, 198, 231–32
See also fragrance
pierced side (of Christ), 170, 190–91, 194, 212
platonism, 19–20, 41, 50, 55–56, 134–35, 136–37, 138, 139, 150
pneumatic body, 13, 218–37
pneumatic language, 36–37, 38, 58, 85, 94, 103–4, 155–57, 183, 197–98, 200, 201, 203, 221
Pneumatomachians, 3–4
power (*dunamis*), 105–6, 107
prophecy, prophets, 56, 78–79, 81–83, 138, 150, 157–58, 189–90, 198–99, 202, 209–10, 211–12, 215, 220, 232
Proverbs 8 78–86, 90, 91, 151
Pseudo-Athanasius, 70–71, 129, 151
Pss. titt., 134–35
purity, purification, 8, 33–35, 40–41, 49, 52, 54, 69–70, 115–16, 138, 154–55, 156, 166, 169, 172, 174, 181–82, 184–85, 189, 195, 208–9, 215, 220–21, 232, 233–34, 235–36

Radde-Gallwitz, Andrew, ix, 5–6, 19, 23, 65–66, 105–6, 131

rank, 87–88, 93, 97–98, 126, 139, 145, 146, 216–17
rebirth, 38, 52–54, 55–57, 61, 67–68, 70, 87, 88, 89, 90–91, 167, 168–69, 171, 197, 198, 213, 214, 215–16, 220, 229–30, 236–37
regeneration, 9–11, 52–53, 54, 60–61, 67–68, 69–70, 72, 74–75, 89, 91, 97, 146, 165–66, 167, 197, 215–16, 219–20, 229–30
See also rebirth
resurrection, 10–12, 73–74, 88, 89–90, 91, 94–95, 97–98, 115, 117–18, 127–28, 143–44, 188, 196–97, 198, 204, 212–13, 215–16, 223–26, 227, 237, 238–39
rhetoric, rhetorical, 3, 14–15, 23, 46–47, 58, 126–27, 129–30, 142, 196, 207, 208, 242
rod, 35, 209–12

Sabellianism, 60–61, 162
sheep, 95, 139–40, 170, 171, 194, 195, 212, 215
See also flock
Silvas, Anna M., 5–6, 61, 193, 194
simplicity, 104–6, 107, 108–9
skopos, 9–10, 14, 39–40, 51, 56–57, 150, 151, 207
Smith, J. Warren 149, 179–80
Solomon, 81–83, 150, 151, 166–67, 219
soteriology
  coherence, 2
  humanistic, 71–72, 75
  physical, 71–72
spear, 170, 190–91
spikenard, 173, 175, 176–78, 210
Spirit-based Christology, 12–13, 29, 96–97, 99–121, 122, 123–31, 132, 133, 134, 142–45, 146–47, 151–52, 170–71, 188, 198, 207, 212, 218–19, 224–25, 226–27, 228, 234, 235, 237, 238–39, 240, 241
spiritual marriage, 33–34, 40, 47, 48–49, 58, 153–54, 165–66, 168–69
spiritual senses, 49–50, 160–61, 162–63, 164–65, 172–75, 180, 193, 238–39
Stoics, 43, 44, 133, 183–84, 193–94
strike, striking, 205, 208, 209–12
See also wound, wounding:

268 INDEX

subjection (of the Son), 225–27, 228, 236
Synesius of Cyrene, 136–37, 139
systematic thinking, 14–18, 27

tension (*tonos*), 43, 44, 193–94
theological interpretation, 242
thirst, 35, 157–58, 170, 196, 198–99, 211–12
Tieleman, Teun, 43
tongues, 156–57, 200, 202
Trin., 12–13, 96–97, 123–30, 143–44, 145, 234, 237
Trinity
  baptismal formula, 60–67
  circular model, 10, 13, 65–67, 75–76, 120–21, 146, 151–52, 185–86, 187, 192–93, 216–17, 218–37
  coherence of, 16–17
  cosmology, [needs more refs], 64–65, 73–74
  economy of salvation, 62, 64, 66, 76
  glory, 10, 12, 13, 62, 65–67, 75–76, 97, 112, 113–14, 120–21, 145–46, 152, 187, 192–93, 197–98, 199, 215–17, 218–37
  immanent Trinity, 66, 76
  incorporative model, 27–28, 185–88
  linear model, 10, 27, 63, 64, 65, 66, 68, 69, 73–74, 75–76, 159, 185–86, 187, 218–19, 236–37
  unified activity, 8–9, 13, 16–17, 62, 63–64, 65, 66, 72–73, 74, 75–76, 98, 146–47, 153–54, 162, 163, 167, 172–75, 177, 181–217, 236–37
tunic, 208–9, 213–14

union (with God):
  objective, 1–2, 13, 22–23, 147, 150, 151–52, 154–55, 180
  subjective, 1–2, 13, 22–23, 28–29, 147, 150, 151–52, 154–55, 180, 216, 218–19

v. Mos., 4–5, 35
vehicle of the soul, 50–51, 136–37, 138, 139, 167–69
veil, 107–8, 126, 184, 208–9, 211, 214, 215, 220–21, 228

virg., 3–4, 7, 9–10, 20, 33–58, 67–68, 74–75, 85, 94, 136–37, 138, 153–55, 165–66, 193, 212–13
  baptism, 33–34, 36, 47, 51–52, 54, 155
  baptismal exegesis, 52–53, 54, 58
  beatific vision, 49, 54, 55
  Bridegroom, 39–40
  Christology, 34–35
  death, 39–42, 44–45, 46, 47, 51–54, 56–57
  demons, 42, 43, 44–45
  extreme virgin ascetics, 41–43, 44–45, 58
  Great Command, 48–49, 50–51
  Holy Spirit, 33, 35, 36, 39, 42, 45–54
  Macedonians, 33–34, 38
  marriage, 39–41, 48–49, 53, 153–54
  Mary, 34–35, 55, 56–57
  spiritual childbearing, 39–40, 55–56
  spiritual marriage, 33–34, 40, 47, 48–49, 58
  symbiosis, 39–40, 48–49
  Trinity, 34–35, 76
  vehicle of the soul, 136–37, 138, 139
  virginity, 39–41, 47–48
  virtue, 42–43, 44–46, 56
virtue, 9–10, 39, 67–68, 74–76, 162–66, 168–69, 172, 173, 174, 175, 176, 182, 191, 201, 203, 205, 211, 216, 227
vivification, 208–12
  See also mortification

water, 35, 52, 54, 67–68, 73–74, 89, 90–91, 94, 134, 135–36, 157, 159, 167, 170–73, 185, 190, 198–99, 211–13, 215–16, 224, 230–31, 232
  See also living water
wind, 26, 50, 81, 85, 138, 169, 170–71, 190–91, 200, 201–3, 215
wings, 38–39, 50, 138, 233
wisdom, 56–57, 78–86, 96, 104–6, 107, 140, 209–10, 229–30
works, 205–8
wound, wounding, 26, 44–45, 207–12

Zachhuber, Johannes, 71–72, 98, 229–30, 241
Zahl, Simeon, 242–43